Education in the Asia-Pacific Region: Issues, Concerns and Prospects

Volume 50

D1807608

More information about this series at http://www.springer.com/series/5888

Nhai Thi Nguyen • Ly Thi Tran
Editors

Reforming Vietnamese Higher Education

Global Forces and Local Demands

 Springer

Editors
Nhai Thi Nguyen
Monash College
Clayton, VIC, Australia

Ly Thi Tran
Deakin University
Burwood, VIC, Australia

ISSN 1573-5397   ISSN 2214-9791   (electronic)
Education in the Asia-Pacific Region: Issues, Concerns and Prospects
ISBN 978-981-13-8920-7   ISBN 978-981-13-8918-4   (eBook)
https://doi.org/10.1007/978-981-13-8918-4

This Springer imprint is published by the registered company Springer Nature Singapore Pte Ltd.
The registered company address is: 152 Beach Road, #21-01/04 Gateway East, Singapore 189721, Singapore

Series Editors' Introduction

This volume by Nhai Thi Nguyen and Ly Thi Tran on *Reforming Vietnamese Higher Education: Global Forces and Local Demands* is the latest book to be published in the-long standing Springer Book Series Education in the Asia-Pacific Region: Issues, Concerns and Prospects. The first volume in this Springer series was published in 2002, with this book by Nhai and Ly being the 50th volume to be published to date.

Reforming Vietnamese Higher Education: Global Forces and Local Demands examines the role of higher education in Vietnam, taking into account its changing dynamics in response to globalisation. Issues that affect its higher education such as quality, access, culture, governance and professional development among others are discussed to give readers a comprehensive overview of the higher education sector of the country. Divided into five main parts, the book enables readers to realise how Vietnam responds to the broader internationalisation and globalisation of higher education systems worldwide.

This book discusses the reforms envisioned for the country's higher education institutions to optimally respond to globalisation while at the same time considering the local demands needed for these to develop. Varied and significant issues such as graduate employability, curriculum and work-integrated learning are examined, while some comparative perspectives to other East Asian countries (in terms of governance) and Australia (for research capacity) are also discussed. Given the rising economic development of Vietnam, this book contributes to the understanding of higher education systems in emerging countries, while taking into account the contextual realities that affect such development.

In terms of the Springer Book Series in which this volume is published, the various topics dealt with in the series are wide ranging and varied in coverage, with an emphasis on cutting-edge developments, best practices and education innovations for development. Topics examined in the series include: environmental education and education for sustainable development; the interaction between technology and education; the reform of primary, secondary and teacher education; innovative approaches to education assessment; alternative education; most effective ways to achieve quality and highly relevant education for all; active ageing through active learning; case studies of education and schooling systems in various countries in the region; cross-country and cross-cultural studies of education and schooling; and the sociology of teachers as an occupational group, to mention just a few. More information about this book series is available at http://www.springer.com/series/5888

All volumes in this series aim to meet the interests and priorities of a diverse education audience including researchers, policy makers and practitioners; tertiary students; teachers at all levels within education systems; and members of the public who are interested in better understanding cutting-edge developments in education and schooling in Asia-Pacific.

The reason why this book series has been devoted exclusively to examining various aspects of education and schooling in the Asia-Pacific region is that this is a particularly challenging region which is renowned for its size, diversity and complexity, whether it be geographical, socio-economic, cultural, political or developmental. Education and schooling in countries throughout the region impact on every aspect of people's lives, including employment, labour force considerations, education and training, cultural orientation, and attitudes and values. Asia and the Pacific are home to some 63% of the world's population of 7 billion. Countries with the largest populations (China, 1.4 billion; India, 1.3 billion), and the most rapidly growing mega-cities are to be found in the region, as are countries with relatively small populations (Bhutan, 755,000; the island of Niue, 1,600).

Levels of economic and socio-political development vary widely, with some of the richest countries (such as Japan) and some of the poorest countries on earth (such as Bangladesh). Asia contains the largest number of poor of any region in the world, the incidence of those living below the poverty line remaining as high as 40% in some countries in Asia. At the same time many countries in Asia are experiencing a period of great economic growth and social development. However, inclusive growth remains elusive, as does growth that is sustainable and does not destroy the quality of the environment. The growing prominence of Asian economies and corporations, together with globalisation and technological innovation, are leading to long-term changes in trade, business and labour markets, to the sociology of populations within (and between) countries. There is a rebalancing of power, centred on Asia and the Pacific region, with the Asian Development Bank in Manila declaring that the twenty-first century will be 'the Century of Asia-Pacific'.

We believe this book series makes a useful contribution to knowledge sharing about education and schooling in Asia-Pacific. Any readers of this or other volumes in the series who have an idea for writing their own book (or editing a book) on any aspect of education and/or schooling, that is relevant to the region, are enthusiastically encouraged to approach the series editors either direct or through Springer to publish their own volume in the series, since we are always willing to assist perspective authors shape their manuscripts in ways that make them suitable for publication in this series.

School of Education   Rupert Maclean
RMIT University
Melbourne, Australia

College of Education   Lorraine Symaco
Zhejiang University
Hangzhou, China
20 April 2019

Acknowledgments

We are indebted to a number of people in the process of shaping this edited book, entitled *Reforming Vietnamese Higher Education: Global Forces and Local Demands*. We the editors, Nhai Thi Nguyen and Ly Thi Tran, would like to express our sincerest thanks to all our colleagues and contributors whose intellectual inputs, passion, and wonderful commitment have been invaluable to this book. We are very grateful to the series editors Rupert Maclean and Lorraine Pe Symaco who saw the value of this book and to Ang Lay Peng and Lawrence Liu from Springer Nature for their great support and assistance throughout this book process. We wish to thank the anonymous reviewers for their valuable comments and suggestions, which help us significantly improve the manuscript. Our special thanks are extended to Professor Martin Hayden for his invaluable editorial assistance in the final stage of our book.

Our gratitude goes to the Asia Pacific Higher Education Research Partnership (APHERP) Senior Research Cluster led by Professor Sheng-Ju Chen and other respectful colleagues, including Professor Molly N. N. Lee, Professor Morshidi Sirat, Professor Rui Yang, Dr. William Yat Wai Lo, Dr. Cheng Cheng Yang, Dr. Akiyoshi Yonezawa, Dr. Jisun Jung, Dr. Edilberto C. de Jesus, and Dr. Yeow-Tong Chia. The transnational research project, Exploring Hybrid Universities in East Asia: Cultures, Values and Changes, has fuelled a critical and productive dialogue on higher education reforms beyond the national boundaries. We would like to thank Professor John Hawkins and Professor Dean Neubauer and the East-West Centre, University of Hawaii, whose intellectual insights, academic wisdom, and mentorship accompanying our research project have contributed tremendously in framing such an innovative conceptual framework for our book. Nhai Thi Nguyen's sincere thanks are extended to Vietnamese academic colleagues who participated in her research project, as well as RMIT Vietnam colleagues and students for having contributed to her project on work integrated learning. This book is in memory of her wonderful former colleagues, Anais Lacouture and Paul Smith, at the Centre of Communication and Design in RMIT Vietnam.

Contents

1 Impacts of Global Forces and Local Demands on Vietnamese
   Higher Education   1
   Nhai Thi Nguyen and Ly Thi Tran

Part I Context for Reform

2 Cultural Modalities of Vietnamese Higher Education.   17
   Nhai Thi Nguyen

Part II VHE Structure, Policy and Governance

3 Vietnam's Progress with Policies on University Governance,
   Management and Quality Assurance   37
   Khanh Van Dao and Martin Hayden

4 University Governance in Vietnam and East Asian Higher
   Education: Comparative Perspectives   51
   Mai Tuyet Ngo

5 Financing Vietnamese Higher Education: From a Wholly
   Government-Subsidized to a Cost-Sharing Mechanism   75
   Hiep-Hung Pham and Huyen-Minh Vu

Part III Curriculum, Equity and Quality Assurance

6 Graduate Employability: Critical Perspectives   93
   Thi Tuyet Tran

7 Work-Integrated Learning for Enhancing Graduate
   Employability: Moving from the Periphery to the Centre
   of the Curriculum 113
   Nhai Thi Nguyen, Ly Thi Tran, and Truc Thi Thanh Le

8   Accreditation, Ranking and Classification in Vietnamese
    Higher Education: The Localization of Foreign-Born
    QA Models and Methods 133
    Quyen Thi Ngoc Do

9   Access and Equity in Higher Education in Light
    of Bourdieu's Theories: A Case of Minority Students
    in Northwest Vietnam 149
    Thuy Thi Ngoc Bui, Nga Thi Hang Ngo, Hoa Thi Mai Nguyen,
    and Hang Thu Le Nguyen

Part IV   HE Research

10 A Comparative Analysis of Vietnamese and Australian
    Research Capacity, Policies, and Programmes 173
    Quy Nguyen and Christopher Klopper

Part V   HE Professional Development

11 Teacher Competence Standardisation Under the Influence
    of Globalisation: A Study of the National Project 2020
    and Its Implications for English Language Teacher
    Education in Vietnamese Colleges and Universities 199
    Mai Tuyet Ngo

12 Professional Learning for Higher Education Academics:
    Systematic Tensions 223
    Hoa Thi Mai Nguyen and Thu Dinh Nguyen

13 Revisiting "Teacher as Moral Guide" in English Language
    Teacher Education in Contemporary Vietnam 245
    Linh Thuy Le and Leigh Gerrard Dwyer

About the Editors

Thuy Thi Ngoc Bui (PhD) graduated from the master's and doctoral programmes in Language Policy in the USA under the Ford Foundation and the East-West Center scholarships. In 2015, she was awarded with the Australian Executive Fellowship to work as a visiting scholar at the University of Sydney, Australia. She has experience working as a senior academic manager, a lecturer, and a researcher. Her research focuses on multilingualism, critical literacy, teacher agency, and the relationship between language and education policies and socio-economic equity. She has published journal articles and book chapters on these topics. Since December 2018, she has been working as a deputy head of the International Affairs Office at Hanoi University of Science and Technology (HUST). Besides her academic positions, she actively works as a community project manager for projects funded by the US and Australian Embassies.

Khanh Van Dao (PhD) is a former personal assistant to the president and deputy director of the International Relations and Project Management, Can Tho University, in Vietnam. Since 2003, he has published journal articles and book chapters (in English and Vietnamese) relating to higher education governance, management, quality assurance, and finance in Vietnam. Between 2009–2010 and 2011–2012, under the supervision of Prof. Martin Hayden, he actively engaged in research and consultancy for the Vietnamese Ministry of Education and Training in the 'New Model University' project, funded by the Asian Development Bank, and the 'Higher Education Master Plan' project, funded by The World Bank. He worked for 2 years as a post-doctoral research fellow in higher education governance and management at Southern Cross University in Australia.

Quyen Thi Ngoc Do (PhD) is a lecturer at Hanoi University of Business and Technology, in Vietnam, and a researcher in higher education studies with interests in educational effectiveness, university governance, quality assurance, and improvement, particularly accreditation and benchmarking. She completed her PhD at the University of Melbourne and has been active in the development of quality assurance and accreditation in Vietnamese universities.

Leigh Gerrard Dwyer (MA) is programme leader in the Foundation Studies Department of Melbourne Polytechnic, Australia, and currently is primarily involved in the Adult Migrant English Programme (AMEP). Formerly director of Studies at Baxter Institute and education team leader in the Republic of Nauru, he has 16 years of classroom experience, including 8 years in management, and is also the owner of his own education consultancy company, Global Education Specialists Pty Ltd. He was an editor of *Knowledge Journeys and Journeying Knowledge*, which is a book of collected academic papers from the 7th 'Engaging with Vietnam: An Interdisciplinary Dialogue' conference. His main academic interests are in the area of philosophy of mind and language, semantics, metaphysics, metacognition, computer-aided learning, and foundation studies.

Martin Hayden (PhD) is professor of Higher Education at Southern Cross University, Australia. He has published extensively on topics related to higher education policy in Australia and in Asia. Since 2005, he has been intensively engaged in research and consultancy in the Southeast Asian region. In 2011–2012, he led a major project supported by the World Bank to develop a master plan for the higher education system in Vietnam. Over the past few years, he has also produced reports on higher education in Southeast Asia for the ADB, the ASEAN Secretariat, the OECD, the World Bank, and the Australian Government.

Christopher Klopper (PhD) is an associate professor and deputy dean of Learning and Teaching for the Arts, Education and Law Group, Griffith University, Australia. His grant and publication record profiles research outcomes in the fields of enhancing teaching quality in higher education through peer review and student evaluations; the exploitation of digital technologies to enhance learning in initial teacher education; creative arts education models, approaches, and professional practice; music education for the non-specialist primary preservice teacher; the intentional provision of music in early childhood settings; academic mobility; musicians' physiological response to prolonged performance; and transnational intercultural musical communication.

Linh Thuy Le (PhD) is a teaching associate at Monash University and is currently the English course coordinator at ATMC Baxter Education Group, Australia. She has been actively involved in English language training and teacher education through her work at Hanoi National University of Education (HNUE) and in various professional development projects in Vietnam and Australia over the last 18 years. Her research interests include teacher education and teacher identity, pedagogy and assessment in TESOL, professionalism in ELT, and, recently, vocational training and education (VET).

Truc Thi Thanh Le (DEd) is a research fellow at Deakin University. Her research activities and publications focus on transnational academic mobility, academic profession, staff professional development and learning, culturally inclusive pedagogy, and English as medium of instruction. She is the coauthor of the 2018 book entitled *Teacher Professional Learning in International Education: Practice and Perspectives from the Vocational Education and Training Sector*, published by Palgrave MacMillan, and of a commentary entitled 'Teacher professional learning is neglected in internationalisation', published in the World University News in May 2018.

Mai Tuyet Ngo (PhD) is a lecturer in ESL/TESOL and Applied Linguistics at Flinders University, Australia. She was a lecturer at Hanoi University since 1994. She has been actively involved in Vietnam's education reform projects since 2000 and received CAMTESOL Innovation Award in 2009, and her paper on management of university-based English Language Programme in Asia's non-native contexts was the best selected paper. In 2014, she was awarded Doctor of Philosophy in Education from the UNSW, Sydney, and received the NSW Institute of Education Research's Beth Southwell Award for Outstanding Doctoral Thesis. Her research interests are TESOL pedagogy, university leadership, and university governance.

Nga Thi Hang Ngo (PhD) is a lecturer in TESOL at Tay Bac University, Vietnam. She has had experience in teaching TESOL and training TESOL preservice and in-service teachers in Vietnam. Her research areas include TESOL pedagogy and teacher education, particularly teachers in disadvantaged areas. She has published various articles in these areas.

Hang Thu Le Nguyen (PhD) is a lecturer in English Language Teacher Education at the University of Languages and International Studies, Vietnam National University, Hanoi. She has been working in both preservice and in-service teacher education in Vietnam. Her major areas of specialisation include teaching methodologies, curriculum development, course design, and quality assurance in higher education. Apart from her university teaching and management experience, she also has 20 years of experience with the Asian Institute of Technology in Vietnam, designing and delivering training courses in training methodologies, organisational management, and generic and language skills for professionals.

Hoa Thi Mai Nguyen (PhD) is a senior lecturer in Teacher Professional Learning at the School of Education, University of New South Wales, Australia. She has experience in teaching and training preservice and in-service teachers in Asia and Australia. Her ongoing research interests have been in the areas of teacher education, teacher professional development, mentoring, TESOL, and sociocultural theory. She has recently published a book entitled *Models of Mentoring in Language Teacher Education* (Springer).

Nhai Thi Nguyen (PhD) is a teacher and unit leader of the Educational Studies stream at Monash College, Australia. She has woven her 16 years of research, teaching, and industry experiences into the design, development, and delivery of higher education, cultural studies, and teacher education. She has won a number of awards and fellowship including Australian Leadership Award, Comparative and International Education Society (CIES) 2016 International Travel Award for Distinguished Service in Educational Reforms in Canada, and CIES 2018 International Travel Award for Emergent Scholars.

Quy Nguyen (DEd) is a lecturer in TESOL and dean (Educational Testing and Quality Assurance) at the University of Foreign Language Studies, the University of Danang, in Vietnam. He obtained a doctoral degree in Education from Griffith University, Australia, in 2015 and became an adjunct research fellow at the Griffith Institute for Educational Research, Griffith University. His research interests are in educational leadership, university policy, research and teaching nexus, research productivity of academics, and English language.

Thu Dinh Nguyen (PhD) is a senior lecturer at the Faculty of Foreign Languages, University of Technology and Education, Ho Chi Minh City (HCMUTE), in Vietnam. His research interests cover TESOL teacher education, preservice and in-service teachers training, teacher professional development, mentoring, and socio-cultural theory in the EFL context of Vietnam.

Hiep-Hung Pham (PhD) currently serves as director of the Center for Research and Practice in Education, Phu Xuan University, Vietnam. In 2017, he was awarded his PhD in International Business Administration from the Chinese Culture University, Taiwan (ROC). In 2013, he was an endeavour research fellow, conducting research at the Centre of Studies in Higher Education, the University of Melbourne. His research interests include international education, tertiary education management, and scientometrics.

Ly Thi Tran (PhD) is an associate professor in the School of Education, Deakin University, Australia, and an Australian Research Council future fellow. She has published widely in the field of Vietnamese higher education and student mobility international education and is frequently invited to speak at conferences, symposiums, and workshops. Her books, *Teaching International Students in Vocational Education: New Pedagogical Approaches* and *International Student Connectedness and Identity: Transnational Perspectives*, won the International Education Association of Australia Excellence Award for Best Practice/Innovation in International Education and third place in the 2019 Best Book Award category from the Comparative International Education Society Study Abroad and International Students SIG, respectively.

Thi Tuyet Tran (June Tran) (DEd) is a mobile researcher. She has worked in three countries, Australia, Vietnam, and Germany, and has developed an interest in interdisciplinary research. Her interests range from labour economics and human resource management to various areas in management and education research such as migrant workplace integration, graduate employability, work integrated learning, university-industry collaboration, language education, and cultural study. She is currently based at the School of Management, RMIT University, working toward her research project, namely 'Workplace Integration in Australia: The Experience of Professional Chinese and Vietnamese Skilled Migrants'.

Huyen-Minh Vu (MEd) is a lecturer at Vietnam National University, University of Language and International Studies, Hanoi. In 2013, she obtained a master's degree in Lifelong Learning from the Institute of Education at the University College London. Her academic interests include university governance, curriculum design, and English teaching.

Abbreviations

ACTFL	American Council on the Teaching of Foreign Languages
ADB	Asian Development Bank
APHERP	Asia Pacific Higher Education Research Partnership
ASEAN	Association of Southeast Asian Nations
ATN	Australian Technology Network
CEFR	Common European Framework of Reference
CETCF	Core English Teacher Competency Framework
CHAT	Cultural-Historical Activity Theory
CHC	Confucian Heritage Countries
CHEA	Council for Higher Education Accreditation
CLT	Communicative Language Teaching
CN	China
CRN	Collaborative Research Networks
DEEWR	Department of Education, Employment, and Workplace Relation
DIUS	Department for Business Innovation and Skills
DoHE	Department of Higher Education
EAL	English as an Additional Language
EFL	English as a Foreign Language
EIL	English as an International Language
ELLT	English Language Learning and Teaching
ELT	English Language Teaching
EMI	English as a Medium of Instruction
EPI	English Proficiency Index
ESL	English as a Second Language
ETCF	English Teacher Competency Framework
EU	European Union
EUEC	University-Enterprise Collaboration
GDETA	General Department of Educational Testing and Accreditation
GDP	Gross Domestic Product
HDI	Human Development Indicators
HEIs	Higher Education Institutions

HEPs	Higher Education Providers
HERA	Higher Education Reform Agenda
HES	Higher Education System
HK	Hong Kong
ILO	International Labour Organization
ILOs	Intended Learning Outcomes
IMF	International Monetary Fund
MNCs	Multinational Corporations
MOET	Ministry of Education and Training
MOET	Vietnamese Ministry of Education and Training
MOLISA	Ministry of Labour, Invalids, and Social Affairs
MOOCs	Massive Online Open Courses
NACIQI	National Advisory Committee on Institutional Quality and Integrity
NAFOSTED	National Foundation for Science and Technology Development
NCATE	National Council for Accreditation of Teacher Education
NEASC-CIHE	New England Association of Schools and Colleges-Commission on Institutions of Higher Education
NFL2020	National Foreign Language 2020 Project
OECD	Organisation for Economic Cooperation and Development
OHEC	Office of Higher Education Commission
PD	Professional Development
PhD	Doctor of Philosophy
PL	Professional Learning
QA	Quality Assurance
SEAMEO	Southeast Asian Ministers of Education Organization
SEOG	Supplemental Educational Opportunity Grant
ST	Student Teacher
TBLT	Task-Based Language Teaching
TDTU	Ton Duc Thang University
TE	Teacher Educator
TESOL	Teaching English as a Second Language
TL	Thailand
TMG	Teacher as Moral Guide
TPP	Trans-Pacific Partnership
UGC	University Grants Committee
UNDP	United Nations Development Programme
UNESCO	United Nations Educational, Scientific, and Cultural Organization
VASS	Vietnam Academy of Social Sciences
VAST	Vietnam Academy of Science and Technology
VCP	Vietnamese Communist Party
VED	Vietnam Education Dialogue
VHE	Vietnamese Higher Education
VHLSS	Vietnam Household Living Standards Survey

VN	Vietnam
VND	Vietnam Dong
VNU-HCMC	Vietnam National University-Ho Chi Minh City
VNU-HN	Vietnam National University, Hanoi
VUN	Vietnam Universities Network
WB	World Bank
WIL	Work-Integrated Learning
WTO	World Trade Organization
NWU	North-West University

List of Figures

Fig. 5.1 Seven aspects in current debate on higher education
financing mechanism. (Source: author synthesized
and extended from ADB 2009) 82
Fig. 5.2 Lorentz concentration curves in accessibility of Vietnam's
higher education in 2004 and 2011 (*Q1* represents
the poorest 20% population of Vietnam while *Q5*
represents the richest quintile) (Pham and Tran 2014) 85

Fig. 8.1 Factors affecting transferability 145

Fig. 12.1 The structure of a human activity system.
(Engeström 1987, p. 78, with permission from
Yrjö Engeström) 226
Fig. 12.2 Two interacting activity systems as the minimal model
for the third generation of activity theory.
(Engeström 2001, p. 136, with permission from
Yrjö Engeström) 227
Fig. 12.3 Academics' professional learning activity system.
(After Engeström 2001) 230

List of Tables

Table 5.1   Tuition fee per student per month at regular state-sponsored
undergraduate courses in Vietnam 78

Table 5.2   Amount of student loan in Vietnam 80

Table 5.3   Comparison of dual track fee system between Vietnam's
public higher education institutions and Johnstone's (2004) 81

Table 5.4   Two selected projects funded by government
with high per-student investment 86

Table 5.5   Results of Top 350 QS University Ranking Asia 2016
at some selected countries in ASEAN 87

Table 8.1   A snapshot of accreditation in the USA,
Australia and Vietnam 138

Table 9.1   Participant information 158

Table 10.1   Statistics of colleges and universities
in Vietnam 2000–2016 176

Table 10.2   International refereed journal articles of researchers
in East and Southeast Asia countries, 2000–2016 179

Table 10.3   The national budget for research and technology
each year (VND Million) 180

Table 10.4   The number of universities of each country ranked
in the World's Top 400 in 2015–2016 and 2016–2017 181

Table 10.5   The number of universities of each country ranked
in the Asia's top 200 in 2015 and 2016 181

Table 10.6   International refereed journal articles of Ton Duc Thang
University and regional universities 182

Table 10.7   International refereed journal articles of academics
in key Australia's and Vietnam's universities, 2000–2016 188

Table 12.1   Eight-step model (Mwanza 2002b, p. 86) 228

Chapter 1
Impacts of Global Forces and Local Demands on Vietnamese Higher Education

Nhai Thi Nguyen and Ly Thi Tran

Abstract The chapter discusses the context of higher education reforms in Vietnam. It sets the scene by exploring the global forces that have shaped and reshaped the landscape of Vietnamese higher education. It then examines how the local demands have affected the higher education sector and concludes with an outline of the book structure.

Introduction

As the world's 14th and ASEAN's third largest nation, with a population of almost 96 million people, Vietnam is well known for a good tradition of teaching and learning as well as a strong family commitment to education. The country has achieved 92% of adult literacy, as compared to the average world adult literacy of 98.06% for those aged between 14 and 25, and an average of 94.51% for those who are 15 years old and older (UNESCO 2015). Despite remarkable achievements in basic education, health and income (Do and Do 2014), Vietnam's Human Development Indicator (HDI) index of 0.683 in 2015 (up from 0.435 in 1990) (UNDP 2011) ranked 128 out of 187 countries (UNDP 2015). However, Vietnam's tertiary education has been identified as the weakest sector in the education system (Nguyen 2018; Tran et al. 2014, 2017; Tran and Marginson 2018a, b).

The Vietnamese higher education (VHE) system is comprised of both junior colleges and universities, which are responsible for awarding diploma, bachelor, master and doctorate credentials. There are two national universities and three regional universities, each with its own distinctive institutional governance arrangements and member universities, and there are a large number of provincial

N. T. Nguyen (✉)
Monash College, Clayton, VIC, Australia
e-mail: Nhai.Nguyen@monashcollege.edu.au

L. T. Tran
Deakin University, Burwood, VIC, Australia

© Springer Nature Singapore Pte Ltd. 2019
N. T. Nguyen, L. T. Tran (eds.), *Reforming Vietnamese Higher Education*,
Education in the Asia-Pacific Region: Issues, Concerns and Prospects 50,
https://doi.org/10.1007/978-981-13-8918-4_1

universities and academic institutes. The system includes nonpublic and foreign-owned tertiary education institutions, accounting for 19.5% of all higher education institutions (Do and Do 2014). The number of universities and colleges in the system has expanded fourfold within the past two decades, reaching 425 by 2015 (UNESCO 2015). It is estimated that over the decade between 2000 and 2010, one new university, on average, was being established every week. Over a 6-year period from 2007 to 2013, 133 new universities were established, of which 108 were upgraded from 2-year colleges (Pham 2015). Vietnam's institution-to-people ratio is estimated currently to be 1:212,000. Rapid and fragmented growth in the number of new higher education institutions with a limited vision of their role has posed significant risks for quality assurance and governance (Do and Do 2014).

To date, the research literature on the VHE system has not explored the role and importance of globalisation in sufficient depth. In a postcolonial country such as Vietnam, it is important to detect transnational linkages, junctures and disjunctures as well as the stoppages residing within the system. This book seeks to advance a conceptual understanding, as well as offering practical insights about the system and the extent of educational reform. The book addresses the following principal question and sub-questions:

Principal question: 'How are Vietnamese higher education institutions responding to globalisation and internationalisation as well as local demands?'
Sub-questions:

(a) What changes have occurred in Vietnam's higher education system as a consequence of the impact of global forces?
(b) What is the nature of the local forces being exerted on the higher education system in Vietnam?
(c) What is the impact of Vietnamese culture and values on Vietnam's higher education system in a context of global forces?
(d) What are implications of local and global forces for reforming Vietnam's higher education system?

Globalisation and Internationalisation

Fundamental to the tracking of VHE's patterns and developments are globalisation and internationalisation, which are identified as global forces in this book. Initially, globalisation may be approached from top-down or bottom-up. The former approach is sensitive to global expansion of free trade and free market ideology. It unpacks the power geometry of supranational agencies such as the World Bank (WB), International Monetary Fund (IMF), UNESCO and the like, as well as the acceleration of multinational corporations (MNCs). The latter proposes an opposite path, understood as the 'grassroots' of globalisation in the words of Ajun Appadurai (2001b). Viewed according to this approach, globalisation must be seen as a complex site which is neither complete nor fixed. Rather, it is the combination of networks of relation, be they economic, cultural or political (Altbach and Knight 2007; Enders

2004; Marginson and Mollis 2011). Essentially, these networks of relation extend beyond the geographical boundaries of the nation-state.

Kenway et al. (2006) argue that the process of deterritorialisation occurring within the nexus of globalisation has made our social life less structured and dependent upon physical territories. Neither does it lie in the particularities of locality or place. Instead, the 'social relations are "stretched out" across ever-widening expanses of space' (Kenway et al. 2006, p. 44). Aspects of social and cultural life have been isolated from the notion of defined 'place', leading further to an advent of a 'new scale of social action and social power' (ibid, p.45). As a result, these scholars urge us to move away from the comfort of spatiality [the local and the nation-state] to a social space which involves and invokes transnational social and cultural activities and formations.

Kenway et al. (2006) also remind us that this social space is embedded with power geometries. As a consequence, scholars must not be completely bounded by local place and time. They must be critically aware of the importance of place and reflexively attend to both embodied and local habits and cultures. These habits and cultures become seen as observant of the '*fluidities* and *mobilities*' alongside with the '*stoppages* and *fixities*' which characterise the social space.

Essentially, globalisation is dispelled at the local production level. The local/the single place and globalisation are inseparable entities. They precondition the existence of the other. Often, the politics of local production are subtly embedded in every activity of supranational production. In Burawoy's (2001) critique, the interconnected political struggles should be tied up to every node of the global production lines. Burawoy (ibid.) therefore urges us to 'replace abstract globalisation with a grounded globalisation but also how that *experience is produced in specific localities* and how that productive process is a contested and thus a political accomplishment' (p. 158, emphasis added). Alongside this political struggle is the need to restore history and agency at the local reception and contestation of the global and further relocate the global as produced in the local. Here globalisation is understood and interpreted as the production of (dis)connections that link and of discourses that travel (Appadurai 1996; Burawoy 2001; Kenway et al. 2006).

Globalisation has posed numerous challenges to sociocultural life. It has changed the ways in which humans normally live (Appadurai 1996, 2001a). One typical example of this change is the vast expansion of individualism in the traditionally so-called collectivist societies. It subliminally conditions *hybridisation of cultural and social tradition* which would have us go beyond economic globalisation to unpack the education system and its patterns and changes (Marginson and Mollis 2011).

Neubauer's (2012) proposal of 'circuit' and 'subcircuit' of exchange upon the profusion of globalisation is useful. This scholar locates globalisation in the landscape of higher education in East Asia, arguing that higher education is actually made of another circuit of exchange. It is constitutive of multiple subcircuits, each of which constitutes and is derivative of the delineated geography of networks. These circuits and subcircuits overlap with one another. Alternatively, according to Neubauer (2012), they are multiple and hybrid. They characterise modern higher education institutions in East Asian countries, including the Vietnamese higher education system (Nguyen and Tran 2017).

Internationalisation in higher education is habituated by globalisation. It constitutes a space where multifarious flows of international students, scholars, knowledges, programs and educational service providers stretch higher education boundaries beyond nation-state. Viewed according to this perspective, internationalisation has become seen as the realisation and the product of social spatiality. In examining the impact of spatiality in internationalisation of higher education, Larsen notes:

> Internationalisation is the expansion of the spatiality of the university beyond borders through mobilities of students, scholars, knowledge, programs and providers. (Larsen 2016, p. 10)

However, internationalisation cannot be hastily or narrowly reduced to student mobility, cross-border education or curriculum-related changes. Jane Knight (2003) proposes three dimensions of globalisation: international, intercultural and global. In examining internationalisation of higher education, she alerts us to the danger of overlooking the complexities of globalisation and internationalisation. Following Knight, globalisation ideologies have been injected into internationalisation. Consequently, international and intercultural dimensions have been prioritised in higher education policies and programs. The rationale behind internationalisation is to ensure this international dimension remains central and sustainable.

Local Responses and Demands

Globalisation, internationalisation, the knowledge economy and the shifting labour market structure have created a demand for reforms of the VHE. Changes to the higher education system are critical to respond to the need to enhance human capital for a globalised knowledge economy. Nguyen and Tran (2017), upon observing globalisation and internationalisation in the Vietnamese higher education system, remark:

> … the influences of global and external forces upon HE in Vietnam are inevitable. Globalisation has created the condition for the reform of VHE to take place. At the same time, the HE system is under the pressure to change in order to respond effectively to the new circumstances brought about by globalisation and internationalisation. (p. 13)

Higher education has been recognised as pivotal to national capacity building. It enhances national economic growth and national competitiveness in the global arena, while also re-enhancing political and cultural power. It prepares, equips and strengthens its citizens' skills, knowledge and competencies, enabling those who are fully prepared to function efficiently in the more competitive global labour market. And yet, Vietnam does not seem to be well prepared for such global integration.

Vietnam's success at the Trans-Pacific Partnership[1] (TPP) on 8 October 2015 would urge researchers and HE policymakers to reframe VHE in ways that it responds more effectively to the mega forces of globalisation and national economic development. In an interview with the *Thanhnienonline* newspaper, the economic specialist, Phan Van Truong (Phan 2015), expressed his concern that Vietnam was not yet well prepared to meet the human resources, strategic planning strategies and international trade relations required by TPP member countries. As Phan argued, mobilising the nation's internal strength (inner agency) and self-determination is a critical strategy in face of TPP and intense economic globalisation.

In 2008, there were 2,162,106 students enrolled in Vietnamese tertiary education; 76% of whom were studying full time (MOET 2009). There were 74,573 lecturers. Only 10.6% of whom held a PhD qualification. The ratio of students to lecturers was comparatively high, at 29 to 1. According to World Bank (2015), the country's tertiary gross student enrolment increased by almost 13 times, from 2% in 1991 to 25% in 2013. Such a rapid growth in higher education has slowed down since 2013. In 2016, it is reported that there were total 2.2 million students enrolling in universities and colleges, a slight decrease compared to that of 2015 and somewhat equivalent to that of 2008. However, what captivates us is the social craze and social mentality towards credentials, that is, the society-wide obsession for securing a place in the Vietnamese universities or colleges tends to fade away (Nguyen 2013; Nguyen and Lehy 2015). The yearning of Vietnamese families and students for higher education credentials appears to be not as strong as it used to be. Instead, Vietnamese families and students have become more selective and rational with their choice of universities and the undergraduate programs massively offered in the market. Never before have we witnessed such a severe competition coming from both public and private sector, with institutions now racing against one another for recruiting students via enormous marketing-driven campaigns and student recruitment strategies. Increasing local demands have been shifted towards the quality of undergraduate programs, the prestige of the university or college and the student employability rate upon graduation.

Universities and colleges in Vietnam have become subject to severe public scrutiny. More often, pressure comes directly from parents and students who have placed higher demands for teaching and learning quality, branding and graduate employability. Universities and colleges are being required to align better with market needs and stakeholder demands; they are seeking to uplift teaching and learning quality, improve graduate employability rates and build their brand identities in the higher education market. The challenges lie on the fact that their

---

[1] Championed as the "21st Century Agreement", the TPP involves 12 countries including the USA and Japan. The TPP block produces 40% of the global trade within this trade agreement. Vietnam successfully signed the TPP agreement on 8 October 2015. Together with other three Southeast Asian countries such as Malaysia, Singapore and Brunei (Hunter Marson, The Diplomat, 25 July 2015), Vietnam is believed to benefit the most from TPP in the fields of garment and textiles (Retrieved from http://thediplomat.com/2015/07/what-the-trans-pacific-partnership-means-for-southeast-asia/)

existing curriculum appears to be fairly out of tune with the labour market, new technologies and international developments in teaching and learning (Tran et al. 2018). Especially, current teaching and learning practices tend to be fairly slow to respond to the demands of the market economy. Preoccupied with pure disciplinary theories and political indoctrination, the VHE curriculum provides insufficient attention to work-integrated learning as well as the development of soft skills and attributes for students (Tran et al. 2014). Critical reflection and creative thinking have been given insufficient emphasis in current HE teaching and learning practices. Scholars have pointed out that many students 'find it hard to think creatively or to respond flexibly to emerging challenges' (Tran et al. 2014, p. 20). This is coupled with the disconnectedness between the VHE institutions and the industry, the decreasing university enrolment rate mentioned previously and the growing concern over university graduates' unemployment (Pham 2015; World Bank 2012).

At the national level, the Vietnamese Government's responses to these challenges have been comparatively aggressive; they have been manifested via a series of decades-long, post-1986 policies in an effort to create a breakthrough in VHE quality (Nguyen and Tran 2017). One of the highlights of these policy texts is Decision No.201/2001/QD-TTG of 28 December 2001. In principle, the Decision is correlated to the 2001–2010 Educational Development Strategy. It stresses the need for the VHE system to 'create a breakthrough in educational quality compatible to international standard and at the same time, fits well into Vietnamese context' (Vietnamese Government 2001).

Resolution No.37/2004/QH11 issued by the National Assembly on 3 December 2004 re-enhances Decision No.201/2001/QD-TTG. Overall the Resolution commands that the Vietnamese universities are supposed to choose amongst a vast array of international advanced programs to develop an advanced modern curriculum, thanks to which the VHE institutions can create through teaching and learning reforms (Vietnamese National Assembly 2004). In 2005, Vietnam's Education Law was officially approved by the 11th National Assembly meeting. The Education Law speculates that the VHE curriculum content must be modern and advanced; in addition, it has to be synched with basic science knowledge, foreign language, information and technology literacy and specialised knowledge. At the same time, it is to meet regional and international standard (Vietnamese Government 2005). The Resolution14/2005/NQ-CP was issued on 2 November 2005; it showcases, amongst other things, the Vietnamese Government's determination to comprehensively innovate the VHE system for the 2006–2020 period and, again, commands the VHE institutions to import and apply the so-called advanced foreign curriculum and programs (Vietnamese Government 2005).

Most prominently, Decision No.145/2006/QĐ-TTg on 20 June 2006 guides and orients VHE institutions towards building a Vietnamese university with an international standard (Vietnamese Government 2006). It is followed by the 10th National Congress's Decision in 2010 and the National Standing Committee of the Vietnamese Communist Party's report, focusing exclusively on transforming education and training. Anticipated to thoroughly renew the VHE system and build an international standard university, it aims to train the Vietnamese talents (Centre

Committee 2010; Vietnamese Communist Party 2010). Further, the higher education law approved by the National Assembly on 18 June 2012 became effective as of 1 January 2013, and it was appended with a Chapter on International Cooperation (Chapter VI with 6 Articles).

The Vietnamese Ministry of Education and Training (MOET) has introduced various policy texts in attempt to respond timely and effectively to the local Vietnamese needs. It, at the same time, has to align well with global trends in higher education. The most prominent policies are the Higher Education Reform Agenda (HERA) – Resolution 14/2005/NQ-CP (Vietnam Government 2005) and Resolution 73/2012/ND-CP, both of which were aimed at VHE's *'fundamental and comprehensive'* reforms (Vietnamese Government 2012). These policies have, nevertheless, been subjected to scrutiny; they are said to lack comprehensiveness, vision and practicality (Hoang et al. 2018; Nguyen and Tran 2017; Tran et al. 2014; Tran and Marginson 2018a). Neither do these policies could help tackle VHE crisis at root, nor can they embody a sophisticated educational philosophy driving higher education reforms. Except for an over-ambitious goal of producing 20,000 PhDs by 2020 regarded as one of strategic human power plans and massive state funding, these alarming issues have posed numerous constraints to government authorities (Harman et al. 2010; Hayden and Lam 2010; Hayden and Thiep 2007; London 2011; Pham 2010; Tran et al. 2014).

The burgeoning local demands for the VHE reforms are clearly felt in the field of university governance and structure, including institutional autonomy, accountability and academic freedom. The lack of autonomy, accountability and academic freedom is rooted in the highly centralised and bureaucratic system with top-down management style and overlapping control of different ministries (Nguyen et al. 2009; George 2011). Consequently, VHE institutional governance falls below standard and expectation and is commonly tied to power hierarchy. Do Minh Hoang and Do Thi Ngoc Quyen (2014) further argue 'the lack of well-planned reforms and synchronic solutions and measures has led to an unmanageable higher education system in terms of educational quality' (p. 48). As a consequence, academics have been familiar with poor autonomy, underpay and lack of research funding and professional development. Limited resources and insufficient empowerment have been commonly cited for hindering Vietnamese academics' commitment to their duties and responsibilities. Many of them have turned to 'informal' sources of income so that they could make their ends meet. More alarmingly, they tend to marginalise their institutional duties rather than seeing them as being core to their professional life. Apart from selecting, developing, resourcing and regulating academics' quality, enhancing academics' commitment to their university and their professional duties is key to ensure teaching and learning quality.

Higher education reforms and massification of the VHE system over the past three decades since economic reforms in 1986 have constrained university leaders and MOET authorities. The VHE institutes appear to fall short of academic staff. The consequence is academic staff's workload has been increased. Further, Decision No.1400/QĐ-TTG (Vietnamese Government 2008) raised the bar of English communication skills and standards required for university lecturers. The Decision was officially approved by the Vietnamese Government to launch Project 2008–2020 on 30 September 2008. It is considered a timely response to the need to teach English for Vietnamese students, public servants and staff nationwide. The project costs approximately VND 9400 trillion, an equivalent of US $540 million.

Alongside with Decision No.1400/QĐ-TTG, in the field of teacher education, there has been a burgeoning need for an effective professional training model for academic staff and professional ethics and morality. This is because this model is expected to improve teacher competences and, thus, assist Vietnamese teachers, especially primary and secondary English teachers, in meeting the new English teacher standard as is outlined in the Joint Circular No.21/2015/TTLT-BGDĐT-BNV by MOET (MOET 2015).

MOET has acknowledged the importance of research in universities and national capacity for shaping an innovative, dynamic economy. Paradoxically, a large number of Vietnamese universities and colleges have been deploying the Soviet higher education model after 1954 in Northern Vietnam and post 1975 in the South of Vietnam. In light of this model, universities and research institutes are separate bodies, those whose domain is to mainly focus on teaching and those whose function is research focussed such as government research institutes. This long-standing Soviet model is criticised for failing to respond to the country's scientific, economic and social needs (Tran et al. 2014). The disconnection between higher education and research institutes, according to World Bank (2012), has been identified as one of five key weaknesses of the VHE system. Albeit massive funding poured into higher education research, limited research achievements have been gained compared to other Asia Pacific developing countries. The Vietnamese HE research capacity tends to lag behind, as is observed by World Bank (2012).

Since Vietnam Economic Reforms (*Doi Moi*) in 1986, numerous efforts have been done to improve higher education equity and equality. However, there exists a gap, especially for the underprivileged and disadvantaged students. Access to tertiary education and quality of tertiary education in general and between regions has been deviated and granted to different student cohorts.

Vietnamese Higher Education in a Globalised Context

The edited collection of chapters is accessible to global readers. It offers an alternative and comparative approach to more critical, sustainable VHE reforms. This is because it, perhaps for the first time, reinvigorates the higher education in Vietnam as a field of knowledge enquiry. Within this field are complexities and geopolitical, historical and economical forces, be they global, national or local. These forces are intertwined, inhibiting in themselves numerous circuits and subcircuits (Hawkins et al. 2013; Marginson 2008; Neubauer 2012). At every node of the global-national-local intersection, it is possible to observe subtle translation and interaction of these forces writing and rewriting the local landscapes including education.

Of particular emphasis of the book is the way in which the book multiplies and shifts its referencing points that locate Vietnamese higher education as an important node in the 'global-national-local' circuit and subcircuits of the network. The edited book chapter advances the conceptual understanding of higher education; it not only contributes theoretically to research scholarship but also holds significant methodological implications for reading and interpreting higher education reforms from a critical and sustainable approach.

Part I proposes a conceptual framework of approaching and interpreting education reforms and puts forward an alternative approach to higher education. Specifically, it utilises an inside-out perspective via looking inwardly into the system structure and agency of Vietnam higher education. Nhai Thi Nguyen, for instance, in Chap. 2 travels the concept of cultural identities, core values, being and becoming into the cultural field of higher education. The author traces the historical development of Vietnamese higher education and identifies the hidden linkages, disconnections, disjuntures, fixities and stoppages residing in this cultural field that have overturned, translated and reshaped the landscape of higher education in Vietnam.

In Part II, the authors address in great detail issues associated with VHE structure, policy and governance including university leadership and management, government policy, university governance and financing. Khanh Van Dao and Martin Hayden in Chap. 3 review a variety of the VHE policy texts on university leadership and management in light of a comparative framework and analyse the sector's prospects up to 2020. Mai Tuyet Ngo in Chap. 4 focuses on four comparative case studies of the models of public university governance in four East Asian countries including Thailand, China, Hong Kong and Vietnam. Her multilevel thematic framework and the cross-case comparisons indicate, to a certain degree, the similar patterns as well as specificities of every single case, proposing a novel model of Vietnamese university governance in the public sector in which academic excellence is promoted and remedies for minimal research-led universities in Vietnam are touted out.

Financing, another key aspect of VHE structure and governance, in the analysis of Hiep-Hung Pham and Huyen-Minh Vu in Chap. 5, has been shifted from being fully government-subsidised to be the cost-sharing one. The new financing model is associated with educational socialisation and differs considerably from the Western model. This is added by the fact that the Vietnamese Government has been no longer solely responsible for financing the VHE institutions. Consequently, educational costs and financial commitments have been shared and transferred to students and their parents. Clearly inherited from Western neoliberalism, these policies raise concerns over social equity and equality and access to higher education as well as quality and sustainability of VHE. Measures for effective HE financing, as Pham and Vu propose, will be addressed meticulously in this chapter.

Part III assembles research studies on curriculum, quality assurance and equity in higher education. Thi Tuyet Tran in Chap. 6 sees the strategic importance of enhancing employability and factors such as higher education massification, traditional features of family/career orientation in Confucian Heritage Countries (CHC), teaching philosophy, and internal and external connectivities within the education system and between the education system and the labour market have been decisive to the Vietnamese graduates' job readiness and employability after graduation. The complex interplay of various parties calls for a society-wide effort in which, a part from other equally important factors, student and their family must take the central role and responsibilities for choosing appropriate discipline, career and university alongside with equipping themselves with a suitcase of generic skills, soft skills and employability skills, in order to make sure that they are job ready and perform well in the field they were trained at university. In the subsequent chapter, Nhai Thi Nguyen, Ly Thi Tran and Truc Thi Thanh Le draw on a case study in an Australian branch campus in Vietnam in which the authors measure the efficiency of this model against their employability and work readiness. The authors also investigate in depth how work-integrated learning (WIL) has been merged into curriculum design, conditioned teaching and learning practices and helped build a robust support system, as well as insinuated and strengthened cross-sectoral staff mobility. The authors urge to relocate the work-integrated learning (WIL) from margin to the centre of curriculum and pedagogy, the heart of teaching and learning practices. Fuelled by high unemployment rates amongst Vietnamese university graduates, the WIL model is expected to make university teaching and learning closer to local market demands, enhance students' work readiness and promote industry linkages. It aims at preparing a generation of graduates equipped with necessary skills, knowledge and a set of generic skills, soft skills and employability skills (Tran et al. 2014). It enables university graduates to fully capitalise on their flexibility, mobility and practicality.

Quyen Thi Ngoc Do, in Chap. 8, addresses another important aspect of VHE, that is, the national quality assurance (QA). The scholar investigates the ways in which various local demands and international practices in QA implicitly inform the importation of foreign approaches and concepts into the education system. While stressing that modification and adaptation of the borrowed policies need to take the 'host' and 'home' contexts into careful consideration, Do concludes that maintaining the core principles of the borrowed model is as equally important as modifying and adapting specific practices.

The development of Vietnam's national quality assurance system is characterized by the import of foreign-born concepts, policies, models and instruments. They have been adapted to different extents to fit local contexts. By looking into the degrees at which original models and methods are adapted, the chapter sheds light on how local demands and international practices have driven the borrowing of foreign approaches and concepts into the local education system. The discussion covers accreditation, a widely known QA instrument, and a mix of ranking and stratification, which is newly introduced into the system. The chapter stresses that adaptation is essential in model transfer. It also argues that during the transfer process, the fundamental principles of the borrowed model or instrument should be retained, while specific practices could be considered for modification and adaptation. It is also recommended that a thorough analysis of the both 'home' and 'host' contexts be conducted for effective transfer.

Drawing on Bourdieu's theory of social reproduction and the notion of educational capital, scholars such as Thuy Thi Ngoc Bui, Nga Thi Hang Ngo, Hoa Thi Mai Nguyen and Hang Thu Le Nguyen in Chap. 9 argue that factors including geographical location and financial and nonfinancial factors have held main responsibilities for maintaining and balancing equity, access and social justice for students in this disadvantaged region, and education capital could support this student cohort to narrow these gaps in Northwest Vietnam.

Part IV is devoted to exploring VHE research. Since research capacity building always plays a pivotal role in national strategic development, attempts have been made to build research-led universities and revitalise research capacity in the VHE institutions. Amongst many others, central to the VHE reform agenda is the strategy to create a giant leap for Vietnamese universities. The agenda indicates an overambitious aim to have a couple of Vietnamese universities listed in the top 200 universities in the world by 2020. Quy Nguyen and Christopher Klopper in Chap. 10 investigate the spectrums associated with research capacity, policy and programs under the impacts of globalised forces. Using a comparative perspective of Australia, Singapore, Hong Kong, South Korea and Vietnam, these scholars reconnoitre research environment, research capability and productivity of academics in HEIs in the above-listed countries and conclude that building research capacity is within our reach if sufficient time allocation, research funding and scholarly resources and the surround support are in attendance.

Part V looks in depth at VHE professional development which is central to national capacity building in the fast-changing context of globalisation and the rise of the knowledge economy. Such external global forces would have every single government to sufficiently train its human resources in ways that they are well equipped with prerequisite skills and knowledge to respond to and thus perform well in the global, national and local labour market. So does English language education in Vietnam. Foreseeing the emergence and the imperative of English language in global economic integration, the Vietnamese Government introduced the National Foreign Language 2020 Project (NFLP2020). Chapter 11, written by Mai Tuyet Ngo, offers a critical lens into the introduction of the new Vietnam English teacher competency standardisation as is commissioned by the NFLP 2020.

Hoa Thi Mai Nguyen and Thu Dinh Nguyen in Chap. 12 investigate the perceptions, beliefs and attitudes of Vietnamese academic staff at the VHE institutions. These authors indicate factors affecting the professional development (PD) of the Vietnamese academics and propose a viable model for lecturers' PD. Alongside with lecturers' PD is the shifting of Vietnamese academic's identity. Conditioned by globalisation and English imperialism, Linh Thuy Le and Leigh Gerrard Dwyer in Chap. 13 use the social positioning theory to investigate the ways in which teachers of English perceive themselves as a moral guide. Their research reveals that Vietnamese teachers are more likely to perceive their moral identity in a less traditional way, and there are criss-crosses, mixing and crossover of their moral guide and other emerging identities borne as a result of globalisation and urge teachers of English to draw on their moral identity as a compass to guide and encourage a fuller understanding, an appreciation and an enactment of moral identity traits in their students.

References

Altbach, P., & Knight, J. (2007). The internationalisation of higher education: Motivations and realities. *Journal of Studies in International Education, 11*(3/4), 290–305.

Appadurai, A. (1996). *Modernity at large: Cultural dimensions of globalisation.* Minneapolis: University of Minnesota Press.

Appadurai, A. (2001a). *Globalisation.* Durham: Duke University Press.

Appadurai, A. (Ed.). (2001b). *Grassroots globalisation and the research imagination.* Durham: Duke University Press.

Burawoy, M. (2001). Manufacturing the global. *Ethnography, 2*(2), 147–159.

Centre Committee. (2010). *Báo cáo chính trị của Ban Chấp hành Trung ương Đảng khoá X tại Đại hội đại biểu toàn quốc lần thứ XI của Đảng.* Hanoi: Vietnamese Government Online Portal Retrieved from http://chinhphu.vn/portal/page/portal/chinhphu/NuocCHXHCNVietNam/ThongTinTongHop/noidungvankiendaihoidang?categoryId=10000716&articleId=10038382

Decree 73/2012/NĐ-CP on International Cooperation and Foreign Investment in Education (2012).

Do, M. H., & Do, T. N. Q. (2014). Policy borrowing. In L. T. Tran, S. Marginson, H. M. Đo, Q. T. N. Đo, T. T. T. Le, N. T. Nguyen, T. T. P. Vu, T. N. Pham, & H. T. L. Nguyen (Eds.), *Higher education in Vietnam: Flexibility, mobility and practicality for national development* (pp. 29–53). Basingstoke: Palgrave Macmillan.

Enders, J. (2004). Higher education, internationalisation, and the nation-state: Recent developments and challenges to governance theory. *Higher Education, 47,* 361–382.

Harman, G., Hayden, M., & Nghi, P. T. (2010). Higher education in Vietnam: Reform, challenges and priorities. In G. Harman, M. Hayden, & T. N. Pham (Eds.), *Reforming higher education in Vietnam: Challenges and priorities* (pp. 1–14). London/New York: Springer.

Hawkins, J. N., Neubauer, D., & Shin, J. C. (2013). Introduction: Four hypotheses of higher education development. In D. Neubauer, J. C. Shin, & J. N. Hawkins (Eds.), *The dynamics of higher education development in East Asia: Asian cultural heritage, Western dominance, economic development, and globalisation (international and development education)* (pp. 1–8). New York: Palgrave Macmillan.

Hayden, M., & Lam, Q. T. (2010). Vietnam's higher education system. In G. Harman, M. Hayden, & T. N. Pham (Eds.), *Reforming higher education in Vietnam: Challenges and priorities* (pp. 15–30). London/New York: Springer.

Hayden, M., & Thiep, L. Q. (2007). Institutional autonomy for higher education in Vietnam. *Higher Education Research & Development, 26*(1), 73–85.

Hoang, L., Tran, L. T., & Pham, H. (2018). Vietnam's government policies and practices in internationalization of higher education. In L. T. Tran & S. Marginson (Eds.), *Internationalisation in Vietnamese higher education* (pp. 19–42). Dordrecht: Springer.

Kenway, J., Kraack, A., & Kickey-Moody, A. (2006). *Masculinity beyond the Metropolis.* New York: Palgrave Macmillan.

Knight, J. (2003). Updating the definition of Internationalization. *International Higher Education, 33,* 2–3.

Larsen, M. A. (2016). Introduction. In *Internationalisation of higher education: An analysis through spatial, network, and mobilities theories* (pp. 1–14). New York: Palgrave Macmillan US.

London, J. D. (2011). *Education in Vietnam.* Singapore: Institute of Southeast Asian Studies.

Marginson, S. (2008). Global field and global imagining: Bourdieu and worldwide higher education. *British Journal of Sociology of Education, 29*(3), 303–315. https://doi.org/10.1080/01425690801966386.

Marginson, S., & Mollis, M. (2011). The door opens and the tiger leaps. *Comparative Education Review, 45*(4), 581–615.

Ministry of Education and Training [MOET]. (2009). (No 760/BC-BGDĐT). Hanoi Retrieved from http://www.moet.gov.vn/?page=1.19&view=1736

MOET. (2015). *Joint Circular No.21/2015/TTLT-BGDĐT-BNV on the code and standards for primary teachers in public schools.* Hanoi Retrieved from https://thuvienphapluat.vn/van-ban/Lao-dong-Tien-luong/Thong-tu-lien-tich-21-2015-TTLT-BGDDT-BNV-ma-so-tieu-chuan-chuc-danh-nghe-nghiep-giao-vien-tieu-hoc-cong-lap-292264.aspx.

Neubauer, D. (2012). Introduction: Giving dimension and direction to mobility and migration in Asia Pacific higher education. In D. E. Neubauer & K. Kuroda (Eds.), *Mobility and migration in Asian Pacific higher education* (pp. 1–20). New York: Palgrave McMillan.

Nguyen, T. N. (2013). *Selling western dreams: Australian transnational education in Vietnam and the formation of students' identities.* Doctor of Philosophy, Monash University, Clayton, Victoria.

Nguyen, T. N. (2018). Transnational education in the Vietnamese market: Paradoxes and possibilities. In L. T. Tran & S. Marginson (Eds.), *Internationalisation in Vietnamese higher education.* Dordrecht: Springer.

Nguyen, T. N., & Lehy, P. (2015). Generalizing the self? Towards an Asian self in Australian transnational education. In P. W. Chan, H. Zhang, & J. Kenway (Eds.), *Asia as a method in educational studies.* Singapore: Sage.

Nguyen, N., & Tran, L. T. (2017). Looking inward or outward? Vietnam higher education at the superhighway of globalisation: Culture, values and changes. *Journal of Asian Public Policy,* 1–18. https://doi.org/10.1080/17516234.2017.1332457.

Nguyen, K. D., Oliver, D. E., & Priddy, L. E. (2009). Criteria for accreditation in Vietnam's higher education: Focus on input or outcome? *Quality in Higher Education, 15*(2), 123–134. https://doi.org/10.1080/13538320902995766.

OECD. (2012a). *PISA 2012 results in focus what 15-year-olds know and what they can do with what they know.* Retrieved from http://www.oecd.org/pisa/keyfindings/pisa-2012-results-overview.pdf

OECD. (2012b). *Snapshot of performance in mathematics, reading and science.* Retrieved from http://www.oecd.org/pisa/keyfindings/PISA-2012-results-snapshot-Volume-I-ENG.pdf

OECD. (2015). *Vietnam: Student performance.* Retrieved from http://gpseducation.oecd.org/CountryProfile?primaryCountry=VNM&treshold=10&topic=PI

Pham, T. N. (2010). The higher education reform Agenda: A vision for 2020. In G. Harman, M. Hayden, & T. N. Pham (Eds.), *Reforming higher education in Vietnam: Challenges and priorities* (pp. 51–64). London/New York: Springer.

Pham, L. (2015). *Ranking makes no sense without differentiation.* Retrieved from https://www.universityworldnews.com/post.php?story=20151014151901972.

Phan, V. T. (2015). *Chúng ta chưa chuẩn bị kỹ lưỡng cho TPP (We have not been well prepared for TPP yet)/Interviewer: T. Hieu.* TPP (Vol 25 October), Thanh Nien Online, Ho Chi Minh.

St. George, E. (2011). Higher educational reform in Vietnam. In J. D. London (Ed.), *Education in Vietnam* (pp. 212–236). Singapore: Institute of Southeast Asian Studies.

Tran, L. T., & Marginson, S. (2018a). Internationalisation of Vietnamese higher education: An overview. In L. T. Tran & S. Marginson (Eds.), *Internationalisation in Vietnamese higher education.* Dordrecht: Springer.

Tran, L. T., & Marginson, S. (2018b). Internationalisation of Vietnamese higher education: Possibilities, challenges and implications. In L. T. Tran & S. Marginson (Eds.), *Internationalisation in Vietnamese higher education.* Dordrecht: Springer.

Tran, L. T., Marginson, S., Do, H., Do, Q., Le, T., Nguyen, N., Vu, T., Pham, T., & Nguyen, H. (2014). *Higher education in Vietnam: Flexibility, mobility and practicality in the global knowledge economy.* Basingstoke: Palgrave Macmillan.

Tran, L. T., Ngo, M., Nguyen, N., & Dang, X. T. (2017). Hybridity in Vietnamese universities: An analysis of the interactions between Vietnamese traditions and foreign influences. *Studies in Higher Education, 42*(10), 1899–1916.

Tran, L. T., Phan, H. T. T., & Marginson, S. (2018). The 'advanced programmes' in Vietnam: Internationalising the curriculum or importing the 'best curriculum' of the west? In L. T. Tran

& S. Marginson (Eds.), *Internationalisation in Vietnamese higher education* (pp. 55–76). Dordrecht: Springer. (Forthcoming).

UNDP. (2011). *About Viet Nam.* Retrieved from http://hdr.undp.org/en/countries/profiles/VNM

UNDP. (2015). *About Viet Nam.* Retrieved from http://www.vn.undp.org/content/vietnam/en/home/countryinfo.html

UNESCO. (2015). *Vietnam: Literacy rate.* Retrieved from http://uis.unesco.org/en/country/vn

Vietnam Higher Education Renovation Agenda – Period 2006–2020, Resolution No.14/2005/NQ-CP on the Fundamental and Comprehensive Reform of Higher Education in Vietnam 2006–2020, (2005).

Vietnamese Commnunist Party. (2010). *Nghị quyết Đại hội đại biểu toàn quốc lần thứ XI Đảng Cộng sản Việt Nam* (The Decision of the 10th National Congress of the Communist Party of Vietnam). Hanoi: The Vietnamese Government Online Portal Retrieved from http://www.chinhphu.vn/portal/page/portal/chinhphu/NuocCHXHCNVietNam/ThongTinTongHop/noidungvankiendaihoidang?categoryId=10000716&articleId=10038365

Vietnamese Government. (2001). *Quyết định số 201/2001/QĐ-TTg ngày 28/12/2001 về Chiến lược phát triển giáo dục giai đoạn 2001–2010* (Decision no. 201/2001/QD-TTG of December 28, 2001 approving the "2001–2010 educational development strategy"). Hanoi: Vietnamese Government Online Portal.

Vietnamese Government. (2005). *Decree 14/2005/NQ – CP on the government resolution on substantial and comprehensive renewal of Vietnam's tertiary education in the 2006–2020 period.* Hanoi: Vietnamese government Retrieved from http://thuvienphapluat.vn/van-ban/Giao-duc/Nghi-quyet-14-2005-NQ-CP-doi-moi-co-ban-va-toan-dien-giao-duc-dai-hoc-Viet-Nam-giai-doan-2006-2020-5013.aspx

Vietnamese Government. (2006). *Quyết định số 145/2006/QĐ-TTg ngày 20/6/2006 về Chủ trương và những định hướng lớn xây dựng trường đại học đẳng cấp quốc tế của Việt Nam* (Decision No. 145/2006/QĐ-TTg, dated June 20, 2006 on the guideline and major orientations for building an international-level university in Vietnam). Hanoi: Vietnamese Government Online Portal.

Vietnamese Government. (2008). *Decree 1400/QĐ-TTg on approving the English language teaching and learning in the Vietnamese education system period 2008–2020.* Hanoi: Vietnamese Government Retrieved from http://www.chinhphu.vn/portal/page/portal/chinhphu/hethongvanban?class_id=1&_page=18&mode=detail&document_id=78437

Vietnamese Government. (2012). *Decree 73/2012/NĐ-CP on International Cooperation and Foreign Investment in Education (2012). Hanoi.* Retrieved from http://vbpl.vn/bogiaoducdaotao/Pages/vbpq-van-ban-goc.aspx?ItemID=27848

Vietnamese National Assembly. (2004). *Nghị quyết số 37/2004/QH11 tại kỳ họp thứ 6 Quốc hội khoá XI về giáo dục* (Resolution No. 37/2004/QH11 of December 3, 2004 on Education). Hanoi: Vietnamese Government Online Portal Retrieved from http://www.moj.gov.vn/vbpq/en/lists/vn%20bn%20php%20lut/view_detail.aspx?itemid=7322

World Bank. (2012). *Vietnam.* Retrieved from http://data.worldbank.org/country/vietnam

World Bank. (2015). *School enrollment, tertiary (% gross).* Retrieved from https://data.worldbank.org/indicator/se.ter.enrr.

Part I
Context for Reform

Chapter 2
Cultural Modalities of Vietnamese Higher Education

Nhai Thi Nguyen

Abstract The chapter adopts an inside-out approach to interpreting the cultural modalities of the Vietnamese higher education. It debunks these modalities in three categories: Vietnamese traditions, Confucianism, and Buddhism. Also, it attends closely to post-1945 nation-state identities dominated by Marxism–Leninism and Ho Chi Minh ideologies. This chapter serves as a cornerstone for subsequent chapters to explore various aspects of higher education reforms.

Introduction

There have been a plethora of policy texts addressing Vietnamese higher education (VHE) and the reforms implemented over the past decades (Nguyen and Tran 2017). Most of the research literature has investigated extensively the crisis and issues associated with higher education reforms. Harman et al. (2010), for example, discuss the challenges and priorities of the Higher Education Reform Agenda (HERA) and other aspects of higher education reforms, such as teaching and learning quality, financing, research, university governance, strategic planning, and management. Insights from these authors' work are useful. However, it is insufficient.

There is a critical need for a more rigorous conceptual tool which helps deconstruct the VHE reform phenomenon in a way that it enables the development of a more nuanced understanding of the decades-long higher education crisis. Equally, few researchers have offered such a philosophically robust ground for which a conceptual lens is erected to meticulously capture various modalities of higher education reforms. This chapter seeks to respond to this challenge. The author is intrigued to move her analysis beyond to a more philosophically grounded understanding of the VHE by uprooting the hidden connectivities between

N. T. Nguyen (✉)
Monash College, Clayton, VIC, Australia
e-mail: Nhai.Nguyen@monashcollege.edu.au

© Springer Nature Singapore Pte Ltd. 2019
N. T. Nguyen, L. T. Tran (eds.), *Reforming Vietnamese Higher Education*,
Education in the Asia-Pacific Region: Issues, Concerns and Prospects 50,
https://doi.org/10.1007/978-981-13-8918-4_2

Vietnamese culture and the centuries-long colonial history of Vietnam (Nguyen 2011, 2013; Nguyen and Lehy 2015).

Central to the framework of this chapter are the notions of cultural identities, core values, being and becoming. Acknowledging other influences of Christianity, Caodaism and Hoahaoism in Vietnamese culture, the chapter will, however, limit its analysis to Vietnamese traditions, Confucianism, and Buddhism, the ones that have been perceived as the prominent characteristics of Vietnamese culture. Marxism–Leninism and Ho Chi Minh ideologies that entered Vietnam after 1945, when the country officially gained independence, will also be brought into discussion.

Vietnamese Cultural Identities and Core Values

Identity is generally understood as the characteristics or the fact which determine who a person or what the thing is. Cultural identities have become seen as core to VHE. Upon conceptualising identities, there are two dominant approaches to uncovering what identities mean and what constitutes identities in the research literature; they are essentialist and non-essentialist. The former suggests that identity may be seen as something static, fixed, unified and predictable throughout a person's life (Hall 1992a, b, 1996a). Most noticeably, the concept of identity is closely linked to the matter of the subject, as Hall (ibid) observes. The concept of subject is derived from the notion of human person as fully centred, unified individual, endowed with reasoning capacity, consciousness, and action. Central to the human person existence is the inner core emerged right after the subject's birth and unfolded with it, whereas its essence stays unchanged, as continuous and identical with itself over its lifetime. Therefore, a person's identity is premised essentially on the centre of the self. Seen in this way, human identity is precisely associated with the full consciousness and the consistency of the centring self as the wholeness.

The essentialist perspective of identity is taken by a number of Vietnamese scholars who see cultural identities as being bounded and relatively solid over the passage of time (Phan 1994, 1998; Tran 1999, 2000, 2003). These scholars advocate for treating Vietnamese identities as being coherent and oneness that remain fairly stable and unchanged throughout a person's life. Identities are therefore interpreted as core identities, or *being*.

The latter approach – the non-essentialist – to interpreting identity differs starkly from the essentialist proposition in a number of ways (Austin 2005; Bhabha 1987; Hall 1987, 1991, 1992a, 1996a, b, 1997). First, the non-essentialist scholars criticise the ethnocentric nature of essentialism on identity in light of the postmodern context, globalisation. Most importantly, Hall (1992b) raises the issue of cultural identity in late-modernity and the crisis of identity as well as what this consists of, and in which direction it is moving. He indicates change forces transforming the modern societies in the late twentieth century. Second, in his line of argument, Hall alerts us that the identities which guarantee our subjective conformity with the objective needs of the culture in this contemporary world are infringing as the result of structural and institutional change (ibid). As a consequence, modernity and its constant, rapid changes have made the process of identification, in which the subject projects itself into cultural identities, problematic and capricious. It results in the birth of the post-modern subject with, describes Hall, no fixed, essential and permanent identities. Identities become a "movable feast", formed and transformed incessantly in the way we are represented and addressed in the cultural systems that bound us. Additionally, identity is defined in resonance with historical conditions. The subject holds multiple identities which are not unified around a coherent "self". Hall, in his discussion of postmodern identities, points, for example, to the paradoxes of identities, arguing that these identities are pulled into different directions so that identifications of identities are continuously being shifted away (ibid. p. 277).

Non-essentialist scholars urge us to resuscitate identity within the context of intensified globalisation. As a result, identity should be viewed as flexible, open, non-static, and even, fragmented under the impacts of globalisation. Ngo Tu Lap (2005) in his article entitled *Cultural Identity: Relativity in Diversity*, argues, for instance, that cultures are ceaselessly changing under numerous impacts of social and natural forces, especially when being conditioned by globalisation forces. These cultures permeate into one another; they are conditional and thus conditioned by the other. In face of these forces and the flows of different cultures occurring both locally and globally, the survival of a community is recognised through its differences and dichotomy with other communities. Despite their need to assert their physical existence, these cultures possess a strong desire to emphasise "who they are" – the critical question of identity.

Additionally, the essentialist approach to identity relates the Vietnamese identities to the geographical, historical and economic conditions which, argue these scholars, have shaped Vietnamese cultural identities (to be discussed in the coming section). This explanation has for long time enjoyed the merit of the whole society. Since Economic Reforms initially introduced in 1986, the country has experienced various transformations in many aspects of life. The wider integration of Vietnam into globalisation is, the more alarming the issue of Vietnamese identity fragmentation seems to be (Tuong Lai 2009). Unfortunately, neither the essentialists nor the non-essentialists can adequately explain the fragmentation of the Vietnamese identities under the conditions of globalisation. This is because new Vietnamese cultural identities are postulated; they are contradictory to the existing Vietnamese identities. They can become "unresolved". Importantly, these identities are pulled into various directions and become fragmented, and the identifications of these Vietnamese cultural identities are constantly shifted, which make the tracking and interpretation of modern Vietnamese identities somehow problematic. This issue of Vietnamese identity fragmentation can be best captured in Hall's remark of modern identities as the result of structural and institutional change in modern societies as follows:

> Correspondingly, the identities which composed the social landscapes "out there," and which ensured our subjective conformity with the objective "needs" of the culture, are breaking up [which means "fragmented"] as *a result of structural and institutional change*. The very process of identification, through which we project ourselves into our cultural identities, has become more open-ended, variable, and problematic. (Hall 1996b, p. 598, emphasis added)

Hall's discussion of identity fragmentation, multiplicity of identity and the notion of identification is inherited by Phan Le Ha who studies cultural identities of TESOL Vietnamese teachers. Adapting a multiple approach to interpreting modern Vietnamese identities, Phan Le Ha (2008) submits to the argument that [Vietnamese cultural] identities must be seen as both *being* and *becoming* (pp. 56–57), fragmented, multiple, changing, and at the same time, stable, continuous and connected with a sense of belonging (pp. 64–65).

However, Phan's study (ibid.) does not discuss yet the current context of Vietnam in regards to globalisation (be it cultural, economic and political) and how global forces, to a greater degree, impact, condition, shape, and reshape modern Vietnamese identities. So, what is actually happening to Vietnamese identities under the impacts of globalisation? Why do most essentialists and non-essentialists fail to provide a satisfactory answer to the emerging issues of identity fragmentation? Why are identities central to the base of the Vietnamese higher education and core to the shaping of and navigating the Vietnamese higher education field?

Welsch (1999) fills in this gap. The scholar critically remarks:

> … recent acceleration of cross-cultural flows and processes of cultural mixture has produced new form of identity. The intensification and diversification of flows in cultural traffic have put into question many of the earlier models for understanding the boundaries of culture and the configurations of identity. It is the failure to recognize this that makes 'the classical model of culture not only descriptively unserviceable, but also normatively dangerous and untenable' (cited in Papastergiadis 2005, p. 54).

Following Welch, the flows and mixture of culture have generated novel forms of identity and challenged the traditional ways of understanding and interpreting culture and identities. Again, the problems of reframing our understanding and interpretation of Vietnamese cultural identities (Hall 1996b; Phan 2008; Nguyen 2011; Welsch 1999) convince the author of this chapter of going beyond the existing parameters to look at the politics of Vietnamese identities as the product of the older traditions and the modern nation-state under the conditions of modernity (Nguyen 2011).

Vietnamese Traditions

Initially, tradition is understood as the collection of ideologies, customs and habits in the thought pattern, lifestyle and behaviours of a certain community. It is gradually formed via that community's history, preserved and relayed from generation to generation (Pham et al. 1996). Traditions form a nation's identity. Although it is difficult to clearly define Vietnamese singular identity, two most striking features are *collectivism* and *nationalism* (Karnow 1983).

Collectivism derived from Vietnam's wet rice growing. This wet rice growing required human labour and urged them to collectively protect crops by building dykes, irrigation systems and many other means. Without collective power, individuals would have not survived under the severe natural conditions (Pham et al.

1996). Collectivism became a powerful driving force for uniting the Vietnamese people and sharpening their self-determination to fight for independence.

Citing Nguyen Van Ngoc's (1991) study, Pham Minh Hac and colleagues show that the nature of their agriculture activities requires them to strengthen community solidarity. So, communalism[1] plays a no less important role in an individual's life. Throughout one's lifetime, a person is closely attached, primarily to her family and then her community. She is supposed to manage her multiple identities, being centred on the individual–family–community–country equation. And yet, communalism appears to reproduce class hierarchy; it is additionally linked to "corruption" practices. For instance, the leading positions in the commune were usually negotiated by the use of money and affluence. Collective values were central to the village's communal life, manifest in administrative meetings and the village's common feasts. As a result, individualism is extremely biased, and thus despised. The following dictums cited by Nguyen Van Huyen (1995, p. 80), a famous Vietnamese scholar, illustrate the point clearly:

> A piece in the middle of the village is as valuable as a great tray in a corner of one's kitchen (*Một miếng giữa làng bằng một sàng xó bếp*).

> One piece from the village is as valuable as a great tray of meat bought at the market (*Miếng thịt làng sàng thịt mua*).

Also, worth noting is that communalism implies a strong sense of origin, rootedness and belongingness. At the same time, it biases and derecognises the "stranger" or the "outsider" within that community. If a person is labelled as a stranger, then it is not uncommon that he or she will be treated with little – or even no – recognition or even discrimination in the community where that person resides. Equally, communalism is itself, in some measure, completely estranged to "cosmopolitanism" in reference to the identification of a person's origin[2] and identity. Since communalism plays an important role in shaping social institutions, it exerts its decisive influence on the formation of Vietnamese social mentality and cultural identities. Nguyen makes an important point that:

> For a Vietnamese, it is always honourable to have a village of origin in a province. Otherwise, one will be labelled by a rather derogatory term, in the eyes of the villagers, *người tứ xứ*, people of the four corners of the world. With the facilities of movement, people can settle down elsewhere, but will always claim to be a native of their original village, they pay their personal tax to the village, they contribute to the communal charges, even they do not enjoy material advantages, they register their children and grandchildren in the village and try to possess at least a portion of land there, although they can give it to poor relatives. Quite a few make effort to secure a plot and to erect a very humble hut for the installation of the altar of their ancestors. (1995, pp. 70–71)

---

[1] Interestingly, communalism is derived from the notion of "commune", defined as "a union of several families grouped into one agglomeration or separated into many individual ones. It is formed not only by those who live there but also by all those who originated there and may return only once or twice in a lifetime, but have the tombs of their ancestors in the commune and their familial temple is maintained by a member of the clan" (Nguyen 1995, p. 70).

[2] Another interesting case in point is, believe it or not, the Vietnamese identity card still spares a space for specifying the card holder's place of origin.

Family and kinship play an equal role in shaping a person's identity. Pham Minh Hac and colleagues remark that "Family spirit was the most essential for Vietnamese people regardless of their social classes. Family means everything to them" and "The core of the Annamite society is the family. It centralizes all benefits and thoughts" (1996, p. 24). Responsibilities tie individuals to family and clan[3], *tộc* or *họ*, family[4], *gia* or *nhà*, *chi* or *phái* and clan to village, and village to country. They result in the Vietnamese religion, particularly the cult of ancestor worshipping: "The most sacred and traditional is ancestor worshipping to Annamite" (Ory 1894, cited in Pham et al. 1996, p. 24).

Apart from being collectivist, communist and nationalist, Vietnamese people are characterised as resilient, harmonious and adaptable (Jamieson 1993; Tran, 2000, 2003). Being largely dependent on the weather conditions in their cultivation activities, Vietnamese people tend to be adaptable and harmonious in their behaviour and resilient in all situations. They are open and amenable to the Other's culture. Also, the Yin-Yang (âm-dương) (Jamieson 1993; Phan 1994, 1998; Tran 1999, 2000, 2003) principle dominates Vietnamese people's life. It constitutes their epistemology in a way that it regulates how they see the cosmos. Furthermore, it informs their ontology to the extent that it principally guides how they lead their life in this cosmos which reaps large the shaping of their national identities: resilience, harmony and adaptability.

Confucianism

In her work, *A Historical-political Approach to Interpreting Contemporary Vietnamese Identity* (Nguyen 2011), the shadow of Confucianism across Vietnam is unquestionable. Following David Marr (1981, 2000) and Nguyen Tai Thu (1997), Nguyen contends that the Confucian intellectual content is deeply embedded in Vietnamese moral teachings. It is engraved in the people's minds and behaviours, serving as a point of reference against which a person's morality is judged. Also, it cements the Vietnamese's values system: benevolence, customs, morality, government and so on.

At the heart of this moral guide are five, *hierarchically structured relationships*, encompassing those between the ruler and the subject, the father versus the son, the husband and the wife, the elder brother versus the younger one, and friend and friend. Each Vietnamese person takes up their role which is strictly defined by Confucian discourses that endorse a vertical hierarchy. Amongst these five key

---

[3] Nguyen Van Huyen (1995) also remarks that clan is the basic social regime of Vietnam, comprising a number of families. It includes all individuals sharing the same stock, đồng tôn, with a common ancestor. The relations of the clan may spread to nine generations, cửu tộc.

[4] The Gia Long code places a high value of the importance of family. It says "The families in the chau or huyen share the land, establish the taxation system, and all families assume the government of the locality" (Nguyen 1995, p. 22).

relationships, family lies in the centre. As a result, family values may hold special meanings not only for individuals but for the stability of the society and the whole nation. Behaviours within a family are strictly disciplined. For instance, a person is expected to maintain *filial piety* (hieu) to his father. And, a father or an elder brother must rule by example (Jamieson 1993; Marr 1981, 2000; Nguyen 1995). In these ways, Confucian teachings shape Vietnamese family morality and ethics.

Specifically, hierarchy has, argues Nguyen Van Huyen (1995), made the basic unit of Vietnamese society. Under Le dynasty, the code, Hồng Đức – which is a rather comprehensive law-making sovereign but considerably differs from the ancient Vietnamese law – was first introduced. Borrowed heavily from Chinese law and appropriated to the Vietnamese context,[5] it specified familial relationships. The code recognised the absolute power of Vietnamese male. For example, article 7(2) of the Hồng Đức code[6] stated that children had to obey and take care of their parents and grandparents. Amongst ten most serious crimes listed, at least one-third of which were about serious breach of moral norms relating to, for example, immorality (bất đạo), disrespect (bất kính) and disloyalty (bất hiếu).[7]

Nguyen (ibid) even moves his analysis deeper, recalling 24 cases of filial piety, *nhị thập tứ hiếu*, a collection of 24 folk stories about filial piety which were used as moral examples[8] to teach young Vietnamese centuries ago. As for the scholar, the Tokin Civil Code of 1931 defines the obligations of filial duties and paternal power. The children and grandchildren were to be dependent on the head of the family. Regardless of age, a child had to honour, obey, and respect his/her parents and grandparents. The Mencius, the famous ancient Chinese philosopher, famously puts that "the duty towards parents is the foundation of all duties" (ibid). Sharing the same indication, Neil Jamieson emphasises:

> Children were taught filial piety (hiếu), to obey and respect and honour their parents. Children were made to feel keenly that they owed parents a moral debt (ơn) so immense as to be unpayable. A child is supposed to try to please his or her parents all the time and in every way, to increase their comfort, to accede to all their wishes, to fulfil their aspirations,

---

[5] The Hồng Đức remained effective until the end of the nineteenth century when Gia Long, in his 11th year of reign, introduced another code constituted by the Hồng Đức code and the Chinese code of the Tsing dynasty (Nguyen 1995).

[6] Retrieved from the following website as of 17 February 2014: http://vi.wikipedia.org/wiki/Lu%E 1%BA%ADt_H%E1%BB%93ng_%C4%90%E1%BB%A9c.

[7] See also: http://pacific.net.vn/Home/NewsDetail.aspx?newsid=31.

Also, disloyalty includes "accusing or abusing one's grand father, grand mother, father or mother; refusing to adequately provide for one's parents; taking a wife during the mourning of one's father or mother; merry-making, or indulging in pleasures and wearing clothes other than the mourning garments; learning of the death of one's grand father or grand father and concealing the news without announcing the mourning; or falsely declaring that one is in mourning for one's grand father or grand mother, one's father or mother" (Nguyen 1995, p. 63).

[8] Nguyen Van Huyen (1995, p. 63) instanced the case of the child "who disowned his child to keep the little quantity of good rice remained for his mother; that of a son who dipped his warm body in the ice-cold river in the hope of catching fish that his parents liked; that of a son who slept in the evening with a naked body to attract all the mosquitoes to himself and to offer peaceful sleep to his father".

to lighten their burden of work and of worry, and to comply with their wishes in all matters, great or small... The parent-child relationship was at the very core of Vietnamese culture, dominating everything else. (1993, pp. 16–17)

As previously reported, in Vietnamese education, Confucianism is an important affective factor determining the roles and conducts of its stakeholders (Huu 2005; Marr 1981, 2000; Nguyen, 1995, 1997, 2011). Analogous to the hierarchy of five relationships, students are inculcated with a fixed set of attributes such as "respecting the teacher, respecting the knowledge". In the classroom, they are expected to be recipients of knowledge and strictly follow what the teacher expects them to do. Meanwhile, teachers' roles are assumed as the source of knowledge, the knowledge transmitter and the moral guide. This teacher–student relation is clearly reflected in the following traditional teaching which reads

To get across the river, you have to build a bridge
To have a well-educated child, you have to respect the teacher.

(*Muốn sang phải bắc cầu kiều*
Muốn con hay chữ, phải yêu lấy thầy.)

Confucianism is extremely influential on the Vietnamese meritocratic system. It is deeply imprinted in the Vietnamese social mentality which has, for its centuries-long existence, wholeheartedly embraced the scholarship of academic achievements. Marr (2000, p. 773) concisely notes that Confucianism focuses on developing the self as a full person. It lays a cornerstone for cultivating both morality and intellectuality. Education becomes a sole means to attain self-transformation. Education co-implies academic excellence and a genuine embrace of the self in the self-forming process.

Confucianism is under the hammer. Since it lays a great emphasis on hierarchical relationships, it is far from unpopular that Vietnamese students are to fulfil their filial piety duties, submitted to their parents' choices of university and future career. The Vietnamese teaching "*Cha mẹ đặt đâu con ngồi đấy*" (A person should do whatever his/her parents want him/her to) makes a clear showcase of this point.

…a bounded domain that includes institutions with cross-border activities in these areas. Although this domain is frayed at the edges by diploma mills, corporate 'universities' and cross-border e-learning – and despite its connections with other social formations – its boundedness and distinctiveness are irreducible. (Marginson 2008, p. 305)

In her cultural study, *Confucianism and its Influences in Vietnam*, Nguyen Thi Thanh Mai (n.d.) scrutinises the limits of Confucianism in Vietnam. She argues Confucianism is deeply embedded with male-dominated idiosyncrasy and gender discrimination. It did injustice to female social status (Marr 2000; Nguyen n.d.; Rambo 2005; Ratliff 2008). A man is, without doubt, expected not only to carry their family surname, but also fulfil their parents' pride by succeeding in the doctoral exam and climbing the ladder of fame. Consequently, education and doctoral exams used to discriminate female, with very few exceptions, whose life was traditionally bounded with domestic duties and strict obedience to her father, her husband and her son.

Precisely, gender differences and/or inequality, social exclusion and filial obligations deeply inform the meritocratic mentality of Vietnamese people, serving as a powerful platform for self-(trans)formation in Confucianism.

Buddhism

While Confucianism is incorporated into the ruler's ideology system and used to define the past, Buddhism may have shaped Vietnamese in popularity regardless of their social classes. It cemented Vietnamese spiritual souls. Tran Van Giap in 1930s even exemplified that there were both a temple and a Confucian Shrine in a village of 500 people. He maintained that:

> Nowadays, if you ask what the Confucian shrine venerates, we can be certain that of those 500 people, only about 50 will know exactly that the Confucian shrine is for the veneration of Confucius and the sages. But if one goes to the temple, all 500 person will know that it is to worship the Buddha. We must recognize that in terms of doing good and avoiding evil, we Vietnamese are more influenced by Buddhism than Confucianism. (McHale 2004, p. 144)

Despite Buddhism reach to all Vietnamese classes, it enjoyed a comparatively long honeymoon period prolonged from Ly to Tran dynasties (1009–1400). Though originating from the Mahaynna Buddhism branch, the Pure Land (*Tịnh Độ*) seemed to exert more influence compared to the Zen (*Thiền*) traditions (McHale 2004; Smith 1968). If the Zen is cultivated upon the "self-reliance" and refuses the external religious objects, the Pure Land argues over the human scantiness of their own capacity and the futility of their times; consequently, salvation can only be "achieved at another time (in the next rebirth), in another place (the Western Pure Land), and through another power (Amitabha Buddha)".

But not all the profound content of Pure Land was translated into Vietnamese Buddhism. Rather, Vietnamese freely picked up the simple Pure Land ideology which best suited their agriculture life and worshipping rituals. For instance, the Pure Land follower believes in the Saha world – this world of suffering made human life miserable. Prayer and faith were commonly noticed to relieve the suffering and being longed for the Nirvana (*Niết Bàn*) after death. The life on earth was just temporary but life in the Nivara is everlasting. Therefore, human should keep themselves off the triple evils: greediness (*tham*), animosity (*sân*) and illusion (*si*).

Vietnamese Identities in Light of Marxist–Leninist and Ho Chi Minh Ideology

In her chapter, entitled *A Historical–Political Approach to Constructing Contemporary Vietnamese Identity*, Nguyen (2011) has pointed out Marxism–Leninism was first introduced into Vietnam in 1932 when the Vietnamese Communist Party (VCP) was founded by Ho Chi Minh. Rationales behind the deployment of Marxist–Leninist prescriptions of the ideal socialist citizens indicate that Ho Chi

Minh and the VCP were aspired to build a novel framework for Vietnamese people after VCP had defeated the French, the Japanese and the Vietnamese feudalism in 1945.

Under the shadow of Marxism–Leninism and Ho Chi Minh ideology, these identities must, argues Nguyen (2011), be aligned with the strategic building of the Socialist Republic of Vietnam within the newly independent context. However, it is noteworthy that this framework shaped largely in light of Marxist–Leninist spirit was confined solely to the North and the Centre of Vietnam. Due to the different and complex historical conditions, the South of Vietnam was not imprinted by Marxism–Leninism until 1975 when the VCP officially united the North, South and the Centre of Vietnam. The VCP correspondingly pushed the American to withdraw their army troops out of South Vietnam as a result of the January 1973 Agreement on Ending the War and Restoring the Peace in Vietnam between the VCP and the US Government. Because of such historical complexities, the Southern Vietnamese were heavily influenced by the French in late 19th and early 20th centuries and the American between 1953 and 1973.

When applying Marxism–Leninism to the new context of Vietnam, Ho Chi Minh and VCP had purposefully retained the fundamentals of Confucian values. Instead of coercing or rubbing Confucianism off, they integrated Confucianism into Marxism–Leninism (Nguyen 2011). Ho Chi Minh made a critical remark:

> … But as far as we are concerned, we Annamites, let us perfect ourselves intellectually through the reading of Confucius, and revolutionarily through the works of Lenin. (Brocheux 2007, p. 38)

Although inheriting Confucian values, Marxism–Leninism applied in post-1945 in Vietnam had witnessed a reversed hierarchy. Confucianism consolidates the Vietnamese conducts and accords them with a set of cardinal virtues such as "benevolence" (*nhân*), "righteousness" (*nghĩa*), "ritual" (*lễ*), "knowledge" (*trí*), "sincerity" (*tín*), "loyalty" to the country and "piety" to the people (*trung với nước, hiếu với dân*) (Dinh and Nguyen 1998; Pham et al. 1996). Recognising and balancing equality and equity amongst three social classes including peasant class, working class and intellectual one, Marxism–Leninism designates the conducts of the intellectual and Communist cadres. These pre-set conducts were, again, heavily imprinted by Confucian values. For instance, if Confucianism stressed loyalty and piety towards the King and the superior, Marxism–Leninism and Ho Chi Minh ideology placed a high value on the people. They regarded them as the bedrock of the nation's wealth and power. Collectivist spirit was boosted. However, it is harmonised with individual, especially the material self-interest via economic production activities; the form of "*hợp tác xã*" and "*khoán*" were popular in the countryside where agriculture still dominated the economy.

Dominant in the Vietnamese individual life is the attachment to family and multiple interest groups, classes, "peoplehood" (*dân tộc*), national citizenship and many others (Marr 1981). A person is expected to cultivate their new citizenship duties while sustaining and promoting their love for the nation. The model of Vietnamese character was ambitiously reconfigured by the Communist Party's Fourth National Congress held in December 1976 and configured a vague model of the Vietnamese characteristics whose aims were to build up a *new life* and *new type of people*. The new type of people demarcated as those with not only a strong commitment and devotedness for the collective mastery principle (Nguyen 2011) but also with a zest for labour, socialist patriotism and affiliation with proletarian internationalism. The novel identities of the Vietnamese described by the VCP in light of Marxism–Leninism are defined as "socialist in content and national in character" (Pelly 2002, p. 122).

Pressed by the quest for national economic development, VCP implemented Economic Reforms (Đổi Mới) in 1986. More remarkably, VCP officially acknowledged individual self-interest as an important constituent among other economic motives for economic development. Two significant studies of Vietnamese traditions on the national scale in 1993 and 1994 conducted by Pham Minh Hac, Phan Huy Le, Vu Van Tao and Le Huu Tang (1996) highlighted a number of emergent Vietnamese characteristics under the impact of series of economic reforms and Vietnam's integration into the global economy as following:

(a) the individual self-interest, values and family interest were prevalent over the collectivist values;
(b) the national interests are more intimate than the international;
(c) the economic interest prevails the spiritual;
(d) the temporary values won over the permanent ones; and
(e) the modern values predominate the traditional.

These scholars outlined a list of Vietnamese values based on the humane traditions, national pride and national essence which are essential to train the future Vietnamese citizens. They include

 (i) the traditions of benevolence, solidarity and interdependence;
 (ii) the tradition of study passion, teacher respect, talent nurturing and national culture treasure;
(iii) professional values including knowledge, skills and benevolence;
(iv) love and well-behaved family;
 (v) individual health and environment and cultural protection;
(vi) the lifestyle principles: hardworking (*cần*), economical (*kiệm*), honest (*liêm*), impartial (*chính*), disciplined (*kỷ luật*) and law-obedient, and (*pháp luật*); and
(vii) gender equality.

Cultural Modalities of VHE: An Example of Confucian Imprints

In the higher education landscape, Johnathan London (2011) discusses the historical roots and current trends of Vietnam education system. He sees the pivotal role of Confucianism which leaves deep imprints in the Vietnamese education system. The scholar writes:

> Confucianism blended education and normative governance. Confucian institutions imposed constraints by linking organized education and the study of classics to governance and authority relations. Confucian ideals and institutions shaped attitudes and behaviours

concerning education, but in non-determinant ways, contingent on actors' interests, capacities, and circumstances. Perhaps most important, the development of education systems in Vietnam, as in China and Korea, occurred in interdependent relation with the development of authority relations – proto national, local and familial. Grasping this helps us to appreciate the historical significance of education in Vietnam. (2011, p. 5)

And London reaffirms his proposition, claiming that:

The practical significance of Confucianism and Confucian institutions with respect to education needs to be clarified. (2011, p. 6)

In the Confucian shadow, education is premised on social exclusion and social hierarchy as is accessible only to a small group of population, often circulated within Vietnamese elites (London 2011; Marr 2000). London (2011, pp. 7–8) makes an important remark:

Although Vietnamese custom did allow education for non-elites, Confucian ideas and institutions nonetheless often promoted and reproduced hierarchies of power, wealth and status.

The author further concludes:

Confucian thought and Confucian-inspired social institutions had wide impacts on the development of education systems in Vietnam and legacies of these impact remains. (ibid, p. 8)

According to Ngo and colleagues, emerging in the university restructuring and changes are key concerns relevant to cultures, values and beliefs and thus power relations when a higher education institute transitions from one system structure to another or restructures the system itself. Vietnam National University, Ho Chi Minh – while inheriting the pre-existing values system – generates a new complex network of relationship and new leadership, let alone the teaching staffs of different disciplines and faculties found it comparatively difficult to adapt to the new culture and the system of belief. Certain clashes in culture, values and beliefs inevitably occur, resulting in chaotic mix, the emergence of sub-cultures and internal contradictions and conflicts. These scholars remark:

The policy cycle and vernacular globalisation contained internal contradictions and conflicts. (p. 235)

And that:

As conflicts occurred both within new groups of teaching staff who came from formerly different faculties or different universities and among groups within the university, it was therefore crucial for the university to have a certain period of time to rebuild its history of shared assumptions so that some degree of culture formation could take place, and so that there could be some harmony between the 'restructuring' and 'reculturing' within the institution. (p. 235)

Without attending to local specificities and responses to globalisation forces at a specific local reception point – in this case, Vietnam National University (Ho Chi Minh city) – we might be caught in the trap of wholeheartedly celebrating globalising discourses of higher education. Local context pays tribunes to higher education reforms. The research done by Ngo and colleagues is useful in the sense that studies in higher education reforms in Vietnam need to meet dual demands. They are to serve challenges of globalisation and the accomplishments of particular national interests, and at the same time, adhere closely to the micro-context so that desired outcomes of higher education reforms could be maximised.

Towards Vietnam higher education field, Ngo Thanh Minh, Bob Lingard and Jane Mitchell (Ngo et al. 2006) examine, for example, the vernacular globalisation, taking into account the impacts of local forces. Using Vietnam National University, Hochiminh as a single case, these scholars remark that developments within the university sector are mediated by both globalisation discourses of higher education reforms and local histories and culture. Pertinent to the micro-politics of implementation, argued Ngo and colleagues, are local factors: institutional size, intra-organisational relations, staff commitment, and capacity and institutional complexities. These factors are significant for enacting institutional responses to the educational policies and appropriating the Western ideas of higher education at almost all levels. What really captivates us is institutional culture and re-culturing, in the analysis of Ngo and colleagues, are detached from legitimate authority structure and power conflict.

Although focusing on two different countries, Ngo and colleagues' observation of VHE intersects with Yang's (2011). Chinese higher education's, in Yang's analysis, route to modernising higher education and the aspiration of building up the world-ranked universities are to a large extent akin to the Vietnamese HE. The scholar interrogates the concept of university and how this concept has evolved over time in China, taking into consideration Western external influences.

Specifically, Yang (2011) speaks assertively of the importance of *"cultural text"* and *the structure of Confucian culture in interpreting Chinese Higher Education development*. Examining the impacts of Chinese traditional way of viewing self, the other and nature of higher education development, especially education reforms, the scholar reveals that it is Chinese traditional culture that has presented obstacles towards indigenising Western concept of the university.

Digging deep into the root of cultural structure, Yang argues Chinese cultural context has been the catalyst for indigenising Western concepts. It is structured by three reciprocal layers: material, social (institutional) and ideological. The last layer, the ideological or psychological, is central. Drawing on Pang Pu (1986), he critically notes:

> Culture is never static. Contacts and communication between cultures begin at the material level and gradually influence social and ideological culture. As material culture is constantly progressing, social and ideological culture are also changing. Culture at the third level is deeply rooted in a nation's tradition and ideology and *is resistant to change*. It is this relative *stability of the core aspect of culture which makes it possible to discuss the variations of culture*. But being stable does not mean that it is static. History moves forward; so does culture. (2011, p. 343, emphasis added)

What remains paradoxical is that, according to Yang (2011), cultural practices of thought have accounted for mismatches and inconsistencies in the process of receiving and appropriating Western thoughts in order to shape Chinese universities. Chinese universities nowadays tend to mobilise the American model of university with incomprehensive knowledge of its root, identities and development trajectories. Insufficient understanding refrains the system from an attempt to retain the "Chinese learning as the essence". Featuring Ruth Hayhoe's work (2005), the scholar sarcastically pens:

> The development of Chinese modern universities has always been confronted with the absence of both classical and modern ideas of a university. While Chinese long-standing traditions never attempted to seek the ontological significance of knowledge, top priority has always been given, consciously and unconsciously, to practical demands. (2011, p. 352)

Rui's discussion of how the cultural context assists in tracking the development of Chinese higher education is philosophically powerful, and thus holds significant implications for Vietnam. Indeed, VHE reform policies tend to offer quick remedies for the surface problems of the system (Nguyen and Tran 2017; Tran et al. 2014; see also Chaps. 3, 4, 5, 7, 10, 12) with limited thoughtful consideration what makes a Vietnamese institution traditionally and in a modern context. This is not to say that its internal dynamics conditioned by an array of complex cultural forces have been exerting unequal, fragmented and ad-hoc power over the VHE institutions. The clashes between the modern and traditions happening within the VHE system, not much of which have been explored in-depth in the research literature, would have us to reinvigorate this field and, more importantly, question the ontological nature of our knowledge about VHE institutions and education reforms, to follow Yang's thesis (ibid). Besides, the cultural features characterised by Confucianism and Buddhism and Marxism–Leninism and Ho Chi Minh ideology discussed above do not have impacts on practices of VHE separately. Rather, these features are represented in united forms at different levels of national, organisational and individual culture. These cultural characteristics, either hindering or facilitating the VHE reforms, will be tackled at root in the subsequent chapters.

Conclusion and Implications for Interpreting Higher Education Reforms in Vietnam

Throughout this chapter, it has become apparent that the cultural approach to deciphering the cultural modalities of the VHE catechises the reciprocity, fluidity and dynamics of the relationship between inward looking and outward looking. An inside-out thinking enables the system to reflect and build on its inner strengths – agency – and the cultural values cultivated over the centuries-long history, the nation's traditions and modernity. It is vested in self-determination to navigate the education system throughout turbulences.

The outside-in thinking attends critically to global forces driving changes in higher education across the globe and Vietnam particularly. Moving this analytical stance beyond the boundaries of a single nation state helps obtain a "big picture" of the global forces appended with globalisation and internationalisation and the complexities of global geography of power (Altbach 1989; Altbach and Selvaratnam 1989; Hawkins et al. 2013a, b; Lee 2006; Yang 2011). They create powerful forces on both the system and the nation state.

Towards an inward versus outward looking, these conceptual notions of identities, core value, and being and becoming help define the internal logics of the VHE field and its modalities to enhance the internal power, that is, the agency of VHE institutes. It leads to the transformation of VHE towards desirable end results of HERA and reform policies. An inward looking complements an outward perspective that encompasses a cross-referencing point. Being at the intersection of making changes responsive to the national demands and catching up with the pace of world universities, such an inside-out versus outside-in looking approach, cultivates cultural values, inner power and self-determination.

Paired with an outward looking is the inward one which examines in retrospect the VHE system by drawing on the centuries-long culture and values of education. It promises a viable philosophical solution for higher education reforms. This is because such an inside-out looking touts out the inner strengths – agency – and the core cultural values while cementing its self-determination to navigate the education system throughout turbulences.

Looking retrospectively into the system of culture and values in higher education is, at the same time, reciprocal to an outside-in perspective, allowing an articulation of a useful cross-referencing point against which VHE institutions bring to the fore a concert of attributes. It encompasses self-reflexivity, the core cultural values, the inner power and self-determination alongside with comprehensive understanding of globalisation forces located within the global geopolitics structure.

Multiplying referencing points overwrites this conceptual framework. It assists in reading education reforms and the history of sociology of higher education. Implied is the narration of Vietnamese history and culture that have been making and remaking VHE as it is nowadays. This resonates an eco-system of higher education and sets the cornerstone for the subsequent chapters to unpack aspects of history and culture in relation to higher education reforms. It partially contributes to the thesis of this book, the inside-out versus outside-in looking and debunks the hidden power of VHE agency.

The referencing points are propelled flexibly. VHE makes an exigent referencing point against which a substantial comparative analysis of higher education reforms is shifted around and relocated across the Asia-Pacific region. It is appended with a variety of subfields. In so doing, cross-referencing VHE with a trans-Asia Pacific comparative perspective does, without doubt, justice to postulate a more nuanced, innovative research approach and methodology. It re-enhances the inward looking versus the outward one. This chapter therefore serves as a catalyst for the coming chapters (from Chaps. 3, 4, 5, 6, 7, 8, 9, 10, 11, 12 and 13) to explore in greater depth various aspects of VHE reforms.

References

Altbach, P. (1989). Twisted roots: The Western impact on Asian higher education. *The International Journal of Higher Education and Educational Planning, 18*(1), 9–29. https://doi.org/10.1007/BF00138959.

Altbach, P., & Selvaratnam, V. (1989). *From dependence to autonomy the development of Asian universities*. Dordrecht: Springer.

Austin, J. (2005). Culture and identity: an introduction. In J. Austin, A. Keddie, A. Hickey, J. Nayler, J. McMaster, K. Howey, M. Lewis, & T. Rossi (Eds.), *Culture and Identity* (2nd ed., pp. 1–16). Frenchs Forest: Pearson Sprint Print.

Bhabha, H. (1987). Interrogating identity. In L. Appignanesi (Ed.), *Identity: The real me* (Vol. 6, pp. 5–12). London: Institute of Contemporary Arts.

Brocheux, P. (2007). *Ho chi minh: A biography. Trans. Claire duiker*. New York: Cambridge University Press.

Dinh, X. L., & Nguyen, V. H. (1998). *Xu huong doi moi trong lich su Viet Nam*. Hanoi: NXB Van Hoa Thong Tin.

Hall, S. (1987). Minimal selves. In L. Appignanesi (Ed.), *Identity: The real me* (Vol. 6, pp. 44–46). London: Institute of Contemporary Arts.

Hall, S. (1991). The local and the global: Globalisation and ethnicity. In A. King (Ed.), *Culture, globalisation and the world system* (pp. 19–39). London: Macmillan.

Hall, S. (1992a). Introduction: Identity in question. In S. Hall, D. Held, & T. McGrew (Eds.), *Modernity and its future*. London: Sage.

Hall, S. (1992b). Cultural studies and its theoretical legacie. In L. Grossberg, C. Nelson, & P. Treichler (Eds.), *Cultural studies* (pp. 227–294). New York: Routledge.

Hall, S. (1996a). Introduction: Who needs "identity"? In S. Hall & P. D. Gay (Eds.), *Questions of cultural identity* (pp. 1–17). London: Sage.

Hall, S. (1996b). Introduction: Identity in question. In S. Hall, D. Held, D. Hubert, & K. Thompson (Eds.), *Modernity an introduction to modern societies* (pp. 596–628). Malden: Blackwell.

Hall, S. (1997). Cultural identity and diaspora. In K. Woodward (Ed.), *Identity and difference* (pp. 51–59). London: SAGE in association with The Open University.

Harman, G., Hayden, M., & Phạm, T. N. (2010). *Reforming higher education in Vietnam challenges and priorities* (Higher education dynamics, Vol. 25). Dordrecht: Springer.

Hawkins, J. N., Neubauer, D., & Shin, J. C. (2013a). *Introduction: Four hypothesis of higher education development*. New York: Palgrave Macmillan.

Hawkins, J. N., Neubauer, D., & Shin, J. C. (2013b). *Is there an Asian hybrid university?* New York: Palgrave Macmillan.

Huu, N. (2005). *Wandering through Vietnamese culture*. Hanoi: The Gioi Publishers.

Jamieson, N. L. (1993). *Understanding Vietnam*. Berkeley/Los Angeles/London: University of California Press.

Karnow, S. (1983). *Vietnam: A history*. New York: Viking.

Lee, M. (2006). Higher education in Southeast Asia in the era of globalisation. In J. J. F. Forest & P. G. Altbach (Eds.), *International handbook of higher education* (pp. 539–555). Dordrecht: Springer.

London, J. D. (2011). *Education in Vietnam*. Singapore: Institute of Southeast Asian Studies.

Marginson, S. (2008). Global field and global imagining: Bourdieu and worldwide higher education. *British Journal of Sociology of Education, 29*(3), 303–315. https://doi.org/10.1080/01425690801966386.

Marr, D. G. (1981). *Vietnamese tradition on trial, 1920–1945*. Berkeley/Los Angeles/London: University of California Press.

Marr, D. G. (2000). Concepts of 'individual' and 'self' in twentieth-century Vietnam. *Modern Asian Studies, 34*(4), 769–796. https://doi.org/10.2307/313131.

McHale, S. F. (2004). *Print and power: Confucianism, communism and Bhuddism in the making of modern Vietnam*. Honolulu: University of Hawaii Press.

Ngo, T. L. (2005). *Ban sac van hoa – tinh tuong doi cua su da dang*. Retrieved from http://www.chungta.com/Desktop.aspx/ChungTa-SuyNgam/Hanh-Dong/Ban_sac_van_hoa-tinh_tuong_doi_cua_su_da_dang/

Ngo, T. M., Lingard, B., & Mitchell, J. (2006). The policy cycle and vernacular globalisation: A case study of the creation of Vietnam National University—Hochiminh City. *Comparative Education, 42*(2), 225–242.

Nguyen, V. H. (1995). *The ancient civilization of Vietnam*. Hanoi: The Gioi Publishers.

Nguyen, T. T. (1997). *Influences of ideologies on Vietnam's culture*. Hanoi: National Politics Publishers.

Nguyen, T. N. (2011). A historical–political approach to constructing contemporary Vietnamese identity. In *Asia Pacific education: Challenges, changes and diversity* (pp. 162–171). Melbourne: Monash E-Publisher.

Nguyen, T. N. (2013). *Asia as method? Towards decolonising research imagination*. Paper presented at the Inter-Asia Studies Conference, The National University of Singapore.

Nguyen, T. T. M. (n.d.). Confucianism and its influences in Vietnam. *Cultural Studies, 2*.

Nguyen, T. N., & Lehy, P. (2015). Generalizing the self? Towards an Asian self in Australian transnational education. In P. W. Chan, H. Zhang, & J. Kenway (Eds.), *Asia as a method in educational studies*. Singapore: Sage.

Nguyen, N., & Tran, L. T. (2017). Looking inward or outward? Vietnam higher education at the superhighway of globalisation: Culture, values and changes. *Journal of Asian Public Policy*, 1–18. https://doi.org/10.1080/17516234.2017.1332457.

Papastergiadis, N. (2005). Hybridity and ambivalence: Places and flows in contemporary art and culture. *Theory, Culture & Society, 22*(4), 39–64.

Pelly, P. M. (2002). *Postcolonial Vietnam: New history of the nation past*. Durham: Duke University Press.

Pham, T. N. (2010). The higher education reform agenda: A vision for 2020. In G. Harman, M. Hayden, & T. N. Pham (Eds.), *Higher education in Vietnam: Reform, challenges and priorities* (pp. 51–64). Dordrecht/Heidelberg/London/New York: Springer.

Pham, M. H., Le Phan, H., Vu, V. T., & Le, H. T. (1996). *Van de con nguoi trong su nghiep cong nghiep hoa hien dai hoa*. Hanoi: NXb Chinh Tri Quoc Gia.

Phan, N. (1994). *Van hoa Viet Nam va cach tiep can moi*. Hanoi: NXB Van Hoa Thong Tin.

Phan, N. (1998). *Ban Sac Van Hoa Vietnam*. Hanoi: NXB. VHTT.

Phan, L. H. (2008). *Teaching English as an international language: Identity, resistance and negotiation*. Clevedon/Buffalo/Toronto: Multilingual Matters Ltd.

Rambo, A. T. (2005). Religion and society in Vietnam. In A. T. Rambo (Ed.), *Searching for Vietnam: Selected writing on Vietnamese culture and society* (pp. 69–108). Kyodai Kaikan: Kyoto University Press.

Ratliff, W. (2008). *Vietnam rising: Culture and change in Asia's Tiger Club*. Oakland: The Independent Institute.

Smith, R. (1968). *Vietnam and the west*. Heinemann/London: Heinemann Educational Books.

Tran, N. T. (1999). *Co so van hoa Vietnam*. Hanoi: NXB. Giao Duc.

Tran, Q. V. (2000). *Van Hoa Viet Nam, Tim Toi va Suy Ngam*. Hanoi: NXB. VHDT.

Tran, N. T. (2003). *Tim Ve Ban Sac Van Hoa Vietnam*. TP Ho Chi Minh: NXB. Tong Hop TP Ho Chi Minh.

Tran, L. T., Marginson, S., Do, H., Do, Q., Le, T., Nguyen, N., Vu, T., Pham, T., & Nguyen, H. (2014). *Higher education in Vietnam: Flexibility, mobility and practicality in the global knowledge economy*. Basingstoke: Palgrave Macmillan.

Tuong Lai. (2009). *Tu tuong Ho Chi Minh sai buoc cung thoi dai*. Retrieved from www.chungta.com/Desktop.aspx/

Welsch, W. (1999). Transculturality - the puzzling form of cultures today. In y. M. Featherstone & S. Lash (Eds.), *Spaces of Culture: City, Nation, World* (pp. 194–213). London: Sage.

Yang, R. (2011). Self and the other in the Confucian cultural context: Implications of China's higher education development for comparative studies. *International Review of Education, 57*(3–4), 337–355. https://doi.org/10.1007/s11159-011-9208-x.

Part II
VHE Structure, Policy and Governance

Chapter 3
Vietnam's Progress with Policies on University Governance, Management and Quality Assurance

Khanh Van Dao and Martin Hayden

Abstract This chapter addresses progress made by Vietnam's higher education sector over the past 30 years in the areas of governance, management and quality assurance. Over the past decade, relatively significant progress is evident in the implementation of quality assurance mechanisms. Regarding governance and management, however, the achievement of progress has been remarkably slow-moving. Though reform aspirations are frequently expressed, a culture of centralised control remains remarkably resilient.

Introduction

Governance, management and quality assurance are important topics in the context of Vietnam's higher education sector. Significant policy progress has been made in these areas during the past 25 years. Pressures associated with globalisation and internationalisation have undoubtedly played an important role in this regard, but there have also been other pressures at work. Ultimately, the Soviet-style centralised system of higher education governance and management which existed in Vietnam up to the mid-1990s had become unviable and needed dismantling. The dismantling process has, however, been slow, and a culture associated with a centrally controlled higher education sector refuses to disappear. This chapter reviews the policy progress which has been made regarding governance, management and quality assurance in the higher education sector and draws attention to several of the ongoing challenges.

K. Van Dao (✉) · M. Hayden
Southern Cross University, Lismore, Australia

© Springer Nature Singapore Pte Ltd. 2019
N. T. Nguyen, L. T. Tran (eds.), *Reforming Vietnamese Higher Education*,
Education in the Asia-Pacific Region: Issues, Concerns and Prospects 50,
https://doi.org/10.1007/978-981-13-8918-4_3

Policy Reform Since the Early 1990s

In *Decree 90/ND-TTG*, issued in 1993, the government signalled clearly that it would not persist in adopting a Soviet model of higher education. Up to that time, higher education institutions (HEIs) were expected to be mono-disciplinary and teaching-focused. *Decree 90* departed significantly from this model. It approved the establishment of a network of national and regional universities that were to be multidisciplinary and to engage in research as well as teaching. The *Decree* signalled that public HEIs would charge tuition fees, that community groups could establish 'non-public' HEIs on a fee-paying basis and that graduates from public universities and colleges would no longer be guaranteed employment by the state. These changes represented a victory for pragmatism. Under Soviet influence, and in light of crippling resource shortages, Vietnam's higher education sector had fallen apart and had become incapable of meeting emerging social needs.

The next significant policy reform occurred in 2005 when the government released a Higher Education Reform Agenda (*Resolution 14/2005/NQ-CP*). The Agenda was ambitious in terms of the raft of reforms proposed. It represented an even more significant departure from the Soviet higher education model. The Agenda indicated that by 2020, there should be the complete removal of line-management control of public HEIs by ministries and other state instrumentalities; there should be the development of key HEIs as major scientific centres; and the private higher education sector should be expanded to a point where it would account for 40% of all higher education enrolments. The Agenda also signalled the need for a boost to the proportion of academic staff members with PhDs, as well as the need for a stronger commitment to the internationalisation of the curriculum.

Given the Communist Party's traditional antipathy to private education, it came as a surprise when the Higher Education Reform Agenda projected a huge increase in the size of the sector by 2020. This expansion has not eventuated, and the sector currently accounts for only about 14% of all higher education enrolments. In 2006, the government decided that all existing and future private HEIs should be corporately governed entities, involving a shareholders' association and a governing board. These institutions were then to be left to manage their own affairs, though subject to national quality assurance and accreditation requirements. In 2013, *Decree 141/2013/ND-CP* subsequently established a mechanism for distinguishing between 'for-profit' and 'not-for-profit' private higher HEIs. Institutions considered to be 'not-for-profit' were defined as those whose shareholders received either no dividend from their shareholdings or, at most, a dividend that fell below the interest rate paid on national bonds. The government indicated that these institutions would have governing boards that were broadly representative of community interests and that it would provide these institutions with access to incentives for development. The nature of these incentives continues to be unclear.

In 2007, the Ministry of Education and Training (MOET) issued requirements for all HEIs to participate in a national quality assurance process requiring the completion of, first, an institutional self-assessment report and, second, an external review leading to accreditation *(Decision 65/2007/QD-BGDDT)*. Ten quality standards and 57 quality criteria formed the basis for the review process. MOET was given responsibility for organising the external review and accreditation process. Later, in 2013, *Decision 37/2013/TTg* reaffirmed the government's commitment to improving the quality of higher education in Vietnam, and MOET issued *Decision 6/VBHN-BGDDT*, promulgating amended regulations regarding the quality criteria for assessing the educational quality of HEIs. Also in 2013, responsibility for the external review and accreditation process was delegated to two accreditation centres, one from each of the two national universities. In 2015, two more of these centres were established, one at Da Nang University and the other attached to the Association of Vietnamese Non-public Universities and Colleges.

In 2010, the government approved a university charter (*Decision 58/2010/QD-TTg*) which prescribed that public universities must work towards establishing university councils that would exercise responsibility on behalf of the state for approving institutional objectives and strategies, guidelines for organisational structures, staff recruitment and training policies and policies regarding institutional finances, property, facilities and equipment. University councils were also given authority to conduct annual performance reviews for rectors and vice-rectors and to approve matters related to tuition fees and institutional scientific and training councils. This legislation was consistent with a growing commitment by the government to the belief that public HEIs should be more self-managing. It was not, however, the first time that the idea of university councils had been proposed. In 2003, a similar policy commitment had been expressed, but few public universities at the time did much to implement the proposal, principally because rectors considered the proposed framework to be unclear. Rectors were also reluctant to be burdened by an additional level of accountability, given that they were already required to report to whichever ministry or state instrumentality had line-management control of their university. In 2014, the *University Charter* was amended (*Decision 70/2014/QD-TTg*), principally with a view to strengthening the role of university councils and to reinforcing their importance within the higher education sector. The amendments did not, however, alleviate the concerns of rectors, and neither did they give any authority to university councils for the appointment of rectors.

In 2012, in what was a significant development for the higher education sector, the National Assembly approved a new *Higher Education Law*. The *Law* acknowledged formally the distinctiveness of the higher education sector within the national education system. It also consolidated a vast amount of regulatory detail concerning higher education that had been approved incrementally since 1993. The new legislation recognised the need for diversity within the sector, stating that some public universities would be elevated to a higher tier within the sector on the basis of their superior research capability and better overall quality. It also clarified that university councils should be given authority to decide institutional development plans, to determine organisational structures for the institution and to supervise the implementation of their own decisions. It gave more seats on university councils to community groups, including the Labour Union and the Youth Association, both extended arms of the Party. No mention was made about university councils having any authority for the appointment of rectors.

In 2013, the Central Committee of the Party declared that, to assist Vietnam to make faster progress with the industrialisation and modernisation of the economy, the education system needed comprehensive renovation (*Resolution 29-NQ/TW*). Of main concern was that the education system was not keeping pace with the needs of the economy. The *Resolution* referred specifically to the higher education sector in this regard, indicating also that public HEIs needed more autonomy as well as better governance and leadership. The *Resolution* expressed concern about the slow progress of reform in the higher education sector.

In 2014, the government issued *Resolution 77/NQ-CP*, which announced the establishment of a pilot scheme under which public universities agreeing to receive no further direct subsidy by the state would be given a greatly increased level of institutional autonomy. These universities would, for example, be able to establish their own training programs and specialisations, determine their own enrolment quotas and determine their own tuition fee levels for different programs – subject to ceiling levels set by the government. The pilot scheme, initially intended to conclude by 2017, was subsequently extended. To date, as many as 23 public universities have accepted self-funding status in exchange for more institutional autonomy. Many questions were, however, left unanswered by the *Resolution*, including questions about the extent of expenditure freedom for the 'autonomous' public universities and the extent of their freedom in making senior staff appointments. The recruitment of senior academic staff members, for example, remained subject to legislation over which the pilot-scheme universities had no control. The ceiling tuition fee levels set by the government have also proven to be restrictive, especially as the universities concerned are highly aspirational, needing much bigger budgets to enable them to become regionally or even globally significant as research-intensive institutions. Another problem recently reported is that the 'autonomous' universities have remained unexpectedly constrained by restrictions imposed on them by Vietnam's highly prescriptive legislative and regulatory culture. Of significance, though, is that in 2016, the Deputy Prime Minister commented that the effect of a requirement of financial self-sufficiency did not mean that the state was completely abandoning these universities and that public funds, provided in targeted ways, would continue to be provided. It is not clearly evident, though, if this form of funding for these universities has eventuated.

In 2016, the Cabinet issued *Resolution 89/NQ-CP*, re-emphasising the government's commitment to the establishment of university councils with genuine institutional autonomy and indicating yet again its intention to remove line-management control of public HEIs by ministries and other state instrumentalities. The *Resolution* indicated that university councils should play a role comparable to that of a board of directors in the private sector and that there should be a clear accountability relationship between a university council and the university's board of rectors (comprised of the rector and vice-rectors). No explanation was provided about how this accountability relationship should function. The *Resolution* also made it clear that all public HEIs must remain under the absolute leadership of the Party.

Most recently, the National Assembly has released an amended draft of the *Higher Education Law*. About one-half of all Articles in the existing *Law* have been proposed for amendment. The proposed amendments are mostly directed at making requirements for institutional autonomy and institutional accountability more explicit. Article 16, for example, is now indicating that a university council, as the governing body of a public university, has responsibility to represent the state as the owner of the university. The university council becomes, therefore, entirely responsible for developing the institution's strategic plan, determining its budget and articulating its approach to teaching, research, international cooperation and quality assurance. Importantly, except at universities concerned with public security and defence, university councils are being permitted to appoint the rector and vice-rectors, subject to final approval given by the relevant line-management authority. University council members are to include the rector, a vice-rector, the Party secretary, the chair of the labour union, the secretary of the youth union, representatives of the staff at the university, a representative of the relevant line-management authority and representatives of external stakeholders (accounting for at least 30% of the membership).

These proposed amendments represent significant policy progress in that they will provide greater clarity about how university governance should occur in public-sector universities. There are, however, important matters yet to be resolved. One of these concerns is the extent of the authority of a university council with respect to both the Party and the relevant line-management authority. Another is that, while direct state control will have been substantially reduced, indirect state control will increase because of an increase in the government's capacity to determine the priorities of the national quality accreditation agencies (see *Circular 04/2016/TT-BGDDT* and *Circular 12/0117/TT-BGDDT*).

Since the early 1990s, therefore, policy reform progress concerning the governance, management and quality assurance of higher education has clearly been evident, but the pace of the reform process has been slow. The reasons for this slow pace of the reform process must now be addressed.

Achieving Autonomy and Accountability

Institutional autonomy is a widely invoked concept in the international literature on higher education governance and management. Tight's (1992) elucidation of the concept is possibly the most relevant to Vietnam's circumstances. He identified institutional autonomy in terms of the freedom: a HEI has to be self-governing; manage its own financial affairs; select and appoint its own academic personnel; select and admit its own students; determine its own curriculum; and assess and accredit the academic performance of its own students.

Considered from this perspective, public HEIs in Vietnam do not yet generally experience a high level of institutional autonomy. For the large majority of these institutions, MOET routinely makes the important decisions regarding curriculum frameworks, quality standards and the introduction of new training programs; the Ministry of Science and Technology (MOST) largely determines their research priorities; and the Ministry of Finance (MOF) is mainly responsible for determining what they can spend. At least 16 ministries and more than 50 other state instrumentalities exercise line-management control over public HEIs, determining their expenditure priorities and appointing their rectors and other senior academic managers. The freedom most available to all of them is that of being able to assess students and accredit student performance.

The two national universities, one based in Hanoi and the other based in Ho Chi Minh City, are exempt in this regard because of their status in being able to report directly to the Cabinet. As reported earlier, there are also now 23 public universities that have accepted self-funding status in exchange for becoming more autonomous. For most public HEIs, however, a traditional form of direct state control remains the norm.

Institutional accountability is another widely invoked concept in the international literature on higher education governance and management. It is often seen as if complementary to institutional autonomy. Santiago et al. (2008, p.89) have identified various forms of institutional accountability that are compatible with institutional autonomy. These include quality assurance, where HEIs are made responsible for the quality of their systems and outcomes; performance-related funding, where the state provides financial incentives for the purposes of achieving desired social outcomes; market mechanisms, where HEIs are required to achieve efficiency by being exposed to market-based forces; participation by external stakeholders on governing bodies, where external stakeholders are given the opportunity to contribute directly to institutional governance; and public disclosure of institutional performance, where public HEIs are required to be transparent in reporting on their use of public funds.

In Vietnam, only two of these forms of institutional accountability have been developed. The first is a national quality assurance framework for the higher education sector. Institutional accreditation is now mandatory for all HEIs, whether public or private, and most HEIs now have their own internal quality assurance units, responsible for fostering a culture of commitment to quality, developing institutional strategies for the appraisal of quality, undertaking periodic appraisals of training programs and so on. An ambitious target has been set for the external accreditation of 95% of all HEIs and training programs by 2020, but this program is known to be running behind schedule because of limited resources. By March 2016, for example, of more than 3000 training programs in Vietnam's higher education sector, only 61 had been fully accredited.[1] The second is the 'three disclosures policy', introduced in 2009 (*Circular 09/2009/TT-BGDĐT*), which requires all HEIs to disclose publicly their commitment to quality, to effectiveness in their teaching and to sound financial management. In general, this policy has had a positive impact on institutional accountability across the sector, though HEIs have generally struggled to report meaningfully about their teaching effectiveness. Some fudging of the data being reported has also been identified, with MOET responding to these occurrences by reducing the enrolment quotas of institutions found to have produced deficient reports.

---

[1] http://www.tienphong.vn/xa-hoi/thanh-lap-trung-tam-kiem-dinh-giao-duc-dau-tien-tai-mien-trung-977359.tpo

Establishing University Councils

As reported earlier, progress in establishing university councils has been slow. The reasons are worthy of exploration because they provide insights regarding the difficulty of achieving reform of the governance and management of higher education in Vietnam.

Much of the delay experienced relates to difficulties associated with accommodating the legitimacy of the Party as the leading force in society with a form of corporate governance in which a university council has authority to govern and, through the rector, manage a public HEI. While the Party does not generally seek to interfere in university affairs, except in relation to the appointment of academic managers, it does have responsibility for approving a public university's strategic plan. If the strategic plan preferred by the Party turns out to be a failure, then it is the rector, on behalf of the university council, who will be held accountable because, under Article 36 of the *University Charter*, it is the rector who is 'the bank account owner of the university' and who is 'entirely responsible to the law'. The Party is above the law and so cannot be held accountable.

This situation presents a predicament for university councils. While they may be expected to exercise corporate governance, focusing on whatever is in the best interests of the institution, they must also be sensitive to Party policies and preferences. Rectors perceive that they can be caught in the middle of this two-way stet of accountabilities. They are also accountable to whichever ministry or other state instrumentality was responsible for their appointment. For rectors, therefore, the preferred option has been to delay the introduction of university councils. Recent legislation has become increasingly insistent, however, about the need for each public HEIs to have its own university council.

Complexities related to accommodating the role of the Party in a culture of corporate governance have not been the only source of delays. There exists in Vietnam a gap between policy articulation and policy implementation, as observed by numerous scholars (see, for example, Hayden and Lam 2007; Dao and Hayden 2010, 2015; London 2011; St. George 2011; Dao 2014; Tran 2014; Do 2014). This gap contributes significantly to delay in matters such as the establishment of university councils. The government routinely attempts to implement higher education reform by promulgating decrees, resolutions, decisions and circulars, but the substance of these documents is often ignored for extended periods for any one of the following reasons: there is insufficient budget to implement the proposed reform; there is a lack of clarity in the legislative and regulatory provisions; the reform proposed is excessively ambitious when considered in relation to the context; and the proposed reform will potentially disrupt well-entrenched vested interests.

Other reasons relate to particular cultural characteristics of public life in Vietnam. Many officials and academic managers may have little or no experience of public management practices beyond Vietnam and so may be unable to comprehend the thrust of reform based on principles of autonomy and accountability. There also exists in Vietnam a culture of 'asking and approving' (*xin-cho*), meaning that officials and academic managers may be reluctant to implement reform processes if they do not perceive some personal benefit as an outcome. There tends to be a 'waiting for guidance and budget' culture, whereby nothing gets done until the framework for the reform process has been fully documented and properly funded. Even rectors will delay making decisions if 'guidance and budget' are not clear. The personal cost for them from making the wrong decision can be high.

A Case Study

A case study of governance, management and quality assurance at a large and nationally significant university in Vietnam serves to illustrate how a changing policy context is being understood and acted upon at a local level. Though undertaken in 2007/2008 (Dao 2014), insights from the case study remain relevant to the contemporary state of governance, management and quality assurance in the higher education sector.

The case study involved semi-structured, in-depth interviews with ten senior and middle-level managers at the site institution, which was selected because it was representative of the leading group of public HEIs in Vietnam. The interviews were supplemented by prolonged observation of the institution's governance, management and quality assurance, as well as by an examination of relevant documentation. Of interest was the institution's experience of institutional autonomy, institutional accountability and quality assurance.

In reporting on the institution, reference will be made simply to 'the University'. In 2007/2008, when data were being collected, the University had over 1000 members of academic staff and as many as 50,000 full-time and part-time students. Most of these students were enrolled in undergraduate degree programs, but the postgraduate programs were expanding rapidly in terms of student enrolments.

The management structure of the University was typical of management structures at public universities across Vietnam. At the top was the Rector's Board, which included the rector and a number of vice-rectors. Next came the Faculty Boards, each chaired by a Dean, with members elected or appointed from within the faculty. At the bottom were the Department Boards, each chaired by a Head of Department and comprised of members appointed and elected from within the department.

Consistent with national political values, the Party played a monitoring role across all levels of management, seeking to ensure that decisions taken were consistent with the expressed policies of the Party. The Party also played a significant role in determining suitability for appointment as an academic manager at the University.

Authority within the institution was highly centralised. The Rector's Board decided all matters of importance to the functioning of the University, nearly always in consultation with the Party Committee. Faculty Boards were informed about the decisions taken and had limited decision-making independence. Department Boards had little or no capacity to make decisions independently, and so their role was primarily administrative and mainly concerned with allocation of teaching responsibilities and the authorisation of compliance reports for consideration at higher levels of authority within the University.

Curiously, more and more faculties and departments were being established each year, resulting in an ever-expanding organisational structure at the University. Subdividing faculties and departments into smaller units seemed to be the preferred strategy of the Rector's Board for the purposes of maintaining control over the University. It was evident that senior managers were aware that this practice was giving rise to problems, and yet it continued. One of the vice-rectors commented, for example:

> [The] organisational structure at the University appears inappropriate. There are too many faculties and [too much] overlapping [of] specialised fields of study available within our institution. Several faculties remain rather weak and academically fragmented. Several deans just allocate around 30% of their time for faculty management. Their power is quite limited.

On this point, a former rector commented:

> This University's management is too heavy and bureaucratic. I cannot understand why there are so many faculties, institutes and centres within it. Surprisingly, even the Department of Registry/Academic Affairs has centres within its Department. Faculties also have their own centres and institutes. The more divisions the University has, the more it has to pay to maintain its operation. Synergy cannot be fully made use of, resulting in waste of time, money and energy.

The University shared with other public universities in Vietnam a commitment to transitioning from a mono-disciplinary profile to one that was multidisciplinary. In 2007, *Decision No 121/2007/QD-TTg* by the Prime Minister had explicitly encouraged HEIs to offer more fields of study, thereby becoming more truly comprehensive. Many mono-disciplinary universities were also keen to become multidisciplinary as a way of distancing themselves from the influence of the Soviet higher education model. The main reason for making the shift, however, was survival. Mono-disciplinary universities had become less able to guarantee the availability of sufficient enrolments to generate the income required to remain fully operational. At the site institution, however, the aspirations to diversify seemed unrealistic: though the institution's core disciplines were business and economics, it had plans to develop training programs in technology, engineering and even biotechnology. A merger with another university might as well have been a more sensible option, but this option was simply ignored, most likely because it would possibly result in a need to consolidate two Boards of Rectors, with possible adverse loss of status and privileges for some existing members of the Board of Rectors.

The University's strategic plan envisaged the development of a comprehensive university with an organisational structure similar to that of the two national (in Hanoi and in Ho Chi Minh City) and three regional (in Hue, Da Nang and Thai Nguyen) universities. However, few of those interviewed appeared to have more than a superficial understanding about how the organisational structure at these universities functioned.

The extent of institutional autonomy at the University was limited. It was evident from comments made, as well as from observations, that the University was very much under control by MOET. A former rector, when describing this situation, drew attention to the implications: inputs to the University in the form of students were tightly regulated, but nobody took responsibility for what was going to happen to these students when they graduated. He commented:

> The paradox here is that institutional autonomy remains modest, but [institutional] account-ability is required to be highly maintained. This is one of the biggest dilemmas in Vietnam's higher education system. I cannot understand why MOET, on one hand, has a very tight control over student admission (input) but, on the other hand, releases the graduates (out-put). No one knows exactly after graduation what types of jobs they will do and if they will be satisfied with the jobs they find.

He observed also that, though academic staff members had lost their right to be permanently employed by the state in 2003, the conditions of their employment had not changed as a consequence, meaning that the incentive for them to take respon-sibility in matters of governance, management and quality assurance was weak and inadequate. He reported:

> For human resources, the policy of permanent recruitment has been abolished since 2003, but the salary rate is still managed in the old way, that is, payment according to positions and working years rather than by job performance. If so, how could institutional autonomy and [institutional] accountability be well maintained?

Many interviewees referred often to 'limited' or 'half-way' autonomy when asked to report on the state of institutional autonomy at the University. They accepted that the University had no authority to decide on the level of student tuition fees or to select its own senior academic managers or to exercise much academic freedom, but most stated that the University now had more expenditure freedom than in the past. In general, they regarded the level of institutional autonomy being provided to the University by MOET to be completely unrealistic.

The University's strategic plan expressed an expectation that MOET would eventually give the University more institutional autonomy. This expectation was said to be consistent with the University's aspiration to become a 'world-class' uni-versity by 2020. At the same time as requesting more institutional autonomy, how-ever, the University was also requesting more funds from the state to enable it to extend its building program. In this regard, its behaviour was consistent with an account given by Chapman and Austin (2002) of the way in which public universi-ties are prone to wanting more independence from state control while at the same time allowing themselves to become more dependent upon state funding. Meanwhile, governments often want public universities to be more financially self-sufficient, but not to become completely free of control by the state. The search for a balance in this regard is, therefore, a challenge.

Institutional autonomy and institutional accountability generally develop hand-in-hand, so that, as freedoms are conferred by the state, checks and balances are implemented to ensure that the freedoms are not being abused. At the site University, it was evident that a governance framework for the exercise of both institutional autonomy and institutional accountability was severely lacking. Though there was a University Council, it remained largely inactive. The role of the Chair of the Council was not at all well-defined, especially in terms of how it related to the rector's role. A former Chair of the University Council described the situation as follows:

> As a University Council chair, I [had] no voice. I did not know what to do because there were no concrete regulations from MOET. Personally, I was under the supervision of MOET but I received no support or guidance from MOET. Therefore, whatever I did, big or small, was fine. One important thing I had in mind is that I should not touch on any complicated institutional issues that might raise conflicts with the Rector's Board or the Party. What I did was to focus on the strategic plan as designated by MOET and that was it. I never interfered in anybody's affairs because I was not stupid. In reality, I participated in all important activities and meetings of the University, but I offered no ideas. I just simply applauded at the end.

The rector had recruited the Chair of the University Council and was also responsible for his remuneration. The role of Chair appeared to be marginalised. As the former Chair admitted:

> I think the establishment of the University Council at the moment is not appropriate at all. Given the condition of limited institutional autonomy and the supreme leadership of the Party, no university council in Vietnam can work properly as required.

Many other interviewees echoed this perspective. It was widely recognised that the University Council had no effective power. Decisions of any consequence could never seem to be taken without 'concrete guidance' from MOET, even though MOET itself often did not always appear to know what to do.

The University was among the first group of universities in Vietnam selected to be involved in the implementation of a national quality assurance program. At the time of the interviews, it had completed both its internal self-assessment and external assessment by a review panel. It was waiting for the outcome of the external review to be released by MOET. The University had already obtained an ISO Certificate issued by the Association for Academic Quality (France). In the opinion of one of the vice-rectors, though, the procedures for obtaining the Certificate had been lax. The University had established its own Department of Quality Assurance, but many university staff members were reported to be unfamiliar with the notion of quality assurance. One middle manager from the Department of Quality Assurance reported:

> I have tried to do many things to enhance staff members' awareness of the importance of the quality assurance program. For example, I myself distributed to all staff members the University's notebooks containing the 53 quality criteria of quality assurance as a reminder that our University is currently implementing this program. Many lecturers, however, said to me that it is unnecessary to implement quality assurance because the current criteria set by MOET are already too high to reach. In their opinions, no university in Vietnam could reach such high standards.

Why did lecturers have this perception? In reality, the 53 criteria referred to were not so demanding and they had been deliberately designed in accordance with Vietnamese, and not international, standards. The question, then, is as follows: how can Vietnam's universities possibly reach international standards of quality if the national standards set for them are already seen to be too difficult to achieve?

This interviewee also expressed concern regarding follow-up to the quality assurance program. He stated:

> I am wondering what we should do after the quality assurance program has been completed. We know our weaknesses, but how can we improve ourselves while being stuck in such a bureaucratic and heavily centralised governance mechanism with limited institutional autonomy. I think we just simply carry out quality assurance assessment and leave everything as it is for the future because we do not have sufficient budget to upgrade our physical facilities and increase staff members' wages.

The case study shows how the governance and management of higher education in Vietnam was in an underdeveloped state as recently as 2007/2008. The legacy of centralised control was manifested in the lack of much institutional autonomy, a reliance on supervision by MOET for the purposes of institutional accountability and a lack of belief in the importance of pursuing a quality assurance agenda. There has undoubtedly been progress made since that time, but, except possibly for those public universities which have elected to be self-funding for the sake of obtaining more institutional autonomy, the extent of the progress made does not appear to be obvious.

Conclusion

In the West, higher education reform is often seen in terms of change to an organisational or corporate culture. Glor (2001, p.5), for example, describes the ability to reform as referring to 'the capability for autonomous direction, and action, growing out of individual self-consciousness, self-identity, values, commitments, knowledge and power' shared by the organisation's members. According to Cummings and Huse (1989, p.421), these cultural elements are seen 'to guide members' perceptions, thoughts, and actions'.

In Vietnam, these elements exist only on the pages of official documents. For reasons that relate to a traditional lack of autonomy, limited capacity in terms of knowledge and skills and the restricted availability of resources, leaders within Vietnam's higher education sector are generally unable to demonstrate the persistent commitment, expertise and capacity to undertake and then achieve significant reforms. Even MOET, which has overall responsibility for the higher education sector, is unable to implement a reform agenda because it must share responsibility for budgeting, planning and the appointment and training of key personnel with multiple other ministries and state instrumentalities, each with line-management control of its own cluster of HEIs. There is also in Vietnam a high level of sensitivity to the preferences of the Party. Indeed, the Party is constitutionally positioned to veto any decision that it considers 'inappropriate' or where the rules of law made by the Party have not been respected. In these circumstances, therefore, Vietnam has been slow to modernise the governance, management and quality assurance frameworks for its higher education sector.

Other factors have also contributed to the general lack of momentum of change. Dao and Hayden (2015) pointed, for example, to 'a high level of institutional paternalism', generally seen in the way in which government ministries and instrumentalities exercise line-management responsibilities for public universities and colleges. They observed that, although governing boards in the public higher education sector are being provided with additional responsibilities for institutional governance and management, they are not given permission to make the critical decisions: 'One of the most important decisions they could make concerns the appointment of the rector, but there is no mention anywhere of this responsibility ever being given to them' (Dao and Hayden 2015, p.331).

Another factor is that senior academic managers of HEIs in the public sector in Vietnam are accustomed to management by an in-line ministry or other state instrumentality, as well as to having subsidised budgets allocated to their institution. In this context, there is a reluctance to take business risks, and it is more politically safe simply to adhere to governmental regulations. There is, in other words, an entrenched mindset within which there exists a 'secure periphery' determined by the laws and regulations issued by the Party and the state. One of the ironies of the current process of approving additional 'autonomous', that is, 'self-funding', universities is to hear concern being expressed by some of the rectors concerned about the loss of protection by a 'parent' ministry. The habits of mind established over the long period of centralised state management of the sector seem unlikely to disappear in a hurry.

When viewed over a 30-year period, however, higher education in Vietnam has made remarkable policy progress. It has now reached a point where 23 public universities can claim to have more institutional autonomy than at any time in the past. While pressures associated with globalisation and internationalisation have contributed to this progress, other pressures have also played an important role. One of these is that the governance and management apparatus of a Soviet model of higher education simply had to be dismantled for the sake of the affordability and efficiency of the higher education sector. This dismantling process, which continues, has, however, been slow and has at times been pursued reluctantly. The government routinely espouses the importance of modernising the structure and processes for the attainment of institutional autonomy, institutional accountability and quality assurance in the higher education sector, but, at least in the public sector, autonomous governing boards are not yet widely evident. The form of institutional accountability relied upon most heavily continues to be direct control by the state. Quality assurance processes continue lack transparency, and there is not yet much evidence of their impact. Though a commitment was made in 2005 in the Higher Education Reform Agenda (*Resolution 14/2005/NQ-CP*) to remove line-management control by ministries and other state instrumentalities of public HEIs, this commitment has not yet been honoured. The culture of the Soviet model seems to be difficult to throw off, especially in Vietnam's higher education sector.

A long-term challenge for the sector is that of finding a way of modernising the sector's governance, management and quality assurance in a context within which the legitimacy of the Party as the leading force in society cannot be not threatened.

As always in matters of good governance and management, the cultivation and maintenance of trust will be essential, as will the need for a shared commitment to the importance of assuring quality.

References

Chapman, D., & Austin, A. (Eds.). (2002). *Higher education in the developing world: Changing contexts and institutional responses*. Westport/London: Greenwood Press.

Cummings, T., & Huse, F. (1989). *Organization development and change* (4th ed.). New York: West Publishing.

Dao, K. V. (2014). Key challenges in the reform of governance, quality assurance, and finance in Vietnamese higher education – A case study. *Studies in Higher Education*. https://doi.org/10.1080/03075079.2013.842223.

Dao, K. V., & Hayden, M. (2010). Reforming the governance of higher education in Vietnam. In G. Harman, M. Hayden, & T. N. Pham (Eds.), *Reforming higher education in Vietnam: Challenges and priorities*. Dordrecht: Springer.

Dao, K. V., & Hayden, M. (2015). Higher education governance reform in Vietnam. In K. M. Joshi & S. Paivandi (Eds.), *Global higher education. Issues in governance*. New Delhi: B.R Publishing Corporation.

Do, H. (2014). Towards more flexible organization. In *Higher education in Vietnam: Flexibility, mobility and practicality in the global knowledge economy*. New York: Palgrave Macmillan. http://www.palgrave.com/page/detail/?sf1=id_product&st1=765663

Glor, E. (2001). Key factors influencing innovation in government. *The Innovation Journal: The Public Sector Innovation Journal, 6*(2), 1–20.

Hayden, M., & Lam, T. Q. (2007). Institutional autonomy for higher education in Vietnam. *Higher Education Research & Development, 26*(1), 73–85.

London, J. D. (2011). Education in Vietnam: Historical roots, recent trends. In J. D. London (Ed.), *Education in Vietnam* (pp. 1–56). Singapore: Institute of Southeast Asian Studies.

Santiago, P., Tremblay, K., Basri, E., & Arnai, E. (2008). *Tertiary education for the knowledge society*. Paris: OECD.

St. George, E. (2011). Higher education reform in Vietnam. In J. D. London (Ed.), *Education in Vietnam* (pp. 1–56). Singapore: Institute of Southeast Asian Studies.

Tight, M. (1992). Institutional autonomy. In B. R. Clark & G. Neave (Eds.), *The Encyclopaedia of higher education* (pp. 1305–1313). Oxford: Pergamon.

Tran, T. T. (2014). *Governance in higher education in Vietnam a move towards decentralization and its practical problems*. Journal of Asian Public Policy, Routledge, http://www.tandfonline.com/loi/rapp20

Chapter 4
University Governance in Vietnam and East Asian Higher Education: Comparative Perspectives

Mai Tuyet Ngo

Abstract This chapter reports on empirical research investigating four case studies of public university governance in four East Asian contexts in Vietnam, China, Hong Kong and Thailand. Guided by the neo-institutional and resource dependency theories, each case study provided insights into its model of public university governance. The cross-case thematic comparative analyses highlight seven transferable lessons acknowledging the urgent needs for actions for Vietnam.

Introduction

University Governance as a Significant Topic for Research and Practice

University governance really matters for the advancement of modern universities. Universities that take the lead in university governance top the global rankings of high-performing universities. Nations at the forefront of university governance reforms advance their national economic growth and lead the world in the fields of science and technology. A strong connection between good university governance practices and university academic excellence has been well acknowledged in the literature (e.g., Aghion et al. 2010; Henard and Mitterle 2009; Shattock 2006). Over the past decades, countries in all corners of the world have thus attached high importance to the way their universities are governed. Vietnam is not an exception. Scholarly and practical attempts, though not many, have been made to innovate Vietnam's contemporary university governance and have caught increased attention of not only Vietnamese higher education scholars (and foreign ones) but also Vietnam's government and higher education reformers aspiring for excellence in

M. T. Ngo (✉)
College of Humanities, Arts and Social Sciences, Flinders University, Adelaide, South Australia, Australia
e-mail: mai.ngo@flinders.edu.au

© Springer Nature Singapore Pte Ltd. 2019
N. T. Nguyen, L. T. Tran (eds.), *Reforming Vietnamese Higher Education*, Education in the Asia-Pacific Region: Issues, Concerns and Prospects 50, https://doi.org/10.1007/978-981-13-8918-4_4

research (knowledge production), teaching (knowledge transfer) and innovation (knowledge application).

This chapter presents some significant findings from the author's PhD study on comparative analyses of public university governance in Vietnam and in three other higher education contexts in East Asia. The study was conducted empirically by the author over four consecutive years, from January 2010 to December 2013, and was published as a PhD thesis in 2014 (Ngo 2014). Specifically, the study made a cross-national comparison of different models of public university governance in four East Asian contexts (one in each context), including Vietnam, representing a *need-help* country because of its current low performing model, and Thailand, China and Hong Kong, representing *offer-help* countries because of their more mature and higher performing models. The findings of the study were based on cross-national comparative analyses of arrangements for university governance, as reflected in legislative and policy documents (at the *macro* levels), institutional documents and university executive leaders' interviews (at the *meso* levels), and empirical survey data from departmental leadership levels (at the *micro* levels).

It is worth noting that, for the purposes of conducting the study, official documents were collected from either relevant university websites or from individuals during the researcher's field trips to the four respective public universities in Vietnam, Hong Kong SAR, Thailand and China where one-on-one semi-structured interviews (with respective universities' executive leaders) and questionnaire surveys (among Departmental leaders) were conducted. To facilitate the data collection from different sources in each of the four different respective universities, many logistical and coordination efforts were made by the researcher prior to each field trip (see Ngo 2014).

Within its limited scope and space, this chapter presents only the most significant findings of the study in relation to cross-national comparative analyses of the two main themes, particularly of contextual and structural arrangements as reflected in analyses of governments' policy documents and respective university documents. Fuller accounts of empirical supporting data (from interviews and surveys) and more comprehensive findings for the two other equally important themes of resource/funding arrangements and university leadership can be found in Ngo (2014).

Conceptualisation of University Governance

Due to its complex multi-faceted nature, defining the concept of university governance is "a troubling task" (Kezar and Eckel 2004, p. 375). University governance can be broadly defined as *a means* of steering and supporting key stakeholders, including academics, towards achieving their dual ends of teaching and research (e.g., Corson 1975; The Carnegie Commission on Higher Education 1973). In a narrower sense, university governance is often conceptualised as formal multi-level arrangements that allow universities to perform effectively towards achieving academic excellence (e.g., Amaral et al. 2002; Bleiklie and Kogan 2007; CHEPS 2010; Kehm 2012; Salmi 2009; Shattock 2006). This study employs the narrow definition of university governance as formal multi-level governance arrangements, which, according to Kehm (2012), consist of formal external arrangements at the macro/system level, and internal arrangements at the meso/university and micro/departmental levels. The study reported here acknowledges the importance of multi-level governance arrangements for any normative model of university governance, with a particular focus on the macro and meso governance arrangements.

University governance arrangements, as the literature suggests, can specifically refer to (i) contextual arrangements (e.g., Asimiran and Hussin 2012; Currie et al. 2003), (ii) governance structural arrangements (e.g., Clark 1983; de Boer and Goedegebuure 2007; Shattock 2014), (iii) resource or funding arrangements (e.g., Gallagher et al. 2009; Hackman 1988; Leisyte 2007) and (iv) university leadership (e.g., Boin and Christensen 2008; Hallinger 2007; Middlehurst 1993). All those four arrangements are of importance for any model of university governance (Ngo 2014). However, within its limited scope and space, this chapter puts under the spotlight only the two most significant governance arrangements, particularly, the contextual arrangements and the governance structural arrangements.

The contextual arrangements and the governance structural arrangements are the two most significant arrangements (e.g., Binsbergen et al. 1994; Clark 1983; Ngo 2014; Shattock 2014) simply because all other arrangements (i.e., resource/funding arrangements and university leaderships) are very much dependent on them as key foundations. *First*, good public university governance is *shaped* by its context and a model of good public university governance, as Ngo (2014, p. 124) argued, "cannot be decontextualised from its own context". More specifically, contexts matter for the quality of teaching and research which can be explained through contextual conditions (Bjorkman 2000). *Second*, evaluating the sufficiency of a university governance model requires significant consideration of its governance structures (Rhoades 1995; Rosovsky 2001; Silverman 1971). For improving university quality, the need for reviewing and modernising governance structures is thus highlighted (e.g., de Boer 1999; Eurydice 2008; Shattock 2014). On those grounds, it is well recommended that if an old model of public university governance puts constraints on its public universities' ability to carry out academic quality improvement, then both the contextual arrangements and structural arrangements of that model must be first under review and modernised.

The Prominent Problem Facing Vietnam's Contemporary Model of Public University Governance

Literature on Vietnam's current model of public university governance, though not extensive, has consistently suggested that its current model is an old state-centralised model adopted from the Soviet model since the 1950s that is no longer fitting for modern Vietnam (e.g., Dao and Hayden 2010; Pham 2012). The way Vietnamese public universities have been governed since the 1950s, in the broadest sense, has mostly remained unchanged, leading to various concerns raised by the country's key actors and governance practitioners. In the preceding chapter – Chap. 3, Dao and Hayden (this volume) pointed out that the Vietnamese higher education system had copied the former Soviet Union's model since 1954 in the North and since 1975 in the South, and highlighted its instability, its slowness and its being largely intact without any dramatic changes. Despite reform attempts, Vietnamese university governance reforms have been highly centralised and slow moving (Dao 2015). In such a centralised model, Vietnamese public universities, as observed by Wilkinson (2008, p. 4), "are the worst in the region".

The most prominent problem facing Vietnam's current model of public university governance is, among others, *an absence of adequate incentives* for academic excellence, producing the sluggishness that paralyses any flexibility in positional leaders' actions, stifles the creativity and innovation of academic staff, and most seriously, impacts university performance (e.g., Dao and Hayden 2010; Fry 2009; Hayden and Lam 2010; Pham 2012). This absence of adequate incentives for academic excellence in Vietnamese public universities has also been politically acknowledged in the Prime Minister's Directive 296/CT-TTg (Vietnamese Prime Minister 2010).

From university governance perspectives, the main reason for the absence of adequate incentives for academic excellence in Vietnam's public universities, among others, is its old model of public university governance with irrelevant features of, namely, disadvantageous contexts, "out-moded" governance structure arrangements, inappropriate resource/funding arrangements and lacks of responsive university leadership. Given its limited scope, this chapter addresses only its governance contexts and its old governance structural arrangements, which are the two most significant features in most urgency of renovation in Vietnam. Vietnam's Minister of Education and Training – Dr. Phung Xuan Nha – appointed in April 2016, publicly voiced the urgent need to renovate Vietnam's current governance contexts and structures to promote incentives for universities' academic staff, managers and leaders who are implementers of fundamental and comprehensive higher education reforms in Vietnam.

Research Aim and Research Question

Given the paramount aim of this study which is to look for a new improved model of public university governance, prioritising improved contextual arrangements and more modernised governance structural arrangements that can hopefully promote more incentives for academic excellence in modern Vietnamese public universities, the main research question is: *what* can modern Vietnam learn from contextual arrangements and governance structural arrangements, as revealed from the global trends and from other more successful (or at least higher performing) empirical models of public university governance in neighbouring East Asian contexts? This research question implies an outward-looking approach placing emphases on the global trends and East Asia's public university governance practices, which are useful sources of reference and of transferable lessons for Vietnam.

Methodological Considerations

Finding answers to the research question formulated above demands an empirical, holistic and comparative study of cross-national models of public university governance, which can be conducted through the use of a case-study approach. In the field of university governance, case study is a useful "reality check", providing insights into issues of university governance (Fielden et al. 2004) and into how good governance comes about (Goedegebuure and Hayden 2007). More importantly, insights gained from an empirical case study can, as Merriam (1998, p. 19) suggested, "directly influence policy, practice, and future research".

Unlike most studies in the literature that have used single case studies which are of a descriptive or explanatory or exploratory nature, this study ambitiously and intentionally used multiple case studies to provide more compelling evidence and more robust findings (e.g., Miles and Huberman 1994; Yin 2003). Multiple case studies conducted in this particular study are of explanatory kinds and comparative by nature because comparison is highly regarded in university governance studies (e.g., Fielden et al. 2004; Shattock 2006). The importance of cross-national comparative studies into higher education governance that include Vietnam is also well acknowledged (e.g., Dao 2015; Dao and Hayden 2010; St. George 2003; Wilkinson 2008). However, there has not been much real cross-national comparison that puts the Vietnamese model of public university governance under spotlight. This study not only attempts to fill in such methodological gap, but it also selects cross-national comparison as an appropriate methodological approach to answer the research question formulated at the beginning of the study.

Despite their strengths, multiple case studies conducted in this research have their limitations. *First*, their substantive focus is limited to the set boundary within the governance of one type of university, namely, *public universities*, not all types of universities across the four territories under investigation. The findings are thus relevant for governance of public universities and should not be generalised beyond this activity, albeit one of major importance. *Second*, this study focuses on the differences *between* models of public university governance employed in different territories, not *within* each territory where each single case study was conducted. The researcher is therefore aware of the study's limited appreciation of diverse and dynamic circumstances within each territory.

Third, mixed documentary datasets in multiple cross-cultural case studies present a methodological challenge in collecting data in different language settings as well as integrating or merging data in each within-case study and across four case studies. The use of a single data source and a single case study may have addressed this challenge although it may have brought about an even more serious shortcoming related to the "single-source bias".

Finally, given the use of a limited number of four case studies, the present study's findings might be open to the charge, as Ragin (1987, p. ix) asserted, "that their findings are specific to the few cases [in this present study, only *four* case studies], and when they do make comparisons and attempt to generalise, they are often

accused of letting their favorite cases shape or at least color their generalisations".
To address this charge, for delimitation, this study did not aim for a generalisation
of findings in other contexts nor let any favourite case shape the findings. Efforts
have been consciously made to ensure creditability and trustworthiness of each case
study. After the findings of each case study revealed, the researcher sent via email
the reported findings of each single case study to those executive leaders and departmental leaders who participated in the research for their final feedback and
comments.

The Outline of the Chapter

This chapter is structured into four main parts. The *first* part introduces the topic of
university governance, and briefly depicts the most prominent problem facing
Vietnam's current outdated irrelevant model of public university governance, highlighting Vietnam's urgency to improve its contextual arrangements and modernise
its governance structures which are the focus of the book chapter. The research aim,
research question and the case study methodology employed in this study to address
the research question are also presented in this part.

The *second* part presents the two main global thematic trends of public university
governance in relation to (1) the new changing global contexts and (2) the new
changing governance structures, as revealed from both the secondary literature and
the good practices of university governance presented in summary reports by the
OECD, the World Bank, governments and higher education institutions.

The *third* part, which is the main part of the chapter, presents cross-case thematic
comparative analyses of Vietnam's current low-performing model of public university governance and three other higher performing ones employed in Thailand's,
China's and Hong Kong's higher education contexts. Drawing from the cross-case
thematic comparative analyses, this part highlights seven transferable lessons for
Vietnam.

The *fourth* part concludes with implications for both further research and practice of modernising Vietnam's current model of public university governance that
promotes more incentives for academic excellence in public universities in Vietnam
and beyond.

Global Trends of University Governance: Changing Contexts and Changing Governance Structures

Many recent studies have addressed the broad topic of global trends of university
governance (e.g., CHEPS 2010, 2015; Christopher 2012: de Boer and File 2009;
OECD 2008) as well as the Asian trends of university governance (e.g., Chan and
Lo 2008; Marginson 2011; Mok 2010; Welch 2009). Such studies indicate many

different interesting global and regional trends which are recently summarised by Ngo (2014) under four main themes: (1) the rapidly changing *contexts* forcing changes in public university governance, calling for higher education governance reforms and a new search for new models of university governance; (2) the new *governance structural arrangements* with the new changing roles of key governance actors; (3) the new *resource arrangements* holding universities accountable to allocations and use of resources; and (4) *new leadership responses* to promote incentives for academic excellence. All these four main global thematic trends capture well the four key corresponding features of university governance. However, within the limited space of this chapter, only the first two global thematic trends are chosen to be focused on as they are concerned with governance contexts and governance structures which, as indicated earlier, urgently need improving in Vietnam. These two thematic trends also provide a guiding framework for cross-national comparative analyses presented later in this chapter.

Global Trend 1: New Rapidly Changing Contexts Forcing Changes in Public University Governance

Internal as well as external contexts have been changing rapidly, impacting the national practices of university governance. *Externally*, university governance everywhere is subject to the influences of the *external* influencing forces, including globalisation of the economy and internationalisation of higher education (e.g., CHEPS 2010, 2015; Eurydice 2008; UNESCO 2006). It is therefore urgent for nations to devote much more resources to both their higher education systems and their higher education institutions. *Internally*, universities everywhere are subject to *internal* influencing forces and challenges, ranging from pressures for the rapid higher education expansion (increased student enrolment), diversification (different types of HEIs), emergence of private higher education, marketisation and commercialisation of higher education to a relative decrease in public funding (particularly, pressures for financial cutbacks or financial stringency due to reduced funding) and the increasing importance of research and innovation in the global knowledge-based economy and wider competition among higher education institutions. Notably, external and internal influencing forces are conflicting as external pressures demand for a substantial increase in resource inputs for universities while the internal influencing forces are calling for a substantial decrease in public funding due to financial cutbacks. This really presents a dilemma for national governments and public universities in many corners of the world.

In the context of globalisation and internationalisation, it can be observed that countries all over the world, including developed ones with internationally recognised universities, are not complacent with the way their public universities are governed; their models of public university governance started to be questioned as being obsolete and no longer fitting for the rapidly changing environment. National higher education policy-makers are abandoning, to a greater or lesser degree, classic models inherited from the past (Asimira and Hussin 2012). Therefore, there is a global trend of re-examining own current models of public university governance and reorientating the higher education sectors, re-designing and embracing new models of university governance (e.g., Capano 2011; Varghese 2012).

Global Trend 2: New Governance Structural Arrangements with the Changing Roles of Governance Actors

Traditional models of university governance, as the global trend suggests, have been shifting towards *new* ones, thus demanding *new* governance features including *new* governance structural arrangements (e.g., Binsbergen et al. 1994; Eurydice 2008; Goedegebuure and van Vught 1994; Shattock 2014). In the words of Shattock (2014, p. 1), "pressures have mounted for a 'modernisation' of governance structures". This is not surprising because governance structures are one of the core features of any model of university governance that need special attention (e.g., Eurydice 2008; Shattock 2014). The new governance structural arrangements found in more mature and higher performing models of university governance are globally characterised as the new structures of more "centralised" decentralisation and deregulation, providing universities with more autonomy and less state intervention accompanied by appearance of a multiplication of intermediary (buffer) governing bodies between government and higher education institutions (e.g., Henard and Mitterle 2009; Varghese 2012); and more strengthening of appointed executive leadership at the central and middle levels of universities which is replacing structures of elected executives and affecting the powers of senates and academic councils (Marginson and Considine 2000).

In addition, it is worth noting that the new governance structural arrangements are characterised by a higher degree of governance structure clarity (reflected in clearer governance rules specifying clearer roles and responsibilities for institutions and stipulating required actions) (Binsbergen et al. 1994; Henard and Mitterle 2009) and a higher degree of governance flexibility allowing universities to adapt to meet society's emerging needs (e.g., CHEPS 2010; Dobbins et al. 2011; Fielden 2008). Empirical examination into governance structures' degrees of clarity is thus needed to see how higher degrees of governance structure clarity can come about in high-performing models of public university governance and what modifications are needed in relation to the governance structures of low degrees of clarity in low-performing models of public university governance.

Accompanying the changes in *new* governance structural arrangements, the human dynamics of university governance structures have changed accordingly. Three observations in relation to the changing roles of key governance actors are (1) the *stronger roles of governments* (more as strategy developers, goal setters, supervisors, regulators and supporters, but less as resource controllers) as the driving forces in university governance (e.g., Fielden 2008; Kehm 2012; Varghese 2012); (2) the *new configuration of actors* with the notable emergence of new actors at the different levels of governance (e.g., the new actors of the European Union and the

World Bank at the supra-national levels and the emergence of buffer governing bodies at the institutional levels, and private investment sectors); and (3) the *more strengthened internal university leadership* as universities are becoming more professionally managed organisations. The changing roles of governance actors have been well captured by Kehm (2012, p. 66, emphasis added) who noted:

> Responsibilities for higher education governance and policy making on the systems level no longer tend to be the exclusive responsibility of national governments. Some responsibilities have *"moved up"* to the supra-national level, others have *"moved down"* to the institutional level through deregulation, and again others have *"moved out"* to independent or semi-independent agencies.

To sum up, the current knowledge revealed from literature on the global thematic trends of university governance suggests that any countries with aspirations for their universities' academic excellence should neither go against such two global thematic trends nor stand still. It follows that a country with its slow-moving university governance model like Vietnam should be well informed of these two global thematic trends to practically and critically reflect on and renovate its own model of public university governance.

Comparative Analyses of Vietnam's and Three East Asia's Models of Public University Governance in the Global Context

Overview

East Asia's successful experience in university governance (Marginson 2011; Wilkinson 2008) is chosen to be under the spotlight in this study, particularly because success in East Asia, as observed by UNESCO (2006), "lies in their reliance on incentives to motivate individuals to change rather than on mandates to comply", whereas an absence of incentives for academic excellence in Vietnamese public universities, as indicated earlier, is the prominent problem facing Vietnam's current model of public university governance. Moreover, the three non-Vietnamese contexts of Thailand, China and Hong Kong, to some extent, have their cultural convergence with and geographical proximity to Vietnam, thus making the research's findings more significant, more culturally relevant and more transferable to Vietnam.

Using thematic comparative analyses, as mentioned earlier, this book chapter is interested in two key relevant themes of (1) the contextual arrangements and (2) governance structural arrangements of public university governance in Vietnam, China, Thailand and Hong Kong. Thematic comparative analyses of Vietnam's model and three non-Vietnamese models in East Asia highlight the specific problems in relation to Vietnam's contexts and its public university governance structures. However, comparative analyses among three non-Vietnamese models in East Asia reveal some converging patterns and suggest some possible solutions or transferable lessons for Vietnam. Using such cross-case thematic comparative analyses, the present study could achieve "a structured, focused comparison" (Bleiklie and Kogan 2000) and draw transferable lessons from foreign experiences (Page 1995).

For cross-case comparison and interpretation, the present study used the four useful notions advanced by Ragin (1987) for case-oriented comparative research, namely, "illusory commonality", "illusory difference", "obvious commonality", and "obvious difference". The two notions of *"obvious commonality"* and *"obvious difference"* are straightforward in meanings; while *"obvious commonality"* refers to both apparently similar features and similar performance outcomes, the notion of *"obvious difference"* refers to both apparently different features and apparently different outcomes across cases under comparison (Ragin 1987). In contrast, *"illusory difference"* refers to "features which appear different but are causally equivalent at a more abstract level" whereas *"illusory commonality"* implies "apparently common features [that] differ dramatically in causal significance" (Ragin 1987, p. 48). All these four notions advanced by Ragin (1987) put emphasis on the *outcomes* of features being compared.

To determine whether particular features of public university governance under comparison are obviously/illusorily common or different across cases, this study uses the simple dichotomy of *low-/high*-performing models of public university governance for grouping models and refers all the three non-Vietnamese models of university governance (in China, Thailand and Hong Kong) to high-performing models with high performance outcomes, whereas the Vietnamese model is categorised as a low-performing model with low performance outcomes. This model grouping is well supported in the literature (e.g., Asian Development Bank 2012; Marginson 2011; Wilkinson 2008). Particularly, comparing models of higher education in Confucian societies of East Asia, that of Vietnam and elsewhere, Marginson (2011, p. 587, emphasis added) stressed the distinctiveness of models outside Vietnam as follows:

> Except for Vietnam, these [East Asian] systems… have created a *distinctive* model of higher education [even] *more effective* in some respects than systems in North America, the English-speaking world and Europe where the modern university was incubated.

More particularly, comparing Hong Kong with other Asian countries, Welch (2010) concluded that Hong Kong's public university governance is very much advanced and more mature. Hong Kong's success story of development of its universities is highlighted in the 2002 Sutherland Report (UGC 2002) and widely acknowledged in the literature (e.g., the World Bank 2012; UNESCO 2006). Thailand has made impressive progress in its public university governance, transforming from being a historically "low" achiever in public university governance (almost at the same level as Vietnam) to being a successful "middle" (adequate) achiever (the World Bank 2012). Thailand's middle path success in achieving a strong modern public university governance system with significant commitments in higher education and research innovation is highlighted in many recent university governance reports and studies (Asian Development Bank 2012; UNESCO 2006; The World Bank 2009, 2012). China, according to Wilkinson (2008, p. 6), "has enjoyed great success in its development of an elite cohort of universities and research institutions".

It is also worth noting that the chosen territories of Thailand, China and Hong Kong are within geographical proximity (to Vietnam) which, as UNESCO (2006, p. iii) asserted, "can make findings more transferable and applicable to Vietnam". In addition, all the four territories of Vietnam represent "a sufficiently wide range of circumstances to allow both sharp contrasts and subtle differences in the modes of governance" (Palfreyman et al. 2009, p. xiii) and therefore to "make comparative findings significant" (Cerych and Sabatier 1986, p. 5).

To draw practical transferable lessons for Vietnam, in this chapter, special attention was paid to relevant points of *"illusory differences"* and/or *"obvious commonalities"* in terms of contexts and governance structure arrangements which contribute to high performance outcomes of the three non-Vietnamese models of public university governance. Such points of *"illusory differences"* and/or *"obvious commonalities"* among case studies in Thailand, China and Hong Kong are under the spotlight because they are at the same time points of "obvious differences" when compared directly with Vietnam. As case studies conducted in all the four territories are repeatedly referred to in comparative analyses, to save presentation space, acronyms have been used, namely, CN for the case study in China, TL for the case study in Thailand, HK for the case study in Hong Kong and VN for the case study in Vietnam.

Cross-National *Comparative Analyses of Contexts: Transferable Lessons 1, 2 and 3*

Comparative analyses of contexts, according to Fraser (2005), involve "multi-layered" contexts, which consist of (i) the territory-layered contexts; (ii) the higher education system-layered contexts; and (iii) university-layered contexts. In this chapter, only the first two layers of contexts will be cross-nationally compared for drawing relevant lessons, with particular attention paid to "illusory differences" and/or "obvious similarities" among the three non-Vietnamese contexts and the "obvious differences" and/or "illusory commonalities" between Vietnam's and three other East Asia's contexts.

Comparing territory-layered contexts and Lessons 1 and 2

For cross-national comparative analyses of territory-layered contexts, Millette (1978) highlighted the importance of historical, socio-political, cultural and economic environment and wrote:

> Anyone who undertakes a transnational comparison and analysis of higher education must at all times be mindful of the history, culture, socio-political structure, the government organization, and the state of economic development in each nation. Many of the differences in higher education must be understood in terms of the particular *historical, cultural social, governmental [political], and economic environment* of each nation (p. 15).

Following Millette (1978), the present study takes into account not only the cultural and historical contexts but also the socio-political and economic contexts in which the four studied models of university governance are employed.

Culturally, Vietnam shares many common aspects of East Asia's cultures. Together with CN, HK and TL, VN has many common features of Buddhism cultural and religious heritage. In addition, VN, HK and CN all belong to Confucian societies (Marginson 2011). It is worth noting that such cultural commonalities have put all the four higher education systems in culturally advantageous contexts attaching high importance to their higher education (e.g., Altbach and Umakoshi 2004; Do and Ho 2010; Vallely and Wilkinson 2009). However, a rich diversity of historical, political and economic contexts seems to overwhelm such cultural commonalities across cases.

Historically, Vietnam is similar to HK and has a long national history of colonisation. However, unlike VN, TL was never colonised by any Western nation while China was historically recorded to be a semi-colonised nation because in the nineteenth and early twentieth centuries, Chinese foreign relations with most major world powerful nations devolved into semi-colonialism. A closer investigation into the historical commonality (of being both colonised) of VN and HK and the different performance outcomes of HK's and VN's models of university governance suggests that it is an "illusory commonality". While Vietnam's long history of being colonised by the Chinese dynasties, the French and the Americans was a long-suffering or non-peaceful struggle against colonists, HK was peacefully ruled by the British for more than 150 years. In this regard, HK's model of public university governance has been situated in a more historically advantageous context of colonisation than VN's.

In addition, despite being both influenced by a long history of *colonisation*, HK has long adopted only one single sustainable model – the British model of public university governance whereas Vietnam was exposed to many different foreign models. Vietnam first adopted the *Chinese* model of public university governance during the feudal period from 938 to 1847, then the *French* model from 1847 to 1954 before adopting the *Soviet* model after gaining independence from the French in 1954. It is worth noting that the historical differences between HK (being colonised) and CN (being semi-colonised) and TL (never being colonised) is an illusory difference as all the three non-Vietnamese contexts are associated with high-performing models of public university governance. This suggests an equal possibility of developing a high-performing model of public university governance in not only a never-colonised context like TL and a semi-colonised context like CN but also in such historically colonised contexts as HK and VN.

Lesson 1: The need for Vietnam to decentralise responsibilities to university levels and to maintain a democratic administration and academic freedom under the Communist Party

Politically, there is a rich diversity across four studied contexts. While TL is a constitutional monarchy under the King with multiple political parties and is governed by a democratically elected government, HK is a capitalist constitutional democratic society. Notably, both VN and CN are among very few countries in the world still under the ruling of a single Communist Party being the only political force constitutionally responsible for leading the state. Like CN, Vietnamese public organisations, including its public universities, are under the leadership of the grass-roots committees of the Communist Party; the Communist Party Committee is embedded in public organisational structures in both VN and CN. Policy documents issued by both the Vietnamese and the Chinese Governments all record the need for the Communist Party consultation or approval.

A closer investigation reveals that the political commonality (of being both ruled by the single Communist Party) between VN and CN is an illusory commonality. Under the Communist Party ruling, while CN's model of public university governance has successfully produced such first-tier universities as the Tsinghua University, the Peking University and the Fudan University (QS University Ranking 2015; Ross and Wang 2016), Vietnam has never seen any of its best universities being internationally recognised in any World University Ranking Lists. At a more abstract level, unlike VN where responsibilities for VN's higher education governance have been borne mainly by the Communist Party of Vietnam and Ministry of Education and Training (VN), CN has decentralised and "moved down" responsibilities for its higher education governance to provincial and university levels (CN).

In addition, a deeper investigation into the administration of CN's and VN's public universities suggests that each political system in VN and CN has its own characteristics. CN's administration of the first-tier and the second-tier universities is a democratic administration laying great emphasis on academic freedom and scientific research (Jianhua 2016) though academics in CN may not enjoy as much academic freedom as their counterparts in Western universities (e.g., publications in social sciences by Chinese scholars tend to be in favour of Chinese Government's policies and suiting Chinese national interests). Whereas VN's administration of public university is still centralised and top-down with the University President as the single most important decision-maker, as at least revealed in the case study in Vietnam. Furthermore, to become a university president, it is a prerequisite that university president candidates in VN must be Communist Party members, and the elected university president is always the head of the Communist Party Committee embedded in the university governance structure. However, it is not the case in CN. University president candidates in the case study in China are not required to be the Communist Party Committee, though similar to VN, they are required to successfully complete a PhD overseas, be qualified for and experienced in university governance. This political illusory commonality between the two Communist regimes of VN and CN can convince us that a high-performing model of public university governance can exist and thrive within a Communist Party's regime though it raises a concern over who is in charge of appointing the university presidents/rectors in CN and VN (i.e., whether the university councils/governing boards or the governmental instrumentalities in line ministries/provinces appoint them) and over what level of intervention from the State/ministerial and provincial governments.

It is also worth noting that the political differences among CN, TL and HK (all associated with their high-performing models of public university governance) are illusory differences. At a more abstract level, responsibilities for higher education governance have been decentralised and "moved down" to provincial and university levels (CN), or "moved down" to university levels (TL), or "moved out" to such semi-independent agencies like the University Grants Committee (HK). This converging trend of devolution of power and responsibilities across the three non-Vietnamese cases offers the first transferable lesson for Vietnam (Lesson 1), which is to decentralise the responsibilities to university levels and to maintain a democratic administration and academic freedom under the Communist Party, as is the case in CN. Supporting empirical data concerning how responsibilities are decentralised and how a democratic administration and academic freedom is maintained are presented more comprehensively in Ngo (2014).

Lesson 2: The need for Vietnam to launch higher education reforms as strong drivers for improving its economic competitiveness.

Economically, there is an "obvious commonality" among cases outside VN which is at the same time an obvious difference between VN's and three other East Asia's economies. Comparing the levels of economic development, HK, TL and CN's levels are all higher than Vietnam's. HK is the highest income economy (the upper income economy) with the highest Gross Domestic Product per capita, followed by CN and TL (the upper middle-income economies) while VN is the lowest income economy, with the lowest GDP per capita. VN is still considered an emerging economy, which adopted an economic policy of transition in 1986 from a centrally planned economy to a market-based economy, albeit with socialist characteristics. It is worth noting that the "higher performing" models of public university governance in TL, CN and HK are *positively* associated with stronger and more competitive economic conditions, whereas the "lower performing" model in VN is *negatively* associated with weaker and less competitive economic conditions. In this regard, Hickling-Hudson (2007) asserted, "wealth confers the *privilege* of being able to choose to pour massive resources for innovation and improvement into aspects of education [including higher education]" (p. xiv).

This comparative analysis of economic development levels across cases highlights the supportive role of economic conditions for higher education and offers the second transferable lesson for Vietnam (Lesson 2). Rather than waiting for a better economy to thrive in Vietnam, Lesson 2 suggests that Vietnam should learn from HK, CN and TL where higher education reforms have been launched as strong drivers for improving its economic competitiveness. This lesson is consistent with what Varghese (2012, p. 41) observed earlier, "in South and East Asia, the [higher education] reforms were aimed at improving the quality of higher education and at repositioning higher education to improve economic competitiveness".

Comparing higher education system-layered contexts and Lesson 3: The need for Vietnam to speed up its comprehensive quality-focused reforms in higher education governance

For comparing higher education system-layered contexts across VN, CN, TL and HK, this study puts under the spotlight their higher education system reforms. A comparison of higher education system reforms indicates that there are "obvious differences" (between VN and three other East Asian contexts) which are "obvious commonalities" across non-Vietnamese contexts of TL, CN and HK. While Vietnamese higher education system reforms seem ceremonial, fragmented and slow-moving with its focus on quantitative goals resulting in a non-transparent higher education system in Vietnam (Dao and Hayden, see Chap. 3), system reforms in TL, HK and CN share the obvious commonalities of being better planned, more strategic, faster moving and, more importantly, more quality focused. Comprehensive quality-focused reforms of higher education were launched early in the 1990s in cases outside Vietnam, as evidenced in the *Higher Education in Hong Kong: Report of the University Grans Committee on the 1995–2001 Triennium* (Sutherland 2002) in HK, in *Action Scheme for Invigorating Education toward the twenty-first Century 1998–2002* (MoE 1998) in CN and in the enactment of *the 1999 National Education Act* in TL. However, VN delayed its comprehensive higher education reforms and it was not until 2005 when the Vietnamese Government officially declared a Higher Education Comprehensive Reform Agenda (HERA 2005) which still targeted at quantitative goals aiming for an expansion of HE system by 45% by 2020 (from 13% in 2006), and a significant expansion of the non-public sector accounting for 40% of all higher education enrolments by 2020. In Chap. 3, Dao and Hayden reported that by the end of 2015, as many as 225,500 postgraduates (both bachelor and master degrees) were unemployed, indicating that a serious HE training quality problem and the HE supplies far exceeding socio-economic demand.

It follows that if Vietnam aspires to catch up with its neighbouring countries in East Asia, Vietnam should learn a transferable lesson from them (Lesson 3), which is to speed up its comprehensive quality-focused reforms in higher education governance. In so doing, factors and underlying issues (e.g., heavy control of the state or the Communist Party, lack of university autonomy granted) that have slowed down the system and higher education governance reforms in VN need to be specifically identified and addressed. In addition, reforms in well-planned stages guided by in-depth analyses, reviews and consultations with internal and external experts and the public, accompanied by different measures and tools used in HK (e.g., introduction of Research Assessment Exercises, quality reviews, teaching audits and management reviews, Periodic Teaching and Learning Quality Process Reviews), in CN (e.g., Initiatives of Excellence through Project 211 & Project 985 for building world-class universities) and in TL (e.g., quality assurance management tools), all provide useful sources of references for VN.

Cross-National Comparative Analyses of Governance Structures: Transferable Lessons 4–7

Comparisons of governance structural arrangements as reflected in government policy document analyses and university document analyses across non-Vietnamese cases in TL, CN and HK suggest four "obvious commonalities" characterised by (i) stratification and differentiation policies of university governance, (ii) increased autonomy for universities due to more centralised decentralisation and less state intervention, accompanied by (iii) the establishments of intermediary or buffer governing bodies between the government and universities and (iv) a higher degree of governance structure clarity. It is worth noting that these four obvious commonalities found in three cases outside Vietnam are all compatible with the global trends reviewed earlier in this chapter. They offer four corresponding lessons (Lessons 4 through 7) that can be practically transferable to Vietnam.

Lesson 4: The need for Vietnam to develop stratification and differentiation policies of university governance

Despite the recent effort of issuing the Decree 73/ND-CP on 8th August 2015 on the stratification and ranking of higher education institutions, the Vietnamese Government tended to treat all of their public universities in almost the same way. However, HK, TL and CN have differentiated their public universities and stratified them into two main tiers: (i) top-tier universities striving to be world-class universities and (ii) universities pursuing the goal of being universities with quality improvement. For example, TL's differentiation policies are reflected in *University Acts and Performance Agreements* between nine National Research Universities in TL and their Thai Government. Similarly, in HK, its eight UGC-funded institutions have eight different *University Ordinances* stipulating different missions for different institutions. In CN, *Project 211 and Project 985* have targeted at developing internationally recognised top universities while concurrently enhancing quality of mediocre universities. Therefore, universities in TL, CN and HK of different tiers are officially allowed to define and differentiate their own mission and goals. Such strategic stratification and differentiation policies concurrently targeting both "good to great" universities and "mediocre to good" universities in TL, CN and HK offer a transferable lesson for VN – Lesson 4 which is to develop similar stratification and differentiation policies of higher education governance for different universities for Vietnam, rather than the current classification into three tiers, as specified in the Decree 73/ND-CP, of basic research, applied research and professionally oriented research. This lesson is well recommended on the reasonable ground that resources are limited and not always available to allow all institutions in a country, regardless of its economic development level, to address all the functions of a university in the same way (Gallagher et al. 2009).

Lesson 5: The need for Vietnam to grant increased autonomy to its public universities

It was not until 2005 that the Decree on Autonomy and Accountability for Public Universities (Decree 115/2005) was issued by the Vietnamese Government to officially grant autonomy to Vietnamese public universities. However, more than a decade later, it is still now controversial over how autonomy should be exercised in Vietnamese public universities and concerns have still been raised over whether Vietnamese public universities are competent enough to be autonomous, whereas university governance reforms in other countries outside Vietnam have granted increased autonomy to public universities since 1990s across HK, TL and

CN. For example, in TL, since 1992, the Office of Higher Education Commission (OHEC) has gradually delegated authority to be responsible solely by the University Council, moving toward full autonomy of universities as so desired. In CN, university autonomy was officially stipulated in China's Law on Higher Education of 1998. In HK, since the 1990s, a university in HK has been treated as a statutorily autonomous body with autonomy granted and the eight universities funded by the UGC have their own Ordinance and Governing Council. In HK, specific tasks such as the assessment of teaching staff performance and institutional policies on staff promotion "fall squarely within institutional autonomy", as stated explicitly in Notes on Procedures (UGC 2010). The common future direction for TL, CN and HK, as their government policies suggest, is to continue to grant full autonomy to public and private universities, reducing state regulations, focusing on policy formulation and post-auditing, and strengthening the governance of University Council and university management (Ngo 2014). Thus, to improve performance outcomes, experience from CN, TL and HK suggests Lesson 5 for Vietnam, which is to grant both substantive autonomy (deciding what to do to fulfil academic functions of universities) and procedural autonomy (deciding how to do it) (Berdahl 1990) to public universities.

It is worth noting that in HK, CN and TL, autonomy is not granted unconditionally. Instead, autonomy is only granted to universities in HK, CN and TL on the key conditions that universities have internal competence to exercise it and, more importantly, must be at the same time under both internal and external reviews. Real autonomy, as experienced from HK, TL and CN suggested, can be granted to universities by concurrently removing unnecessary government's intervention in micro-managing internal university affairs and empowering internal governing bodies (i.e., University Councils, the Senate, and others) to make decisions, especially those in relation to promotion of incentives for academics to achieve academic excellence. This has been clearly stated in HK's Sutherland report (2002, p. 6):

> The best research ideas are *not* the product of intrusive government direction. The best teaching builds upon the creative talents of lecturer and professor. Such ideas, such talents, are best fostered where *autonomy* is balanced by the acceptance of responsibility.

This transferable lesson (Lesson 5) is consistent with what was consistently suggested in the literature highlighting the urgency for increased autonomy for universities as an essential element of good university governance (e.g., Clark 1983; Eurydice 2008; Fielden 2008; Henard and Miterlle 2009; van Vught 1993). For example, Van Vught (1993) argued that more autonomy granted to universities can more effectively trigger innovative behaviour and thus suggested, "government should provide the *general* (not too detailed) rules within which the institutions can use their autonomy" (p. 358). More detailed government policy document analyses in CN, TL, and especially HK provide more empirical supporting evidence of such "general" rules (see Ngo 2014).

Lesson 6: The need for Vietnam to establish intermediary or buffer governing body both externally (at the macro level) and internally (at the meso level)

One of the prominent good university governance features at the macro levels across high-performing contexts of TL, CN and HK is their establishment of *"buffer"* agencies who represent the government and supervise the governing of their public universities. Examples of buffer governing bodies are the Office of Higher Education Commission (OHEC) in TL, the University Grants Committee (UGC) in HK and Project Management Units (for Project 211 and Project 985) in CN. With the established buffer agencies, governments in TL, CN and HK play indirect roles of supervising and supporting universities by "steering from a distance" whereas the government in VN represented by Ministry of Education and Training is still playing the direct role of controlling their public universities and no such buffer agencies as those found in CN, HK and TL can be found in VN.

The establishment of "buffer" agencies and accompanied delegation of decision-making powers to them, as the global trend and practice indicates, have long been the preferences in many world countries and are now being adopted elsewhere (Fielden 2008). Particularly, the most common global practice, according to Fielden (2008), is to remove all the detailed operational issues from relevant Ministry of Education and pass all matters (relating to funding and operational management) to the buffer body or bodies which can be more than just one principal buffer body. In doing so, the government is free from charges of over-intervention in universities' internal academic affairs, focusing more on policy issues and encouraging more institutional autonomy while the buffer body is allowed to develop more in-depth understanding of the higher education sector, making better-informed decisions, providing more supervision and support for public universities.

Concurrently, at the meso/university level, in cases outside Vietnam, another obviously common feature is concerned with the establishment of University Councils, which are still in absence in Vietnam. University Councils in public universities in HK, TL and CN, as revealed from the government policy documents, are empowered by their national governments (by law) to act as the highest governing body or the highest decision-maker of the university. University Councils' engagement in university governance can help adjust the managerial self-governance dimension to a higher level. In this way, governance is distributed across the higher education institution in HK, TL and CN and does not reside in either one level of hierarchy or in one purpose-built body; collective responsibilities for university governance are thus promoted. However, in VN, although the obliged requirements for establishing University Councils was clearly stated in Vietnam's University Charter (Decision 58/2010/QĐ – TTg) issued in 2010, many public universities in Vietnam have not yet had their University Council established.

Lesson 7: The need for Vietnam to ensure a "higher" degree of governance structure clarity at both the macro levels and the meso levels for Vietnam

The case study in Vietnam suggests that the current clarity degree of both its macro and meso governance structure is low, as evidenced in both its government's and its university's documents. With reference to a legal document of the *Higher Education Law 2012*, Dao and Hayden in Chap. 3 raised concerns over its lack of clarity as to relations between the Party and the governing boards as well as to what kind of institutional autonomy was to be given to institutions that achieve a higher rank than the others. However, the corresponding comparative analyses of governments' and universities' documents across three cases outside Vietnam reveal an "obvious commonality" of having a high degree of their corresponding macro and meso governance structure clarity. It follows that if VN wants to improve its current low-performing model of university governance, the experience from HK, CN and TL suggests Lesson 7 for VN that needs to ensure a "higher" degree of its macro and meso governance structure clarity by simultaneously ensuring consistently "higher" degrees of clarity of its "academic excellence" goals, tasks, power and incentive rules as stipulated in both its national government's and university's documents.

More specifically, to make this lesson realistically transferable, experience from TL, CN and HK suggests that Vietnam needs to specify in its government policy documents and university documents (1) a clearer *goal* toward achieving "academic excellence" or quality improvement at both the macro/meso level through the use of stratification and differentiation policies; (2) clearer and more specific *tasks* for universities to fulfil so as to promote incentives for academic excellence at the macro/meso level by providing rationale, arguments, delegations of tasks, best practices and guidance for performing such tasks; (3) clearer *power* (both substantive and procedural autonomy) granted to universities and departments so as to promote incentives for academic excellence by empowering internal university leaders (at both executive levels and departmental levels) more and reducing state intervention and (4) clearer and more specific rules specifying adequate incentives for academic excellence at the macro/meso level by linking merit-based incentives with performance assessment and reporting tasks. Empirical evidence of how such four indicators of high-clarity degrees of governance structure are reflected in governments' and universities' document analyses in CN, HK, and TL is provided in Ngo's (2014) study.

Conclusion

The two global trends and thematic cross-case comparative analyses across four case studies of public university governance in Vietnam, Thailand, China and Hong Kong in this chapter have provided answers to the original research question formulated at the beginning of the study as to *what* Vietnam can learn from contextual arrangements and governance structure arrangements in neighbouring East Asian contexts. Answers to the research question are presented in forms of seven transferable lessons, highlighting the urgent needs for action by the Vietnamese government and other concerns, and suggesting that Vietnam should give top priority to changing or at least modifying its current contextual arrangements (through Lessons 1, 2 and 3 in relation to its decentralisation of responsibilities to university levels, democratic administration and academic freedom under the Communist Party regime, improvement of economic competitiveness through higher education reforms and quality-focused higher education reforms) as well as its governance structural arrangements (through Lessons 4–7 in relation to stratification and differentiation policies, increased university autonomy, establishment of intermediary governing bodies and higher degree of governance structure clarity).

To make these seven lessons realistically transferable, the Ministry of Education and Training (MOET) representing the government of Vietnam should acknowledge the needs for changing both the contextual and structural governance, as specified in each drawn lessons, and be determined to renovate its outdated model of university governance by looking outwardly at the higher performing models of university governance and taking into serious considerations how to realise those needs. Rather than tightly controlling the governing of universities, MOET should progressively grant more autonomy and freedom to universities who can make their own academic and non-academic decisions while being held accountable to MOET for all their decisions made. In doing so, Vietnam's current public university governance model of central control can be reorientated into a new modernised model of supervision and support. Such a new model will be better shaped by improved contextual arrangements and modernised governance structures and MOET's new supervising and supporting roles, rather than controlling ones, to create better mechanisms for promoting more incentives for academic excellence in public universities in Vietnam.

The present study has significant implications for both practice and further research. For public university governance practice, at the *macro level*, Vietnamese policy-makers may use the research findings (i.e., Lessons 1 through 7) to guide their design of the newly proposed model of public university governance. At the *meso levels*, it is imperative for university executive leaders to make changes in the institutional level governance structures. Unless all the seven changes (as reflected in the seven transferable lessons) are made at both the macro and the meso level, the performance of the Vietnamese model of public university governance would remain inertia and fail to promote incentives for academic excellence.

It is important to note that the findings are significant not only for Vietnam as the "need-help" country in focus but also for those three other East Asia's participating countries of China, Hong Kong and Thailand and even beyond. Given its comparative nature, the present research encourages high-performing practitioners and actors at all levels across Thailand, China and Hong Kong to appreciate their domestic models as well as to critically reflect on their own model and practices, and to learn from other studied territories outside theirs. In this way, this study facilitates the exchanges of lessons and experiences within, between and among the societies under investigation and even beyond. However, as this study is limited to a small number of four case studies in East Asia, the findings of the study, though significant, might be applicable in the limited number of countries. For further research, a larger number of case studies guided by relevant university governance theories (e.g., the neo-institutional theory, the resource dependency theory, the stakeholder theory) are needed to facilitate a generalisation of its findings on a larger scale. More in-depth comparative analyses between Vietnam and China is crucial for Vietnam because both countries share more things in common than Thailand and Hong Kong. Notably, further investigation into other factors, especially the non-governance ones that might slow down the implementation of each of the seven lessons suggested in this chapter, is highly recommended, simply because good university governance, though a necessary and significant factor, is not sufficient in itself and not the only factor involved in assuring high-quality academic performance of universities.

References

Aghion, P., Dewatripont, M., Hoxby, C., Mas-Colell, A., & Sapir, A. (2010). The governance and performance of research universities: Evidence from Europe and the US. *Economic Policy, 25*(61), 7–59.

Altbach, P. G., & Umakoshi, T. (2004). *Asian universities: Historical perspectives and contemporary challenges*. Baltimore/London: The John Hopkins University Press.

Amaral, A., Jones, A., & Karseth, B. (2002). *Governing higher education: National perspectives on institutional governance*. Dordrecht: Kluwer.

Asian Development Bank. (2012). *Administration and governance of higher education in Asia: Patterns and implications*. The Philippines: Asian Development Bank.

Asimiran, S., & Hussin, S. (2012). *University governance: Trends and models*. Kuala Lumpur: University of Malaya Press.

Berdahl, R. (1990). Academic freedom, autonomy, and accountability in British universities. *Studies in Higher Education, 15*(2), 169–180.

Binsbergen, P., De Boer, H., & van Vught, F. A. (1994). Comparing governance structures of higher education institutions: Towards a conceptual framework. In L. Goedegebuure & F. A. van Vught (Eds.), *Comparative policy studies in higher education*. Utretcht: Centre for Higher Education Policy Studies.

Bjorkman, L. B. (2000). Why universities need leaders: The importance of department leaders. In J. Brennan, J. Fedrowitz, M. T. Huber, & T. Shah (Eds.), *What kind of university? International perspectives on knowledge, participation and governance*. Philadelphia: Open University Press.

Bleiklie, I., & Kogan, M. (2000). Comparison and theories. In M. Kogan, M. Bauer, I. Bleiklie, & M. Henkel (Eds.), *Transforming higher education: A comparative study*. Dordrecht: Springer.

Bleiklie, I., & Kogan, M. (2007). Organisation and governance of universities. *Higher Education Policy, 20*, 477–493.

Boin, A., & Christensen, T. (2008). The development of public institutions: Reconsidering the role of leadership. *Administration and Society, 40*(3), 271–297.

Capano, G. (2011). Government continues to do its job. A comparative study of governance shifts in the higher education sector. *Public Administration, 89*(4), 1622–1642.

Cerych, L., & Sabatier, P. (1986). *Great expectations and mixed performance: Implementation of European higher education reforms*. Stoke-on-Trent: Trentham Books.

Chan, D., & Lo, W. (2008). University restructuring in East Asia: Trends, challenges and prospects. *Policy Futures in Education, 6*(5), 641–652.

CHEPS. (2010). *Progress in higher education reform in Europe: Governance reform*. Retrieved from http://www.utwente.nl/mb/cheps/publications/Publications%202010/Governance%20Reform/GOV%20vol%201%20Executive%20Summary.pdf

CHEPS. (2015). Analysing the regional component of the influence of university's structural configuration on its performance. In M. Sanchez-Barrioluengo, & P. Benneworth (Eds.), *CHEPS working paper*. University of Twente, the Netherlands: Center for Higher Education Policy Studies.

Christopher, J. (2012). Governance paradigm of public universities: An international comparative study. *Tertiary Education and Management, 18*(4), 335–351.

Clark, B. (1983). *The higher education system: Academic organisations in cross-national perspectives*. Berkeley: University of California Press.

Corson, J. J. (1975). *The governance of colleges and universities: Modernizing structure and processes*. New York: McGraw Hill Book Company.

Currie, D. J., De Angelis, R., De Boer, H., Huisman, J., & Lacotte, C. (2003). *Globalising practices and university responses*. Westport/London: Praeger.

Dao, V. K. (2015). Key challenges in the reform of governance, quality assurance, and finance in Vietnamese higher education – a case study. *Studies in Higher Education, 40*(5), 745–760.

Dao, V. K., & Hayden, M. (2010). Reforming the governance of higher education in Vietnam. In G. Harman, M. Hayden, & T. N. Pham (Eds.), *Reforming higher education in Vietnam*. London/New York: Springer.

Dao, V. K., & Hayden, M. (this volume). Vietnam's updated policies on university governance, management and quality assurance. In N. T. Nguyen & L. T. Tran (Eds.), *Reforming Vietnamese higher education: Global forces and local demands*. Dordrecht: Springer.

de Boer, H. F. (1999). Changes in institutional governance structures: The Dutch case. In J. Brennan, J. Fedrowitz, J. M. Huber, & A. Shah (Eds.), *What kind of university? International perspectives on knowledge, participation and governance*. Buckingham: SRHE: Open University Press.

de Boer, H., & File, J. (2009). *Higher education governance reforms across Europe*. Enschede: Centre for Higher Education Policy Studies, University of Twente.

de Boer, H., & Goedegebuure, L. (2007). "Modern" governance and codes of conduct in Dutch higher education. *Higher Education Research and Development, 26*(1), 45–55.

Do, H. T., & Ho, T. M. (2010). Governance reform in higher education of Vietnam.

Dobbins, M., Knill, C., & Vogtle, E. M. (2011). An analytical framework for the cross-country comparison of higher education governance. *Higher Education, 62*(5), 665–683.

Dudzik, D. L. (2008). English policies, curricular reforms and teacher development in multilingual, postcolonial Djibouti. Dissertaion Abstracts International, 69, 1652.

Eurydice. (2008). *Higher education governance in Europe: Policies, structures, funding and academic staff*. Brussels: Eurydice.

Fielden, J. (2008). *Global trends in university governance*. Washington DC: World Bank.

Fielden, J., Middlehurst, R., & Schofield, A. (2004). *A final report to the CUC on: Good practice in six areas of the governance of higher education institutions*.

Fraser, K. (2005). *Education development and leadership in higher education: Developing an effective institutional strategy*. London/New York: Routledge Falmer.

Fry, G. W. (2009). Higher education in Vietnam. In Y. Hiroshato & Y. Kitamura (Eds.), *The political economy of educational reforms and capacity development in South East Asia*. The Netherlands: Springer.

Gallagher, M., Hasan, A., Canning, M., Newby, H., Saner-Yiu, L., & Whitman, I. (2009). *Thematic review of tertiary education*. OECD.

Goedegebuure, L., & Hayden, M. (2007). Overview: Governance in higher education: Concepts and issues. *Higher Education Research and Development, 26*(1), 1–11.

Goedegebuure, L., & van Vught, F. A. (1994). Comparative higher education policy studies. In L. Goedegebuure & F. A. van Vught (Eds.), *Comparative policy studies in higher education*.

Hackman, J. D. (1988). Power and centrality in the allocation of resources in colleges and universities. In M. W. Peterson (Ed.), *ASHE reader on organisation and governance in higher education*. Washington, DC: Ginn Press.

Hallinger, P. (2007). 21st century school leadership development: Global trends and challenges.

Hayden, M., & Lam, Q. (2010). Vietnam's higher education system. In G. Harman, M. Hayden, & T. N. Pham (Eds.), *Reforming higher education in Vietnam* (Vol. 29, pp. 15–30). London/New York: Springer.

Henard, F., & Mitterle, A. (2009). *Governance and quality guidelines: A review of governance arrangements and quality assurance guidelines*. Paris: OECD.

HERA. (2005). Vietnam higher education reform agenda: Period 2006–2020.

Hickling-Hudson, A. (2007). Foreword. In M. Bray, B. Adamson, & M. Mason (Eds.), *Comparative education research*. Hong Kong: Springer.

Jianhua, L. (2016). The Message from the President.

Kehm, B. (2012). *What is university governance and does it matter?* Paper presented at the International conference: Responding to the 21st Century demands for educational leadership and management in higher education.

Kezar, A., & Eckel, P. D. (2004). Meeting today's governance challenges: A synthesis of the literature and examination of a future agenda for scholarship. *Journal of Higher Education, 75*(4), 371–399.

Leisyte, L. (2007). *University governance and academic research: Case studies of research units in Dutch and English universities.* University of Twente.

Marginson, S. (2011). Higher education in East Asia and Singapore: Rise of the Confucian model. *Higher Education, 61*, 587–611.

Marginson, S., & Considine, M. (2000). *The enterprise university: Power, governance and reinvention in Australia.* Cambridge: Cambridge University Press.

Merriam, S. (1998). *Qualitative research and case study applications in education.* San Francisco: Jossey-Bass.

Middlehurst, R. (1993). *Leading academics.* Buckingham: Society for Research into Higher Education.

Miles, M. B., & Huberman, M. A. (1994). *Qualitative data analysis: An expanded sourcebook.* Thousand Oaks: Sage Publications.

Millett, J. (1978). *New structures of campus power: Success and failures of emerging forms of institutional governance.* San Francisco: Jossey-Bass Publishers.

MoE. (1998). *Action scheme for reinvigorating education toward the 21st century.*

Mok, K. H. (2010). *The search for new governance of higher education in Asia.* New York: Palgrave Macmillan.

Ngo, T. M. (2014). *A quest for a new model of Public University governance that promotes incentives for academic excellence for modern Vietnam: Lessons from multi-site comparative case studies in East Asia.* (Doctor of Philosophy in Education). The University of New South Wales, Sydney.

OECD. (2008). *OECD thematic review of tertiary education.* Paris: OECD.

Page, E. C. (1995). Comparative public administration in Britain. *Public Administration, 73*(1), 123–141.

Palfreyman, D., Tapper, T., & Thomas, S. (2009). Series editors' introduction. In J. Huisman (Ed.), *International perspectives on the governance of higher education.* New York/London: Routledge.

Pham, T. L. (2012). The renovation of higher education governance in Vietnam and its impact on the teaching quality at universities. *Tertiary Education and Management, 18*(4), 289–308.

QS University Rankings. (2015). *Top universities in Asia and in the world.* http://www.topuniversities.com/university-rankings/world-university-rankings/2015

Ragin, C. C. (1987). *The comparative method: Moving beyond qualitative and quantitative strategies.* Berkeley: University of California Press.

Rhoades, G. (1995). Rethinking and restructuring universities. *Journal of Higher Education Management, 10*(2), 17–30.

Rosovsky, H. (2001). Some thoughts about university governance. In W. Z. Hirsch & L. E. Weber (Eds.), *Governance in higher education: The university in a state of flux.* London/Paris/Geneva: Economica.

Ross, H., & Wang, Y. (2016). What does innovation mean and why does it matter? Innovation in Chinese higher education in global era of. In S. Guo & Y. Guo (Eds.), *Spotlight on China: Changes in education under China's market economy.*

Salmi, J. (2009). *The challenge of establishing world-class universities directions in development.* Washington, DC: World Bank.

Shattock, M. (2006). *Managing good governance in higher education.* Maidenhead: Open University Press.

Shattock, M. (2014). *International trends in university governance: Autonomy, self-government and the distribution of authority.* University of London, United Kingdom: Center for Higher Education Studies, Institute of Education.

Silverman, R. J. (1971). The invitational seminar on restructuring college and university organization and governance. *Journal of Higher Education, 42*(6), 442–445.

St. George, E. (2003). *Government policy and changes to higher education in Vietnam: 1986–
1998: Education in transition for development?* Canberra: Australian National University.

Sutherland, S. R. (2002). *Higher education in Hong Kong: Report of the University Grants
Committee*. Hong Kong: University Grants Committee.

The Carnegie Commission on Higher Education. (1973). *Governance of higher education: Six
priority problems*. New York: McGraw-Hill.

UGC. (2002). *Higher education in Hong Kong: Report of the University Grants Committee*. Hong
Kong: UGC.

UGC. (2010). *Notes on procedures*. Hong Kong: UGC.

UNESCO. (2006). *Higher education in South-East Asia*. Bangkok: UNESCO Bangkok.

Vallely, T., & Wilkinson, B. (2009). Vietnamese higher education: Crisis and response.

van Vught, F. A. (1993). *Patterns of governance in higher education concepts and trends*. Paris:
Centre for Higher Education Policy Studies.

Varghese, N. V. (2012). Drivers of reforms in higher education. In B. Adamson, J. Nixon, & F. Su
(Eds.), *The reorientation of higher education: Challenging the east-west dichotomy*. Hong
Kong: Springer.

Vietnamese Prime Minister. (2010). *University Charter (Decision 58/2010/QĐ-TTg*.

Welch, A. (2009). *Higher education in Southeast Asia. Blurring borders, changing balance*.
London: Routledge.

Welch, A. (2010). Internationalisation of Vietnamese higher education: Retrospect and prospect.
In G. Harman, M. Hayden, & T. N. Pham (Eds.), *Reforming Vietnamese higher education* (Vol.
29, pp. 197–214). London/New York: Springer.

Wilkinson, B. (2008). *Choosing success: The lessons of east and Southeast Asia and Vietnam's
future. A policy framework for Vietnam's socioeconomic development, 2011–2020*. Harvard
Vietnam Program.

World Bank. (2009). *The challenge of establishing world-class universities directions in development*. World Bank: Washington, DC.

World Bank. (2012). Benchmarking the Governance of Tertiary Education Systems.

Yin, R. K. (2003). *Applications of case study research* (Vol. 34). Thousand Oaks: Sage publications.

Chapter 5
Financing Vietnamese Higher Education: From a Wholly Government-Subsidized to a Cost-Sharing Mechanism

Hiep-Hung Pham and Huyen-Minh Vu

Abstract Over the last three decades, Vietnam's higher education has transited radically from an elite to a mass system. Under this circumstance, the financing system in higher education has shifted significantly, from a wholly government subsidy system to a cost-sharing mechanism. This chapter traces such an evolvement of financing polices and proposes implications for policy-makers in Vietnam.

Introduction

Cost sharing, which refers to the transition of a certain proportion of the higher education cost burden from government to other stakeholders, including students, parents, donors and so forth, has been a significant trend occurring to higher education across the world in previous decades (Johnstone 2004). This is not only true with capitalist-oriented countries but also with socialist-oriented countries or contingent European countries.[1]

Embracing the ideology of socialism, Vietnam believed education, including higher education, was public good and therefore should be provided by the state. Prior to the 1970s, Vietnam's Government used to cover tuition fees for any student entering university. Better still, those studying in northern Vietnam (i.e. The Democratic Republic of Vietnam) were even given living allowances and free accommodation at university dormitories. In the mid-late 1980s, when the economy slumped and inflation hit to a three-digit number, the government budget could not

---

[1] Johnstone (2004) called contingent European countries as the "last bastions of generally free higher education".

H.-H. Pham (✉)
Center for Research and Practice on Education, Phu Xuan University, Hue, Vietnam

H.-M. Vu
Faculty of Linguistics and Cultures of English Speaking Countries, VNU Hanoi University of Foreign Languages and International Studies, Hanoi, Vietnam

© Springer Nature Singapore Pte Ltd. 2019
N. T. Nguyen, L. T. Tran (eds.), *Reforming Vietnamese Higher Education*, Education in the Asia-Pacific Region: Issues, Concerns and Prospects 50, https://doi.org/10.1007/978-981-13-8918-4_5

afford to continue its generous subsidy for the expanding higher education sector. To compensate for the deficit, policy-makers had to agree to introduce some preliminary forms of cost sharing such as medical and sanitation fees or construction "contributions" (London 2011, p. 27). Since then, the way higher education is financed has undergone an irreversible shift to cost sharing, despite the country's continued embrace of socialism.

At the beginning of the twenty-first century, the demand of social demand for higher education was greater than ever. This demand has put urgent pressure on the Vietnamese Government to create a higher education landscape that simultaneously achieves targets of quality, accessibility and equality. Consensus about the importance of these targets is widely shared, but disagreement exists regarding which financing mechanism is appropriate to enable them to be achieved. While the notion of free higher education still seems to be attractive to the general population and to senior government officers, most policies promulgated over the past three decades have tended to move in the direction of cost sharing under the framework referred to euphemistically as the "socialization" (*xã hội hoá*) of higher education.

This chapter starts with a brief review of the evolution of the cost-sharing mechanism in Vietnam since the late 1980s. It then presents an analysis of the issue of cost sharing, drawing upon an ADB (2009) framework for developing member countries.[2] The final section addresses implications for policy-makers. The chapter's focus is on the financing of teaching and related activities, which accounts for most of Vietnam's higher education budget. The financing of other activities (e.g. research, facilities investment or construction) is not addressed by the chapter.

Trends Since the Late 1980s

Throughout the past century, the world has seen a remarkable growth in the higher education sector. It is estimated that the worldwide population of tertiary students in 2000 was around 100 million, accounting for 200-fold times the respective figure 100 years ago (Schofer and Meyer 2005). And it is forecast that by 2025 the corresponding figure will reach to 262 million (Maslen 2012).

This unprecedented cascade in student population stems from both the individual level (i.e. students and parents) and governmental level (Johnstone 2004). In parallel, higher education becomes costlier. Consequently, these phenomena resulted in a significant deficit in maintaining a continuing financial support to higher education institutions, especially support from taxpayers. Under this circumstance, a pervasive trend occurring globally is the shift from a government-subsidized financing system into a cost-sharing system. Johnstone (2004) categorized cost sharing into six different forms as following: (1) the introduction of tuition fee where higher education used to be completely free, an increase in the existing tuition fee; (2) the allowance of dual track system, where personal tuition fee track is added in juxtaposing to the traditional free higher education; (3) the decrease of student grants and

---

[2]Vietnam is a member of these developing countries.

scholarships; (4) the introduction of student loans; (5) the imposition of "user charge" principle in which students, but not government, are those who have to pay for living expenses; and (6) the introduction of wholly fee-based private higher education sector.

The financing regime in Vietnam's higher education[3] also reflects this pattern. Along with the Economic Reform (*Đổi Mới*) in 1986, due to the unprecedented growth of population at university age and the demands of the newly emerging market, higher education in Vietnam has undergone radical changes of which the most notable is the rapid expansion of the system. Between 1987 and 2009, the number of higher education institutions (i.e. universities and colleges) increased nearly four times (from 101 to 376) and the number of students 13 times (from 133,000 in 1987 to 1,719,500) (Pham 2011).

Under this circumstance, the government became unable to fund the whole higher education system as it had previously done. As a result, a number of cost-sharing policies have been steadily introduced and implemented over the last three decades. However, the term "cost sharing" was rarely adopted in official documents. Vietnamese policy-makers have used the term "socialization" (*xã hội hoá*) of higher education instead. The meaning of "socialization" in this context, indeed, does not align with regular understanding of "socialization" in western culture (i.e. process of acquiring culture) but refers to "broad-based social mobilization of resources for education, not public finance of education" (London 2011, p. 26). In fact, the issue of "socialization" of education and other traditional public services such as culture and public health already appeared in Vietnam's policy practices in late 1980s but it was mentioned officially only for the first time in government's Resolution No. 90/CP in 1997. Particularly in education, Resolution No. 90/CP placed the emphasis on some cost-sharing features such as: the role of parents and students as alternative sources of revenue, apart from government subsidy; the role of student loan in ensuring the accessibility and participation in education and the importance of non-public sector, including foreign investors and private sector as well.

In the following subsections, we outline some notable examples of such cost sharing or "socialization" policies in higher education in Vietnam which were issued and implemented before and after the scheme identified by Resolution No. 90/CP.

Some Notable Policies on Cost Sharing or "Socialization" in Vietnam's Higher Education System Since the 1990s

Policies on Tuition Fee at Public Higher Education Institutions Prior to 1993, tuition fee at traditionally public subsidized programmes in Vietnam was strictly free. However, universities and colleges were allowed to levy some additional fees

---

[3] The current Vietnamese higher education inherits from the system of North Vietnam prior to 1975. Therefore, in this chapter, Vietnamese higher education financing system refers to this in the unified country after 1975 and that in North Vietnam between 1954 and 1975.

Table 5.1 Tuition fee per student per month at regular state-sponsored undergraduate courses in Vietnam

| Year | Regulative documents | The cap of monthly tuition fee at government subsidized programmes at different clusters of disciplines | | |
		Social Science, Economic, Law, Agriculture, Forestry, Fishery[a]	Science, Engineering, Technology, Sport, Fine Art, Hospitality, Tourism	Medicine
Before 1993		Tuition fee waived; administrative fee allowed		
1993–1998	241/QĐ-TTg	Not identified clearly		
1998–2008	70/1998/QĐ-TTg 54/1998/ TTLT-BGDĐT-BTC	50,000–180,000		
2009–2010	1310/QĐ-TTg	50,000–240,000		
2010–2011	49/2010/NĐ-CP	290,000	310,000	340,000
2011–2012		355,000	395,000	455,000
2012–2013		420,000	480,000	570,000
2013–2014		485,000	565,000	685,000
2014–2015		550,000	650,000	800,000
2015–2016	86/2015/NĐ-CP	610,000	720,000	880,000
2016–2017		670,000	790,000	970,000
2017–2018		740,000	870,000	1,070,000
2018–2019		810,000	960,000	1,180,000
2019–2020		890,000	1,060,000	1,300,000
2020–2021		980,000	1,170,000	1,430,000

Source: Author synthesized from Vietnamese regulative documents
Unit: VND; 1 USD~22,000 VND
[a]Agriculture, Forestry and Fishery were included since academic year 2015–2016

such as: construction fee, admission fee or graduation fee (Decision No. 248-TTg issued by Prime Minister in 1973). However, these fees were usually small and did not contribute significantly to the overall revenues of higher education institutions. In 1993, along with the implementation of Decision No. 241-TTg issued by Prime Minister, a tuition fee was officially introduced for the first time in Vietnam at public higher education institutions. Since then, the policy on tuition fee has been adjusted and increased regularly. Table 5.1 draws attention to some major regulatory documents on tuition fees in Vietnam since 1993. By the academic year of 2015–2016, the regulation stipulated that students at public subsidized programmes had to pay up to 610,000 VND, or 720,000 VND or 810,000 ND (per month), respectively, according to their disciplines of study.[4] And these caps of tuition fees are expected

---

[4]Since 2014, 23 public universities across the country have been selected as parts of a so-called governmental Resolution 77 on piloting of rennovation of operational mechanism at public higher

to increase by approximately 10% per year until academic year of 2020–2021. According to governmental explanation, this annual increase aims to recover the expected inflation rate in the country in the next few years (Tieu 2015).

The Allowance of Private Sector in Higher Education By 2013, among 421 higher education institutions across the country, there were 83 private ones, accounted for 19.7%. Regarding student population, these non-public institutions enrol 14.3% out of total 2,177,299 students nationwide (Bộ Giáo dục và Đào tạo 2013). These figures completely contrast to what was accounted in 1987 (the first year after Economic Reform – *Đổi Mới*). In 1987, the correspondent figures were both "nil" (institutions and students). As a socialist-oriented country, Vietnam used to only have public institutions. However, due to the mismatch between the increasing demand from students and parents and the capacity of public higher education providers, the Vietnamese Government eventually allowed for the establishment of the private institutes in higher education sector with the first approval of Thang Long Center for higher education (the former name of the current Thang Long University). Subsequently, in 1993, the first regulation (i.e. Decision No. 240-TTg by Prime Minister) on private higher education institutions was released. After that, until 2012, the regulations on non-public higher education sector have been adjusted several times with the promulgation of a plethora of legal documents. Thus, the nature of ownership of non-public higher education institutions has also been regulated accordingly with different names (e.g. people-founded, semi-public and private). Under the current regulation (i.e. Law of Higher Education 2012 and Charter of University issued along with Decision No. 70/2014/QĐ-TTg by Prime Minister), there is only single type of non-public higher education in Vietnam: private higher education. And this sector, subsequently, is divided into two sub-sectors: not-for-profit private higher education and for-profit private higher education.

The Introduction of Student Loan Programmes In 2002, the government introduced a loan programme aiming to support disadvantaged people in general, among which students from lower income families were one of the eligible recipient groups (Decision No. 78/2002/QĐ-TTg). Until 2007, Vietnam introduced the first-ever student loan designated for secondary and post-secondary levels under the tenure of the former Minister of Education Nguyen Thien Nhan (Decision No. 157/2007/QĐ-TTg). This, indeed, is a mortgage-type of loan with the annual interest rate of 0.5%. And all students, regardless of their gender, ethnicity, economic situations and household registration, have the right to apply for the loan. The maximum amount of loan was set at 800,000 VND per month per student when it was first released in 2007 and it was increased steadily since then to recover the inflation rate.

---

education institutions between 2014 and 2017. Under this scheme, the 23 selected public universities are granted more institutional autonomy at the expense of cease of receiving recurrent subsidy. Among indentified aspects of institutional autonomy, autonomy on setting tuition fee above the predefined caps as represented in Fig. 5.1 is one of the most important powers granted to the selected universities.

Table 5.2 Amount of student loan in Vietnam

Year	Amount of loan	Interest rate
2007	800,000 VND per month per student	0.5% per year
2009	860,000 VND per month per student	0.5% per year
2010	900,000 VND per month per student	0.5% per year
2013	1,100,000 VND per month per student	0.5% per year
2015	1,350,000 VND per month per student	0.5% per year

Source: Ha (2015)
1 USD~22,000 VND

In 2015, the corresponding amount of loan for students is 1,350,000 VND per month per student (see Table 5.2 for details). According to Vietnam Bank for Social Policies, which is the agency in charge of this student loan, there have so far been 3.3 million students accessing to this programme between 2007 and 2015 (Ngân hàng Chính sách xã hội 2016).

The Allowance of Dual Fee Track System in Public Institutions According to Johnstone (2004), the dual track fee system in public higher education has two components: the traditionally free higher education and the newly added tuition fee-based higher education. In Vietnam, there is also a dual track fee system in public higher education; however, the Vietnamese system seems to be different from Johnstone's model. Indeed, the dual fee track system in public universities and colleges in Vietnam refers to two ways to finance a student's study: (i) the regular track: government-subsidized track and (ii) the newly added track: self-funding track. Under the first track, students pay partially for their college while the government subsidizes the rest – which is recurrently allocated to universities based on their approved quotas of enrolment, historical budget and degree type.[5] Their tuition fee scheme has been discussed in the first paragraph of this section. In the official document, we call this track as "*students within quotas of enrolment*" or "*students within governmental subsidy*". Under the second track, students have to pay the whole fee by themselves and are not subsidized by the government. These students are referred to as "*students outside the quotas of enrolment*" or "*students without the governmental subsidy*". Table 5.3 presents the dual track fee system in the public sector of Vietnam higher education in comparison to that of Johnstone (2004).

The Introduction of Policies on Philanthropy and Charity in Education Although anecdotal evidence shows that charity in education has been a common practice for several decades (e.g. students suffering from natural disaster often receive donations from community), the philanthropy does not contribute significantly for the overall income of universities in Vietnam. For instance, available data show that about 90% of total revenue from Vietnam National University-Hanoi, one of the most reputable higher education institutions in Vietnam, comes from state allocation and tuition fees.

---

[5]According to current scheme, the amount allocated to undergraduate students at regular government-subsidized programmes is 6,133,680 VND per year (Nguyen, 2014a, b).

Table 5.3 Comparison of dual track fee system between Vietnam's public higher education institutions and Johnstone's (2004)

	Vietnam's	Johnstone's (2004)
Track 1	Students have to pay tuition fee as indicated in Table 5.1 but still receive subsidy from government	Free
Track 2	Students have to pay tuition fees that cover the whole cost	Students have to pay tuition fees that cover the whole cost

Source: Author synthesized

It does mean that the remaining revenue, including science-technology transfer and donations, only accounts of 10%.

The modest share of income from donations might stem from two reasons:

First, for several years, there has been a lack of appropriate policies in encouraging advantaged people to involve in philanthropy activities. Decree No. 30/2012/NĐ-CP was regarded as the first comprehensive policy that aims to mobilize the endowment and donations from society for higher education sector as well as other public service sectors. Notable features promulgated by Decree No. 30/2012/NĐ-CP includes tax deduction and the student's right in receiving additional state allocation apart from self-raising fund. Nevertheless, the limitation of Decree No. 30/2012/NĐ-CP is that it only allows philanthropists to donate money to charity funds rather than to universities directly. Thus, this regulation results in unnecessary complexity in terms of procedure and, in many cases, discourages people who want to donate money.

The second reason refers to cultural factor. Many education observers argued that Vietnamese culture is a key factor inhibiting the development of philanthropy and charity activities in Vietnam. For instance, in a round-table conducted in 2014, Giap Van Duong, Hanoi-based famous educator, asserted that "*endowment is familiar with European and American people, but alien from the culture of Eastern people, especially Vietnamese people*" (Nguyen 2014b). Duong concluded that, within Vietnamese culture, people have tendency to invest on their descendants rather than on community.

Current Debate on Higher Education Financing Mechanism in Vietnam

Financing mechanism for higher education institutions in Vietnam has undergone radical changes over previous decades. From a wholly government-subsidized system in the late 1980s, we can find an array of cost-sharing mechanisms such as tuition fee, student loan or dual track fee system at the current time. However, in official documents released by Vietnamese authorities, the term "cost sharing" is rarely recognized and officially utilized. Instead, policy-makers have selected

Fig. 5.1 Seven aspects in current debate on higher education financing mechanism. (Source: author synthesized and extended from ADB 2009)

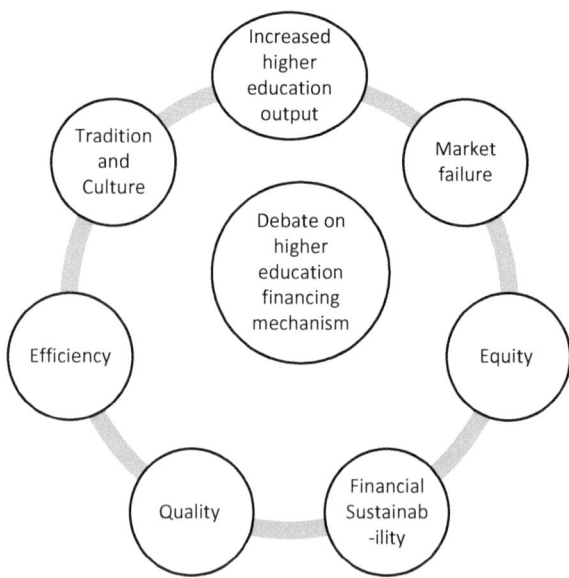

"socialization" as a euphemistic term to refer to cost sharing. A review of the current debate on higher education financing mechanism in Vietnam in this section will provide us the insights into why this euphemism is used. The debate, as identical to other countries across the world, involves two opposite groups: proponents to subsidy and proponents to cost sharing. To illustrate this debate, we adopt and extend the ADB's (2009) framework with seven perspectives: (1) increased higher education student output; (2) market failure/merit good; (3) equity; (4) financial sustainability; (5) quality; (6) efficiency and (7) tradition and culture[6] (see Fig. 5.1).

Increased Higher Education Student Output

Consensus is widely achieved that higher education in Vietnam is suffering from underinvestment. Without sufficient funding, Vietnamese higher education institutions are unlikely to be able to pay competitive salaries for qualified faculty nor afford modern infrastructure and facilities. These disadvantages will continue to churn out graduate students who do not meet the increasingly demanding socio-economic growth. Among the identified weak outputs, increasingly jobless graduates and graduate unemployment rate are given the most attention and criticism from public (see Tran, Chap. 6). A report issued by Institute of Science Labour and Society estimated that in the first quarter of 2015, the number of jobless graduates with a bachelor's or a master's degree was 178,000, which increased 10% compared

---

[6]Given the importance of culture in all socio-economic aspects, we include culture as one of the important dimensions into the ADB (2009)'s framework, along with tradition.

to the correspondent figure in 2014 (Thanh Hoa 2015). Similarly, data obtained by Tradingeconomics (2016) also revealed that unemployment rate among youth population increased significantly over the last 5 years (from 5.17% in the fourth quarter of 2011 to 7.30% in the third quarter of 2015).

However, discrepancy on solution to this issue has still been a topic for debate between proponents to governmental subsidy and those favouring cost-sharing mechanism. In recent years, there has been an increase of scholars suggesting cost-sharing-like mechanism to solve the problem of underinvestment in higher education. For instance, in a working paper, Pham (2012) computed that a reasonable unit cost (i.e. total investment per student per year from governmental subsidy, tuition fee and other sources) for developing countries like Vietnam should be around 120% the correspondent GDP per capita, much higher than the actual proportion of 57% (as estimated by Pham in 2009). To fulfil the gap between the estimation (120%) and the actual figure (57%), Pham suggested a so-called "two high" policy, i.e. high tuition fee coupled with high loan or scholarship for students. Components of "two high" policy, indeed, are features of cost-sharing mechanism as described above. Since the suggestion of Pham (2012), scholars and experts also recommended similar solutions (Nguyen and Pham 2014; Hayden et al. 2012; Vietnam Education Dialogue 2015). However, the suggestion of such cost-sharing mechanism often becomes subject of criticism by the public as well as educators. For instance, the recommendation of Vietnam Education Dialogue (2015)[7] to dismantle the predefined cap of tuition fees applying for all public higher education institutions ignited a heated debate on Vietnamese media in 2015 between proponents and opponents of cost-sharing policy in higher education.

In analogous to the majority part of the world, the above debate in Vietnam remains unresolvable. However, while empirical studies undertaken in different countries have proved counterproductive of free higher education policy (e.g. Ben 2008; Bergh and Fink 2008), there has been yet any research on the correlation between equity and tuition fee using actual data obtained in Vietnam context. Given this, such study is worthwhile and would, without any doubt, provide insights for policy-makers and educators in Vietnam.

Market Failure

ADB (2009) mentioned two dimensions of market failure while discussing about the issue of cost sharing in higher education. These are: (1) the positive externalities as a nature of higher education accrue to students; and (2) the principle of higher

---

[7]Vietnam Education Dialogue (VED) is an initiative led by famous Prof. Ngo Bao Chau, mathematics Field awardee in 2010. VED, unified by a dozen of Vietnamese scholars living in Vietnam and abroad, aims to provide policy-makers and governments proposals for the reform of higher education in particular and education in general.

education as market imperfections. The former relies on the comparison between the social rate of return and personal rate of return appearing when an individual completes his or her university education. If the social benefit is higher than a personal one, public expenditure is a favoured mechanism and vice versa. The latter bases on the assumption that within higher education context, the consumer (i.e. student) does not have enough information about the service providers (i.e. institutes of higher education), and therefore he or she would bear a "short-sighted" behaviour and reluctant to invest in education that does not ensure a reasonable return in the long run.

Few numbers of proponents to governmental subsidy solution have argued the topic from the perspective of market failure. For instance, Pham (2009) emphasized the role of public intervention on higher education, given the nature of market failure of the sector.

Among proponents to cost-sharing mechanism, "Vietnam: Higher education and skills for growth" (World Bank 2012) is one of the first attempts that tried to conduct an empirical analysis from the perspective of positive externalities. Based on the 2004 Vietnam Household Living Standards Survey (VHLSS)[8] data, the authors of the World Bank's report revealed that an additional year of schooling at tertiary level might lead to an increase in earnings of approximately 10%. Although this report does not compute the social rate of return bearing with a university graduate, the result with high personal rate of return on higher education implies that cost sharing is an appropriate mechanism that would be suitable for Vietnam's higher education financing system.

Equity

In terms of equity, data obtained from ADB (2012) indicates that the most dilemma that Vietnam is facing is the widening gap in opportunities to access in higher education between students from richer and poorer families but not other issues (e.g. gender equality). Supporters of governmental subsidy argue that if state support is cut down, students from lower income families would not afford the cost of study, and therefore, would be excluded from higher education. This point of view also reflects the opinion of policy-makers in Vietnam over previous three decades. Indeed, in previous decade, Vietnam is an outlier case in Asian region in which growth in per-student support from government outpaces the growth of student population. Between 2001 and 2008, student enrolment in Vietnam rose 1.7-folds from 974,100 to 1,675,700 while recurrent per-student subsidy increased 2.83-folds from 1,845,806 VND to 5,222,892 VND per year (ADB 2012). However, Pham and Tran (2014) argued that, given the current capacity of higher education providers that under match the student demands, increasing governmental allocation only results

---

[8]VHLSS is a longitudinal survey conducted by General Statistics Office of Vietnam, asking more than 30,000 Vietnamese households on income, expenditures, economic activity, education, healthcare and available infrastructure.

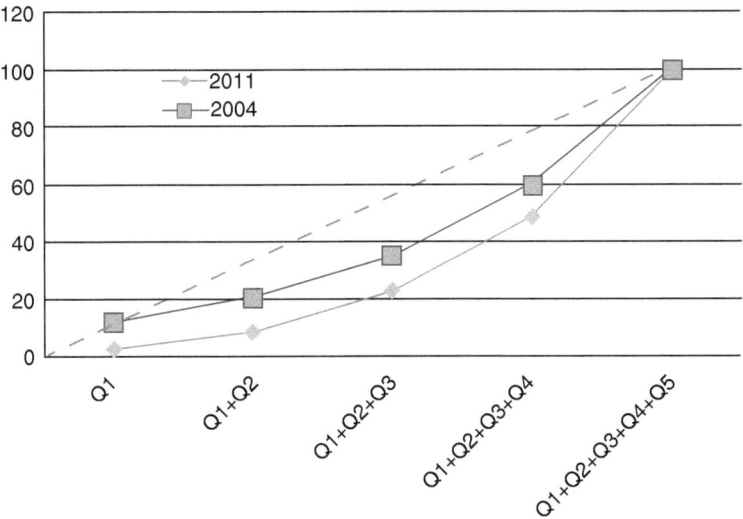

Fig. 5.2 Lorentz concentration curves in accessibility of Vietnam's higher education in 2004 and 2011 (*Q1* represents the poorest 20% population of Vietnam while *Q5* represents the richest quintile) (Pham and Tran 2014)

in regressive consequence in equity. Through drawing Lorentz concentration curves of student shares between five different quintiles according to their families' income in 2004 and 2011, Pham and Tran (2014) revealed that the level of inequity in higher education opportunities across household wealth quintiles has been widening over the period from 2004 to 2011. In other words, economic disparity has become a more and more visible trouble for Vietnam's higher education system (Fig. 5.2).

Financial Sustainability

State budget has been the main source of income of higher education institutions in Vietnam. Currently, even with increasing tuition fee, the government still contributes approximately 55% flow of revenue for public higher education institutions (Hayden et al. 2012). However, the central role of state budget is only justified and viable within the context that unit cost is maintained as low as per se (i.e. around 500–700 USD per year). Anecdotal evidences have shown that all endeavours to enhance unit cost via increasing state allocation in Vietnam are not sustainable due to limited resources and commitments of government. Table 5.4 summarizes two most recent and notable initiatives funded by Vietnamese Government agencies that aim to enhance the quality of higher education since 2007. The purpose of these two projects, one hosted by Ministry of Education and Training and another hosted by Vietnam National University – Hanoi, is to

Table 5.4 Two selected projects funded by government with high per-student investment

No.	Name of project	Scope of project	Source of funding	Average per-student governmental subsidy
1	Advanced programmes (in Vietnamese: *Chương trình tiên tiến*)	Some selected undergraduate courses at nine leading higher education institutions	Ministry of Education and Training	38,000,000 VND per year
2	Strategy programmes (in Vietnamese: *Nhiệm vụ chiến lược*)	Some selected undergraduate and graduate courses at Vietnam National University, Hanoi	Ministry of Finance	24,000,000 VND per year

Source: Author adopted from Nguyen (2014a, b)
1 USD~22,000 VND

establish several university courses that meet international standards. The strategies of these two projects are similar and their key activities are three-folds: (1) Adopting curriculum, syllabus and textbook from a partner university from developed countries such as the USA, France and Singapore; (2) inviting professors from partner university to Vietnam and give lectures to students and mentor local lecturers in pedagogy or conduct co-research; and (3) sending local lecturers to partner university for internship or short-course trainings. However, by mid-2016, both these two initiatives have arrived the final steps of the projects and there have been any signals that Vietnamese Government would continue to invest or extend these two programmes. Thus, this implies that government does not have both adequate resources and commitment to maintain qualified higher education system. Given the current difficulties of government budget, cost sharing is widely recognized as a more feasible and more sustainable solution from a perspective in which unit cost is increased to provide enough resources for higher quality of education and this increasing cost is to be shared by different stakeholders, including government, students, parents and society.

Quality

Traditionally, most proponents to government subsidy have insisted on the central role of government and call on the government to allocate more resources to promote higher education quality. However, an increasing number of proponents to cost sharing express their hope in emerging private providers to fix some part of the hole-ridden system that almost public providers have failed to. Regardless of differences in their points of view, however, both sides agree that the current quality of higher education is poor, and more investment is therefore prerequisite and urgent. The number of Vietnamese universities listed in Top 350 QS Asia 2016,

Table 5.5 Results of Top 350 QS University Ranking Asia 2016 at some selected countries in ASEAN

Country	Number of higher education institutions listed in Top 350 QS Asia 2016	Position of higher education institutions with highest ranking
The Philippines	8	70
Indonesia	11	67
Malaysia	20	27
Thailand	13	45
Vietnam	5	139

Source: Author synthesized from QS (2016)

compared to other developing countries within the region, partly reflects the quality of status quo of quality of Vietnam's higher education system (see Table 5.5).

Efficiency

Ziderman (2002) believed that, in general, students who have to pay fully or partly the cost of their studies would be more committed to their choices and their study. In the same vein, institutions which serve fee-paying students would have a tendency to be more responsive and responsible to their students (ADB 2009). By contrast, the regime in which universities receive funding recurrently from government is regarded as the root of bureaucracy and inefficiency, which creates a more wasteful mechanism. In Vietnam, Vietnam Education Dialogue's (2015) report is among the few endeavours considering the above issue from the efficiency perspective. In its report submitting to the government, Vietnam Education Dialogue asserted: *"market mechanism should be regarded as the most powerful motivation to enhance quality of higher education, to mobilize income and utilize resources effectively. Adopting market as motivation means granting higher autonomy, facilitating for universities (public and private) to compete in educational quality, tuition fee and student enrolment; and thus serve society better"* (Vietnam Education Dialogue 2015).

Tradition and Culture

As discussed at the outset of this chapter, education, including higher education, has been traditionally free in Vietnam. This stems from the depth culture of Vietnam, which always highlights the importance of talents for national benefit. Given this circumstance, it is not easy for the general population to accept a non-free higher education landscape. This partly explains why policy-makers in Vietnam avoid using term "cost sharing" in their regulative documents over previous decades. Also, most current policy-makers and university leaders in Vietnam are now used to being beneficiary of government subsidy higher education regime. Thus, these factors, without doubt, have resulted in significant obstacles for the transition to a full-fledged cost-sharing mechanism.

Discussion and Conclusion

Over the last three decades, Vietnam has transitioned from a solely governmental subsidized to a cost-sharing higher education system. This phenomenon is a reasonable and necessary consequence of a rapid massification of higher education and inability of the state in maintaining finance for the sector. Nevertheless, in official term, cost sharing appears to be not widely used. Instead, "socialization" (xã hội hoá) has been used as a euphemist term in mostly all regulative documents issued by government authorities. This, on the one hand, reflects an official unrecognition of Vietnamese policy-makers towards cost-sharing policies in particular and the concept of market-based higher education in general. On the other hand, this reflects the insistence of Vietnam's political leaders and policy-makers on the ideology of socialism in the country's development: in a socialist-oriented country, there is no legitimate room for cost sharing or the concept of education as private good. Regardless of this unofficial recognition, cost sharing in Vietnamese higher education is still alive and well, being practiced in the forms of tuition fee, student loan and private higher education establishment, to name a few. It implies that with increasing demand from learners, Vietnam's policy-makers must unwillingly adopt a cost-sharing mechanism and refer to it with another term: "socialization". Given this, we call the current financing mechanism in Vietnam's higher education a "passive" cost sharing. The term "passive" denotes that the promulgation of policies in "socialization" over previous decades has been a compelled response of policy-makers to the increasing demands from society in post-secondary education level. And because of its "passive" nature, Vietnamese policy-makers do not seem to fully exploit the advantages of cost-sharing options in particular and dynamic features of market role in general.

Thus, among different objectives of higher education, the combination of existing options of cost-sharing policies in Vietnam over previous decades seems to result in only the increase of participation of higher education. The other objectives, i.e. quality/outcome and equality, as discussed earlier in this chapter, tend to be deteriorated and decline.

Under such circumstances, to attain a massive higher education system but qualified and equal, it is suggested that Vietnamese policy-makers should adopt more proactive cost-sharing choices. For instance, on the one hand, the current regulation on cap of tuition fee applying for public higher education institutions might be dismantled to help universities to seek enough financial source to maintain competitive quality. On the other hand, the issue of inequality, which might emerge as a consequence of no tuition fee cap policy, might be resolved by need-based student loan and merit-based scholarship programmes facilitated at the national level.

Whatever new cost-sharing option is to be determined, other caveats, which have been untapped or under-tapped for a long time, should be addressed immediately by policy-makers and researchers. These, as addressed throughout this chapter, are relevant data, information and empirical analysis to the issue, such as Gini index (an indicator representing the level of inequality in access to higher education) and personal vs. social rate of return in different subjects in higher education or unit cost analysis (a minimum investment per student that ensures competitive quality to other countries). As cost sharing is still a controversial topic as emphasized by ADB (2009), the collection of the above information is paramount because it would provide transparent evidence for both proponents and opponents of cost sharing.

References

ADB. (2009). *Good practice in cost sharing and financing in higher education*. Mandaluyong City: Asian Development Bank.

ADB. (2012). *Counting the cost: Financing Asian higher education for inclusive growth*. Mandaluyong City: Asian Development Bank.

Ben, M. M. (2008). Credit constraints in education: Evidence from international data. *Journal of Applied Economics, 11*(1), 33–60.

Bergh, A., & Fink, G. (2008). Higher education policy, enrollment, and income inequality. *Social Science Quarterly, 89*(1), 217–235.

Bộ Giáo dục và Đào tạo [Ministry of Education and Training]. (2013). *Thống kê giáo dục 2013* [Education statistics 2013]. Retrieved June 24, 2016, from http://moet.gov.vn/?page=11.11&view=5251

Ha, M. (2015). Điều chỉnh mức vay tín dụng học sinh, sinh viên [Adjustment on loan for pupils, students]. *Nongnghiep*. Retrieved June, 24, 2016 from http://nongnghiep.vn/dieu-chinh-muc-cho-vay-tin-dung-hoc-sinh-sinh-vien-post153221.html

Hayden, M., Pham, P., Lam, Q. T., Pettigrew, A., Meek, L., Ryan, N., et al. (2012). *Master plan for Vietnam's higher education system*. Hanoi: Southern Cross University.

Johnstone, D. (2004). The economics and politics of cost-sharing in higher education: Comparative perspectives. *Economics of Education Review, 23*(4), 403–410.

London, J. D. (2011). Education in Vietnam: historical roots, recent trends. In J. D. London (Ed.), *Education in Vietnam* (pp. 1–56). Singapore: Institute of Southeast Asian Studies.

Maslen, G. (2012). Worldwide student numbers forecast to double by 2025. *University World News*. Retrieved June 24, 2016 from http://www.universityworldnews.com/article.php?story=20120216105739999

Ngân hàng Chính sách Xã hội [Vietnam Bank for Social Policies]. *Tăng mức cho vay học sinh, sinh viên lên tối đa 1,25 triệu đồng/tháng* [The maximum amount of student loan is increased to 1.25 million VND/month]. Retrieved October, 12, 2016 from http://vbsp.org.vn/tang-muc-cho-vay-hoc-sinh-sinh-vien-len-toi-da-125-trieu-dongthang.html

Nguyen, T. H. (2014a). Hoàn thiện cơ chế quản lý tài chính đối với các chương trình đào tạo chất lượng cao trong các trường đại học công lập Việt Nam [Improving financing management for high-qualified courses at public higher education institutions in Vietnam]. Unpublished doctoral dissertation. National University of Economics, Hanoi.

Nguyen, V. P. (2014b). *Đại học tư thục phi lợi nhuận: vì sao họ làm được còn chúng ta thì chưa?* [Non-profit university: Why can they do it but not us?]. Retrieved June 24, 2016 from http://www.thesaigontimes.vn/Home/diendan/ykien/112457/Dai-hoc-tu-thuc-phi-loi-nhuan-Vi-sao-ho-lam-duoc-con-chung-ta-thi-chua?.html

Nguyen, M. H., & Pham, H. H. (2014). Tín dụng sinh viên – kinh nghiệm quốc tế và khuyến nghị cho Việt Nam [Student loan – International experiences and implications for Vietnam]. *Tạp chí nghiên cứu Tài chính kế toán* [*Journal for study of Finance Accounting*], *2*, 127.

Pham, D. C. (2009, December). *Vai trò quản lý của Nhà nước trong giáo dục đại học – góc nhìn từ lý thuyết kinh tế học hiện đại* [The role of state management in higher education from modern economics perspectives]. Trình bày tại Hội thảo quốc tế về chính sách cho giảng viên và các nhà lãnh đạo giáo dục trong quá trình đổi mới giáo dục, Trường đại học giáo dục, Đại học Quốc Gia Hà Nội [Paper presented at the International workshop on policies for teachers and educational leaders in innovative educational process, College of Education, Vietnam National University, Hanoi].

Pham, H. (2011). Vietnam: Young academic talent not keen to return. *University World News*. Retrieved June 24, 2016, from http://www.universityworldnews.com/article.php?story=20110722201850123

Pham, P. (2012). *Đầu tư và chia sẻ chi phí trong giáo dục đại học Việt Nam* [Investment and cost-sharing in Vietnam's higher education]. Báo cáo thường niên về giáo dục [Annual report on education]. Hà Nội: Nhà xuất bản Đại học Quốc Gia Hà Nội [Hanoi: Vietnam National University, Hanoi's Publisher].

Pham, H. H., & Tran, N. A. (2014). *Chia sẻ chi phí: rào cản hay tiền đề cho phát triển giáo dục đại học ở Việt Nam* [Cost-sharing: Obstacles or premises for the development of Vietnam's higher education system]. Retrieved June 24, 2016, from https://hocthenao.vn/2014/09/04/chia-se-chi-phi-rao-can-hay-tien-de-cho-phat-trien-giao-duc-dai-hoc-o-viet-nam-pham-hung-hiep-tran-ngoc-anh/

QS. (2016). *QS university rankings: Asia 2016*. Retrieved June 24, 2016, from http://www.topuni-versities.com/university-rankings/asian-university-rankings/2016#sorting=rank+region=+country=+faculty=+stars=false+search=

Schofer, E., & Meyer, J. W. (2005). The worldwide expansion of higher education in the twentieth century. *American Sociological Review, 70*(6), 898–920.

Thanh, H. (2015). Gần 178.000 cử nhân, thạc sỹ thất nghiệp [About 178,000 bachelor, master holders unemployed]. *VnExpress*. Retrieved June, 24, 2016 from http://vnexpress.net/tin-tuc/thoi-su/gan-178-000-cu-nhan-thac-si-that-nghiep-3251443.html

Tieu, H. (2015). Các trường đại học đồng loạt tăng học phí: liệu phụ huynh có kham nổi? [Universities enhance tuition fees simultaneously: Are parents able to afford?]. *Phunuonline*. Retrieved June, 24, 2016 from http://phunuonline.com.vn/thoi-su/xa-hoi/cac-truong-dh-dong-loat-tang-hoc-phi-lieu-phu-huynh-co-kham-noi-7120/

Tradingeconomics. (2016). Vietnam youth unemployment rate 2011–2016. Retrieved October 16, 2016 from http://www.tradingeconomics.com/vietnam/youth-unemployment-rate

Vietnam Education Dialogue. (2015). *Tổng kết về phương hướng cải cách đại học ở Việt Nam* [Review on studies of higher education reforms in Vietnam]. Retrieved June 24, 2016 from https://hocthenao.vn/2015/06/11/phuong-huong-cai-cach-dai-hoc-o-viet-nam-doi-thoai-giao-duc/

World Bank. (2012). *Vietnam: Higher education and skills for growth*. Washington, DC: The World Bank.

Ziderman, A. (2002). Alternative objectives of national student loan schemes: Implications for design, evaluation and policy. *Welsh Journal of Education (Special International Issue), 11*(1), 37–47.

Part III
Curriculum, Equity and Quality Assurance

Chapter 6
Graduate Employability: Critical Perspectives

Thi Tuyet Tran

Abstract This chapter discusses the issues beyond the skill agenda provided by higher education. It argues that graduate employability in Vietnam is a complex issue and that the effort of sole universities will not create a positive change. It calls for a more productive collaboration and better understanding of mutual responsibility among all related stakeholders in enhancing graduate employability in Vietnam.

Introduction

The notion of employability has been high on the political agenda for higher education, not only in advanced western economies but also in the economies with lower level of development in Africa and Asia (Artess et al. 2011; Hager and Holland 2006; Tomlinson 2012). A number of employability and career guidance frameworks have been created to reinforce the relevance of higher education and training to the workplace; these include Canadian Blueprint,[1] Australian Blueprint for Career Development,[2] US National Career Development Guidelines,[3] European Lifelong Guidance Policy Network[4] and Competences for Lifelong Learning: European Reference Framework.[5] The issue of graduate employability is given a special concern in the context of a shifting interrelationship between higher education and the labour market, the current climate of wider labour market uncertainty and the

---

[1] Canadian Blueprint: http://206.191.51.163/blueprint/home.cfm

[2] Australia Blueprint for Career Development: http://www.blueprint.edu.au/

[3] US National Career Development Guidelines: http://www.learning4liferesources.com/Nationalcareerdevelopmentguidelines/Aftergraduation_000.pdf

[4] European Lifelong Guidance Policy Network: http://ktl.jyu.fi/ktl/elgpn

[5] Competences for Lifelong Learning: European Reference Framework: http://www.scribd.com/doc/33445618/Key-Competences-for-Lifelong-Learning---A-European-Framework

---

T. T. Tran (✉)
RMIT University, Melbourne, VIC, Australia
e-mail: june.tran@rmit.edu.au

© Springer Nature Singapore Pte Ltd. 2019   93
N. T. Nguyen, L. T. Tran (eds.), *Reforming Vietnamese Higher Education*,
Education in the Asia-Pacific Region: Issues, Concerns and Prospects 50,
https://doi.org/10.1007/978-981-13-8918-4_6

changing regulation of graduate employment (Department for Business Innovation and Skills (DIUS) 2008; Tomlinson 2012). Universities have gradually moved their focus on enhancing graduate employability. Modules have been developed, and practices have been implemented, all with the same aim: to equip students with knowledge and skills desired by prospective employers.

In Vietnam, making university relevant to the workplace or, in other words, providing skilled workers for industrialization and modernization of the country has long been the central mission of the higher education system (HES). Nonetheless, due to the loose connection between the HES and the industry, the knowledge and skills which universities have equipped students with have increasingly been considered irrelevant to the needs of the contemporary labour market. The HES is still struggling to find ways to address the problem.

This chapter will review the relevant international literature in the first part to explain why graduate employability has become popular in many university practices. It will also differentiate the notion of employability from the notion of employment and argue that enhancing the work-readiness of students does need the collaboration and input from enterprises in the labour market. The second part of this chapter will discuss the issues of employability and employment in the specific context of Vietnam and suggest that the situation of students with poor employability and high unemployment tendency will remain unless a more effective and sustainable connection between higher education and enterprises is developed.

Graduate Employability in the International Context

It has been argued that the connection between the knowledge and skills students acquired from universities and those required by employers has been traditionally flexible, loose and open-ended (Tomlinson 2012). This has also not presented problems for either graduates or employers when higher education remained elite (Little and Arthur 2010). However, over time, this traditional relationship has been reshaped. The expansion of higher education with a more heterogeneous mix of graduates (Scott 2005) coupled with an increasing intensification in the labour market in a globalized competition for skilled labour force and the pressure from neoliberal government to maximize the output of universities (Brown and Lauder 2009) have created a strong impact on the role of higher education in meeting the new needs of employers, graduates and the governments. The call for HESs to make explicit the task of developing students with skills and knowledge required by the contemporary employers has been clear and loud. The key structural changes both to higher education and the labour market have shifted their interrelationship (Tomlinson 2012).

The most obvious change higher education has experienced over the past few decades is its massification. This is resulting in a wider body of graduates in a crowded graduate labour market (Tomlinson 2012). Mass higher education also raises the concern around the traditional mission of HE as to 'prepare the elite to govern the nation', to 'provide an institutional basis for research into all forms of knowledge' (Jarvis 2002, p. 43) and to facilitate access to desired forms of employments (Scott 2005). In the early twentieth century, when higher education remained elite, Clark (1930) had already argued that educated people could earn more with better employment positions, not because they were educated but because they were scarce. Now the oversupply of graduates caused by mass higher education will result in the fall of earnings capacities. Higher education credentials do not seem to be a sufficient condition for obtaining employment, let alone a desired form of employment. Brown et al. (2003) seem to be right when they argue that employability is ultimately about the state of demand for labour in the market and the amount of competition of other applications.

Together with massification, universities have also moved towards greater autonomy and accountability. In most countries, the state commitment to public financing of higher education has been decreasing. Students increasingly have to pay tuition fees for their study and have somehow become 'customers' of the services provided by universities. Evidence suggests that employability is increasingly important in student choice of institution (Artess et al. 2011). This is not only because of the increasingly competitive graduate labour market but also because students realized the changes required by employers when recruiting skilled labour. On the one hand, students and graduates increasingly see themselves as the ones in charge of their own employability. Being a graduate and possessing graduate-level credentials no longer warrant access to a desired form of employment, as so many others share similar educational and pre-work profiles (Tomlinson 2012). In other words, graduates see a disrupted link between higher education participation and their future returns caused by mass higher education (Brooks and Everett 2009; Little and Arthur 2010). On the other hand, graduates also experience increasingly demanding recruiting requirements from employers. Under the impact of globalization and neoliberal policies, economies have become more competitive and flexible, which are now characterized by more intensive competition, deregulation and lower employment tenure (Tomlinson 2012). Market rules have dominated the market; and employers, in competitive market conditions, and allowed by a crowded pool of graduates, become more selective in their choices. They are no longer willing or no longer have to seek and train their workers and are able to recruit work-ready graduates. Many even can recruit graduates to positions previously been filled by school leavers (Brown et al. 2003). This gives them a significant cost saving but places challenges for new graduates and, in turn, challenges for universities to provide work-ready graduates.

Taking on-board employability has become universities' 'pragmatic response' (Clarke 2008) to the competition among universities and to the requirements of both students and employers. In many universities, employability has now become 'a standard mode of discourse – not only for the media and government ministries, but also academics marketing their institution on parent-centred University Open Days' (Taylor 2013, p. 851). Apart from students and employers, universities are also under the state pressure to be more responsive to the needs of the economy and to be able to provide graduates who can be able to adapt to their working environment and are adaptable within it (Cable 2010). In many countries, the state continues to exert pressures on the HES to enhance outputs, quality and the overall market responsiveness (Department for Education 2010; European Commission 2003, 2005, 2011; Tomusk 2004). Governances have different ways to make sure universities taking on board the employability agenda, e.g. through public funding, program measurement and audit. In most HESs now, universities's performance in terms of employability has been linked to quality assurance (Knight 2001). In short, all related stakeholders, including policy makers, employers and students, have created a strong influence on the higher education agenda in order to ensure that graduates leaving the system are fit-for-purpose (Harvey 2000; Teichler 2007).

What Is Graduate Employability and How to Best Address It in Higher Education Curriculum?

Employability has attracted increasing attention from researchers and policy makers in higher education agenda. However, there has been no common definition of this terminology in the research literature. Harvey (2001) suggests, for instance, that employability definitions can be grouped into two broad groups. The first relates to the ability of the student to get and retain work after graduation (e.g., see Hillage and Pollard 1998). Nonetheless, from the employers' perspective, employability is often placed in relation to the requirements and contribution to the workplace (e.g., see Australian Chamber of Commerce and Industry & Business Council of Australia 2002). However, as Boden and Nedeva (2010) argue, it seems impossible to define precisely the content of employability as that is where different employers' needs and graduate attributes meet, and this varies in different places and over time.

However, there is a need to differentiate between employability and employment. Harvey (2001, pp. 97–98) emphasizes that employability is the 'propensity of the individual student to get employment', or in other words, it is equipped for a job, rather than it is actually getting a job. Being employed means having a job, but being employable means having the qualities necessary for one to gain and maintain employment and progress in the workplace (Weligamage 2009). Employability is often regarded as the fitness for graduates to join the labour market. It may increase opportunities for graduates to obtain desired jobs, but does not assure them (Cabellero and Walker 2010; Clarke 2007; Helyer et al. 2011; Knight and Yorke 2004; Leong and Kavanagh 2013; Yorke 2006). This is because gaining employment does not only depend on the knowledge and skills one possesses, but it also depends on the general economic conditions and the context of the current labor market, as well as on one's personal circumstances and characteristics (Clarke 2007; McQuaid 2006).

The next question is how to enhance graduate employability in the higher education context. The current trend is to develop a list of skills desired by employers and create initiatives/activities to enhance those skills. The list of skills claimed to be desired by contemporary employers have been expanded with different umbrella terms such as generic skills, soft skills, transferable skills, cross-disciplinary skills, graduate attributes, core skills, key skills, basic skills, cross-curricular skills, common skills, essential skills, enterprise skills or even employability skills (Caballero et al. 2011; Cabellero and Walker 2010; Hager and Holland 2006; Lowden et al. 2011; Rust and Froud 2011). These types of skills are claimed to be important for any individual in the changing context of life, and especially essential for graduates in the employment context, as these skills are important to make them "'prepared' and 'ready' for success in rapidly changing work environment" (Cabellero and Walker 2010, p. 16). Moreover, these skills are also claimed to be important for the competitiveness of the national economy:

> National competitive advantage is increasingly dependent on the skill base of the workforce, and more specifically, on the ability of both firms and individuals to engage in innovative activity and in new economic activity. This has created an imperative for both general skills, as these, it is suggested, are related to innovation, and for specific enterprise skills, which are related to new venture creation. (Hytti and O'Gorman 2004, p. 11)

Universities worldwide have gradually taken up the employability agenda. Strategies have been developed and employed with the aim to enhance graduate work-readiness. Students and academic staff are required to share responsibility for developing employability skills. Initiatives such as engaging prospective students to determine the role employability plays in decisions over course of study, making use of alumni network, applying credit to employability activities, highly evaluating the value of extracurricular activities or the engagement with employment have been reported rather popular across HESs around the world. These initiatives have started quite early in developed countries such as the UK, USA, Australia or Europe. Nonetheless, the effort of universities has not been paid off yet. There still exists a skill perception gap between universities and employers. For example, Bisoux (2015) finds that while 96% of university presidents in the USA believed that their graduates were adequately prepared for the workforce, only 33% of senior executives had the same view. Similarly, a global study finds that 72% of interviewed education providers responded that they were adequately preparing their students for the labour market; in contrast only 42% of employers shared this opinion (Mourshed et al. 2012). A study in the Middle East and North America also reveals a similar gap when almost all the interviewed education providers believed that their graduates had the necessary skills for the employment market; only 20–35% of employers agreed with this view (Kandri et al. 2011). A study about graduate employability in Asia also suggests that the perspectives of universities and employers differ when it comes to the issue of skills students acquired before entering the labour market. While, in most cases, universities considered their students to be well prepared for employment, employers often complained about the lack of vital skills graduates possess before negotiating their transition to employment (UNESCO 2012).

The literature also suggests a broad mismatch between the skills developed by universities equip and those required by the industry. Various studies, such as Handel (2003); Sala (2011); Tran (2012a); Nicolescu and Paun (2009); Dewey et al. (2008); and Hernández-March et al. (2009), have reported different perspectives and different expectations students, employers and universities hold, in terms of work-oriented skills and abilities developed through higher education. Interestingly, some skills such as interpersonal, presentation skills or project management skills are often claimed to be developed during university time; nonetheless, these skills somehow differ from the interpersonal, presentation skills or project management skills desired by employers (Dewey et al. 2008). Some reasons have also been suggested in the literature. First, universities have not shifted the focus to applied learning and functional skills and remained their focus rigidly on academically orientated provision and pedagogy (Tomlinson 2012). Second, the notions of graduate 'skill', 'competencies' and 'attributes' often convey different things to different stakeholders, i.e. students, universities and employers (Barrie 2006; Handel 2003; Knight and Yorke 2004; Sala 2011; Tran 2012a). The perception gap is often reported to be wide, and a research reported by McKinsey and The Conference Board (2012, p. 23) even provides a negative conclusion that 'there is an issue with education systems that fail to produce future workers with the kinds of skills required by today's organizations – let alone those of tomorrow'.

Stakeholder collaboration is also suggested in the literature as an important area that needs to be tackled in order to improve the situation and bridge the perception gaps among stakeholders. There is a need to increase communication and mutual understanding among universities, graduates, employers and policy makers, and university-enterprise collaboration (UEC) is considered an important way to improve the authenticity of the process of enhancing graduate employability (Gibbs et al. 2011; Stone et al. 2013; Tran 2015a). Secondly, the UEC should be designed to provide students with experiential learning, which is considered vital in enhancing the preparation and success of students in the entry-level market (Gault et al. 2000). Employers have been reported to highly evaluate graduates' work experience, and they often view it as an indicator of workplace readiness (Andrews and Higson 2008). Thus, it is suggested pre-graduate work experience in the forms of internships, work placement, co-ops and other related activities enables students, on the one hand, to develop their skills by experiencing real-world challenges and applications (Cooper et al. 2010; Ferns et al. 2014; Ferns and Moore 2012; Smith et al. 2010) and, on the other hand, to have opportunities to understand the real needs of the employment market and gradually develop the right skills that is desired in that market (Ferns et al. 2014; Kogan et al. 2011). It is not surprising when different forms of UEC have been focused in the literature on graduate employability and work-based learning and work-integrated learning are viewed as particularly effective approaches to promote the employability of graduates (Etzkowitz 2004; Lowden et al. 2011; World Bank 2012).

Graduate Employability Issue in Vietnam

Vietnamese Higher Education and the Mission of Providing Skilled Workers for Industrialization and Modernization of the Country

Although Vietnam has opened its door to the world economy since 1986, its economy and the HES are still at much lower stages of development compared with the developed countries in the West. The central mission of the HES is still limited in training skilled labour force for the development of the country (George 2010; Tran 2006). Unlike higher education in the West, the Vietnamese HES has been 'fundamentally designed to meet the needs of the labour market' (George 2010, p. 34) with different small, mono-disciplinary universities operating under both their Line Ministries and the Ministry of Education and Training (MOET) (Tran 2012b). Now, under the impact of the globalization, the West-East influence and the mass higher education movement, coupled with the recognition about the needs to provide flexibility and more choices for students and the aim to prepare skilled labour force for a knowledge economy, multidisciplinary universities, both the state and the private ones, have been founded. Vietnam seems to achieve its goal of expanding the HES. The number of students enrolling in the system in the school year 2014–2015 had increased more than 200% compared to the school year 2000–2001, and the number of HEIs increased from 178 to 436, with the number of universities nearly tripling (increased from 74 universities in 2000 to 219 in 2015). This is not to count the other 30 HEIs who are under the Ministry of Military (MOET 2013, 2015; Vietnamese Government 2015). The expansion of the HES with the aim to strengthen a knowledge economy and to increase graduates' adaptability to new technologies and flexible market (Lee and Healy 2006) is claimed to be essential for Vietnam to become 'a major player on the world scene economically, culturally, and intellectually' (Pham and Fry 2004, p. 329).

Nonetheless, mass higher education also comes along with its problems. When the system has been expanded rapidly, and when the resource and experience in managing the growing system is still limited, the HES is struggling to maintain their capability to provide high-skilled labour force for the industry. This, coupled with the loose connection with the labour market which has been developed fast in an increasingly open market economy, has kept the HES far behind the development of the economy. The HES has gradually failed to implement their central mission of providing high-quality labour force for the modernization and industrialization of the country. The claim about the poor capability of universities in enhancing or equipping students with the knowledge and skills required by the employer has been loud (Pham 2008; Tran 2006; Tran and Swierczek 2009; Tran 2013c). The rate of unemployed graduates has also increased rapidly. In 2010, the number of unemployed HE graduates aged from 21 to 29 was less than 60,000. Despite the fact that the number of students enrolling in the system has remained rather stable since 2010 (MOET 2013), by the end of 2015, the number of unemployed graduates had reached 225,500 (Ministry of Labor – Invalids and Social Affairs & General Statistics Office 2015).

To be fair, mass higher education is not the only reason painting the dark picture of the transition to employment among university students in Vietnam. Although the HES in Vietnam has expanded rapidly recently, it is claimed that the number of graduates from the system are still lower compared to the high demand of skilled labour force from an increasingly integrated economy (Tran 2016; World Bank 2008, 2012). Looking from the overall employment market, the ratio of the workforce with higher education qualifications is still very low (currently around 9% of the workforce) and much lower than the ratio in its labouring countries such as China or Thailand (Ministry of Labor – Invalids and Social Affairs & General Statistics Office 2016; Nguyen 2014; Tran 2016). It is suggested that the labour market can still absorb more university graduates, given the condition that university education are more relevant to the workplace requirements; nonetheless, this remains a work in progress (Postiglione 2011). Vietnam seems to share a common characteristic of the education systems in developing countries where the focus has still been on teaching basic cognitive skills and facts, labour market skills are still equated with technical skills and employers continue to lament the difficulties in finding employees with required skills for the contemporary competitive labour market (Cunningham and Villaseñor 2014).

Research into the issue of graduate employability among Vietnamese university students has indicated the inadequate quality of students and graduates (Fatseas 2010; Nguyen 2014; Tran 2006, 2015a; Tran and Swierczek 2009; Truong 2006). There is also a common support to Tran and Swierczek's (2009, p. 580) claim in naming the reasons for the low level of responsiveness of the higher education to the demand of the labour market: the primary focus of university on explicit knowledge, the design of the curriculum depriving the market orientation and the lack of or the ignorance of the need of employers in most universities. In 2006, the World Bank's Vietnam Development Report found that skills and education of available workers ranked third in the list of constraints of doing business in Vietnam (World Bank 2008). However, in 2012, skills and education become the biggest obstacle in the business climate in Vietnam (World Bank 2012, p. 41). Then in 2015–2016, Vietnam higher education and training (one of the efficiency enhancers of the economy) is ranked low – 95th in 140 countries in the World Competitiveness Index – and the inadequately educated workforce has become the third problematic factor for doing business in Vietnam (World Economic Forum 2015, p. 366).

Research of Tran (2014) has also identified the key quality deficits among Vietnamese graduates. These are the poor and outdated professional knowledge, the lack of experience/practice to apply the learnt knowledge in the real context of work, the poor foreign language skills (especially English) and the lack of work experience. She also suggests that the main reasons for the situation come from the loose connection between the HES and the labour market, the weak capability and limited resources of universities to enhance graduate employability, the interference of Vietnamese cultural features and also the weak capability of the industry to absorb the increased number of graduates.

The Effort of the HES to Address the Problem

The Vietnamese HES has also recognized its weaknesses and has made some efforts to address the problem. This is clearly evident in many documents, policies and instructions recently issued by MOET and the government. In 2005, the Vietnamese government launched an ambitious reform, namely, 'Fundamental and Comprehensive Reform of Higher Education in Vietnam 2006 – 2020' (also known as Higher Education Reform Agenda or HERA) (HERA 2005). The reform promotes an agenda which maintains and emphasizes a strong focus on job orientation, in which up to 80% of students will enrol in professional-oriented programs and only 20% in research oriented by the year 2020. HERA also aims to develop a curriculum that has strong professional orientation with the shift from the instructional to the learning paradigm and pays special pedagogical consideration to bring higher education training more align with the demand of the labour market (Harman and Nguyen 2010; Pham 2010). If this is to be followed, the involvement of enterprises in university practices should be the main focus in the educational reforms in Vietnam.

Indeed, some measures have been taken to drive universities towards better communication and collaboration with employers. According to MOET's circular number 37/2012/TT-BGDĐT, universities are required to consult employers when designing university curricular and evaluating university practices. They also have to report on the rate of employed recent graduates, to provide evidences of consulting employers' opinions and contribution towards developing or revising syllabus/curriculum and to take into account market demands into university everyday practices. These are part of the quality assurance criteria that MOET has urged each and every university in the system to follow. MOET has issued another circular[6] requiring, again, the involvement of employers in university curriculum design. In addition to this, in 2008, the Vietnamese government launched the US$450 million National Foreign Language 2020 Project (Project 2020) in order to reach an ambitious aim of upgrading the language capability of its students so that by 2020 most students can use a foreign language (especially English) confidently in their daily communication (MOET 2008). These efforts all aim to address the problems and overcome the deficits mentioned by Tran (2014) in the above section.

It is now more than a decade since the launch of HERA and Project 2020; however, positive indicators for the change in the outcome quality of the system seem to be underachieved reversely, the number of unemployed graduates has non-stop increase and complaint about the mismatch between what graduates can offer when negotiating employment and what employers expect from them has been getting louder. Reports have been issued and submitted; universities are still going their ways which are not always the same as reported. It is suggested that there is a lack of sustaining policies which can help translate the political wills into practice in the system (Pham et al. 2013).

---

[6]Circular 12/2017/TT_BGDĐT

Nonetheless, in some universities, especially the top state and private universities, there are growing evidence of cooperation between universities and enterprises. For example, the collaborations between technical universities like the Hanoi University of Science and Technology; Ho Chi Minh City University of Technology; University of Engineering and Technology – Vietnam National University, Hanoi; University of Communications and Transport; University of Civil Engineering; and enterprises in petroleum, electric power, telecommunications, information technology and transportation are increasing. However, in general, private universities take more initiatives towards collaboration with industry partners. This is easy to understand as the competitions to attract students among private universities are more 'serious' than among state universities. In the top-ranked private universities such as the Haiphong Private University, Duy Tan University, Lac Hong University or FPT University, the integration of theory and practice in teaching and the collaboration with employers in developing curriculum and internships have become one of their central missions. Nonetheless, the impact of the effort from these universities on the whole system seems to be modest, and reports on effective and sustainable cooperation between universities and firms to enhance the practical knowledge and skills for students remain rare.

Clearly, Vietnamese universities are weak in enhancing employability for their students. However, other related factors also need to address and to be taken into account to develop appropriate steps in enhancing graduate employability in the Vietnamese context. Some of such factors are discussed in the following section.

Other Related Factors

The Interference of Cultural Features

Vietnam is a typical Confucian Heritage Culture (CHC)[7] country, where the Confucian values such as respecting elders and the 'face saving' culture remain alive (Tran 2013b). In Vietnam, power distance or 'the extent to which the less powerful members of institutions and organisations within a country expect and accept that power is distributed unequally' is very high (Itim international's HOFSTEDE CENTRE 2014). In that context, children are still taught and expected to respect older people and to obey parental guidance and orders (Ramburuth and McCormick 2001). There is still popular the case where parents interfere into or even decide personal matters for their children: parents decide which school children go, which job children should follow or even who children should get married to. In short, Vietnamese children, the same as children raised in other Eastern culture countries, are traditionally and normally more protective than Western children (Chalamwong et al. 2012).

---

[7]Examples of CHC countries are Vietnam, China, Singapore and Japan where they have strong influence of Confucianism; children in CHC are often expected and taught to respect people who are older or who have higher ranks, i.e. parents, elders and teachers (Nguyen et al. 2005; Ramburuth and McCormick 2001; Tran 2013b).

This tradition has somehow made the child obedient and passive, and this is viewed as a negative factor affecting students' transition to employment (Tran 2015a). On the one hand, it has created the expectation from the students that their schools or universities should equip them with enough knowledge and skills necessary for them to negotiate their transition to employment. This hinders their efforts to make full use of extracurricular activities, to get involved in different volunteering and community work, to expand their network and to increase their understanding about the outside world during the time at university. These activities would all help them to enhance the skills appreciated by the employers in the labour market (Tran 2014). On the other hand, the deep interference of parents who may not fully understand their child's interests, strengths and weaknesses and who may have limited understanding about the change in the industry may mislead the child. Evidence suggests that it takes longer for some students to find their ways to their first stable and satisfactory job because they have to follow their parent's guidance and orders to learn in the discipline that they do not like and to work in a position/ place that they do not find suitable (even when their parents have to spend much money to geese the machine and place them in that position). In many cases, parents virtually become an obstacle preventing students from deciding their own matters and being in charge of their own career management.

The Weak Career Services Inside and Outside the Education System

To be fair, Vietnam is a fast developing society, and globalization and an open policy for people to get access to the Internet have reduced the cases of parents interfering into children's own matters. Moreover, parents are getting busier; they have less time than their children to update information about the tendency in the labour market; some of them also understand that they should empower their children to make their own decisions. Thus, more and more children are allowed to decide their own career management issues now. Nonetheless, when being given the right to manage the career route, many young people are struggling. They seem to hover the zone of unknown. They are not sure which job they should follow, which university they should apply for, how to enhance the knowledge and skills desired by employers and how to approach the labour market and deploy their assets in a way to resonate employers (Tran 2014). Career services are virtually absent or ineffective in both high schools and universities. In addition to that, the function of easing the transition to work among young people of employment centres outside the education system does not seem to work effectively either. Seeking the help of the employment centre is one of the least methods used by youth when they need job advice or when they look for a specific job (Tran 2015b).

The Low Stages of Development of Both the HES and the Labour Market

When suggesting the reasons for the low employability among Vietnamese university graduates, there is a need to mention the low levels of development of not only the HES but also of the Vietnamese economy in general and of the employment market in particular. The weak capability of employment centres mentioned above is somehow reflected a weak function of the Vietnamese labour market. Apart from the weak capability to manage the incoming labour force, the Vietnamese labour market, especially the public sector, has still inherited many characteristics of the central command economy where corrupted recruitment procedures are still rife. Evidence of using money, bribery, gifts, offspring or relative relationships to gain access to employment and be promoted at work are still popular (Tran 2013a). This has created more confusion for the young people who are wobbling around to find their ways to employment.

The increased number of unemployed and underemployed university graduates also indicates the weak capability of the labour market to absorb the increased number of young people finishing higher education training (Elder 2014). In the knowledge economy era, only around 9% of the working age population are university graduates (Ministry of Labor – Invalids and Social Affairs & General Statistics Office 2016), but the claim of 'thừa thầy thiếu thợ' (too many masters, too few labourers) is still popular. This somehow indicates the low level of development of the economy in general and of the skilled labour market in particular. The labour market does not seem to run their functions well. At the current stage, it is still unclear which jobs are or will be of high demand and how many new jobs are created each year. In the last few years, it is claimed that the number of new jobs is even less than the number of jobs that disappeared as a result of the economic crisis. Moreover, the oversupply of graduates in some fields, and the undersupply of graduates in other fields, was another issue (UNESCO 2012). Adding to the dark picture is the low qualifications of the majority employers and their limited knowledge of human resource (Nguyen 2014; Tran 2014). Clearly, the Vietnamese economy and its labour market also have many problems needed to be addressed and tackled.

When both the employment market and the HES still have many internal problems needed to be settled, and when enterprises do not think enhancing graduate employability is their mission (Le and Truong 2005), the loose connection between them is understandable. Nonetheless, without an effective and strong university-enterprise collaboration, it is hard to enhance the integration of theories and practices, an essential condition to enhance graduate employability in a neoliberalised economy (Etzkowitz 2004; Lowden et al. 2011; World Bank 2012). In other words, the solo effort of the university will never bring the desired outcome when it comes to the issue of enhancing graduate employability.

Interestingly, Vietnamese universities often complain that the active involvement of employers in the collaborations with universities is rare. Apart from approaching universities for recruitment of graduates, for scholarship sponsoring, sometimes for sponsoring students' extracurricular activities and advertising their company images or products, not many enterprises actively approach universities to discuss the collaboration in teaching or training (either for their staff or for university students) or for research collaboration (Huynh 2012). Many employers still keep the thought that the university-enterprise cooperation mainly brings benefits for universities and students, not for firms; thus, they are not really actively involved in that collaboration (Pham 2013). In many state organizations, the recruitment process is still unclear and interfered by corruption which has created a certain negative impact on students who believe that money, social connection and luck are essential for them to negotiate their transition to employment (Tran 2013a).

Moreover, at the current stage, when the HES in Vietnam was still dominated by state universities, who are mostly still managed in similar ways like in the central command economy before, the government grants most of the university expenses, staff salary included, and students' tuition fees are very low. Thus, most university entrance exam takers aim to go to the state universities. The internal competitiveness is, therefore, low. Most state universities are not under real pressure to increase students' employability to attract new students. The market share for the private universities is very small as the tuition fees in this sector are often much higher than in the state universities. Recently many private universities are struggling to attract enough students to maintain their teaching and learning practices (Hanh 2016). Some of them have made effort to initiate the collaboration with firms to enhance employability for students and consider this as a way to attract new students. Nonetheless, the impact of such effort is still considered modest.

Conclusion

The development of the Vietnamese HES shares some similarities as elsewhere under the impact of neoliberalism and the mass higher education movement. The size of the system is getting bigger with more requirements and pressures from students, employers and the central government for university responsibility and accountability. Nonetheless, when in most developed countries, universities now seem to accept enhancing graduate employability as its subset mission and have been working towards developing university-enterprise collaboration to integrate theories and practices, the Vietnamese higher education does not seem to fulfil its traditional duty of training and providing high-skilled labour force for the industry. Despite some internal efforts and the pressure coming from educational policy makers, there have been, conversely, increased indicators for the poor and mismatched knowledge and skills students equipped during university time and the ones required by the industry. Both the number and the ratio of unemployed graduates have significantly grown year after year. The claim of the employers over the general quality of graduates has become louder. The dissatisfaction of most related stakeholders over the inadequate teaching and learning at the HES has become popular. In short, all eyes are on the HES, and most stakeholders see higher education as the one who needs to take responsibility for the low employability and employment rate among recent graduates.

The Vietnamese HES, indeed, is weak in enhancing employability for its students. The limited resource, experience and understanding to manage the change internally (the growing number of enrolling students) and externally (the changes in the market-led economy) are considered the key problem the Vietnamese HES has to face in order to address the issue of employability at the current stage. In addition to this, the lack of internal competitiveness and the low interest from enterprises in cooperating with universities to create more practical lessons for students both have negatively impacted on the university process of enhancing graduate employability in Vietnam. Evidence suggests that even when MOET is struggling to find ways to increase the responsiveness of the HES towards the needs of the industry, there is still an absence of a practical and sustaining policy or measure to change the wills into practice.

Nonetheless, the university cannot take the sole blame for recent graduates' difficulties in finding and retaining employment. The discussion in this chapter suggests that universities are not the only stakeholder that has impacted on the employability development of their students. Efforts by universities, if any, will not work without the cooperation and input of other related stakeholders during this transitional period of the economy. Other related stakeholders, including employers, students and their families, all need to acknowledge the changes in society. They should be aware of the cultural features affecting the university-workplace transition and should recognize their responsibility in this process. Without mutual efforts and understanding to bridge the gap between theories and practices, to build a sustainable university-industry collaboration to provide and prepare students with skills and knowledge desired by the industry, the transition to the workplace of Vietnamese university graduates will remain to be a painful process.

References

Andrews, J., & Higson, H. (2008). Graduate employability, 'soft skills' versus 'hard' business knowledge: A European study. *Higher Education in Europe, 33*(4), 411–422.

Artess, J., Forbes, P., & Ripmeester, N. (2011). *Supporting graduate employability: HEI practice in other countries* (BIS Research Paper Number 40). London: BIS.

Australian Chamber of Commerce and Industry & Business Council of Australia. (2002). *Employability skills for the future.* Canberra: Department of Education, Science and Training.

Barrie, S. C. (2006). Understanding what we mean by the generic attributes of graduates. *Higher Education, 51*(2), 215–241.

Bisoux, T. (2015). *Business education jam: Continuing the conversation.* Retrieved 20 September, 2015, from www.bizedmagazine.com/special-coverage/aacsb-deans-conference-2015/business-education-jam

Boden, R., & Nedeva, M. (2010). Employing discourse: Universities and graduate 'employability'. *Journal of Education Policy, 25*(1), 37–54.

Brooks, R., & Everett, G. (2009). Post-graduate reflections on the value of a degree. *British Educational Research Journal, 35*(3), 333–349.

Brown, P., & Lauder, H. (2009). Economic globalisation, skill formation and the consequences for higher education. In S. Ball, M. Apple, & L. Gandin (Eds.), *The Routledge international handbook of sociology of education* (pp. 229–240). London: Routledge.

Brown, P., Hesketh, A., & Williams, S. (2003). Employability in a knowledge-driven economy. *Journal of Education and Work, 16*(2), 107–126.

Caballero, C. L., Walker, A., & Fuller-Tyszkiewicz, M. (2011). The work readiness scale (WRS): Developing a measure to assess work readiness in college graduates. *Journal of Teaching and Learning for Graduate Employability, 2*(2), 41–54.

Cabellero, C. L., & Walker, A. (2010). Work readiness in graduate recruitment and selection: A review of current assessment methods. *Journal of Teaching and Learning for Graduate Employability, 1*(1), 13–25.

Cable, V. (2010). A new era for universities *Speech delivered by the Secretatry of State on Higher Education*: Department for Business, Innovation & Skills and The Rt Hon Dr Vince Cable.

Chalamwong, Y., Hongprayoon, K., Suebnusorn, W., Doung, N. A., Chan, S., & Dyna, H. (2012). *Skills for employability: Southeast Asia*. Washington, DC: Thailand Development Research Institute (TDRI).

Clark, H. F. (1930). Economic effects of education. *The Journal of Higher Education, 1*(3), 141–148.

Clarke, M. (2007). Understanding and managing employability in changing career contexts. *Journal of European Industrial, 32*(4), 258–284.

Clarke, M. (2008). Understanding and managing employability in changing career contexts. *Journal of European Industrial Training, 32*(4), 258–284.

Cooper, L., Orrell, J., & Bowden, M. (2010). *Work integrated learning: A guide to effective practice*. New York: Routledge.

Cunningham, W., & Villaseñor, P. (2014). *Employer voices, employer demands, and implications for public skills development policy* (World Bank Policy Research Working Paper 6853). World Bank.

Department for Business Innovation and Skills (DIUS). (2008). *Higher education at work – High skills: High value*. London: HMSO.

Department for Education. (2010). *Securing a sustainable future for higher education (the Browne review)*. London: HMSO.

Dewey, J. D., Montrosse, B. E., Schröter, D. C., Sullins, C. D., & Mattox, J. R. (2008). Evaluator competencies What's taught versus What's sought. *American Journal of Evaluation, 29*(3), 268–287.

Elder, S. (2014). *Labour market transitions of young women and men in Asia and the Pacific*. Geneva: International Labour Office.

Etzkowitz, H. (2004). The evolution of the entrepreneurial university. *International Journal of Technology and Globalisation, 1*(1), 64–77.

European Commission. (2003). *The role of the universities in the Europe of knowledge*. Brussels: European Commission.

European Commission. (2005). *Mobilising the brainpower of Europe: Enabling universities to make their full contribution to the Lisbon Strategy*. Brussels: European Commission.

European Commission. (2011). *Supporting growth and jobs – An agenda for the modernisation of Europe's higher education systems*. Brussels: European Commission.

Fatseas, M. (2010). Research-industry cooperation supporting development in Vietnam: The challenge of translating policy into practice. In G. Harman, M. Hayden, & P. T. Nghi (Eds.), *Reforming higher education in Vietnam: Challenges and priorities* (pp. 103–116). London: Springer.

Ferns, S., & Moore, K. (2012). Assessing student outcomes in fieldwork placements: An overview of current practice. *Asia-Pacific Journal of Cooperative Education, 13*(4), 207–224.

Ferns, S., Campbell, M., & Zegwaad, K. (2014). Work integrated learning. In S. Ferns (Ed.), *Work integrated learning in the curriculum* (pp. 1–6). Milperra: Higher Education Research and Development Society of Australasia HERDSA.

Gault, J., Redington, J., & Schlager, T. (2000). The benefits of undergraduate business internships: Implications for the student, university, and business community. *Journal of Marketing Education, 22*(1), 45–53.

George, E. S. (2010). Higher education in Vietnam 1986–1998: Education in transition to a new era? In G. Harman, M. Hayden, & P. T. Nghi (Eds.), *Reforming higher education in Vietnam* (pp. 31–50). London: Springer.

Gibbs, S., Steel, G., & Kuiper, A. (2011). Expectations of competency: The mismatch between employers' and graduates' views of end-user computing skills requirements in the workplace. *Journal of Information Technology Education, 10*(1), 371–382.

Hager, P., & Holland, S. (2006). *Graduate attributes, learning and employability*. Dordrecht: Springer.

Handel, M. J. (2003). Skills mismatch in the labor market. *Annual Review of Sociology, 29*, 135–165.

Hanh, H. (2016). *The need to restructure colleges and universities who are facing difficulties in recruiting students* (Sẽ cơ cấu lại các trường đại học, cao đẳng gặp khó khăn về tuyển sinh). Retrieved 26 April, 2016, from http://dantri.com.vn/giao-duc-khuyen-hoc/se-co-cau-lai-cac-truong-dh-cd-gap-kho-khan-ve-tuyen-sinh-20160104084626021.htm

Harman, G., & Nguyen, T. B. N. (2010). The research role's of Vietnam's universities. In G. Harman, M. Hayden, & P. T. Nghi (Eds.), *Reforming higher education in Vietnam* (pp. 87–102). London: Springer.

Harvey, L. (2000). New realities: The relationship between higher education and employment. *Tertiary Education and Management, 6*(1), 3–17.

Harvey, L. (2001). Defining and measuring employability. *Quality in Higher Education, 7*(2), 97–109.

Helyer, R., Lee, D., & Evans, A. (2011). Hybrid HE: Knowledge, skills and innovation. *Work Based Learning e-Journal, 1*(2), 18–34.

HERA. (2005). *Vietnamese government resolution on substantial and comprehensive renewal of Vietnam's tertiary education in the 2006–2020 period* (No 14/2005/NQ-CP).

Hernández-March, J., Martín del Peso, M., & Leguey, S. (2009). Graduates' skills and higher education: The employers' perspective. *Tertiary Education and Management, 15*(1), 1–16.

Hillage, J., & Pollard, E. (1998). *Employability: Developing a framework for policy analysis*. London: Department for Education and Employment.

Huynh, N. L. (2012). *Đào tạo đáp ứng nhu cầu thị trường lao động* (Training for the employment market). Paper presented at the Đào tạo, nghiên cứu khoa học và chuyển giao công nghệ gắn kết với nhu cầu doanh nghiệp (Training, research and technology transfer vs enterprise demands), Dong Nai, Vietnam.

Hytti, U., & O'Gorman, C. (2004). What is "enterprise education"? An analysis of the objectives and methods of enterprise education programmes in four European countries. *Education and Training, 46*(1), 11–23.

Itim international's HOFSTEDE CENTRE. (2014). *Hosftede center: Vietnam*. Retrieved 8 March, 2016, from http://geert-hofstede.com/vietnam.html

Jarvis, P. (2002). The changing university: Meeting a need and needing to change. *Higher Education Quarterly, 54*(1), 43–67.

Kandri, S.-E., Bjarnason, S., & Elsadig, A. (2011). *Education for employment: Realizing Arab youth potential*. Washington, DC: International Finance Corporation, World Bank Group.

Knight, P. (2001). Employability and quality. *Quality in Higher Education, 7*(2), 93–95.

Knight, P., & Yorke, M. (2004). *Learning, curriculum and employability in higher education*. London: Routledge Falmer.

Kogan, I., Noelke, C., & Gebel, M. (2011). *Making the transition: Education and labor market entry in Central and Eastern Europe*. Stanford: Stanford University Press.

Le, C. T., & Truong, Q. (2005). Human resource management practices in a transitional economy: A comparative study of enterprise ownership forms in Vietnam. *Asia Pacific Business Review, 11*(1), 25–47.

Lee, M. N., & Healy, S. (2006). *Higher education in South-East Asia: An overview*. Bangkok: UNESCO.

Leong, R., & Kavanagh, M. (2013). A work-integrated learning (WIL) framework to develop graduate skills and attributes in an Australian university's accounting program. *Asia-Pacific Journal of Cooperative Education, 14*(1), 1–14.

Little, B., & Arthur, L. (2010). Less time to study, less well prepared for work, yet satisfied with higher education: A UK perspective on links between higher education and the labour market. *Journal of Education and Work, 23*(3), 275–296.

Lowden, K., Hall, S., Elliot, D., & Lewin, J. (2011). *Employers' perceptions of the employability skills of new graduates*. London: SCRE Centre/Edge Foundation, University of Glasgow.

McKinsey & Company, & The Conference Board. (2012). *The state of human capital 2012: False summit – Why the human capital function still has far to go* (Research Report No. R-1501-12-RR). McKinsey and Company, The Conference Board.

McQuaid, R. W. (2006). Job search success and employability in local labor markets. *The Annals of Regional Science, 40*, 407–421.

Ministry of Labor – Invalids and Social Affairs, & General Statistics Office. (2015). *Newsletter for Vietnam's Labour Market Update* (Vol. 5, Quarter 1–2015). Hanoi: Ministry of Labor - Invalids and Social Affairs.

Ministry of Labor – Invalids and Social Affairs, & General Statistics Office. (2016). *Newsletter for Vietnam's Labour Market Update* (Vol. 10, Quarter 2–2016). Hanoi: Ministry of Labor – Invalids and Social Affairs.

MOET. (2008). *National Foreign Language 2020 Project*. Hanoi: Vietnamese Ministry of Education and Training.

MOET. (2013). *Thống kê 2013* (2013 statistics). Retrieved 14 October, 2015, from http://www.moet.gov.vn/?page=11.11&view=5251

MOET. (2015). *Education and training statistics report 2011–2015*. Hanoi: Ministry of Education and Training.

Mourshed, M., Farrell, D., & Barton, D. (2012). *Education to employment: Designing a system that works*. Washington, DC: McKinsey Center for Government, McKinsey & Company.

Nguyen, H. L. (2014). *Nghiên cứu đánh giá mức độ hài lòng của doanh nghiệp về chất lượng đào tạo nhân lực trình độ đại học ở Việt Nam* (Business satisfaction levels for the quality of manpower training at universities in Vietnam). Doctor of Philosophy, Hanoi University of Science and Technology, Hanoi.

Nguyen, P.-M., Terlouw, C., & Pilot, A. (2005). Cooperative learning vs Confucian heritage culture's collectivism: Confrontation to reveal some cultural conflicts and mismatch. *Asia Europe Journal, 3*(3), 403–419.

Nicolescu, L., & Paun, C. (2009). Relating higher education with the labour market: Graduates' expectations and employers' requirements. *Tertiary Education and Management, 15*(1), 17–33.

Pham, T. H. (2008). *Higher education in Vietnam: A look from labour market angle*. Hanoi: Vietnam Development Forum.

Pham, T. N. (2010). The higher education agenda: A vision for 2020. In G. Harman, M. Hayden, & P. T. Nghi (Eds.), *Reforming higher education in Vietnam: Challenges and priorities* (pp. 51–64). London: Springer.

Pham, T. L. (2013). *Quan điểm của doanh nghiệp về hợp tác với các trường đại học ở Việt Nam* (Enterprises' perspective of the collaboration with universities in Vietnam). Hanoi: POHE Project, Ministry of Education and Training.

Pham, L. H., & Fry, G. W. (2004). Universities in Vietnam: Legacies, challenges, and prospects. In P. A. Altbach & T. Umakoshi (Eds.), *Asian universities: Historical perspectives and contemporary challenges* (pp. 301–331). Baltimore: Johns Hopkins University Press.

Pham, T. L., Bui, A. T., & Dongelmans, B. (2013). *Vietnamese higher education responsiveness toward the needs of the industry: Impact evaluation of the POHE projects and questions for developing university-industry interaction.* Paper presented at the university-industry interaction conference proceedings: Challenges and solutions for fostering entrepreneurial universities and collaborative innovation, Amsterdam.

Postiglione, G. A. (2011). Global recession and higher education in eastern Asia: China, Mongolia and Vietnam. *Higher Education, 62*(6), 789–814.

Ramburuth, P., & McCormick, J. (2001). Learning diversity in higher education: A comparative study of Asian international and Australian students. *Higher Education, 42*, 333–350.

Rust, C., & Froud, L. (2011). 'Personal literacy': The vital, yet often overlooked, graduate attribute. *Journal of Teaching and Learning for Graduate Employability, 2*(1), 28–40.

Sala, G. (2011). Approaches to skills mismatch in the labour market: A literature review. *Papers: revista de sociologia, 96*, 1025–1045.

Scott, P. (2005). Universities and the knowledge economy. *Minerva, 43*(3), 297–309.

Smith, J., Meijer, G., & Kielly-Coleman, N. (2010). Assurance of learning: The role of work integrated learning and industry partners. In M. Campbell (Ed.), *Work integrated learning: Responding to challenges* (pp. 409–419). Perth: Australian Collaborative Education Network (ACEN) Incorporated, Curtin University of Technology.

Stone, G., Lightbody, M., & Whait, R. (2013). Developing accounting students' listening skills: Barriers, opportunities and an integrated stakeholder approach. *Accounting Education, 22*(2), 168–192.

Taylor, P. (2013). Putting theory to work–aka 'if you don't like academia, why don't you leave?'. *Ephemera: Theory & Politics in Organization, 13*(4), 851–860.

Teichler, U. (2007). Does higher education matter? Lessons from a comparative graduate survey. *European Journal of Education, 42*(1), 11–34.

Tomlinson, M. (2012). Graduate employability: A review of conceptual and empirical themes. *Higher Education Policy, 25*(4), 407–431.

Tomusk, V. (2004). Three bolognas and a pizza pie: Notes on institutionalization of the European higher education system. *International Studies in Sociology of Education, 14*(1), 75–96.

Tran, N. C. (2006). *Universities as drivers of the urban economies in Asia: The case of Vietnam* (Policy Research Working Paper). World Bank.

Tran, T. T. (2012a). Graduate employability: Interpretation versus expectation. In N. Brown, S. M. Jones, & A. Adam (Eds.), *Research and development in higher education: Connections in higher education* (Vol. 35, pp. 317–325). Hobart: HERDSA.

Tran, T. T. (2012b). Vietnamese higher education and the issue of enhancing graduate employability. *Journal of Teaching and Learning for Graduate Employability, 3*(1), 64–78.

Tran, T. T. (2013a). Count the uncounted: Rumors, corruption and luck in job seeking by Vietnamese university graduates. *Journal of Asian Critical Education, 2*, 3–12.

Tran, T. T. (2013b). Is the learning approach of students from the Confucian heritage culture problematic? *Educational Research for Policy and Practice, 12*(1), 57–65.

Tran, T. T. (2013c). The perception of employability and the subsequent role of higher education in Vietnam. *Journal of the World Universities Forum, 6*(1), 1–11.

Tran, T. T. (2014). *Graduate employability in Vietnam: A loose relationship between higher education and employment market.* Hamburg: Anchor Academic Publishing.

Tran, T. T. (2015a). Is graduate employability the 'whole-of-higher-education-issue'? *Journal of Education and Work, 28*(3), 207–227.

Tran, T. T. (2015b). *Youth transition to employment in Vietnam: A vulnerable path of transition.* Paper presented at the 20th international research conference on business, economics and social sciences, IRC-2015, Istanbul, Turkey.

Tran, T. T. (2016). Chất lượng đầu ra của giáo dục đại học (The outcome quality of Vietnam higher education). In CERA (Ed.), *Báo cáo thường niên giáo dục Việt nam 2015* (Vietnam Annual Education Report 2015) (pp. 78–104). Hanoi: Vietnam National University Press.

Tran, Q. T., & Swierczek, F. W. (2009). Skills development in higher education in Vietnam. *Asia Pacific Business Review, 15*(4), 565–586.

Truong, Q. D. (2006). Quality of business graduates in Vietnamese institutions: Multiples perspectives. *Journal of Management Development, 26*(7), 629–643.

UNESCO. (2012). *Graduate employability in Asia.* Bangkok: Asia Pacific Regional Bureau for Education, UNESCO Bangkok.

Vietnamese Government. (2015). *Về việc thực hiện Luật Giáo dục đại học và vấn đề giải quyết việc làm cho sinh viên tốt nghiệp* (Report on the implementation of higher education law and the issue of employment for recent graduates) (Report Number 174/BC-CP).

Weligamage, S. S. (2009). *Graduates' employability skills: Evidence from literature review.* Kelaniya: University of Kelaniya.

World Bank. (2008). *Vietnam: Higher education and skills for growth* (p. 195). Hanoi: Human Development Department East Asia and Pacific Region.

World Bank. (2012). *Putting higher education to work, skill and research for growth in East Asia* (World bank East Asia and Lacific Regional Report, p. 195). Washingon, DC: The World Bank.

World Economic Forum. (2015). *The global competitiveness report 2015–2016.* Geneva: World Economic Forum.

Yorke, M. (2006). *Employability in higher education: What it is – What it is not* (Vol. 1). York: The Higher Education Academy.

Chapter 7
Work-Integrated Learning for Enhancing Graduate Employability: Moving from the Periphery to the Centre of the Curriculum

Nhai Thi Nguyen, Ly Thi Tran, and Truc Thi Thanh Le

Abstract The chapter draws on an Australian branch campus case in Vietnam. It addresses how work-integrated learning (WIL) is incorporated into curriculum, pedagogies and institutional support. The findings show that WIL enhances students' work readiness, strengthens industry linkages and improves graduate employability. WIL should therefore be shifted from the periphery to the core of curriculum, teaching and learning, and institutional policy making. It calls for a joint effort of different stakeholders including students, academics, institution support staff, employers, policy makers and related communities.

Introduction

Since the introduction of Economic Reforms (Doi Moi) in 1986 and the promotion of the socialist-oriented market economy, Vietnamese universities have been facing numerous challenges such as market competition, higher education massification and consumerism (Nguyen 2018). Under pressure to become more commercially driven institutions, Vietnamese universities must respond timely and effectively to the labour market needs while engaging immensely with the local communities. Importantly, they have to warrant that their graduates are employable after graduation.

Widely applied in medicine, law, physiotherapy, nursing and teaching, work-integrated learning (WIL) has been seen as an important strategy for enhancing university graduates' employability skills so that these graduates can successfully

N. T. Nguyen (✉)
Monash College, Clayton, VIC, Australia
e-mail: Nhai.Nguyen@monashcollege.edu.au

L. T. Tran · T. T. T. Le
Deakin University, Burwood, VIC, Australia

© Springer Nature Singapore Pte Ltd. 2019   113
N. T. Nguyen, L. T. Tran (eds.), *Reforming Vietnamese Higher Education*,
Education in the Asia-Pacific Region: Issues, Concerns and Prospects 50,
https://doi.org/10.1007/978-981-13-8918-4_7

practise their occupation after graduation (Department of Innovation Universities and Skills 2008; Ministry of Education and Training 2008; Nguyen et al. 2016a, b). WIL bridges the gap between university curriculum and industry's needs and demands; it also links academic domain to the professional world (Fleming 2015; Jackson 2015; Orrell 2011; Patrick et al. 2008). It has various forms, ranging from fieldtrips, internships, work placements, practicum, project-based learning experience to voluntary work in industry. Additionally, it varies from physical to online and virtual modes. Except for teacher education and medical education, WIL has been far from being fully integrated into the VHE curriculum.

Drawing on a case study at an Australian branch campus in Vietnam, this chapter addresses how WIL has been translated into curriculum design, teaching pedagogies and support system. It starts with a critical literature review of WIL and its relation to higher education curricula, followed by an explication of research design. Subsequently, it will present and discuss key research findings on WIL in relation to intended learning outcomes (ILOs), WIL pedagogies and support system and the changing roles of lecturers as well as cross-sectoral career mobility. The chapter finally puts forward implications for curriculum design, teaching and learning as well as institutional and governmental policy making.

Work-Integrated Learning

Initially, Patrick et al. (2008) describe WIL as an overarching term that defines a plethora of approaches and strategies. These approaches and strategies combine theories and practice in the curriculum which is often designed with a defined purpose (Patrick et al. 2008; Vallely and Wilkinson, 2008). Therefore, WIL must serve as a purposeful component of teaching pedagogy and curriculum rather than a non-intentional or an add-on feature (Patrick et al. 2008; Atkinson et al. 2005).

WIL programs or experiences align theories with work experiences (Fleming 2015; Jackson 2015; Orrell 2011; Patrick et al. 2008). WIL can be done either onshore or offshore and can be paid or unpaid work. It has various forms such as work placements, internships, practicum, field work, service learning, work-based project, industry project, industry experience, work experience, co-operative education, sandwich course and job shadowing (Smith et al. 2009; von Treuer et al. 2010; Jackson 2013). It can occur either on campus or in off-campus settings which are industries, health sectors, schools and government offices. It may have different durations, and its learning outcomes can or cannot be identified and assessed (Smith et al. 2009). Furthermore, WIL may or may not involve placements in a workplace or a community.

According to Orrell (2011), WIL can be either non-credited or credited. On the one hand, WIL can be a non-credited subject and is comprised of both academic theories and practice if its objective is merely for students to gain some work experience. On the other hand, WIL programs may encompass on-campus or workplace learning activities to earn credits (Beard and Wilson 2006; Reeders 2000, cited in Orrell 2011, p. 5).

WIL can warrant success on the condition that sufficient preparation is provided for students and staff (Freudenberg et al. 2010, 2011; Armatas and Papadopoulos 2013; Tran and Soejatminah 2016, 2017). For instance, research confirms that students' insufficient preparation and lack of necessary generic skills have actually impeded WIL (Freudenberg et al. 2010, 2011). Conjointly, limited resources, excessive number of students and student diversity in WIL programs present challenges for WIL implementation. Simpson and Gates (2014) are in agreement with this point, listing a number of difficulties for implementing WIL such as compliance with accreditation, professional membership, risk management, network building, training of workplace supervisors, student supervision during and after workplace, management of students in multiple campuses and the design of WIL in new courses where WIL has not traditionally been a component of the learning programs.

HE Curriculum and WIL

VHE reforms have received enormous government funding and investment (Nguyen and Tran 2017). Unfortunately, higher education quality remains far from satisfaction. VHE curriculum appears to inadequately and timely respond to the changing society's needs and demands for high-quality human resources. Indeed, the VHE curriculum does not seem to meaningfully relate to the socialist-oriented market economy, local demands and increased regional and international integration (Pham 2011; Tran 2006; Tran et al. 2014b).

In other words, the disconcertedness between curriculum, industry needs and labour market demands has been commonly cited for this issue, resulting in an increase in unemployment amongst university graduates (Nguyen et al. 2016a; Tran and Nguyen 2011; Tran et al. 2014a, b, 2017; Tran and Marginson 2018; Tran and Swierczek 2009; Tran 2013). For instance, the International Labour Organization (ILO) reported that the Vietnamese university graduates' unemployment rate had been doubled within just 4 years, from 2010 to 2014 (Ngan 2015). The Ministry of Labour, Invalids and Social Affairs, MOLISA for short (MOLISA, March 2016), estimated that in the first quarter of 2016, there were around 417,000 unemployed people. Further to this point, World Bank's survey found that up to 60% of university graduates were not work-ready. In fact, they needed re-training (Tran n.d.). The paradox is, as the World Bank pointed out, despite a high graduate unemployment rate (Pham 2015; World Bank 2012), there was a significant lack of qualified personnel and practitioners both in companies and in trades (World Bank 2012). The USAID Connecting Mekong through Training and Education (USAID COMET) shares similar findings. It indicated that amongst 70% of employers in the Mekong Region, only 16% of them could find graduates with the skills they needed (USAID, 2019). The USAID stressed the importance of gaining necessary skills required of young people in the Lower Mekong region to meet the market demands. In a similar vein, the Profession-Oriented Higher Education (POHE) project funded by the Dutch Government interviewed 350 Vietnamese academics concerning university-business collaboration (UBC) in 2015. It found that there was a skills gap and a mismatch between the supply-side universities and the demand-side business. Universities tended to have very limited knowledge of what the business demanded and vice versa (Littooij 2015a, b).

Bisland and colleagues (Bilsland et al. 2014, 2015), who researched WIL in a foreign university in Vietnam, support this line of argument. They showed that there was an absence of a dialogue between university and workplace supervisors. Nor was there an intersectoral conversation amongst students, workplace supervisors and university academic advisers. Consequently, the disconnection amongst these stakeholders tended to impede the impacts of placement and its "capacity of internship placements to deliver desired workplace learning practice and capability development to interns" (Bisland et al. 2015, p. 188). Echoing Tran's (2012) study, these scholars critically noted:

> The lack of university involvement in the work placement establishment or process leads to unsystematic, unstructured internships. The learning experience of the intern is fortuitous rather than targeted and planned. (ibid.)

Apart from that, the existing VHE curriculum appears to rely heavily on formal academic learning, which overemphasises theoretical knowledge and political indoctrination. At the same time, it pays insufficient attention to improve practical knowledge, work readiness, soft skills and other important attributes which are imperative for graduates' employability (Tran 2013; Tran and Swierczek 2009). The problem lies in the fact that political content – a compulsory component of the curriculum, occupies around 25% of the total curriculum content (Vallely and Wilkinson 2008). Besides, the current curriculum seems to be too slow to catch up with rapid global changes, technological innovations and international developments (Ministry of Education and Training 2003, 2008; Tran et al. 2014a, b; Vietnamese Government 1993, 2005).

To tackle these problems at root, various strategies in an attempt to align the VHE curriculum with labour market needs and demands have been prioritised in the Vietnam's Strategy for Education Development 2011–2020 (Thủ Tướng Chính Phủ 2012). To illustrate, the national high-stake examinations have been shifted from traditional testing and assessment methods to incorporate more practical assessment tasks. These new assessment tasks require students to demonstrate critical, reflective thinking and creative learning (Tran et al. 2014a, b). Active teaching and learning practices have emerged as a remedy for the traditional passive learning culture and rote memorisation of factual knowledge. Tran et al. (2014a, b) observe that these teaching and learning practices remain largely fragmented and ad hoc due to the lack of a coherent, systemic support structure, albeit this remarkable change in the practices of critical thinking and deep learning across the sector.

The Ministry of Education and Training (MOET) issued the Circular 07/2015/ TT-BGDĐT on 16 April 2015, which required both public and private universities in Vietnam to involve industry representatives and employers in developing and evaluating undergraduate and postgraduate curricula. In other words, different stakeholders, especially industry leaders and professional organisations, were to be given a voice in shaping the VHE curriculum. Curriculum content, pedagogy and assessment must be appropriated and/or renewed in a way that they arm university graduates with practical knowledge, experiences, soft skills, professional attributes and professional portfolios required for the world of work. Tran et al. (2014a, b) take this point further, emphasising the importance of increasing industry engagement and making the curriculum closer to the labour market's needs. This can be done via introducing practicum and internship, balancing theory and practice and putting more weight on job-related training in a specialised subject. Another research conducted by Pham and Tran (2013) attests to this line of argument and claims work-integrated learning programs, such as alumni engagement, career networking events and employment advisory capability, are equally important for improving graduate employability. Tran et al. (2014a, b) are in agreement with this point, calling for the need to

> set up a basic guiding framework for the subject-specific syllabus, which stipulates work skills and generic skills, meanwhile raising wider social awareness of the potency of work placement because of its present significant contribution to national capacity building and social development. (2014a, b, pp. 104–105)

Successful stories of WIL projects have been witnessed in the Vietnamese universities and colleges. For example, the University of Economics in Ho Chi Minh City and Hanoi Foreign Trade University are amongst the pioneering higher education (HE) providers which partner with local industry to support work-integrated learning programs (Lam 2013, cited in Bilsland et al. 2014, p. 148). In addition, five Vietnamese higher institutions have joined the MekongSkills2Work Network, together with seven others in the Lower Mekong region. They have adopted a work-integrated learning training model to help students master new job-focused skills and to better prepare them for relevant and productive employment.

The Study

The research is stemmed from a two-year case study research conducted in an Australian branch campus in Vietnam between 2014 and 2016. It investigated the lecturers' perspectives on work-integrated learning (WIL) and its impacts on teaching pedagogies, curriculum design and support system. It also examined students' viewpoints on the extent to which WIL impacts their employability after university graduation.

The primary author is the principal research investigator. She conducted semi-structured interviews with over 20 lecturers across a number of disciplines: professional communication, design, fashion merchandising, accounting, economics, marketing and engineering. Between 2015 and 2016, she led a team of junior student scholars and conducted in-depth interviews with over 40 students in Ho Chi Minh City and surveyed 173 university graduates and alumni nationwide.

The data used in this book chapter is extracted from the first research participant category, the university lecturers, which explored in great depth their perception of WIL and how they integrated WIL in curriculum design and teaching practices as well as support system. The research participants represented a mixture of local Vietnamese academics and expatriates, ranging from novice teachers with less than 3 years of teaching experience to the very experienced who have at least 15–20 years of teaching and industry experiences.

Each interview required approximately 1 hour. By means of interviews, the research participants shared their insights into how they embedded WIL in curriculum design, course materials development, teaching practices, student support, and their shifting roles of a lecturer, alongside cross-sectoral career mobility.

Data was collected from a number of supplementary sources, such as university-wide WIL workshop series, flagship internship programs and a series of career-oriented programs, which were rolled out by the Career Centre at the branch campus in addition to personal observation.

Findings and Discussion

Translating Industry's Demands and Requirements into WIL's Curriculum and Intended Learning Outcomes (ILOs)

As said, WIL used to be offered in few vocational programs. It has now been expanded to massive undergraduate and postgraduate programs in many countries with explicit intended learning outcomes (ILOs) which serve as the beginning and the end result of curriculum design and teaching practices. Kennedy and colleagues remark that:

> … As noted, however, programs within higher education come to increasingly focus on specific outcomes of the provision of practice based experiences is shifting from being included in a limited select number of occupations to a wider range and number of programs and it [practice bandwagon including practice-based learning and work-based learning] sometimes seems almost universally, as there emerge imperatives to make employment relevant programs that have no specific outcomes. Hence, it becomes a concern for nearly all discipline areas within universities. (Kennedy et al. 2015, p. 6)

Allen, Pavlin and Van der Velden (2011, cited in Pavlin 2013) researched how graduates' employment is correlated with, amongst many other factors, *the learning outcomes approach* (DEHEMS Project 2013). They argued traditional teaching must be intertwined with problem-based learning, assessment modes and support system so as to inform employers and graduates about what is expected of university graduates. In doing so, this learning outcome approach can partially garner WIL's success (Pavlin 2013).

Our research findings on the interconnectedness between ILOs and WIL success are resonated with Allen and colleagues' research in a number of ways. First, the overall response to how lecturers align course and curriculum design in our research appears to be positive. Most research participants agree that central to WIL curriculum design is identifying what learning outcomes are intended for students. Second, for a number of the research informants, these intended learning outcomes (ILOs) become principles for improving, appropriating, and/or redesigning course and renewing curriculum. Third, lecturers are required to consider the needs of all stakeholders – students and industry partners – together with learning goals underpinning WIL as is guided in the Branch Campus Online Toolkit. As a result, subject matter knowledge and the skills set must be updated on a regular basis allowing students to prepare and transition smoothly into the workplace. These practices extend curriculum beyond to respond to students' emerging needs and to meet changing demands of the local labour market, especially in creative industries such as professional communication, design and fashion. One of the lecturers recalls how she aligned her Strategic PR Planning course design with ILOs. She enthusiastically shared:

> But with Strategic PR Planning course, WIL really aligns with ILOs. Most of the ILOs in this course are to get students ready for their work. They would be able to apply their knowledge and skills in the real projects, and they have to respond to the client requirements and they could apply creativity into the project. So they totally match with one another. (Female lecturer, Professional Communication)

Admitting that integrating WIL in curriculum design is a challenge for the lecturers and that it can be applied to a particular course, she added:

> For other courses, it will be more challenging. Because when you designed WIL, you have to think of what kind of activities, what kind of topics you gonna apply. I find that it will be a lot easier if WIL is applied to some capstone courses, the courses that students will have to generate the project rather than the contextual course and the foundation course. (Female lecturer, Professional Communication)

Interestingly, another lecturer explicated how ILOs had been aligned to her course when designing curriculum and syllabus. As for her, she followed closely the university and the branch campus guidelines to make sure of consistency across these campuses. This lighthoused her teaching plan, in-class and extra-curricular activities. She enthusiastically shared:

> Before I design any assignments, I actually look at the University Course Outline carefully first and then I will make sure that I fulfil all the course outlines…then I will design a week 1-12 what I am going to do, what are my expectations, what are my assignments all that all in one document and put it on my Google document and share with them. So they will know what is going to happen right from week 1 to week 12. (Female lecturer, Design)

As the above excerpt indicates, ILOs have become the springboard for making pedagogy-related decisions. Besides, ILOs are not meant solely for serving students' needs and interests. Nor are they determined by institution and lecturers. Rather, they must respond to industry's demands and requirements. One research participant spoke of the importance of industry involvement and feedback in designing and implementing novel courses of the undergraduate program. Subsequently, industry's feedback and comments have been well received, responded appropriately in a timely manner, translated into designing curriculum, defining intended learning outcomes, selecting assessment and evaluation and, finally, choosing relevant teaching and learning materials. The case of the Vietnamese for Professional Communication is an example. One lecturer expanded this diameter of WIL, saying that:

> The course (Vietnamese for ProfComm Professional Communication) was designed as a response to the industry feedback and request. You know most of the students here have to learn in English. When they go to work in the industry, they have to speak and use Vietnamese most of the time. This is a big problem for them. They need to communicate with the media, the client and also writing articles for companies in Vietnamese. (Male lecturer, Professional Vietnamese)

Apart from designing new courses to respond in a timely fashion to industry's demands, a number of our research participants subscribed to the perspective that industry linkages hold significant implications for curriculum design and teaching pedagogies. One form of this linkage is, mentioned by a large number of research participants, introducing industry guest lecture series, industry mentoring and coaching projects to course delivery. Other effective forms include capstone courses such as industry-based projects (Nguyen et al. 2016a, b). Upon introducing these industrial linkage projects, the research participants stressed the importance of discussing with industry's experts and leaders on how the project could be embedded effectively with practical work experiences.

The connection between curriculum and industry is further enhanced by the 'Profession-Oriented Higher Education' (POHE) project funded by the Dutch Government (Littooij 2015a, b). The POHE validates the role of involving industry in designing and implementing the curriculum; it also appreciates lecturers' contribution to curriculum design. For example, the employers participating in the project were invited to co-design the curriculum and help student transition into industry smoothly. The lecturers conducted interviews and implemented workshops and discussions with industries. As a result, they could stocktake what industry's expectation and requirement of their graduates are. Further to this point, they were able to bridge both academic knowledge to professional knowledge and skills. These lecturers and their teaching teams and management then redesigned the curriculum incorporating the state-of-the art knowledge and connecting theories with practice.

Our research also corroborates, to a certain extent, with the USAID COMET (USAID, 2019) project. Implemented in the Mekong provinces in Southern Vietnam, the USAID COMET project stressed the role of linking comprehensively the Vietnamese higher institutions and their students with employers. With 20 higher institution participants, the project researched the regional labour market, and assessed and identified priorities, challenges and opportunities emergent in this region. It interviewed employers, education institutions and job-seekers. Subsequently, participants were trained with skills in demand in the Lower Mekong region. The outcomes of the project have been reported to be highly impactful for 34,000 student participants from Burma (Myanmar), Cambodia, Laos, Thailand and Vietnam in 2016.

Precisely, ILOs and industry's demands and requirements have been central to every stage of WIL. Industry representatives have worked closely with university lecturers on speculating clearly the intended learning outcomes, course content, mode of delivering brief, mentoring and support scheme. These industry guests are invited to walk in, deliver the brief and supervise projects in collaboration with the lecturers. Additionally, they contribute to outlining key performance indicators (KPIs) for course assessments as well as evaluate and provide feedback on students' performance. The coming section will explore how lecturers WIL embed pedagogies in delivering WIL curriculum while pinpointing cross-sectoral staff mobility as a direct result of WIL.

WIL Pedagogies

WIL pedagogy involves selecting relevant teaching content, designing effective teaching materials, choosing a wide range of modes of instructions and teaching activities, and creating a vibrant, caring learning environment for students. It is combined with practice-led learning activities in which students obtain more hands-on experiences. These are coupled with simulated learning such as imagined and real cases and scenarios. The Centre for Innovation in Learning and Teaching, Flinders University[1] (n.d.) supports this point and states that:

> In cases where placement in professional work situations cannot be arranged, Work-Integrated Learning topics should be designed to provide for placements in settings that simulate professional work situations as realistically as possible.

Effective implementation of WIL pedagogy accelerates positive learning experiences for students. It insinuates useful simulated learning contexts and activities. The university outlines, for instance, the benefits of applying simulated workplace in teaching practices in which WIL teaching activities are planned as a compensation for the lack of placements and internships. This is because a simulated learning context offers the best choice when there are concerns and hesitations relating to ethics, safety and professional reasons in placement and/or internship. These environments simulate real workplaces in their function, equipment and mode of operation so that students can experience a variety of scenarios and activities similar to the real workplace. In this process, industry partners are proactive to co-constructing curriculum and providing feedback to students. In disciplines with a heavy practice-based component such as engineering, medicine, communication, design, law, chemistry, simulated workplaces equipped with labs, studios, courts and mock hospital wards become paramount. These activities could be either on-campus or off-campus, online or offline (University's WIL Guide).

When interviewing how Professional Communication and Fashion Merchandising lecturers incorporated WIL in their teaching pedagogies, what truly captivates our interests is that a large proportion of our research informants agree that WIL has to

---

[1] Retrieved from https://www.flinders.edu.au/ppmanual/teaching-course-management/guidelines-design-work-integrated-learning.cf

be incorporated into every aspect of teaching and curriculum in the Professional Communication and Fashion Merchandising courses. Most of them embrace *authentic WIL experiences* gained through a series of bona fide tasks and genuine interactions with real industry experts. The majority of lecturers require students to attend client brief, research consumer insights via doing field work, conduct surveys and face-to-face interviews, set up networks with industry experts, and finally, deliver client pitch. More to the point, lecturers encourage more direct exposure to the real world of work. One lecturer asserts that "So basically, it's [WIL] just the real thing. Testing with the real people and working with the real department." Clearly, popular vocabularies as "real-life examples", "practical application of theories", "real client", "real project", to name a few, have been repeatedly mentioned in numerous interview excerpts. The overall responses suggest that pertinent to the lecturers' viewpoint is WIL serves as a doorway to professionalism. Students are treated as real professionals with specific codes of conduct, high quality of work and productivity. The collection of lecturers' voices delineates the point vividly in the following excerpts:

> Definitely yes. As I mention, instead of getting students to do simulated scenarios, we get students to work with real clients. We get client briefing and the student can obtain the requirements from the client. I can tell they are very much the same as the reality, the client briefing in reality. Also students have client meeting and the pitching. They have to pitch their ideas to the client. Also, I have some in-class activities that equip students with skills. *.. So basically, it's just the real thing. Testing with the real people and working with the real department.* (Female lecturer, Professional Communication, emphasis added)

One female research participant reinvigorates this perspective and comments that:

> Yes, we got an activity where students have to visit the company, interview the head or the manager and then they come back to report the outcomes to me. Then they've got to do the client project. At the end of the course, they have to present the project to the client and send the result to this client. From that, you can monitor the process and the project and try to improve their professionalism. They also represent the image of University A. *So they need to work in a very professional way. They are not just a student. Now they are also the professionals [who are] working for University A.* So they need to work in a correct way with the high-quality product and outcome. (Female lecturer, Professional Communication, emphasis added)

Another research participant reemphasised the value of practical application of theories in practice. She remarks that there had been a practical component embedded in the course she taught which clearly assisted the local students in comprehending the knowledge provided in the textbooks written in foreign countries. She succinctly accentuated that:

> The course is managed by coordinator and they already incorporate some real-life examples, about the *practical application of certain types of theories* that travels their knowledge from the academic textbook written in a foreign, estranged country to the local students. (Female lecturer, Professional Communication, emphasis added)

One male design lecturer accepted this point and added that:

> Yes, I want it [the design course] to be practical. (Male lecturer, Design)

This opinion is further supported by another female research participant in professional communication who underlined the connection between her industry work experiences which help connect theories to the real practices for students to quality WIL learning. She shared:

> And a lot of cases have I could say this from my experience, I experienced this before and I know how it works... *This is a really real experience and I think it makes a lot more sense for the students.* (Female lecturer, General Manager of an advertising agency, Professional Communication, emphasis added)

As an overall most of the research informants tend to align their WIL teaching practices with students' future occupation, industry connection and the real world of work outside of the university which had been discussed previously. One lecturer explained how her industry experiences had paid tribute to enhancing WIL class activities. Her WIL pedagogy, or so to speak, asserts the role of appropriating the prescribed curriculum at the branch campus. She critically noted:

> So in the materials, *we localize the materials and the cases relevant to the context of Vietnam.* For my teaching, I also share with them some of my industrial experiences in the workplace, what PR involves and what advertising involves in my workplace so that they could recognize this difference straightaway. (Female lecturer, General Manager of an advertising agency, Professional Communication, emphasis added)

Findings of this research resonate with WIL pedagogies utilised in the USAID[2] COMET project (2019). In this project, the student participants learned how to explore real-world problems through project-based learning and a plethora of work-based learning activities. The students accessed online experiential learning toolkit and had internships as part of the curriculum. Also, they engaged with employers in novel approaches. Teaching in these pilot universities offered various formats and exposed students to authentic situations in real businesses (Littooij 2015a, b). The project has created region-wide impacts on students' employability.

The power of using WIL pedagogies is additionally validated by the POHE project[3]. Overall the POHE project developed competency-based education applied in pilot universities. In conjunction with enhancing professional capacities for the Vietnamese students, the project had implemented 50 training programs in these pilot universities. Nearly 2000 students have graduated from the POHE's training programs, 85% of whom were successful in finding jobs within 3 months after graduation (Vietnam News 2016). The POHE project team surveyed over 4000

---

[2] The USAID COMET project aims to help 20 higher education institutions and train 120,000 youths with skills in demand in the Lower Mekong region. Countries participating in and benefitting from this project include Burma (Myanmar), Cambodia, Laos, Thailand and Vietnam. These skills are, lists USAID, the ability to adapt to the new technologies, team work, communication and interpersonal skills. Via the MekongSkills2Work Network, university and vocational instructors were trained in dynamic classroom approaches. Intel, Cisco and Microsoft participated as industrial partners and provided mentorship, workshops for "women in technology" and externship to Austin, Texas, and build professional network within this Lower Mekong region.

[3] The POHE project was funded by the Dutch Government. It tackled the challenges that Vietnamese graduates had been facing when entering the labour market.

students and employers in 2013 and found that 80% of employers were satisfied with the graduates from these programs (Littooij 2015a, b).

Clearly, industry involvement cannot garner success if WIL preparation provided by the lecturers is either limited or absent. This means that there must be a radical shift in teacher's roles and duties compared to how they have been traditionally positioned. Immense engagement with industry experts and professionals has brought about increasing cross-sectoral career and staff mobility, which will be discussed in the subsequent section.

Shifting Lecturer's Roles and Duties and Mobilising Cross-Sectoral Staff

University lecturers play a central role in designing and implementing WIL (Kennedy et al. 2015, p. 5). Prominent in our research findings is that there has been a shifting role of the lecturer's duties and cross-sectoral staff mobility brought about by WIL. Primarily, there are a considerable number of industry experts and professionals who have been directly engaged in designing and delivering WIL curriculum, teaching, assessment and evaluation, as well as supervision of student placement as both university lecturer and placement supervisor. In fact, industry experts and professionals have increasingly been holding various teaching and support positions in WIL-related courses; they can be part-time lecturers, guest speakers or sessional teaching staff. The essence of WIL implementation at the branch campus suggests a radical shift in the traditional perspective of and the complex and overlapping lecturer's roles and duties (Kennedy et al. 2015). To illustrate, one lecturer accentuates that wearing dual hats as a part-time lecturer and a general manager of a leading advertising agency in Ho Chi Minh City has allowed her to pass her decades-long industry experiences onto students.

> It's all about change. I worked in client service for 10 years and then I moved on to management for a while … After 20 years, you feel like "I don't want to do it, I'm too tired", "I want to do something different" … I like to coach people in my role before I do the training for staff as well so maybe something I will share my experience and my knowledge to young people. (Female lecturer and General Manager of an advertising agency)

However, WIL does not stop short at that. As one research participant mentioned, WIL bridges industry with the future workforce. She headhunted for her advertising agency. As a HR manager of a famous global advertising agency, teaching in university undergraduate program was the best way to headhunt junior talents for her organisation and the industry.

Besides, cross-sectoral career mobility is intertwined with an aspiration of doing something different and generating impacts on the future generation of professionals. She accepts enthusiastically her new role and new identities as an industrial coach for undergraduate students. The following excerpt best illustrates her point:

… I'm desperate before when I interview people and I'm like why can't I find the good people? Where is the next generation for advertising? It's so hard to find here you know and uh, why I need to do something about it. (Female lecturer and General Manager of an advertising agency)

In other words, there has been a cross-sectoral staff mobility, be it temporal or permanent, with wider and more active participation of industry experts and professionals in conducting every step of WIL curriculum. This is appended with an aspiration of creating positive changes in the future professional generation and of headhunting talents at university when industry experts and professionals undertake part-time or casual teaching positions.

In addition to cross-sectoral career mobility, lecturer's roles have been navigated towards building a caring lecturer–student relationship. Another research informant gives prominence to lecturer–student relationship building, in which the lecturer's high expectation on students, student empowerment and equality are fundamental. Interestingly, one research participant pinpointed how Asian culture and particularly the Vietnamese one shaped the ways in which she saw herself as a "master" in Chinese culture or a "sensei" in Japanese culture. To the lecturer, having a high expectation for students, pushing them hard, giving them full autonomy and providing sufficient support and assistance along the way whenever students need is imperative to her WIL pedagogies. She noted:

What I love about Asian culture and Vietnam is the sensei in Japanese, or the master in Chinese is that the teachers expect all the students to surpass him/her. It's what I know from Asian culture. It's what I accept and it's what I actually look for from the students. Because most of the time, being honest to you, as a student, I didn't reach that point. So it's pushing them but at the same time, setting them free to fly and supporting them because they don't know how to fly. So, hey, *I'm here to catch you if you need me.* ... (Female lecturer, Fashion Merchandising, emphasis added)

Our research points to another interesting finding. Shifting the lecturer's roles in WIL implementation is extended to building an equal lecturer–student relationship. This equality informs teaching principles and practices. For instance, one research participant accepted this point and drew particular attention to exploring the ways in which equality influenced her students in her Design course. Her principle of pedagogy and teaching philosophy rests on a strong belief that "Everybody is equal. There is no such thing as hierarchy" (to cite the participant's voice as an illustration). These hold significant implications for her as a lecturer. To interpret the participant, her roles and duties must accord with the principles of teacher–student equality, teacher's non-dictatorship teaching style, student empowerment and creativity. She says:

It [the distance between the lecturer and students] doesn't work that way. *If you actually in the creative environment, everybody is equal. There is no such thing as hierarchy. Once there is a hierarchy, people will feel there is a barrier and they will not be open to share so they will not be open to share their ideas which defeats the purpose so it wouldn't work.* I am not going to dictate them, tell them: you must do this, you must do that. It's pointless because design is a very personal project or a very personal outcome so in the end I want them to create their own style, their own way of finding out. I might give them a rough framework about how they should do but in the end they have to find their own way. (Female lecturer, Design, emphasis added)

Precisely, lecturers' roles and duties have been reoriented towards WIL implementation in regard to specific courses and units at the branch campus. New roles and duties have been appended to the lecturers' traditional responsibilities and identities such as coaching, aspiration, headhunting, lecturer–student equality and renewed lecturer's identities. Moreover, teachers' non-dictatorship style, student empowerment and creativity go hand in hand with the lecturer's high expectation placed on students and a creation of a comprehensive support system which is accessible to all students. In addition, WIL has resulted in increasing cross-sectoral career and staff mobility with intensive participation of industry experts and professionals in conducting every step of WIL including pre-WIL, during-WIL and post-WIL stage. The coming section will address how building the support system is significant for WIL success.

WIL Support System

Our research, while largely agreeing with Tran's argument (Tran 2013), validates the point that university lecturers play an equally important role in improving graduate employability (Bilsland et al. 2014, 2015). Paradoxically, academic lecturers' involvement and supports are often unrecognised in Vietnamese universities. Our observation at the branch campus reveals the opposite. Most of the lecturer participants were receptive to WIL; they considered it an integral part of their teaching duties and roles. They argued that lecturers' support must be intensified, individualised and specialised, and that no one could do it better than the lecturers themselves. The level of details, comprehensiveness and diversity of extra-curricular activities can, in the research participants' opinions, help bring students closer to the industry. As a result, it motivates students to learn about, to raise their awareness and thus, to be fully prepared for the standards and the expectations of the industry in which they are entering. Lecturers advocated strongly for utilising diverse sources of support, which range from coaching, mentoring and extra training to building industry-student linkages.

I've been really supportive. If you want to see me any time, I say "ok. 15 minutes." So I've been really flexible… But anyway, we want them to be the best. Also, their own success is reflecting your success. (Male lecturer, Design)

Again, I am not sure of the term transformational learning. *But for the transformational leadership, I do not give the students' daily tasks but inspire them…*We could push them hard and get them do the task. But at the end of the day, they do need to maintain their enthusiasm. I know it's difficult. Using the transformational leadership, *I tried to inspire them and give as much support as I could. Informal support and not providing them with clear task.* (Female academic, Professional Communication, emphasis added)

As indicated by the research participants' excerpts above, WIL support has been provided in a number of ways. It is accompanied with lecturers' teaching practices such as being understanding and flexible with students. It is integrated with the less autocratic classroom management styles in which the lecturer is flexible and empathetic with students. More interestingly, lecturer's support is accorded with transformational leadership style, the style which immensely motivates and inspires students to maintain their enthusiasm and complete the tasks, according to a number of research participants.

Furthermore, imperative for WIL's success is the institutional provision of extra-curricular activities. Sattler and Peters (2013) assured that WIL assisted students a great deal in transitioning from university to workplace, especially in the fields requiring high skills. WIL, argued these scholars, oriented their career plan towards building resilience and abilities in time of economic downturns, uncertainties and life challenges. It simultaneously stimulated engagement across sectors (Sattler and Peters 2013). Our research points towards the core elements of extra-curricular activities at the branch campus. They include Career Edge program designed to enhance soft skills and on-campus career advising and career planning services. These WIL multimodalities exemplify how WIL thickens students' industry-related experiences and at the same time boosts their work readiness and employability.

It should be noted that Vietnamese cultural modalities have been more or less present in this research, especially in relation to students' and family's awareness and attitudes towards their career trajectories. However, from the participating lecturers' perspectives, most of whom are foreign expats and have been living and working in Vietnam for a comparatively long time, the cultural traits, such as Confucianism, Buddhism, Marxism and Leninism as elaborated by Nguyen (2018) in Chapter 2, did not seem to be prominent and/or hinder WIL success. The branch campus has its own curriculum independent of the top-down, centralised curriculum imposed by the Ministry of Education and Training (MOET). The institutional autonomy and its independence of the politically doctrined curriculum in the mainstream universities appear to determine the accomplishment of WIL in this branch campus.

Conclusion: Connecting the Dots Beyond WIL

WIL enacts high-quality teaching pedagogies; it is therefore useful to capitalise on student human capitals and enhance their work readiness. WIL is perceived to unpack a suitcase of fundamental generic skills and attributes, knowledge of the field and the workplace so that they could cope well with the labour market and industry challenges upon graduation, especially at times of economic turmoil. WIL, with its work-related activities implemented across a range of disciplines, is able to link all stakeholders together: students, parents, academics, industry and communities. Curricula and pedagogies must encourage students to seek and enhance their knowledge in the reciprocity and interrelatedness of graduates' employment and between universities and industry (Pavlin et al. 2009).

The epicentre of pedagogical considerations in curriculum and syllabus design links WIL with the intended learning outcomes (ILOs). Providing that WIL is promoted properly within university curriculum and syllabus – and if done creatively – it exposes students and lecturers to valuable industry linkages and meaningful work-related experiences. Also, WIL curriculum enhances significantly graduate employability skills, professionalism, self-efficacy and teamwork skills and capability to learn in context and reflect on practice. It is therefore crucial to ensure the 'authenticity' of WIL placements, alignment of learning activities and assessments with integrated learning, and to provide a robust, consistent and thorough internal support system in designing and implementing WIL.

WIL builds university's pipelines to industry. It encourages increasing cross-sectoral staff mobility by engaging industry's experts in serving in the university's industry board of advisors; these advisors participate in every step of the university's teaching and learning practices and policy making, ranging from curriculum design, program renewal, teaching and learning, and supervision of student placements. Put it differently, WIL creates more opportunities for mobilising not only knowledge but also staff across different sectors, as is mentioned in the branch campus case.

Institutions must provide a comprehensive support system and an assortment of enriching extra-curricular activities. Particularly, Vietnamese higher education curriculum must move away from being theoretically oriented towards a more pragmatic landscape where curriculum, syllabus, intended learning outcomes, materials, teaching pedagogies and assessments are synchronised with effective WIL teaching practices to enhance student employability and work readiness apart from equipping them with knowledge, skills and attributes. To harvest WIL's benefits, institutional support system needs to be in place and adequately administered. It, in Brown's words, is grounded in "a holistic whole-institution approach to WIL" and is "supported through policy and coordinated practice" (2010, p. 508). As a result, WIL must be embedded into institutional strategic goals. Equally, it must encourage staff to share resources, challenges and examples of good practice.

Preclude to WIL are issues associated with equity and equality. Any justifications, design and implementation of WIL must take into consideration disadvantaged and disabled students. Any decisions relevant to the type and how long WIL should be as well as professional accreditation requirements should be consulted thoroughly. Equally important is being aware of the unnecessary undue hardship for students that WIL might create.

The WIL model, implemented successfully at an Australian branch campus, is potentially useful for VHE institutions. However, it may not guarantee similar impacts and success. WIL implementation has, therefore, to be thoroughly and thoughtfully planned. It must consider a whole range of cultural factors listed by Nguyen (2018) in Chapter 2 and Tran (2018) in Chapter 6 and involve immensely students and their parents. Apart from changing their beliefs and values towards career and employability, students and parents should, however, be proactive to gaining employment and shaping their career pathway.

The WIL case implemented at an Australian branch campus discussed extensively in this chapter can generate more positive impacts and desired learning outcomes, providing that institutional autonomy is granted (see Dao and Hayden 2018, Chapter 3 and Ngo 2018, Chapter 4); the curriculum is independent of political wills; and academic staff are empowered and proactive to taking WIL initiatives. This means academic staff should be empowered to execute their autonomy in deciding curriculum, learning outcomes, teaching materials, designing teaching and learning activities, alongside with introducing more enriched extra-curricular activities. The labour market-friendly curriculum should replace theoretical knowledge with increasing learning opportunities to enhance industry connections, build a robust system of support to help students become work-ready, and finally, minimise negative impacts of the Vietnamese cultural traits. Given political sensitivity in Vietnam in regard to granting full autonomy, especially in relation to the mainstream curriculum, this WIL case of the branch campus showcases a strong link between quality and good governance in HEIs. It validates the point earlier made by Ngo in Chapter 4, stressing that when autonomy is warranted, good HE quality and governance accompany.

The WIL implemented in the Australian branch campus suggests the Triple Helix concept proposed by Etzkowitz (1994) and Etzkowitz and Leydesdorff (1995). Specifically, there must be a paradigm shift in how universities are repositioned in relation to government and industry. In light of this triadic relationship, the Vietnamese universities should no longer be seen as the sole provider of knowledge and skills, but one of the central agents contributing to the socioeconomic development of the society. This means that universities and other institutions must take lead in joint initiatives in partnership with government and industry (Etzkowitz and Leydesdorff 2000). They are required to be more proactive to connecting with industry not only in mobilising knowledge such as producing, circulating and renewing knowledges but also in incorporating industry's voices in teaching, learning, curriculum development, and the process of institutional policy making as well as embracing partnership opportunities and opening their door wider to host cross-sectoral staff mobilities. At the same time, it has to engage immensely with industry experts in every step of their teaching, learning and curriculum development. Equally important is that government policies have to be in place to make sure of an incentive environment in which universities and industry are genuinely, equitably and equally supported.

References

Armatas, C., & Papadopoulos, T. (2013). Approaches to work-integrated learning and engaging industry in vocational ICT courses: Evaluation of an Australian pilot program. *International Journal of Training Research, 11*(1), 56–68. https://doi.org/10.5172/ijtr.2013.11.1.56.

Atkinson, L., Rizzetti, J., & Smith, S. (2005). *Online resources for work integrated learning: A case study in re-usability and flexibility*. Paper presented at the meeting of the Australian Society for Computers in Learning in Tertiary Education, Brisbane, QLD.

Beard, C., & Wilson, J. P. (2006). *Experiential learning: A best practice handbook for educators and trainers*. London/Philadelphia: Kogan Page Publishers.

Bilsland, C., Nagy, H., & Smith, P. (2014). Planning the journey to best practice in developing employability skills: Transnational university internships in Vietnam. *Asia-Pacific Journal of Cooperative Education, 15*(2), 145–157.

Bilsland, C., Nagy, H., & Smith, P. (2015). Planning the journey to best practice in developing employability skills: Transnational university internships in Vietnam. *Asia-Pacific Journal of Cooperative Education, 15*(2), 145–157.

Brown, N. (2010). WIL[ling] to share: An institutional conversation to guide policy and practice in work-integrated learning. *Higher Education Research and Development, 29*(5), 507–518. https://doi.org/10.1080/07294360.2010.502219.

Dao, V. K., & Hayden, M. (2018). Vietnam's progress with policies on university governance, management and quality assurance. In N. T. Nguyen & L. T. Tran (Eds.), *Reforming Vietnamese higher education: Global forces and local demands.* Dordrecht: Springer.

DEHEMS Project. (2013). *Project DEHEMS – Network for the development of higher education management systems.* Ljubljana–Vienna (International). http://www.dehems-project.eu. 15 June 2013.

Department of Innovation Universities and Skills. (2008). *The learning revolution.* UK: Retrieved from https://www.gov.uk/government/uploads/system/uploads/attachment_data/file/238731/7392.pdf

Etzkowitz, H. (1994). Academic-industry relations: A sociological paradigm for economic development. In L. Leydesdorff & P. van den Besselaar (Eds.), *Evolutionary economics and chaos theory: New directions in technology studies* (pp. 139–151). London: Pinter.

Etzkowitz, H., & Leydesdorff, L. (1995). The triple helix—University-industry-government relations: A laboratory for knowledge-based economic development. *EASST Review, 14*, 14–19.

Etzkowitz, H., & Leydesdorff, L. (2000). The dynamics of innovation: From national systems and 'mode 2' to a triple helix of university-industry-government relations. *Research Policy, 29*(2), 109–123.

Fleming, J. (2015). Exploring stakeholders' perspectives of the influences on student learning in cooperative education. *Asia-Pacific Journal of Cooperative Education, 16*(2), 109–119.

Freudenberg, B., Brimble, M., & Cameron, C. (2010). Where there is a WIL there is a way. *Higher Education Research & Development, 29*(5), 575–588.

Freudenberg, B., Brimble, M., & Cameron, C. (2011). WIL and generic skill development: The development of business students' generic skills through work-integrated learning. *Asia-Pacific Journal of Cooperative Education, 12*(2), 79–93.

Jackson, D. (2015). Employability skill development in work-integrated learning: Barriers and best practice. *Studies in Higher Education, 40*(2), 350–367. https://doi.org/10.1080/0307507 9.2013.842221.

Kennedy, M., Billett, S., Gherardi, S., & Grealish, L. (Eds.). (2015). *Practice-based learning in higher education: Jostling cultures.* Dordrecht: Springer.

Littooij, S. (2015a). *University Business Collaboration to enhance graduate employability in Vietnam.* Paper presented at the SEAMEO RETRAC 2015 International Conference, Hochiminh City, Vietnam.

Littooij, S. (2015b). *Business engagement to enhance young people's skills in Vietnam.* Paper presented at the Open University 1st International Conference "Business Corporate Social Responsibility (CSR) and Sustainable Business Development (SBD)", Hochiminh City, Vietnam.

Ministry of Education and Training. (2003). *University charter.* Hanoi: Retrieved from http://www.moj.gov.vn/vbpq/en/lists/vn%20bn%20php%20lut/view_detail.aspx?itemid=7322

Ministry of Education and Training. (2008). *Proposing the advance programs in Vietnamese universities between 2008 and 2015.* Hanoi: MOET.

Ngan, A. (2015). After four years, the unemployment rate doubles. Vietnamnet, 24 April, 2015, Retrieved on 20 September, 2015 from http://vietnamnet.vn/vn/giao-duc/234129/sau-4-nam%2D%2Dcu-nhan-that-nghiep-tang-gap-doi.html

Ngo, M. (2018). University governance in Vietnam and East Asian higher education: Comparative perspectives. In N. T. Nguyen & L. T. Tran (Eds.), *Reforming Vietnamese higher education: Global forces and local demands.* Dordrecht: Springer.

Nguyen, T. N. (2018). The cultural modalities of the Vietnamese higher education. In N. T. Nguyen & L. T. Tran (Eds.), *Reforming Vietnamese higher education: Global forces and local demands*. Dordrecht: Springer.

Nguyen, N., & Tran, L. T. (2017). Looking inward or outward? Vietnam higher education at the superhighway of globalisation: Culture, values and changes. *Journal of Asian Public Policy*, 1–18. https://doi.org/10.1080/17516234.2017.1332457.

Nguyen, H. T. N., Phan, L. N. H., Nguyen, T. T. S., Tran, N. A. L., & Nguyen, T. N. (2016a). *Vietnamese students' perception of employability: An empirical study*. Paper presented at the Global education dialogue: Innovation for employability: University-industry partnership for sustainable economic development, Ho Chi Minh City, 15–16 June 2016.

Nguyen, T. N., Nguyen, H. T. N., & Phan, L. N. H. (2016b). *"Ecology of social innovation" in Vietnamese higher education context: Insights and possibilities*. Paper presented at the Global education dialogue: Innovation for employability: University-industry partnership for sustainable economic development, Ho Chi Minh City, 15–16 June 2016.

Orrell, J. (2011). *Good practice report: Work-integrated learning*. Sydney: Australian Learning and Teaching Council.

Patrick, C.-J., Peach, D., Pocknee, C., Webb, F., Fletcher, M., & Pretto, G. (2008). *The WIL (work integrated learning) report: A national scoping study [Final Report]*. Brisbane: Queensland University of Technology.

Pavlin, S. (2013). *Considering university-business cooperation from the perspective of graduates' early careers*. Paper presented at the 10th International workshop on higher education reform (WHER), Faculty of Education, University of Ljubljana. https://www.eurashe.eu/library/mission-phe/EMCOSU_paper%20Pavlin%2020130901_CEPS_PAVLIN_FINAL.pdf

Pavlin S., Akkuyunlu, A., Kovačič, H., & Svetlik, I. (Eds.). (2009). *Report on the qualitative analysis of higher education institutions and employers in five countries: Development of competencies in the world of work and education*. Hegesco Project. Ljubljana: University of Ljubljana. Access: http://www.decowe.org/static/uploaded/htmlarea/finalreportshegesco/Qualitative_Analysis_of_HEIs_and_Employers_in_Five_Countries.pdf. 30 Aug 2013.

Pham, H. M. (2011). *Triết Lý Giáo Dục Thế Giới và Việt Nam* [Educational philosophy: International perspectives and Vietnam]. Viện Khoa Học Giáo Dục Hà Nội: Nhà Xuất Bản Giáo Dục Việt Nam.

Pham, L. (2015). *Ranking makes no sense without differentiation*. Retrieved from https://www.universityworldnews.com/post.php?story=20151014151901972.

Pham, H. H., & Tran, L. T. (2013). Develop graduate skills, knowledge and attributes for the world of work: The case of the translation curriculum in Vietnam. *Language, Culture and Society, 36*, 1–15.

Sattler, P., & Peters, J. (2013). *Work integrated learning in Ontario's postsecondary sector: The experiences of Ontario's graduates*. Toronto: Higher Education Quality Council of Ontario.

Simpson, M. D., & Gates, A. (2014). *Exploring workplace learning in university education through a 'slow innovations' framework: Curation, innovation and exemplary practice*. Sydney: Australian Government Office for Learning and Teaching.

Smith, M., Brooks, S., Lichtenbergy, A., McIlveen, P., Torjul, P., & Tyler, J. (2009). *Career development learning: Maximising the contribution of work-integrated learning to the student experience*. Project Report, University of Wollongong, Careers Central, Academic Services Division. Wollongong, Australia.

Thủ Tướng Chính Phủ (Prime Minister). (2012). *Quyết định số 711/QĐ-TTg, 13/6/2012, Chiến lược phát triển giáo dục 2011–2020* [Decision number 711/QĐ-TTg, 13/6/2012, strategies for education development 2011–2020]. Hanoi, Vietnam.

Tran, N. C. (2006). *Universities as drivers of the urban economies in Asia: The case of Vietnam*. Hanoi: World Bank.

Tran, T. T. (2012). Vietnamese higher education and the issue of enhancing graduate employability. *Journal of Teaching and Learning for Graduate Employability, 3*(1), 2–16.

Tran, T. (2013). Limitation on the development of skills in higher education in Vietnam. *Higher Education, 65*(5), 631–644. https://doi.org/10.1007/s10734-012-9567-7.

Tran, T. T. (2018). Youth transition to employment in Vietnam: A vulnerable path. *Journal of Education and Work, 31*(1), 59–71. https://doi.org/10.1080/13639080.2017.1404011.

Tran, B. T. (n.d.). Đào tạo nhân lực ở Việt Nam (Human resources development in Vietnam). *Tạp chí Nghiên cứu Văn hóa, 4.* http://huc.edu.vn/vi/spct/id123/ DAO-TAO-NHAN-LUC-O-VIET-NAM/.

Tran, L. T., & Marginson, S. (2018). Internationalisation of Vietnamese higher education: An overview. In L. T. Tran & S. Marginson (Eds.), *Internationalisation in Vietnamese higher education.* Dordrecht: Springer.

Tran, C. N., & Nguyen, H. V. (2011). Vietnam: Current debates on the transformation of academic institutions. In G. Bo & B. Claes (Eds.), *Universities in Transition: The changing roles and challenges of academic institutions* (pp. 119–142). New York: Springer.

Tran, L. T., & Soejatminah, S. (2016). 'Get foot in the door': International students' perceptions of work-integrated learning. *British Journal of Educational Studies, 64*(3), 337–355.

Tran, L. T., & Soejatminah, S. (2017). Work-integrated learning for international students: From harmony to inequality. *Journal of Studies in International Education., 21*(3), 261–277.

Tran, T. Q., & Swierczek, F. W. (2009). Skills development in higher education in Vietnam. *Asia Pacific Business Review, 15*(4), 565–586.

Tran, T. L., Marginson, S., & Nguyen, T. N. (2014a). Internationalising Vietnam higher education. In L. T. Tran, S. Marginson, H. M. Đo, Q. T. N. Đo, T. T. T. Le, N. T. Nguyen, T. T. P. Vu, T. N. Pham, & H. T. L. Nguyen (Eds.), *Higher education in Vietnam: flexibility, mobility and practicality for national development.* Basingstoke: Palgrave Macmillan.

Tran, T. L., Tran, T. T. T., & Nguyen, T. N. (2014b). Curriculum and pedagogy. In L. T. Tran, S. Marginson, H. M. Đo, Q. T. N. Đo, T. T. T. Le, N. T. Nguyen, T. T. P. Vu, T. N. Pham, & H. T. L. Nguyen (Eds.), *Higher education in Vietnam: flexibility, mobility and practicality for national development.* Basingstoke: Palgrave Macmillan.

Tran, L. T., Ngo, M., Nguyen, N., & Dang, X. T. (2017). Hybridity in Vietnamese universities: an analysis of the interactions between Vietnamese traditions and foreign influences. *Studies in Higher Education, 42*(10), 1899–1916.

von Treuer, K. M., Sturre, V. L., Keele, S. M., & McLeod, J. E. (2010). *Evaluation methodology for work integrated learning - placements: A discussion paper.* Paper presented at the ACEN 2010: Proceedings of the 3rd Biannual Australian Collaborative Education Network National Conference, Rockhampton, Queensland.

USAID. (2019). *Connecting the Mekong through Education and Training.* Retrieved from https:// www.usaid.gov/asia-regional/documents/connecting-mekongthrough-education-and-training.

Vallely, T. J., & Wilkinson, B. (2008). *Vietnamese higher education: Crisis and response.* Memorandum: Higher Education Task Force, Harvard Kennedy School.

Vietnam News. (2016). *Schools, firms work to make grads employable.* Retrieved from http://vietnamnews.vn/society/273931/schools-firms-work-to-make-gradsemployable. html#380RhIUGFTE9Cg3u.99.

Vietnamese Government. (1993). Decree No. 90/CP, dated November 24, 1993. Hanoi: The Vietnamese Government Online Portal.

Vietnamese Government. (2005). *Decree 14/2005/NQ – CP on the government resolution on substantial and comprehensive renewal of Vietnam's tertiary education in the 2006–2020 period.* Hanoi: Vietnamese Government. Retrieved from http://thuvienphapluat.vn/van-ban/ Giao-duc/Nghi-quyet-14-2005-NQ-CP-doi-moi-co-ban-va-toan-dien-giao-duc-dai-hoc-Viet-Nam-giai-doan-2006-2020-5013.aspx

World Bank. (2012). *Vietnam development report 2012: An overview.* Retrieved from https://www. worldbank.org/en/news/feature/2012/01/12/vietnamdevelopment-report-2012-an-overview.

Chapter 8
Accreditation, Ranking and Classification in Vietnamese Higher Education: The Localization of Foreign-Born QA Models and Methods

Quyen Thi Ngoc Do

Abstract This chapter discusses major questions of importing foreign-born Quality Assurance models and policies into the local higher education contexts, specifically focusing on accreditation, ranking and classification (also referred to as stratification). The discussion provides insights into the evolvement of the local higher education quality assurance system and implications about how to develop a better established system in the future. Since educational model and policy borrowings have gained increased popularity, the analysis through the lens of model borrowing should be useful for local higher education policymakers in the national educational reform.

Introduction

The Vietnamese Government has carried out educational reforms continuously during the past several decades. While its first reform efforts were mostly targeted at general education, recent initiatives have been deployed in higher education. The focus of reform has also been diverted from quantitative issues, including system scale and size to qualitative matters. A national Quality Assurance (QA) system in place is among the most remarkable developments in higher education.

The country's educational reform continually demands innovative ideas and methods while local policymakers are attracted by QA practices in developed higher education systems. The borrowing of models and methods is inevitable. The import and introduction of foreign concepts and models into the local system is similar to the transplantation of an exotic plant into a garden, where the soil needs examining if it is suitable for the plant. It is also critical to determine if any soil improvement or genetic modification is required.

Q. T. N. Do (✉)
Hanoi University of Business and Technology, Hanoi, Vietnam

© Springer Nature Singapore Pte Ltd. 2019
N. T. Nguyen, L. T. Tran (eds.), *Reforming Vietnamese Higher Education*,
Education in the Asia-Pacific Region: Issues, Concerns and Prospects 50,
https://doi.org/10.1007/978-981-13-8918-4_8

In reality, some QA methods have been borrowed to meet various needs of the local higher education system. They all have been 'modified' to a certain extent. In addition, a legislative QA framework has been created for fostering these 'seeds'. Many questions are of concern, for example, how the borrowed methods and models have been adapted, whether the adaptations are appropriate, whether the modified methods and models are effective or generate any adverse effects and whether provided contextual elements such as regulations and laws are adequate.

In this chapter, these questions are to be discussed at different levels of depth for some model borrowing cases with a focus on accreditation, ranking and classification (also referred to as stratification). The discussion provides insights into the evolvement of the local higher education quality assurance system. It is also a critical review through which implications about how to develop this system in the future can be drawn. The implications through the lens of model borrowing should also be useful to local higher education policymakers in the system's recent reforms, given that educational model and policy borrowings have been widespread.

An Overview of the National QA System

The Department of Higher Education (DoHE) in the Ministry of Education and Training (MoET) is the state agency that manages the quality of higher education. In addition, the General Department of Educational Testing and Accreditation (GDETA), also belonging to MoET, monitors higher education quality through accreditation, a state management instrument (Quyen-Do et al. 2017). GDETA has played a major role in constructing and developing the national accreditation system.

Accreditation is the key instrument for QA, and four independent accrediting agencies undertake the accreditation of local higher education institutions (HEIs). Besides accreditation, MoET also employs Licensing and Public Provision of Data; however, the effectiveness of these tools is still questioned. A National Qualification Framework has not yet been developed. MoET has also encouraged universities and colleges to conduct student surveys. Many institutions have deployed student surveys using their own questionnaires, which are not based on the same indicators or a common template, survey results do not inform higher education managers and researchers about students' experience at the systemic level.

In September 2015, the government promulgated Decree 73/2015/NĐ-CP stipulating new regulations on the stratification and ranking of HEIs and ranking standards. The job of ranking HEIs is currently assigned to independent accrediting agencies.

Among these QA methods, key instruments including accreditation, ranking and stratification will be examined in detail in this chapter.

The Adoption of Accreditation: US Accreditation Model

According to Nguyen et al. (2009), the first dialogue in the local higher education system about quality and quality management dates back to the Dalat conference in 2000. Between 2000 and 2004, much discussion was about a QA model that would be a point of reference for developing a national QA system. US accreditation was selected despite doubts about the suitability of this model due to considerable contextual differences between the two systems. Nguyen et al. (2009) reveal three reasons why the US accreditation system was considered: (1) it is the oldest; (2) it is the largest and most diverse and (3) US education has always been seen as being of high quality.

So, the adoption of the US accreditation was both internally driven by a local need and externally driven by the advantages of this model over others. Many features of the source model were retained and have been operational in the local model; some originally were not retained but have been added on and some were abolished and replaced with those that were more suitable with the local contexts.

Accreditation Principles, Approaches, Methods and Procedures: Original US System vs. Borrowed Vietnamese System

Principles and Approaches

'Independence' and 'Self-Regulation'

> In the United States, accreditation is carried out by private, non-profit organizations designed for this specific purpose. External quality review of higher education is a nongovernmental enterprise. (Eaton 2012, p. 1)

The implementation of accreditation in the US system is undertaken by approximately 60 accrediting agencies, which are in most cases associations of universities and colleges. These organizations include six regional accrediting agencies, such as New England Association of Schools and Colleges (NEASC-CIHE)-Commission on Institutions of Higher Education, four national faith-related accrediting agencies, two national career-related accrediting agencies and 46 programmatic accrediting agencies (Council for Higher Education Accreditation [CHEA] 2016). They are recognized by CHEA, Council for Higher Education Accreditation. The US Government and Department of Education rely on CHEA and NACIQI, National Advisory Committee on Institutional Quality and Integrity, in monitoring and managing the quality of higher education without direct interference in the accreditation process. NACIQI provides recommendations to the Secretary of Education regarding how to use accreditation results (Studley 2012). Accreditation is therefore implemented independently of the state management bodies and US Government. According to

NACIQI, examining the extent to which higher education providers (HEPs) and programs accomplish their missions and commitments if the responsibility of HEPs and accreditation is a mechanism for institutional self-regulation (Studley 2012).

Accreditation when first imported into the Vietnamese higher education did not operate on an independent basis. During the 10 years of pilot implementation, Ministry of Education and Training, via GDETA, organized and led the accreditation of the first 40 universities. The set of accreditation standards and criteria and procedures were developed and promulgated by MoET. This government body also issued accreditation certificates. Under the pressure of international and national scholars and organizations, the accreditation was made independent in principle in 2014 and has been transferred to 'independent' accrediting agencies. Of the four centres, three were established within national and regional universities. The establishment of these organizations, as well as the appointment of directors of these agencies, was approved by MoET. This mechanism of appointment raises a question about how independent these centres can be of the universities and MoET. Early 2016, the first accrediting centre was established as an agency of the Association of Vietnamese Universities and Colleges. This centre is expected to implement the 'independent' principle determined by the system.

With regard to internal QA, quality assurance activities inside universities and colleges are mostly compliance-driven, rather than improvement-led. Accreditation results are mainly for (1) compliance with MoET's regulations and guidelines and (2) publicity. They are rarely used for improvement and self-regulation.

'Voluntary'

The participation of HEPs in accreditation in the US higher education is on a voluntary basis; however, mechanisms to promote participation are in place. 'The accreditation system serves as a critical element in providing information about academic quality to satisfy the federal interest in assuring the appropriate use of federal funds' (Studley 2012, p. 2). Accreditation serves a gatekeeping function for the determination of eligibility for federal funds. To participate in accreditation, HEPs applies for membership of accrediting agencies and pay annual fees to maintain the membership status. In fact, many US HEPs have been accredited though some of them are not entitled to Title IV[1] funds. This shows that there are motives for accreditation other than finance and funding.

---

[1]Title IV funds are federal student aid funds, which are from federal student aid programs administered by the US Department of Education. Title IV funds include Direct Subsidized/ Unsubsidized Loan, Direct Graduate PLUS Loan, Direct PLUS Loan, Federal Pell Grant, Federal Supplemental Educational Opportunity Grant (SEOG) and Federal Perkins Loan. It does not include scholarships from the University or other private organizations.

In the Vietnamese higher education, Education Law 2005 specifies that accreditation is obligatory for all HEIs. In practice, during the past 10 years, for various reasons this 'obligation' principle has not yet come into effect. The government has been consistent in accreditation policy, and it is expected that the policy will take effect once the accreditation system is fully developed.

'Peer Review'

Since the launch of accreditation in the US system in the late nineteenth century, the instrument has always been peer-based. According to Eaton (2012, p. 4), 'accreditation review is conducted primarily by faculty and administrative peers in the profession; these colleagues review the self-study and serve on visiting teams that review institutions and programs after the self-study is completed; peers constitute the majority of members of the accrediting commissions or boards that make judgments about accrediting status'. HEPs that are members of associations of universities and colleges are entitled to all activities organized by the association from workshops and conferences to peer assessment.

Taking the US model, Vietnamese accreditation is somewhat based on peer review in the way that external reviewers are also faculty or administrative peers in the profession. However, there is a difference in the way that they are selected and recruited. Unlike in the US accreditation system, Vietnamese external reviewers are certified and licensed by MoET. Certified external reviewers, who are experts, scholars and managers from universities and colleges are recruited and employed by accrediting agencies as independent reviewers on a case-by-case basis. In the USA, all members of the external review panel are volunteers and are generally not compensated (Eaton 2012).

'Continuous Improvement'

US accreditation is said to help enhance accountability and facilitate continuous improvement. In principle, improvement is believed to happen as a result of the self-evaluation process and through implementing recommendations based on self-evaluation findings. In practice, post-accreditation activities are not followed up. For this reason, that accreditation is for continuous improvement is still a claim, not only in the US accreditation system but in others as well.

In Vietnamese higher education, the focal aim of accreditation is to enhance accountability. As previously mentioned, QA activities inside HEIs are compliance-driven than improvement-led. The focus of the accreditation process, including self-evaluation and site visits, is examining the level at which an HEI or a programme meets prescribed standards and criteria.

Accreditation Procedures and Methods

The US accreditation procedure includes five main steps: registration, self-evaluation, site visit, feedback on external review results and decision granting. As a result of this process, two important deliverables are self-evaluation and external review reports. They are both submitted to accrediting agencies and their decision to grant accreditation status to HEPs is made based mainly on the site visit report provided by external reviewers. Before this decision is made, HEPs have a chance to give feedback on external review results.

In the Vietnamese accreditation system, the process and steps are similar to those in the US system (Table 8.1). The key methods used are also self-evaluation and site visit. It can be said that in terms of method and procedure, Vietnamese accreditation is identical to US accreditation.

Table 8.1 A snapshot of accreditation in the USA, Australia and Vietnam

	US accreditation	Australian accreditation	Vietnamese accreditation
Accrediting agencies	Associations of universities and colleges	TEQSA (Tertiary Education Quality and Standards Agency) – a state organization	Established within national and regional universities
	Professional associations		Association of universities and colleges
Principles	Independence	Independence	Independence[a]
	Self-regulation		
	Voluntary	Obligatory	Obligatory[a]
	Peer review	Risk-based	
	Continuous improvement	Continuous improvement	Peer review
Procedure	1. Registration → 2. Self-evaluation → 3. Site visits → 4. Feedback on external review report → 5. Accreditation decision	1. Application + submission of evidence and documents → 2. Site visit → 3. Feedback on external review report → 4. Accreditation decision	1. Registration → 2. Self-evaluation → 3. Site visit → 4.Feedback on external review report → 5. Decision
Communication	Conventional correspondence and email	Online (via an e-portal for Higher Education Providers)	Business correspondence, paper-based (email but limited)

Source: Aggregated by author
Note: [a]Not fully in operation

The Degree of Adaptation of the Vietnamese Accreditation System

The adoption of the US accreditation is apparently a result of a 'cross-national attraction' described in Ochs and Phillips (2002) and is a typical case of model borrowing in education. The analysis of the differences between the USA and Vietnamese accreditation shows that copying and emulation, adoption without changes and imitation, are not the case. Accreditation has been modified to a certain extent, though it is not clear if these changes and amendments were aimed at harmonizing the instrument with local contexts.

The decision-making process in relation to the adoption of US accreditation at the early stage was based primarily on experts' judgment rather than on findings of empirical studies (Nguyen et al. 2009). Kim Nguyen et al. have expressed concern over the suitability of the US model and its features in Vietnamese higher education, given significant differences between the two countries' political, social and educational backgrounds. Specifically, they caution against the use of peer review as one of the methods of evaluation.

Model borrowing that disregards the differences in the background contexts between lender and borrower systems may not bring desired changes. Scholars like Steiner-Khamsi (2004), Waldow (2012) and Park et al. (2014) have warned policymakers and educators against a wide range of problems related to model borrowings. At one end of the spectrum, borrowing is not copying (Steiner-Khamsi 2004, p. 5), implying that exact transfer is not recommended. At the other end, Waldow (2012) points out a problem of 'borrowing' without involving the transfer of content. Park et al. (2014) mention the distortion of borrowed policies and models as one of the risks. While there is no rule of thumb for how much adaptation is appropriate, it is strongly recommended that borrowed models and methods be adapted with adequate caution. For the model not to be excessively modified or distorted into a new one, its fundamental principles should be retained while specific practices can be adjusted to suit local contexts.

The analysis in the previous section shows several significant differences between the Vietnamese and US accreditation. First, while the US accreditation is implemented on a voluntary basis, accreditation in Vietnam is obligatory by law. Second, US accreditation is independent of the government and HEPs while this principle has been defined only recently in the Vietnamese accreditation and is still challenged. Since these two important principles of accreditation are not maintained, the method may be modified substantially. This modification may divert accreditation from being improvement-led to compliance-driven. The effects of accreditation on quality assurance in the two systems may be completely different.

The Vietnamese Ranking and Stratification

The Introduction of the Vietnamese Ranking and Classification

In September 2015, Vietnamese Government officially launched stratification and ranking in an attempt to introduce more rigorous instruments for higher education quality management. This movement was a result of lengthy discussions at the national level on developing a ranking system for local HEIs. The dialogue about local rankings started in as early as the mid-2000s with some efforts to develop ranking indicators. In 2009, Vietnam Universities Network (VUN) organized a national workshop on higher education evaluation and ranking in Ho Chi Minh City with the participation of hundreds of higher education policymakers, scholars, leaders and managers. The workshop discussed all aspects in relation to the ranking of universities and colleges. At this workshop, T. N. Quyen-Do (2010) proposed a criterion-based bi-dimensional classification-ranking system, which helps to maintain the institutional diversity of the system, instead of simple rankings. The discussion was still going on until 2015 when Decree 73/2015/NĐ-CP was promulgated. By specifying the standards and criteria, the framework and procedures for classification and ranking, the Decree has activated the two approaches in the local system (Thủ tướng Chính phủ [Prime Minister] 2015).

Top-Down Approaches and Compliance-Driven QA

All of the QA methods and instruments that have been adopted so far by MoET are top-down measures with an emphasis on institutions, rather than academic programmes. A large number of standards and criteria means that many requirements are imposed by state management agencies for HEIs to meet. The administrative work involved in the process towards proving that these requirements are satisfied is a huge workload.

Before classification, ranking and certification were introduced, the job of QA staff at HEIs was already mainly about complying with MoET's QA requirements (Quyen-Do 2016; Quyen-Do et al. 2017). While there are few institutional QA methods and instruments, the advent of more top-down external QA tools will probably promote further conformity. The risk for being increasingly compliance-driven in institutional QA is real.

Original Concepts and Model vs. Localized Definitions and Model

Original Version

Both classification and ranking originate from Western higher education. While rankings are globally used, classification is much less popular. In the European U-Map project, 'higher education classifications are descriptive tools that allow categorisations and comparisons of higher education institutions on the basis of a set of dimensions and indicators' (van Vught et al. 2010, p. 19). van Vught et al. (2010) note that classifications are not rankings, which are defined as 'an established technique for displaying the comparative ranking of organizations in terms of their performance' (Vlăsceanu et al. 2007, p. 79). Associated with rankings are league tables, which are often made public in press, specialized journals and on the Internet. In Western education systems, classifications and rankings which are used separately for these two instruments are meant to do different things. Classifications are often descriptive while rankings are judgmental. Furthermore, classifications help to assure institutional diversity while rankings tend to limit diversity (van Vught et al. 2010).

Localised Version

Decree 73 defines Classification as 'an arrangement of HEIs into groups by missions and goals' according to the standards specified by the Decree. Specifically, HEIs are grouped into three layers of research-oriented, professional and practice-oriented HEIs. This Decree also defines Ranking as an arrangement of HEIs in descending order by quality, which is assessed and scored, within each layer of classification. It specifies a ranking frame consisting of three groups HEIs. Class 1 includes 30% of HEIs with highest quality scores, Class 2 includes the middle 40% and Class 3 includes the last 30% of those institutions with the lowest scores.

It should be noted that the Decree neither defines quality, by which HEIs are scored and ranked, nor refers to any previously issued legal documents. Therefore, it is not clear how quality is defined and measured for rankings. In the most recent legal documents, Circular 38 and 62, quality is defined as 'the fitness for purpose' (Ministry of Education and Training [MOET] 2012, 2013). If this Decree implicitly employs this definition, then the questions would be how the standards and criteria for accreditation are different from those for ranking and whether there are overlaps between these QA mechanisms. Regardless of how quality is defined in this instrument, the move to the hybrid model of stratification and ranking is step away from this 'one size fits all' approach and recognizes the diversity of the Vietnamese higher education system.

Furthermore, unlike global rankings, Vietnamese ranking is delegated to accrediting agencies. It is important to note that these agencies are established not as quality assurance organizations.

A Hybrid of Ranking and Stratification

With this Decree, Vietnam's MoET combines these two instruments and introduces them together. By grouping ranked HEIs into classes, ranking in Vietnamese higher education is, in essence, the categorization of HEIs by scoring them against a set of indicators. In practice, the model in place now is 'ranking within stratification', which may help to curb the pitfalls of rankings. Nevertheless, there are technical matters that need tackling to avoid adverse effects, bureaucracy, overlaps and compliance in QA.

First, the grouping of HEIs by ranking results deviates the local ranking far away from the original instrument. Global rankings simply rank HEIs. They neither explicitly attach the ranking results with excellence or performance nor label HEIs with a quality certificate. By grouping HEIs into three classes 1, 2 and 3, by their ranking scores, this model labels HEIs with a quality stamp, which may provide biased information and implications to students and stakeholders.

Second, original forms of rankings often use aggregate indicators. Interestingly, the Decree 73 states a long list of ranking standards including rather specific criteria such as the rate of graduates having major-matching jobs within 12 months from graduation, the number of master programs, teacher-student ratio, the number of accredited programs and detailed institutional accreditation results. It can be seen that some of these criteria are outcomes while some are inputs. And it is not convincing to say that all of these criteria reflect quality.

Third, an important question is whether the specification of classification and ranking standards and criteria might further promote compliance among local HEIs. At this moment, it is too early to have an adequate answer to the question. It can be only examined after these instruments have been in operation for some years. Nonetheless, it sounds obvious that a race for better ranks amongst local HEIs will be ignited.

The government's launch of a hybrid of classification and ranking in higher education obviously shows a high level of adaptation of the two approaches. A question open for discussion is that whether they are still the classification and ranking known in Europe or the USA. Vietnamese classification is probably relatable to the source models, but it is in doubt whether ranking is.

Discussion

The import of such foreign-born models and instruments into the local education system is part of an inevitable movement in the context of internationalisation of higher education. HEIs and the national authority are both under the pressure of change and innovation in the integration process. Interestingly, the borrowings of

QA models and policies were brought in by the World Bank as the sponsor, so it was a submissive initiative at the beginning. Coincidentally, submissiveness is often found common in Vietnamese culture. This property results from the influence of Confucianism that is pointed out by Nguyen in Chapter 2 as a factor that regulates the behaviour of Vietnamese individuals and organizations in every aspect of work and life. In the implementation of accreditation and other QA models, the submissiveness of the system has been consistent with the top-down approach to QA. That is, the top-down approach has worked out well given the submissiveness of HEIs in the search for QA solutions. This approach will still work in the short term.

A Confusing 'Matrix' of Standards and Criteria

Before the launch of ranking and classification, Vietnamese HEIs were supposed to be evaluated against accreditation standards, which include 61 criteria covering almost all areas of the university life. In addition, licensure standards, conditions for opening institutions and programmes are still valid. Decree 73 adds to the list approximately 30 more criteria for ranking and classification. Most recently, Circular 24/2015/TT-BGDĐT, effective from November 2015, specifies eight national standards of an HEI (Ministry of Education and Training [MoET] 2015). This is a form of certification. Apart from standards on facilities and campus, teaching staff, curriculum and program and finance, there are requirements on institutions' accreditation and ranking results. Apparently, the Circular was a MoET's move to implement Decree 73 by the government. With these instruments in place, a complicated matrix of criteria has been formed.

There are several issues in relation to this matrix of criteria. Overlaps among the standards and criteria for accreditation, licensure, classification, ranking and certification are inevitable. The matrix is made of three levels of standards. At the lowest level are accreditation and licensure standards. At the middle level, ranking standards include requirements on accreditation results. And at the top level, national standards for certification comprise requirements on both ranking and accreditation results. Some of the criteria are repeatedly seen in two or three levels of standards such as teacher-student ratio and the number of publications in international and local journals. For university QA practitioners and managers, who are supposed to deal with these standards and criteria directly, this multi-level matrix may be confusing enough.

A Risk-Based Regulatory Approach: The Future Development of Quality Assurance

While both external and internal QA activities in the world higher education have been moving towards continuous improvement, Vietnamese QA is still mainly for accountability and is compliance-driven. Bureaucracy has also been pointed out in such a system. Two strategies at the systemic level can be considered for adoption. One is to promote bottom-up improvement-led approaches at the institutional level. Another is to adopt a risk-based approach to external QA and regulation.

The risk-based approach has been a basis for developing Australian accreditation. In 2011, Australia shifted from audit system to obligatory accreditation (termed institutional registration and course accreditation). Under TEQSA Act 2011, TEQSA must observe three basic principles when exercising a power: (1) regulatory necessity; (2) reflecting risk and (3) proportionate regulation (Australia's Office of Parliamentary Counsel 2014). Underlying these principles is the risk-based approach. This requires TEQSA to focus on higher risk providers while 'allowing higher quality, lower risk providers to operate without unnecessary intrusion' (Department of Education-Employment and Workplace Relation [DEEWR] 2011, p. 2). Specifically, those institutions deemed as 'low risk' will be granted a self-accrediting status. TEQSA developed a Regulatory Risk Framework, consisting of risk indicators to assess the risk level of HEIs.

The Higher Education Funding Council for England (HEFCE) adopted a similar approach to the quality assurance of higher education in England in 2012 (University Learning Teaching and Student Experience Committee 2012). It is noteworthy that in its report to the US Department of Education in 2015, NACIQI recommended a 'risk-based regulatory approach' to the US accreditation allowing accrediting agencies to 'establish less burdensome access to Title IV funding for high-quality, low-risk institutions' (Recommendation 9, 2015 Accreditation Policy Recommendations) (Phillips 2015).

The risk-based regulatory approach has grown in popularity for some reasons. One is that it is considered as a sensible move away from a 'one size fits all' approach (Grove and Havergal 2015). Nevertheless, how the approach is implemented in different systems is not identical. In other words, how and to what extent high-quality, low-risk HEPs in the USA, UK and Australia are liberated from the accreditation burden would be different. These cases can be relevant examples for Vietnamese higher education policymakers to refer to if this approach is considered. Given Vietnam's diverse mix of long-established public universities and a vast majority of newly founded public and private universities, many of which upgraded from provincial colleges and technical schools, this approach helps to maintain institutional diversity in the system. Once again, it is strongly recommended that a thorough analysis and examination of the local contexts of those policies and practices be conducted prior to the adoption of this approach and relevant practices.

Impact Assessment Prior to Model Transfer

Recent discussions by Vietnamese scholars, such as D. K. Nguyen et al. (2009) and Thao-Vu and Marginson (2014), about model borrowings in education have recommended caution to be taken in adopting and transferring foreign-born models and methods into the local system. At the institutional level, a pilot study or an experiment can be conducted to examine the appropriateness and possible effects of the methods or instruments indented for transfer. At the systemic level, as the scope of work may extend to a much larger scale, there is a need for a form of pre-project impact assessment. The purpose of these assessments is to identify potential challenges and inhibitors, as well as possible effects, both negative and positive, of the adopted model or method on relevant stakeholders and beneficiaries.

Such an analysis informs decision-makers in customizing the borrowed model or method to the local contexts and needs. It provides evidence for any adaptations that may be made to the borrowed method and model. Though the pre-transfer assessment may not eliminate all potential issues, it helps to anticipate problems and challenges, which allows adopters to take appropriate measures to address the problems. By so doing, it helps to save time and resources and enhance the effectiveness of educational reforms.

Implications from Model Borrowing Theories

Dolowitz and Marsh (1996) review the literature on transferability in model borrowing and summarize the factors that constrain the process. The factors cluster in the complexity of the borrowed model, past models, cultural and political contexts of the host country, technological ability and economic resources. On the basis of this summary, Quyen-Do (2016) further elaborates the framework so that it better suits the specific context of higher education. The framework (Fig. 8.1) includes four areas as follows:

Fig. 8.1 Factors affecting transferability

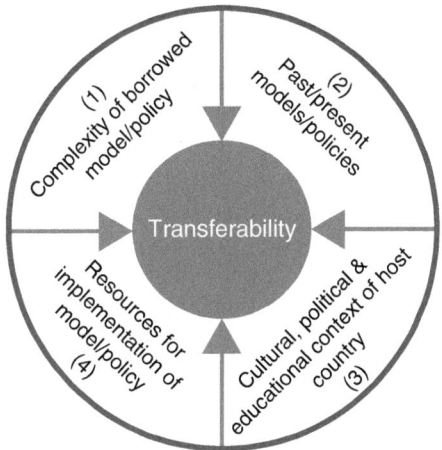

1. *The complexity of the borrowed model/policy*: e.g. (reflected in) goals; relationship between problem and solution; perceived side effects; outcomes; techniques and technical issues.
2. *Past and/or current models/policies:* what can be transferred or borrowed; what to look for when doing model/policy borrowing or transfer.
3. *Cultural, political and educational context of the host country*: e.g. dominant political ideology and values.
4. *Resources for implementation of model/policy*: e.g. human capital, finance, facilities, data, equipment and technologies.

The framework suggests that many elements be considered and examined prior to the adoption of a foreign-born QA mechanism. The examination and assessment of these factors may help to enhance the viability and sustainability of the instrument in the Vietnamese higher education. The framework can also be used to guide an impact assessment prior to adoption and borrowing.

Conclusion

The adoption of accreditation, ranking and classification in the national QA system are typical examples of the borrowing of foreign-born methods and approaches in education. These borrowings have happened along with the development of the QA system and were driven, above all, by the local needs. The attraction of the foreign models and methods that are dominant and trendy in international QA is irresistible for local QA practitioners and policymakers. The analysis in this chapter indicates different levels of adaptation made to the borrowed methods. The adaptations have been based on expert judgment referring to reviews of the methods in other systems, rather than empirical evidence. For this reason, constant reviews and revision along with the implementation of the methods are recommended.

It is noteworthy that even though a number of QA methods have been in place in Vietnamese higher education, none has been fully operational. These external QA instruments have not brought actual effects on either quality improvement or accountability enhancement at the national scale. The long delays in putting them in full operation, for over 10 years in the case of accreditation, may make these methods, together with their model and procedures, obsolete before deployed. Therefore, the discussion about how borrowed QA methods should be adapted is important, but seemingly not adequate in the Vietnamese QA dialogues.

References

Australia's Office of Parliamentary Counsel. (2014). *Tertiary Education Quality and Standards Agency Act 2011* (amended June 2014) [TEQSA Act 2011]. Canberra.

Council for Higher Education Accreditation [CHEA]. (2016). *2015–2016 Directory of CHEA-recognized organizations*.

Department of Education-Employment and Workplace Relation [DEEWR]. (2011). *Tertiary education quality and standards agency (consequential amendments and transitional provisions) bill 2011 – A guide to the exposure draft*. Australia.

Dolowitz, D. P., & Marsh, D. (1996). Who learns what from whom: A review of the policy transfer literature. *Political Studies, 44*(2), 343–357.

Eaton, J. S. (2012). *An overview of US accreditation*. http://www.chea.org/pdf/OverviewofUSAccreditation2012.pdf. Accessed 25 Sept.

Grove, J., & Havergal, C. (2015). *Is 'risk-based' quality assurance too risky?* Times Higher Education. Retrieved from https://www.timeshighereducation.com/features/is-risk-based-quality-assurance-too-risky

Ministry of Education and Training [MOET]. (2012). *Thông tư 62/2012/TT-BGDĐT ban hành Quy định về quy trình và chu kỳ kiểm định chất lượng giáo dục đại học, cao đẳng và trung cấp chuyên nghiệp* [Circular promulgating accreditation procedure and cycle for universities, colleges and professional high schools]. Hanoi: MOET.

Ministry of Education and Training [MoET]. (2013). *Thông tư 38/2013/TT-BGDĐT Ban hành Quy định về quy trình và chu kỳ kiểm định chất lượng chương trình đào tạo của các trường đại học, cao đẳng và trung cấp chuyên nghiệp* [Circular promulgating programmatic accreditation procedure and cycle for universities, colleges and professional high schools]. Hanoi: MoET.

Ministry of Education and Training [MoET]. (2015). *Thông tư 24/2015/TT-BGDĐT quy định chuẩn quốc gia đối với cơ sở giáo dục đại học* [Circular specifying national standards of higher education institutions]. Hanoi: MoET.

Nguyen, D. K., Oliver, D. E., & Priddy, L. E. (2009). Criteria for accreditation in Vietnam's higher education: Focus on input or outcome? *Quality in Higher Education, 15*(2), 123–134. https://doi.org/10.1080/13538320902995766.

Ochs, K., & Phillips, D. (2002). *Towards a structural typology of cross-national attraction in education*. Lisbon: Educa.

Park, C., Wilding, M., & Chung, C. (2014). The importance of feedback: Policy transfer, translation and the role of communication. *Policy Studies, 35*(4), 397–412. https://doi.org/10.1080/01442872.2013.875155.

Phillips, D. S. (2015). *2015 accreditation policy recommendations*. Washington, DC: National Advisory Committee on Institutional Quality and Integrity (NACIQI).

Quyen-Do, T. N. (2010). Vietnamese higher education: Rankings or classification? In *National workshop on evaluation and ranking of Vietnamese colleges and universities, Ho Chi Minh City, 2010* (pp. 156–163). Hanoi: Vietnam Universities Network.

Quyen-Do, T. N. (2016). *Benchmarking for continuous improvement: A study in the domain of university governance*. Doctoral dissertation. The University of Melbourne, Parkville, Australia.

Quyen-Do, T. N., Huong-Pham, T., & Kim-Nguyen, D. (2017). Quality assurance in the Vietnamese higher education: A top-down approach and compliance-driven QA. In M. Shah & T. N. Quyen-Do (Eds.), *The rise of quality assurance in Asian higher education*. Oxford: Chandos Publishing.

Steiner-Khamsi, G. (2004). Globalisation in education: Real or imagined? In G. Steiner-Khamsi & T. S. Popkewitz (Eds.), *The global politics of educational borrowing and lending*. New York: Teacher College Press.

Studley, J. S. (2012). *2012 Accreditation policy recommendations* (U.S. Department of Education, Ed.). Washington, DC: National Advisory Committee on Institutional Quality and Integrity (NACIQI).

Thao-Vu, T. P., & Marginson, S. (2014). Policy borrowing. In L. Tran, S. Marginson, H. Do, Q. Do, T. Le, N. Nguyen, et al. (Eds.), *Higher education in Vietnam: Flexibility, mobility and practicality in the global knowledge economy* (Palgrave Studies in Global Higher Education). London: Palgrave Macmillan.

Thủ tướng Chính phủ [Prime Minister]. (2015). *Nghị định 73/2015/NĐ-CP Quy định tiêu chuẩn phân tầng, khung sếp hạng và tiêu chuẩn xếp hạng cơ sở giáo dục đại học* [Decree specifying stratification standards, ranking framework and ranking indicators for higher education institutions]. Hanoi.

University Learning Teaching and Student Experience Committee (Higher Education Funding Council for England). (2012). *A risk-based approach to quality asurance* (2012/27). Retrieved from http://www.ncl.ac.uk/ltds//assets/documents/com-rep-ultsec-12nov-docE.pdf

van Vught, F. A., Kaiser, F., File, J. M., Gaethgens, C., Peter, R., & Westerheijden, D. F. (2010). *U-Map – The European classification of higher education institutions*. Enschede: Center for Higher Education Policy Studies [CHEPS].

Vlăsceanu, L., Grunberg, L., & Pârlea, D. (2007). *Quality assurance and accreditation: A glossary of basic terms and definitions* (2nd ed.). Bucharest: UNESCO-CEPES.

Waldow, F. (2012). Standardization and legitimacy – Two central concepts in research on educational borrowing and lending. In T. Seddon, J. Ozga, & G. Steiner-Khamsi (Eds.), *Policy borrowing and lending in education* (World yearbook of education). Oxon: Routledge.

Chapter 9
Access and Equity in Higher Education in Light of Bourdieu's Theories: A Case of Minority Students in Northwest Vietnam

Thuy Thi Ngoc Bui, Nga Thi Hang Ngo, Hoa Thi Mai Nguyen, and Hang Thu Le Nguyen

Abstract The chapter unpacks access and equity in higher education for minority students in Northwest Vietnam. A combination of factors including financial struggles, institutional constraints, socio-cultural and geographical barriers, and language barriers are reported to significantly affect students' aspirations, access and success in higher education. The chapter suggests the need for policy change for minority students seeking higher education, which is strictly built upon the constant negotiation of their linguistic, socio-economic and educational struggles.

Introduction

The discourse of global inter-independence and demographic shifts in the contemporary era has urged various nations, especially those in the Asia-Pacific region, to orient their focus towards education as a prerequisite economic commodity for country development in the forms of marketization, decentralization and expansion. Throughout the above-mentioned region, the process of enhancing and expanding education is gravitating towards Vietnamese higher education (VHE) and policy reform. However, central to the proliferation of the higher education is how a country with rapid VHE policy reform can effectively respond to access and equity in a wider population (Hawkin 2011).

T. T. N. Bui (✉)
Hanoi University of Science and Technology (HUST), Hanoi, Vietnam

N. T. H. Ngo
Tay Bac University, Sơn La, Vietnam

H. T. M. Nguyen
University of New South Wales, Kensington, Australia

H. T. L. Nguyen
Vietnam National University, Hanoi, Vietnam

© Springer Nature Singapore Pte Ltd. 2019
N. T. Nguyen, L. T. Tran (eds.), *Reforming Vietnamese Higher Education*,
Education in the Asia-Pacific Region: Issues, Concerns and Prospects 50,
https://doi.org/10.1007/978-981-13-8918-4_9

Participating in a strong movement of VHE reforms across countries in Asia and worldwide, the Vietnamese education has gone through outstanding policy changes. Orienting HE towards practical, flexible and mobile discourse (Tran et al. 2014), the government has both magnified and intensified the internalization of HE (Thủ tướng chính phủ (Prime Minister) 2012a) by initiating multidimensional and multi-segmented layers of education reform aimed at fostering diverse foreign collaborations and investment in education, both domestically and internally (Thủ tướng chính phủ (Prime Minister) 2012a). Recently, the Prime Minister (2012a) has emphasized general and systematic reform towards standardizing, modernizing, socializing and democratizing education while continuing to foster internalization. This process further elucidates the government's emphasis on educating young generations with high morality, life skills and creativity for industrializing and modernizing the country. Generally speaking, the broad aim of VHE reforms is to enhance the quality of higher education in order to educate skilled, creative, independent and responsible citizens to meet the needs of the ever-changing national, regional and international job markets. In particular, the VHE's target is to ensure that 70% of the labour force graduate from vocational and university programmes by 2020 (Thủ tướng chính phủ (Prime Minister) 2012b).

In addition to the significant education shift towards a marketized and internationalized discourse, there have been significant efforts by the central government to reaffirm the right of all citizens to pursue and have equal access to education regardless of ethnicity, religion, gender, family status or economic circumstances (Thủ tướng chính phủ (Prime Minister) 2007). In particular, students from the country's remote, rural and mountainous areas and those of ethnic minority status will have the incentive of a lower university entrance examination cut-off score. Moreover, a number of students from socio-economically disadvantaged groups will be permitted to study at the assigned public universities without first taking any university entrance exams. Furthermore, the government is collaborating with multiple banks to support student credit programmes for higher education (Thủ tướng chính phủ (Prime Minister) 2007). In Vietnam, HE has undergone massive change, which demonstrates the government's ongoing effort to become a knowledge society, guided by multi-collaborations, multi-disciplines and multi-education models that will support both individual and national development. A knowledge society further places a great emphasis on life-long learning and creating skilled and intellectual resources for the course of the country's modernization (Decision 89/QD-TTg).

Developing critical research studies in the context of the rapid expansion of higher education, scholars of equity and access in higher education in various areas in Asia and other regions (e.g. McCowan 2015; Mestan and Harvey 2014; Neubauer and Tanaka 2011; Yu and Ertl 2010) consistently caution that the proliferation of higher education worldwide will not necessarily alleviate access and equity problems due to wide-ranging financial and non-financial challenges. Rather, resolving matters ensuring access and equity in HE has been contested and complex; it could induce new forms of inequitable concomitance. Issues that bar students from accessing quality higher education are often related to students' academic performance, university admission policies and family support (e.g. Espinoza and

González 2013; Kanno and Varghese 2010; Kim and Kim 2013). In addition, cost–benefit barriers, cash-limitations and debt aversion barriers are among the main monetary predicaments impeding young people's access and equity opportunities for tertiary education.

While empirical research into issues of equity and access has been widely undertaken elsewhere (e.g. Mayer et al. 2013; Neubauer and Tanaka 2011; World Bank 2009), it has received minimal attention in Vietnam where HE has undergone dramatic and multifaceted reform. The existing studies of access and equity in Vietnam mainly focus on enrolment quotas, or on measurement of the level of access to higher education in a broader national scope (Fry 2009; Holsinger 2009; Oliver et al. 2009; World Bank 2009). Thus, factors that influence higher education access and equity, especially for those from minority backgrounds in a specific region, have yet to be comprehensively investigated. This study builds upon the backdrop of Vietnam's major higher education reforms to address the increasingly recognized limitation of the research literature on higher education access and equity. In particular, this study seeks to determine the degree to which these and other policy shifts will affect access and equity for minority students in Northwest Vietnam. Furthermore, it aims to offer practical recommendations for improving social and equity issues in the Vietnamese higher education and beyond. In order to pursue these major purposes, the study centres on the following research question:

> What are the factors (if any) that affect equity and access of minority students to higher education in Northwest Vietnam?

In order to provide a larger context of the study, the following section reviews relevant studies to identify the major factors impacting on access and equity in other contexts. This is followed by a conceptual framework that guides the research to interpret the factors impacting on minority students' access and equity.

Access and Equity in Higher Education Across Contexts

In higher education, access depends upon policy decisions and the commitment of a government to ensure that educational facilities and opportunities are provided to individuals in both public and private institutions (Jacobs 2013; Jalava 2013). According to Neubauer and Tanaka (2011), access intrinsically links to equity, resources and future social development. In multiple contexts, access addresses a process, and the inaction of HE policy via-à-vis central questions include: Who should obtain access and under what conditions? And, who is obtaining access and under what conditions? Along with access, equity in higher education promotes individual differences within wide-ranging institutional environments. Within these environments, higher education should support individuals to pursue their social and intellectual capacities and gifts from diverse settings that will help to maximize their best possible potential (McCowan 2015; Neubauer and Tanaka 2011).

The systematic expansion of higher education has been driven by the neoliberalism agenda in education, which manifests as educational decentralization, programme diversification and cost shifting to the masses. This has given rise to the tension between: (a) equity and efficiency; (b) public and private; (c) humanity and potential; and (d) the advantaged and underrepresented groups (Mayer et al. 2013; Tanaka 2011). Research studies exploring higher education confirm that issues related to access and fairness, which have become prevalent across countries (Jacobs 2013; Jalava 2013; Neubauer and Tanaka 2011), derive from the following major mechanisms: financial struggles, institutional constraints, socio-cultural and geographical barriers and language struggles.

Financial Struggles

Studies in the USA, Taiwan, China, Indonesia, South Korea, Colombia, Africa, Brazil and Chile (Espinoza and González 2013; Kanno and Varghese 2010; Kim and Kim 2013; Nieuwenhuis and Sehoole 2013; Somers et al. 2013; Yang and Cheng 2011) consistently argue that financial factors constitute a prevailing barrier that drives equity and fairness of HE access to the margins. Monetary issues are of deep concern for students from ethnic, limited socio-economic, undocumented and immigration and refugee backgrounds. They have resulted in both governments and students looking increasingly towards the private sector for resources and tuition fees. Kim and Kim (2013), with reference to Korea, argue that this capitalist acceleration of higher education, in fact, illuminates economic intention rather than solving social inequity. Socio-economically disadvantaged students tend to be either excluded from universities or compelled to attend low-resourced institutions. Likewise, in China, the shifting of education from elitism to the masses demonstrates greater effort to promote quality assurance and educational access. However, as Zhong (2011) contends, resolving the educational gap between the dominant and socio-economically limited groups, such as Tibetans, remains daunting and will remain unsolved for some time to come. As a consequence, and due to the heavy financial burden involved, rural school-aged children miss out on opportunities to obtain university entrance. This is particularly concerning given that 80% of them drop out of education systems after they have completed their primary or secondary education (Yang 2007). In Indonesia, the neoliberal framework of raising education fees and eliminating government support for university education has made higher education a "luxury". Evidence reveals only 15%–18% student participation: this is because "the vast majority of parents are not able to send their children to university" (Abdullah 2011, p. 80). Relating to financial constraints, although South Africa has made tremendous efforts to maximize higher education participation for the disadvantaged students by providing loans and supporting programmes, Nieuwenhuis and Sehoole (2013) report that the equality of outcomes is still far from meeting expectations. The country has the lowest rate (10%) of HE under-resourced student graduates in South Africa, resulting in racial, social and gender inequity.

Institutional Constraints

Today many states continue to cling to the myth that expanding education could ensure solutions to deep-seated socio-economic problems and safeguard egalitarian orientation to education (e.g. Zhong 2011). Structural constraints, however, serve as a form of underlying surveillance, authorizing those who seek education vis-à-vis the type of education they may access and to what extent in both developed and developing education systems. Structural constraints are systematically interrelated and highly complex. They range from: (a) admission quotas of certain groups to exams (e.g. in China, Ireland, Egypt); (b) national exam scores and previous academic performance, writing samples, personal statements and references (in Australia, Brazil); and, (c) previous academic achievements, references, writing samples and interviews (e.g. in Norway and Canada). However, it is often argued that such structural mechanisms exacerbate HE participation opportunities for those on the periphery when they strongly manifest students' socio-economic, educational and demographic characteristics. Due to these structural constraints, Chankseliani (2013) argues that, in Georgia, students from rural areas, minor language backgrounds and students graduated from state schools are significantly less likely (64%) to obtain higher education admissions than their urban counterparts. An increasingly similar trend was found in Korea where students from higher social mobility groups have higher chances of accessing higher education (Kim and Kim 2013). Thus, institutional admission mechanisms not only exacerbate social inequality but also reaffirm and maximize power and opportunities for the already advantaged groups.

Socio-Cultural and Geographical Barriers

Other related social issues such as parental educational background and ethnicity could significantly engender students' unequal participation opportunities. Yang and Cheng's (2011) study undertaken in Taiwan indicates a strong correlation between parents – especially mother with Masters Degrees – and their children attending highly prestigious universities. But there is no correlation between those who ended their schooling at senior high, junior high or elementary levels. Likewise, the dominant mainlanders were reported to make up most of the freshman cohort with the highest enrolment rate while the Hakka and Taiwanese aborigines had significantly lower chances to study in top universities. More severe racial and ethnic examples were found in South Africa where as many as 90% of black African students are excluded from university education due to racial and ethnic discrimination (Bitzer 2010).

Moreover, students' places of residence create a significant impact on their participating and education equity. Students from rural areas, who are more often likely to be experiencing economic hardship, have fewer opportunities to access tertiary education. Compared with those of urban families, rural students are often economically disadvantaged, and thus they are by far underrepresented in tertiary education. The more prestigious the universities in Korea and China, the lesser the likelihood of rural students gaining entry (Kim and Kim 2013). Furthermore, the World Bank (2009) indicates that the limited distribution of universities in the rural and remote areas of Vietnam (only in major cities), Cambodia (mostly in Phnom Penh) and Thailand (44% of universities are in the Bangkok area) further attributes to unequal access of rural students to high-quality education.

While cultural factors have yet to be widely investigated, some ethnic groups believe that only certain age groups and males should be sent to school. Children, especially ethnic females, are often discouraged from going to college due to various problems including early marriage (e.g. Madurese people in Indonesia) (Suryadarma et al. 2006). In some countries, gender stereotypes lead to investing in education for sons (in China and Laos, Cambodia, Vietnam and Thailand) (World Bank 2009) considered during this gendered selection of who should be educated are women's physical characteristics, personal traits and capacities in society. Such stereotypes can influence the gender-based choice of study fields, close the door of access and eliminate fairness in universities.

Language Barriers

Although linguistic challenges have not been rigorously reported as a roadblock to HE education in Asian contexts, it has been a grave concern for English as second language (ESL) immigrant, undocumented and refugee minority populations in various settings when they learn through the legitimized language. Recent studies by Bui (2008), Kanno and Varghese (2010) and Trang (2016) nominate language constraints as one of the inhibitors impeding minority students' entrance to university. Kanno and Varghese (2010) maintain that we cannot underestimate the linguistic challenges of ESL students as they face tremendous academic difficulties in the areas of reading, specialized vocabulary and academic writing. Thus, they are challenged to achieve the content knowledge in a legitimized language of instruction. Other studies of immigrant students show the profound impact of academic language on the students' learning and success in their institutions (Harklau and Siegal 2009). Immigrant students have a tendency to "self-eliminate" (Kanno and Varghese 2010, p. 323) themselves from the system. The above researchers and others (Davis 2009; Helot and O'Laorie 2011) call for providing students with intensive but welcoming linguistic support, working on the core principle that "every teacher is a language teacher among college faculty" (Kanno and Varghese 2010, p. 324). They further call for addressing literacy needs through applying multilingual practices in the content areas while mobilizing multilingual and multicultural wealth as resourceful capital.

Generally speaking, various countries have made ongoing efforts to ensure higher education expansion and promote initiatives towards equitable and accessible education for all. This has been especially so in the case of minority and socio-economically disadvantaged students. However, rapid acceleration in higher education has created tremendous consequences for ethnic and socio-economically disadvantaged students as they tend either to be highly underrepresented in this field or face high rates of repetition or dropout (Bitzer 2010). Those who gain entry to universities are often stranded in under-resourced institutions while the rich people occupy the most prestigious universities (Kim and Kim 2013). Moreover, many students are seen to be stratified into less desirable fields, isolated and intimidated (Kanno and Varghese 2010). Thus, rather than working towards ensuring democratization in education, maximizing human capital and moving towards greater social equity, higher education expansions have a tendency to reproduce serious consequences that threaten students' jobs, social status, human rights and well-being (Nieuwenhuis and Sehoole 2013).

Our survey of the literature on access and equity in higher education revealed some potential gaps that need to be addressed. First, a great number of the studies explore issues related to participation and equity with socio-economically disadvantaged and minority students on a broad-scale rather than focusing on a particular group of students. While we suspect that minority students face similar issues to those indicated, we, in fact, know very little about the challenges that minority students in a particular region, such as those in this study, cope with in order to access and gain admission to tertiary education. Second, most of the studies reviewed included generated policies and quantitative analysis. Therefore, in addition to methodologies, we argue that gaining qualitatively in-depth and rigorous understanding from different stakeholders (including minority students, their lecturers and administrators) of what specific groups of minority students encounter when aspiring to higher education is essential. Third, the dearth of studies on access and equity among minority groups, especially those who constitute the largest population in Northwest Vietnam, has rendered this study of paramount importance. Thus, the current study attempts to fill these gaps by investigating factors that possibly hinder minority students' higher education access and equity.

The results of the study could effectively support policy-makers, education investors, practitioners and teachers to gain deeper insight into offering practical support to minority students' higher education built on the centrality of their historical, cultural and socio-economic realities. In order to explore this research inquiry, we draw upon Bourdieu's (1986) theory to frame our study, and towards which to orient our analysis. This theory is further discussed in the next section.

Bourdieu's Theories of Social Reproduction and Language as Symbolic Power

Addressing ways in which practices within educational and other social institutions mirror larger social and political agendas and educational inequality, researchers across disciplines have drawn on Bourdieu's (1986) social reproduction theories. The theories involve the intersection of censorship, symbolic power, capital, field and habitus (Grenfell 2012).

Analysing critical socio-political issues and educational inequality across disciplines, scholars widely employ social reproduction theories (Bourdieu 1986). According to Bourdieu, *habitus* reflects individuals' success in a certain field as it resembles one's dispositions. Such dispositions are framed through one's socialization that engenders his/her own ways of seeing, being and successful social interaction. In language, *habitus* represents speakers' social and mental abilities that differentiate their ways of communicating, behaving and interacting in a given discourse from others (Hanks 2005). Bourdieu maintains that if speakers wish to perform successfully in a specific discourse, they must learn forms of formalities reflected of that field. Since such forms and formalities are decided by the upper class, it often legitimizes certain ways of speaking while muting others. This process automatically and de facto intimidates speakers of lower classes. Bourdieu equates this process as a "censorship naturalization" – "the muting of critique and individual expression according to what is rewarded or sanctioned in the field" (Hanks 2005, p. 76). Bourdieu (1991) critically points out that educational discourses including mandates, standards, testing and the uniform curriculum further camouflage language's symbolic power. This type of symbolic power not only refers to the sanctioning and naturalization of language and education policies, but also other forms of powers in society.

Bourdieu's theory of cultural reproduction also reflects *cultural capital* and *economic capital. Cultural capital* is legitimized by a certain political discourse and cultural milieu, resembling the interrelated forms of knowledge, dispositions and educational qualifications. Bourdieu argues that different forms of capital are interwoven and transferable. Hence, cultural capital, for example, can be translated into abundant *economic capital* such as economic capital (money, salary and property), symbolic capital (social status and position) and social capital (relationships and networks) in certain socio-political regimes.

Generally speaking, social reproduction theory reflects interrelated positions that help one to occupy certain social spaces legitimized by a certain discourse or regime. Bourdieu takes schools as an example of intersecting social spaces that one can achieve success or encounter failure. Success or failure is determined by how much capital she/he has (Davis 2009; Hanks 2005; Kramsch 2008). Application of social reproduction theory suggests scholars to delve into the extent to which one could obtain knowledge, language and literacy at school as these manifest larger systems of power relations and equal social access and success both in and out of school (Grenfell 2012; Kramsch 2008).

Bourdieu's theories of social reproduction help this study interpret issues related to access and equity in relation to the expansion of higher education in Vietnam. In particular, his theories offer insight into the operation of social reproduction within financial and non-financial factors. We seek to determine academic preparation, educational policies, college preparation and personal motivation endow minority students with sufficient cultural, social and linguistic capital for them to obtain access and equity in higher education. We inquire into whether these factors could shape students' way into social, educational and economic advancement or at least not disadvantage them. With regard to financial factors, Bourdieu's theories guide this study to investigate whether economic issues, personal and family resources, scholarship and loan policies could advance or restrict their higher education equity. In the following section, we first discuss the method guiding the study. Then we explore the factors that affect minority students' higher education participation and equity.

Methodology

Research Site

This study was undertaken at a regional university in Northwest Vietnam, which we identify as West University (WU). WU is in charge of training human resources and transferring modern technology and research for five provinces in Northwest Vietnam. At the time of undertaking this study, 60% of the students enrolled at this university were minority students. WU was chosen as the research site because one of its fundamental duties is to train minority students. The university offers higher education to at least 40% minority students out of the total number of students who gain admission.

Participants

Nine participants, three per group including managers, lecturers and students, participated in the study on a voluntary basis. With regard to the manager group, two of the managers were vice-deans of faculty and the third was the dean. The three lecturers had achieved three different majors: English as a foreign language, information technology and psychology. The student group comprised of students from different villages who majored in physical education, economics and political studies. The participants were selected from a pool of volunteers and there were wide-ranging variations in their disciplines, roles and educational experiences. Information about the participants is summarized in Table 9.1.

Data Collection and Analysis

The data for this paper was extracted from a larger project which aims to design an instrument suited to exploring the issues of minority students' learning experience. For the purpose of this chapter, our main goal is to gain an in-depth understanding of minority students' opportunities to access higher education from different perspectives. Individual interviews were used to collect data. The interview

Table 9.1 Participant information

Participants	Position	Disciplines	Gender	Ethnic background
Trung	Lecturer	English as a Foreign Language	Male	Kinh
Vy	Lecturer	Psychology	Female	Kinh
Hung	Lecturer	Information Technology	Male	Kinh
Tuan	Second-year student	Physical Education	Male	H'Mong
Thong	Second-year student	Political Study	Male	H'Mong
Tu	First-year student	Economics	Male	Ha Nhi
Duan	Vice-Dean	History	Male	Kinh
Khoi	Vice-Dean	Agriculture	Male	Kinh
Lam	Dean	Economics	Female	Kinh

questions focused on the advantages and disadvantages that minority students experienced when attempting to access higher education. Given the level of the participants' English language proficiency, all of the interviews were conducted in the Vietnamese language to ensure that their content was understood by all interviewees. Following their conclusion, all of the interviews were theme-coded inductively using Nvivo version 10. Pseudonyms were used to ensure the participants' anonymity.

The process of data analysis involved both induction and deduction processes. First, adopting the grounded theory approach to data analysis and interpretation, we pursued an inductive and recursive process. This required reading and rereading the interview transcripts to make sure that patterns, themes and categories emerged from the data (Berg 2001; Strauss and Corbin 2008). Then the data were analysed using a deductive method. More specifically, the themes were consistently aligned with Bourdieu's (1986) theory. In the following section, we present the findings of the study. This is followed by a discussion based on Bourdieu's (1986) forms of capital to interpret the factors that impact on minority students' capacity to obtain equity and access in higher education in Northwest Vietnam.

Findings and Discussion

Data from our interviews with the managers, lecturers and students were analysed and interpreted based on the foundation of the grounded theories developed in this chapter. This enabled us to identify the support and challenges that minority students either received or had to content with when attempting to access higher education. The following themes emerged: (a) Linguistic factors; (b) Economic factors; (c) Geographical factors; (d) Academic factors; and (e) Socio-cultural factors.

Linguistic Factors

The reflections of all three groups of participants showed that language barrier was among the more defining inhibitors of minority students' academic performance. Their ability to use both Vietnamese and English was identified as a significant challenge for minority students attempting to access higher education. Regarding their Vietnamese language proficiency, all of the participants, including managers, lecturers and students, agreed that the minority students had insufficient Vietnamese language ability. Similarly, all of participant students admitted that they had limited proficiency in spoken Vietnamese, particularly in pronunciation. In addition, the lecturers emphasized the students' problems with writing in Vietnamese. These linguistic challenges stemmed from a complex language situation: minority students have to learn and use Vietnamese, not their mother tongue, at schools. Vietnamese is the official language and the medium of instruction. As a result, minority students face significant challenges when speaking and writing in Vietnamese. Trung, a lecturer who taught this group of students, said "They [minority students] normally have wrong spellings and they cannot express their ideas in written form deeply". Language challenges, according to the lecturers and managers, could impede the students' efforts to communicate effectively, comprehend course content and achieve academic success. The following quotes lend additional support to this point: "It is hard for minority students to have in-depth-understanding of the materials because of their limitation in Vietnamese language" (Duan, manager). Or "Due to language obstacles, most of minority students' graduate point average is not high" (Hung, lecturer).

Students not only face the challenges of having to learn using Vietnamese; English is an additional burden with which they have to contend. Both the managers and the lecturers expressed concern regarding the students' ability to learn the English language, especially given that they have to learn it via a language (Vietnamese) in which they lack academic competence. As one manager reasoned, "English is the most challenging to minority students. Given that their Vietnamese language is not good, learning English is impossible for them" (Duan, manager). Another lecturer expressed his concern: "English is the most difficult subject for minority students, especially listening skill" (Trung, lecturer). However, while both the managers and lecturers expressed concern regarding the students' English-learning ability, only one of three students reported challenges to learning English. It could be that the students had more immediate linguistic problems with their use of the Vietnamese language because the Vietnamese language has more impact on their study than the English language.

Economic Factors

Prior to their attempts to access university education, economical capital was both the driving force and the barrier impeding minority students' ability to access higher education. All of the participants emphasized that a successful study in higher education would allow them to overcome their current challenging financial situations. As one student reflected, "My parents are poor. I want to learn to get a good job and a better life" (Tuan, student). Hung, a lecturer commented "Minority students takes higher education with a desire to obtain a diploma to apply for a job, which allows them to earn a living and support their parents". The above quotes indicate that financial problems play a motivating role in the students' desire to access higher education.

Their respective financial situations were considered to be barriers to the students' aspirations to quality university education. The participant students said that their families could not afford for them to study in Vietnam's big cities. It would cost too much, particularly in food and rent. For this reason, all of the participant students chose the teaching discipline because it was fee-free. Regrettably, however, they showed no interest in teaching as a job.

The students' academic paths seemed even harder when most of them had to financially rely on their parents and relatives to fund their higher education study. According to a manager, "a majority of minority students come from very poor family in mountainous areas. For those living in these areas, earning a living is hard" (Duan, manager). All of the participants said that the main financial source was the family. The following quotes lend support to this position:

> Minority students receive limited financial aids. Their parents support them by loaning from grants for minority students. (Hung, lecturer)

> One of the biggest barriers for me is my family's financial problem. My parents have to save all their income for me to study. (Thong, student)

Underpinning the above quotes is the negative impact of financial problems on the minority students' higher education. It becomes clear that due to their families' scant financial resources, the minority students find it hard to pursue their higher education.

According to minority students, they can access some sources of financial support at their institution; but these sources seem to be unsustainable. All of the participants reported that minority students received financial aid from the government and tuition waivers. There was also some aid from provincial organizations. For example, one student said "I received 1 million VND [about $50] from the provincial inspiring learning organization when I got an offer from the university. I heard that the Education Department could provide some financial support, but I did not receive any notice about that" (Tuan, student). Another student said that he did not receive any financial aid, as he did not qualify: "My academic result is low so I do not get any grants" (Tu, student). These narratives reveal that aid for minority students was either unreliable or difficult to achieve.

In their attempts to deal with their financial problems, minority students took part-time jobs. However, jobs for students in the mountainous areas were scarce. In addition, all of the managers, lecturers and students said that the only jobs available to students were hard work such as workers and waiters. This was because NWU is located in an area in which jobs are generally scarce. This made it even harder for minority students with limited Vietnamese language competence to get a good job such as tutoring. Moreover, one of the lecturers realized that working part time negatively affected the minority students' study. They could face difficulty meeting their academic deadlines, and showed limited concentration and poor participation in the class. He commented, "Earning money for living and study has negative impact on the students' physical and mental health, time, and study achievement" (Trung, lecturer).

Academic Factors

Their lack of academic background was another challenge for the minority students trying to access higher education. All the participant students claimed that they could not attend the tutor classes because they could not afford them. In addition, they perceived that the quality of teaching in their villages was not high enough to prepare the students to gain access to universities. Given this lack of preparation, it came as no surprise when we learned that two of three participant students were only the first or second in their villages to gain university entrance. It appears that students from remote villages found higher education access limited, and being pioneers put considerable pressure on them. They had to work hard to fulfil not only their families' expectation but also those of the people in their villages. While Thang (student) said "I need to learn to show that I can do as people in other places can", Tu (student) recalled what his family said to him "Our family is poor and you are the only one going to university. You must try your best".

Despite being given two bonus marks for the entrance exam, the minority students lacked institutional support once they entered the university. First, according to all of the participant managers and lecturers, there was no curriculum specifically designed for minority students. Thus, they had to study the same programmes as advantaged students. This practice was considered a barrier to their understanding of the content. The following quotes illustrate this fact:

> The curricular were designed to all students so they were hard to the minority students. (Hung, lecturer)

> The curricular were designed according to the criteria for national tertiary programs. The curricular were not appropriate for minority students, although considerations of the regional relevance were taken. For example, the general program required to have 15 credits for English language subject, this number was reduced to 10 because minority students could not meet that requirement. (Duan, manager)

The reality was that the "one size fits all" methodological practice threatened to double the minority students' burden once they entered university. The teachers at NWU did not receive any comprehensive training on how to work with students from diverse socio-linguistic backgrounds. In effect, the teachers taught the minority students using the same methods that they used with other students, despite the former's disadvantaged linguistic and social backgrounds. Thus, it is hardly surprising that the minority students found it difficult to keep up with the advantaged students. As one lecturer said, "In the class, the minority students get slower progress than other students" (Vy). Although one manager argued that all of the students should learn the same curriculum to ensure the right of everyone to access the same programmes, other lecturers and managers suggested providing curricular and teaching methods appropriate to the minority students' backgrounds.

Geographical Factors

All three participant students conceded that living in remote areas impeded their opportunities to access higher education. Being isolated from other areas was said to limit the students' exposure to up-to-date information and modern media. In addition, having to commute was inconvenient. These conditions hindered minority students' choices vis-à-vis universities in the big cities. One student said that he chose NWU because "NWU is the one closest to my village; I save much when I do not need to travel a long distance" (Tu, student). This viewpoint was consistent with those of managers and lecturers who noted that in addition to the quality of the university, the main reason why minority students opted to this particular university was its location. Although NWU was much closer to their villages than other universities, minority students still had to live far from family when they entered NWU, while they became more independent. On the other hand, they were negatively affected by the social environment. Duan (manager) commented, "Many minority students were attracted by unhealthy life (e.g., attracted entertaining service such as video games) and paid no attention to their study. Consequently, some of them were involved in social evils." In addition, many participant students found it hard to adapt to the new environment. It was markedly different from the small villages where they were born and grew up. It seems, therefore, that living in remote areas not only limited the students' choice of universities, but they also had to face additional challenges when getting accustomed to their new learning environment.

Socio-Cultural Factors

Another barrier that minority students faced was associated with socio-cultural factors. According to Trung (lecturer), some minority people's reluctance to have their children accessing higher education was due to the traditional thinking that university was not the place for females. Their duty was to stay at home and get married. Trung provided an example of how minority parents' customs hindered their children access to higher education. He said: "Early marriages among minority students affect their study as they need to take care of their family while studying". Further to the gender issue, Khoi (manager) considered the perceived inequality between males and females a barrier to the latter's accessing of higher education. Because females had to spend so much time on housework, they had less time for study. Among other factors that impacted on the minority students' study routines was the New Year festival. Duan (manager) observed that the H'mong students often took a month off to enjoy their New Year festival. This temporary discontinuation of their studies affected their learning. So, in addition to pecuniary hardship, the students' cultural background was a further barrier impeding their higher education access from the perspectives of their lecturers and managers. The fact that the students may be unaware of this impact on their study suggests a need to alert them to the problems that cultural factors can cause.

In addition, data emerged from the interviews indicating that minority students lacked both networks and connections, and this restricted them from taking advantage of opportunities and resources. Due to living in remote areas, the participant students claimed that they could not access information about different disciplines and universities. This led them to choose NWU, which was geographically appropriate to for them. In addition, the minority students' participation in activities outside their villages and their ability to access modern technology were limited. For example, as one lecturer noted "In general, the minority students live far from the center, they are limited to expose to update information and social communication. As a result, they cannot learn as well as other students" (Trung). His comment was confirmed by Tua, a student, who said that one of the minority students' challenges was exposure to the modern world. It becomes clear that limited chances to networking with the outside world were among the hindrances experienced by minority students.

Once they entered university, the minority students' backgrounds seemed to constrain them from connecting with other people and learning about the environment. One of the lecturers observed that minority students seemed to lack self-efficacy. In class, as all of the lecturers said, minority students were shy; they did not dare to express their ideas, mainly because "They did not have chance to communicate with outside world out of their village since they were small" (Khoi, manager). Similarly, the participant students also told us that they felt isolated living far from their families as they had limited communication skills. One student commented "I do not feel confident because of my knowledge and communication skills" (Tuan, student). Therefore, in addition to their other limitations, the minority students' academic achievements were low. Many of them failed to meet the requirement to graduate. As all of the lecturers noted, most of the minority students obtained average graduate points. But three managers reported that only approximately 60% of the total minority students graduated every year. Apart from their lack of success in the academic sphere, the minority students self-eliminated from participating social activities. All of the participant lecturers and managers found that minority students lacked the confidence to actively participate in community activities. Therefore, once again the minority students' backgrounds appear to hinder their involvement where they achieve success.

Discussions and Policy Implications

The results of the study indicate various factors that potentially affect minority students' access and equity in higher education. It may be that their linguistic, economic, socio-cultural and geographical challenges are greatly congruent with the linguistic, cultural, economic and social forms of capital espoused in Bourdieu's theories. However, the abundant capital that determines the minority students' ways of being, seeing and occupying social space and success seems to dispossess any concrete form of capital authorized by the current social milieu due to interrelated socio-cultural, economic and social challenges.

With regard to the linguistic capital, Bourdieu (1991) claims that certain forms of linguistic behaviour (e.g. accent, intonation, vocabulary) determine one's position in the social hierarchy if such behaviour is legitimized by those who wield power. However, due to the contested and complex linguistic dilemmas reported by the students (e.g. different accent; Vietnamese, not their minority language as a medium of instruction; and learning English as a compulsory subject via the national language that minority students cannot fully comprehend), they seem to become locked into a complicated circle that not only critically limits their chances to gain access to higher education, but continues to act as a de facto barrier even when they get privilege to pursue university education. Bourdieu's notion of capital further illuminates that minority students do possess heritage language capital but they are not recognized and legitimized. Rather, it seems to be a tremendous challenge for the students to become competent language users or gain language capital endowed from the current HE discourse. Thus, when language does not equate to power, for the minority students to obtain HE participation, socialize and achieve academic success, it can be said that they have insufficient linguistic capital that could seriously threaten their ability to thrive over the process of access, completion and gaining equity in higher education at large.

Bourdieu (1986, 1991) views that economic capital can be inherited through the family foundation or through concrete cultural capital gained from a recognized education system. Unlike rich linguistic capital inherited (but not legitimized) from home, the minority students do not seem to possess strong economic capital from their parents. Such unfavourable economic conditions together with the scant institutional financial support they receive repeatedly deter the students from maintaining their higher education aspirations and threaten their ability to complete their degrees. Thus, one can easily picture a weak route to educational equity and success in the future because, for the most part, the students' extremely limited economic capital cannot result in lucrative socio-economic opportunities that are critical for ensuring their equity within their higher education institution and later in life.

Regarding cultural capital, it becomes clear that the history of limited education quality and the university entrance exam mechanism further disturbs the students' pursuit of higher education. Participants reported having limited conditions in which to prepare for the national university entrance exam. They felt doubly challenged due to a set of institutional issues including a mismatched curriculum, uniform teaching pedagogies and contested language issues. A combination of these factors resulted in a low percentage of graduates with the requisite quality. Aligning these issues with Bourdieu's cultural capital, we will suggest that society attributes the minority students' insufficient educational capital to their lack of legitimate knowledge and skills, which leads to their failure to access to higher education institution. This fragile linkage between lack of cultural capital and HE struggles is supported by numerous studies in the USA, Taiwan, China, Indonesia, South Korea, Colombia, Africa, Brazil and Chile (Espinoza and González 2013; Kanno and Varghese 2010; Kim and Kim 2013; Nieuwenhuis and Sehoole 2013; Somers et al. 2013; Yang and Cheng 2011). In other words, this study concurs with these aforementioned studies to argue that rather than relying on schooling as a resourceful space to secure the minority students' cultural capital, it could de facto diminish the students' hope of turning their academic qualifications into the social dispositions, knowledge and skills sought after by the globalized job market.

Finally, since Bourdieu's forms of capital are interrelated and transformable, the minority students' social capital could literally be generated from the above forms of capital. In reality, flimsy linguistic, cultural and economic capital, together with the geographical hindrances, feelings of isolation and a limited academic network in their university, signal their deficient social capital. It could greatly inhibit the students' smooth academic trajectory through higher education and weaken the existing and future network that will secure their social participation and success.

In summary, wide-ranging socio-economic, linguistic and cultural factors determine minority students' opportunities to take up fragile forms of capital within and outside the higher education setting. A combination of these factors threatens minority students' aspirations, access and success in higher education. That is to say, despite ongoing efforts to provide access to equal education for all, the expansion of higher education in Vietnam seems to continue to disadvantage the minority students' access and success in a new form. This seems attributable to a vast array of factors including minimal academic preparation for the university entrance exam, different educational expectations and college knowledge, limited support for tertiary planning, and the students' sense of uncertainty and isolation in the university environment. These factors combine to restrict minority students from obtaining the requisite cultural, social and linguistic capital that will later enable them to negotiate social, educational and economic advancement and equity.

The findings of the study thus strongly suggest the need for policy change for minority students seeking higher education, which is strictly built upon the constant negotiation of their linguistic, socio-economic and educational struggles. Within the scope of this study, we specifically focus on three major recommendations directly relevant to the distinct nature of the students and the provinces from which they come. First, in terms of linguistic support, we suggest that students should be assisted with basic Vietnamese language in their primary or secondary education, scaffolded by certain components of their minority languages. We concur with Kanno and Vargehese's (2010) notion of every lecturer as a language lecturer. In other words, lecturers should be sensitive to their students' linguistic challenges and offer ample chances for students to improve their work. Furthermore, multilingual and critical scholars (Hélot and O'Laoire 2011; Ruiz 1984) strongly argue for embedding minority and immigrant students' languages and cultures as rich resources and effective teaching methods. Thus, we suggest integrating students' languages, cultures and ways of learning into everyday teaching. This will help students build a strong academic foundation, and to draw comparisons between the new knowledge and the existing epistemologies rooted in their languages and cultures. Such approaches, it is argued, enrich students' meta-cognitive and meta-linguistic skills and alleviate their burdens of isolation and intimidation in their new learning environment.

We agree with Bui (2008), Bui and Nguyen (2016) and Kanno and Varghese's (2010) proposal that education policy-makers should be encouraged to adopt a holistic approach when dealing with access and equity issues for minority and low-income students. This encourages analysing structural and economic factors that prevent underprivileged students from university access and success. Increasing educational opportunities for socio-economically underrepresented populations engenders justice and fairness. We call for interdisciplinary support from various institutions, starting at the local level and moving out from there. Universities should collaborate with institutions to offer favourable financial support to students in the forms of scholarships, tuition waivers or affordable student loans. Furthermore, building on the lack of information about the financial experience of some the students in this study, we further recommend that HE institutions should clearly publicize policies appertaining to financial support for socio-economically disadvantaged students. Universities' financial aid should also be publicized in the local centres of the students' communities. This will ensure that parents and students are informed regarding the extent to which they will be financially supported and further enable the parents to plan higher education for their children.

While the minority students in this study enjoy the privilege of being able to participate in higher education, a large number of their fellows are left behind in their remote villages due to wide-ranging socio-economic and financial burdens. At the same time, countries in Asia including Vietnam are on the move, shifting their economies from agrarian-based to more diverse economic models (e.g. Erling 2014), requiring various sets of skills. Therefore, we strongly recommend that interdisciplinary policy-makers diversify and intensify their multiple training programmes affiliated with local and regional universities and organizations. To ensure equity and success, such training programmes will need to be sustainably and carefully structured around people's needs, the nature of their land, cultures, history, as well as a range of socio-economic, educational and linguistic factors.

References

Abdullah, I. (2011). Equity and access in a constantly expanding Indonesian higher education system. In D. Neubauer & Y. Tanaka (Eds.), *Access, equity, and capacity in Asia-Pacific higher education* (pp. 71–82). New York: Palgrave Macmillan.
Berg, B. L. (2001). *Qualitative research methods for the social sciences*. Boston: Allyn and Bacon.

Bitzer, E. M. (2010). Some myths on equity and access in higher education. *Unisa Press, 24*(2), 298–312.

Bourdieu, P. (1986). The forms of capital. In J. Richardson (Ed.), *Handbook of theory and research for the sociology of education*. New York: Greenwood.

Bourdieu, P. (1991). *Language and symbolic power*. Cambridge: Polity Press.

Bui, T. N. T. (2008). Minority students need unique classes. *Vietnam News*, available at: http://vietnamnews.vnanet.vn/showarticle.php?num=01EDU061008

Bui, T. N. T., & Nguyen, T. M. H. (2016). Standardizing English for educational and socio-economic betterment – A critical analysis of English language policy reforms in Vietnam. In K. Robert (Ed.), *English language education in Asia* (pp. 363–388). New York: Springer.

Chankseliani, M. (2013). Higher education access in Post-Soviet Georgia: Overcoming a legacy of corruption. In H. Mayer, E. John, M. Chankseliani, & L. Uribe (Eds.), *Fairness in access to higher education in a global perspective* (pp. 171–188). Rotterdam: Sense Publishers.

Davis, K. A. (2009). Agentive youth research: Towards individual, collective, and policy transformations. In T. G. Wiley, J. S. Lee, & R. Rumberger (Eds.), *The education of language minority immigrants in the USA* (pp. 202–239). London: Multilingual Matters.

Decision 89/QD-TTg. Phê duyệt Đề án "Xây dựng xã hội học tập giai đoạn 2012 – 2020". Retrieved from http://hanoi.edu.vn/phong-gd-thuong-xuyen/quyet-dinh-phe-duyet-de-an-xay-dung-xa-hoi-hoc-tap-giai-doan-2012-2020-c559-2664.aspx

Erling, E. (2014). *Role of English in skill development in South Asia: Policies, interventions, and existing evidence*. New Delhi: British Council.

Espinoza, O., & González, L. E. (2013). Accreditation in higher education in Chile: Results and consequences. *Quality Assurance in Education, 21*(1), 20–38.

Fry, G. W. (2009). Higher education in Vietnam. In Y. Hirosato & Y. Kitamura (Eds.), *The political economy of educational reforms and capacity development in Southeast Asia: Cases of Cambodia, Laos and Vietnam* (pp. 237–265). New York: Springer.

Grenfell, M. (2012). Bourdieu, language and education. In M. Grenfell, D. Bloome, C. Hardy, K. Paul, K. Rowsell, & B. Street (Eds.), *Language, ethnography and education: Bridging new literacies and Bourdieu* (pp. 50–70). New York: Routledge.

Hanks, W. F. (2005). Pierre Bourdieu and the practices of language. *Annual Review of Anthropology, 34*(1), 67–83. https://doi.org/10.1146/annurev.anthro.33.070203.143907.

Harklau, L., & Siegal, M. (2009). Immigrant youth and higher education. In M. Roberge, M. Siegal, & L. Harklau (Eds.), *Generation 1.5 in college composition: Teaching academic writing to U.S. educated learners of ESL* (pp. 25–34). New York: Routledge.

Hawkins, J. (2011). Variations on equity and access in higher education in Asia. In D. Neubauer & Y. Tanaka (Eds.), *Access, equity, and capacity in Asia-Pacific higher education* (pp. 15–30). New York: Palgrave Macmillan.

Hélot, C., & O'Laoire, M. (2011). *Language policy for the multilingual classroom (bilingual education and bilingualism)*. London: Channel View Publications.

Holsinger, D. B. (2009). Inequality in the public provision of education: Why it matters. *Comparative Education Review, 49*(3), 297–310.

Jacobs, L. (2013). A vision of equal opportunity in postsecondary education. In H. Mayer, E. John, M. Chankseliani, & L. Uribe (Eds.), *Fairness in access to higher education in a global perspective* (pp. 41–56). Rotterdam: Sense Publishers.

Jalava, M. (2013). The finish model of higher education access: Does egalitarianism square with excellence? In H. Mayer, E. John, M. Chankseliani, & L. Uribe (Eds.), *Fairness in access to higher education in a global perspective* (pp. 97–94). Rotterdam: Sense Publishers.

Kanno, Y., & Varghese, M. M. (2010). Immigrant and refugee ESL students' challenges to accessing four-year college education: From language policy to educational policy. *Journal of Language, Identity & Education, 9*(5), 310–328.

Kim, J., & Kim, H. S. (2013). Globalisation and access to higher education in Korea. In H. Mayer, E. John, M. Chankseliani, & L. Uribe (Eds.), *Fairness in access to higher ducation in a global perspective* (pp. 129–152). Rotterdam: Sense Publishers.

Kramsch, C. (2008). Pierre Bourdieu: A biographical memoir. In J. Albright & A. Luke (Eds.), *Pierre Bourdieu and literacy education* (pp. 33–49). New York: Routledge.

Mayer, E., John, M., Chankseliani, M., & Uribe, L. (2013). *Fairness in access to higher education in a global perspective* (pp. 129–152). Sense Publishers: Rotterdam.

McCowan, T. (2015). Three dimensions of equity of access to higher education. *Compare: A Journal of Comparative and International Education, 46*(4), 645–665. https://doi.org/10.1080/03057925.2015.1043237.

Mestan, K., & Harvey, A. (2014). The higher education continuum: Access, achievement and outcomes among students from non-English speaking backgrounds. *Higher Education Review, 46*(2), 61–79.

Neubauer, D., & Tanaka, Y. (2011). *Access, equity, and capacity in Asia-Pacific higher education.* New York: Palgrave Macmillan.

Nieuwenhuis, J., & Sehoole, C. (2013). In H. Mayer, E. John, M. Chankseliani, & L. Uribe (Eds.), *Fairness in access to higher education in a global perspective* (pp. 189–202). Rotterdam: Sense Publishers.

Oliver, D. E., Pham, X. T., Elsner, P. A., Nguyen, T. T. P., & Do, Q. T. (2009). Globalisation of higher education and community colleges in Vietnam. In L. Rosalind & J. Edward (Eds.), *Community college models globalisation and higher education reform.* New York: Springer.

Ruiz, R. (1984). Orientations in language planning. *NABE: The Journal for the National Association for Bilingual Education, 8*(2), 15–34.

Somers, P., Morosini, M., Pan, M., & Cofer, J. E., Sr. (2013). Brazil's radical approach to expanding access for underrepresented college students. In H. Mayer, E. John, M. Chankseliani, & L. Uribe (Eds.), *Fairness in access to higher education in a global perspective* (pp. 203–223). Rotterdam: Sense Publishers.

Strauss, A., & Corbin, J. (2008). *Basics of qualitative research: Techniques and procedures for developing grounded theory* (2nd ed.). Thousand Oaks: SAGE.

Suryadarma, D., Widyanti, W., Suryahadi, A., & Sumarto, S. (2006). *From access to income: Regional and ethnic inequality in Indonesia.* Jakarta: SMERU Research Institute.

Tanaka, Y. (2011). The dilemma of higher education policy choices. In D. Neubauer & Y. Tanaka (Eds.), *Access, equity, and capacity in Asia-Pacific higher education* (pp. 99–114). New York: Palgrave Macmillan.

Thủ Tướng Chính Phủ (Prime Minister). (2007). Quyết định số 157/2007/QĐ-TTg, 27/9/2007, về tín dụng cho sinh viên hoàn cảnh khó khăn (Decision No. 157/2007/QĐ-TTg, 27/9/2007, Credits for the disadvantaged student. Hanoi, Vietnam.

Thủ Tướng Chính Phủ (Prime Minister). (2012a). Quyết định số 73/ 2012/ND-CP, 26/9/2012, về đầu tư và hợp tác nước ngoài trong giáo dục (Decision number 73/ 2012/ND-CP, 26/9/2012, Foreign cooperation and investment in education. Hanoi, Vietnam.

Thủ Tướng Chính Phủ (Prime Minister). (2012b). Quyết định số 711/QĐ-TTg, 13/6/2012, Chiến lược phát triển giáo dục 2011–2020 (Decision number 711/QĐ-TTg, 13/6/2012, Strategies for Education Development 2011–2020). Hanoi, Vietnam.

Tran, L., Marginson, S., Do, H., Do, Q., Le, T., Nguyen, N., et al. (2014). *Higher education in Vietnam: Flexibility, mobility and practicality in the global knowledge economy.* Hampshire: Palgrave Macmillan.

Trang, T. (2016). *Maintaining in transforming: Bilingual identity of ethnic minority students in the Central Highlands of Vietnam.* (Unpublished PhD), The University of Queensland, Australia.

World Bank. (2009). *Literature review on equity and access to tertiary education in the East Asia Region.* Retrieved from http://siteresources.worldbank.org/EDUCATION/Resources/278200-1099079877269/547664-1099079956815/547670 1276537814548/WorldBank_EAR_Equity_LitReview.pdf

Yang, J. (2007). The one-child policy and school attendance in China. *Comparative Education Review, 51*(4), 471–495.

Yang, S., & Cheng, S. Y. (2011). Social justice, equal access, and stratification of higher education in Taiwan. In D. Neubauer & Y. Tanaka (Eds.), *Access, equity, and capacity in Asia-Pacific higher education* (pp. 139–154). New York: Palgrave Macmillan.

Yu, K., & Ertl, H. (2010). Equity in access to higher education in China, the role of public and nonpublic institutions. *Chinese Education and Society, 43*(6), 36–58.

Zhong, H. (2011). Returns to higher education in China: What is the role of college quality? *China Economic Review, 22*(2), 260–275.

Part IV
HE Research

Chapter 10
A Comparative Analysis of Vietnamese and Australian Research Capacity, Policies, and Programmes

Quy Nguyen and Christopher Klopper

Abstract The chapter explores the research capacity of academics within the contexts of Vietnamese and Australian universities in the following ways: (1) research productivity, (2) the research policies that support the engagement of academics in research, and (3) the national programmes that aim to enhance the research capacity of the academics. It provides insights and recommendations that have the potential to stimulate research activities that promote both the quantity and the quality of research outcomes for all.

Introduction

Higher education plays an important role in every country. Under the influences of globalisation in HE, there have been, to date, not only a significant transformation in the manner of how universities teach students but also changes to the roles of academics. In particular, the responsibility of undertaking research by academics beyond the traditional role of teaching is emphasised (Brew 2006). Some researchers indicated that a combination of teaching and research can enhance teaching quality – a desirable aim of most universities (Brew 2003; Brew and Boud 1995; Hattie and Marsh 1996; Jenkins et al. 1998). The general assumption that a synergistic relation exists between the research productivity of academics and their teaching quality is probably appropriate because universities nowadays aim to produce student learning, not to provide teaching instruction as they used to (Rice 2006). Scott (2004), as cited in Harman and Nguyen (2010), argued that teaching and research should be linked together because the integration of teaching into research

Q. Nguyen (✉)
The University of Danang-University of Foreign Language Studies, Da Nang, Vietnam

Griffith Institute for Educational Research, Griffith University, Brisbane, QLD, Australia
e-mail: nhquy@ufl.udn.vn

C. Klopper
Griffith University, Brisbane, QLD, Australia

© Springer Nature Singapore Pte Ltd. 2019
N. T. Nguyen, L. T. Tran (eds.), *Reforming Vietnamese Higher Education*,
Education in the Asia-Pacific Region: Issues, Concerns and Prospects 50,
https://doi.org/10.1007/978-981-13-8918-4_10

helps to validate the university's academic authority. According to Brew and Boud (1995, p. 264), teaching and research are closely related to each other through the act of learning from each other, 'Doing research is not likely to enhance pedagogical skills, but it is likely to enhance a teacher's knowledge, interest in and enthusiasm for the subject' (p. 264). Similarly, research enhances the knowledge and competence of academics, which, in turn, strengthens capacity to supervise research projects of students, particularly postgraduate students (Lindsay et al. 2002). Supporting the above arguments, Jensen (1988) examined the 'unity of research and teaching' through interviews with about 50 teachers at higher education institutions in Denmark and found 3 significant influences of research to teaching. First, research 'fertilises teaching with new topics and methodological advances'. When academics bring research knowledge in teaching practices, they apply a student-focused teaching approach to facilitate student learning and make a conceptual change of phenomena. Second, research 'provides teachers with a personal engagement of great pedagogic significance'. And, third, 'university teaching, via research carried out by staff, maintains connections with developments in the world of international research' (Jensen 1988, p. 20). In recognition of the importance of academic research, the Vietnamese Government has made a reform known as Higher Education Reform Agenda (HERA) in order to develop a learning society. The HERA emphasises on the quality of teaching and learning and aims to develop curriculum that strongly supports research of academics and upgrade teaching materials that link to research practices.

In order to maintain a competitive edge in the global HE sector, many universities work towards being identified as high-performing universities through the research pursuits of academics. Academics nowadays are not simply knowledge transferors but more importantly, they must be knowledge creators. Due to such demands, academics are increasingly required to engage in both teaching and research in alignment with the expectations of their level of employment at universities (Brew 2006). This can be very challenging for academics that so many of them find it difficult for them to perform satisfactorily in both core missions. It is anticipated that with such increased expectations, all academics have to modify their working practices, attitudes, behaviours, and academic identities from teaching-focused to research-focused to meet the expectations of the twenty-first-century universities.

Universities continue to contribute significantly to the development and competitiveness of a country through the generation of knowledge, and collaboration with industry to conduct joint research and development projects (Cummings 2014). Universities are places that not only transfer knowledge, but also produce knowledge. Importantly, knowledge creation requires a network of scholars and academics that actively engage in future-focused research activities. It is projected that globalisation in HE has resulted in universities to experience greater external pressures to their operation and development and a greater sense of accountability for all academics. Research productivity of academics has become an important indicator used in the evaluation of research performance and serves a multiplicity of purposes such as recruitment, job security, promotion, and salary increase, as well as of universities' rankings.

This chapter explores the research capacity of academics within the contexts of Vietnam and Australia universities in the following ways: (1) research productivity, (2) the research policies that support the engagement of academics in research, and (3) the national programmes that aim to enhance the research capacity of the academics. Additionally, the chapter compares Vietnamese academics' research capacity and productivity with those in the Association of Southeast Asian Nations (ASEAN) and other East Asian countries such as China, Japan and South Korea – these countries used to have similar historical, social, economic, and educational background with Vietnam 30 years ago. Albeit Vietnam's growth over the last 30 years, there remains a significant gap in higher education between Vietnam and other Asian countries. The inclusion of them into this chapter provides an overall picture of research capacity and productivity of the Vietnamese academics in comparison to other neighbouring countries. The chapter begins with a review of the social, political, and economic changes in Vietnam over the past 30 years, which subsequently has impacted on Vietnamese Higher Education.

Social, Political, and Economic Changes in Vietnam and Their Impacts on Vietnamese Higher Education

Since the end of the Resistance War against America in 1975, the North and the South of Vietnam united under the name of Socialist Republic of Vietnam. Between 1975 and 1985, Vietnam encountered numerous challenges and difficulties due to the sanctions and embargos imposed by the United States of America. Acknowledging the urgent need for changes, during the Sixth Congress of the Vietnam Communist Party in December 1986, the leaders of Vietnam launched an 'Economic Reforms' in the economy (widely known as Đổi Mới). The main purpose of the Economic Reforms was to create an environment which was conducive to transformation to occur. Such transformation aimed to convert the economy from a centralised and planned one, mostly founded on imports and subsidisation, to a socialist-oriented market economy. Through this Renovation, the Government of Vietnam 'made a commitment to increased economic liberalisation and structural reforms were implemented to modernise the economy and develop competitive, export-driven industries' (Westerheijden et al. 2010, p. 183). This change opened pathways for Vietnam to gradually take part in the world economy, align with the international development trends, and for the influence of globalisation to permeate in all sectors and industries in Vietnam. The VHE was not immune to this. Since that time, the economy of Vietnam has been improving incrementally and as a result, the standard of living for most Vietnamese people has increased. The Renovation opened opportunities for Vietnam to (re)-establish its diplomatic relations with the United States of America after a period of interruption and to forge new relations with other

Table 10.1 Statistics of colleges and universities in Vietnam 2000–2016

Year	2000	2006	2012	2016
Colleges				
Number of colleges	104	183	214	219
Number of students	186,723	367,054	724,232	449,558
Number of academics, *of which:*	7843	15,381	26,008	24,260
Doctorate	109	216	693	633
Master's	1468	3669	10,015	12,365
Universities				
Number of universities	74	139	207	203
Number of students	731,505	1,173,147	1,453,067	1,753,174
Number of academics, *of which:*	24,362	38,137	61,674	69,591
Doctorate	4454	5666	8869	13,598
Master's	6596	14,603	28,987	40,426

Source: Data collected from statistics of the Ministry of Education and Training over different years

countries. The Vietnam's increasing participation in the international organisations and associations such as the Association of Southeast Asian Nations (ASEAN) and the World Trade Organisation (WTO) has gradually strengthened its position in the global map.

Due to Economic Reforms in 1986 and various social and economic changes, the VHE has made positive advancements. The higher education system in Vietnam has been restructured to meet students' demands and to enhance the higher education quality. There have been diverse types of HE institutions (HEIs – Cơ sở giáo dục đại học trong hệ thống giáo dục quốc dân) existing across the higher education sector. According to the Article 7 of the Law of Higher Education 2012, HEIs include: (a) college (trường cao đẳng), (b) university (trường đại học) and institute (học viện), (c) regional university (đại học vùng) and national university (đại học quốc gia), and (d) research institute that is allowed to train doctoral candidates (viện nghiên cứu khoa học được phép đào tạo trình độ tiến sĩ).

Over the last 20 years, Vietnamese higher education has expanded dramatically. Table 10.1 provides an overview of the changes in 2000, 2006, 2012, and 2016. The number of colleges, universities, and academics since 2000 has increased significantly. Table 1 signposts that the number of colleges in 2016 has doubled, reaching 219 colleges compared to 104 colleges in 2000. Universities have tripled within 16 years (2000–2016), from 74 universities in 2000 to 203 universities in 2016. Although the number of academics at colleges and universities increased as a result of rapid expansion of universities and colleges, such increases have not caught up with the booming student enrolment demands of HE in Vietnam (Hayden and Thiep 2010).

Two hundred and three universities in Vietnam have been classified in three administratively hierarchical classes from top to bottom[1]: (1) national university (đại học quốc gia), (2) regional university (đại học vùng), and (3) university (trường đại học). National and regional universities have been established since 1990s on the basis of amalgamating several long-standing colleges and universities that already existed in the five key cities during that period. Currently, Vietnam has two national universities and three regional universities. The mission of the two national universities is to produce highly qualified human resources and talents for the industrialisation and modernisation of the whole country, while the three regional universities have been in charge of three regions where they are located. Under the globalised forces such as the need to join in the global knowledge society, which Nguyen and Tran (Chap. 1, p. 16) consider good conditions for the implementation of the higher education reform in Vietnam, these national and regional universities are expected become the research-oriented universities of Vietnam by 2020 (Thủ tướng Chính phủ 2012a). The establishment of such research-oriented universities helps to develop an effective academic system in order to improve the reputation and competitiveness of VHE on the world stage of higher education.

The period between 2012 and 2016 witnessed a colossal increase in the number of doctoral academics working at universities, from 8869 people in 2012 to 13,598 people in 2016. Despite the large number of doctorates, the average percentage of doctoral academics among teaching staff at HEIs remains comparatively low (10–25%), with the exception of the two leading universities of Vietnam: Vietnam National University-Ha Noi (VNU-HN) and Vietnam National University-Ho Chi Minh city (VNU-HCMC). As of 2016, the percentage of the doctoral holders over the total number of academic staff at VNU-HN is 47.62% (VNU-HN 2016) and at VNU-HCMC is 38.46% (VNU-HCMC 2016). Although two national universities of Vietnam[2] have the highest concentration of doctoral academics, such percentages are considered low compared to universities in other countries where approximately 90% of academics hold a doctoral degree (Altbach 2011).

Research Capacity, Policies, and Programmes in Vietnam

The next sections present the research capacity, policies, and programmes in higher education of Vietnam and Australia. Although analysis of each country will be made separately, a contrastive analysis between these two countries will be reflected during the presentation.

---

[1] Vietnamese Higher Education does not have a professional framework for classifying universities like the Carnegie Classification of Institutions of Higher Education in the USA.

[2] They are considered the top universities of Vietnam.

Research Capacity of Vietnamese Academics

Although Vietnam has implemented the Higher Education Reform Agenda since 2005 (see the section of Research Policies in Vietnam for further information), the research capacity of the Vietnamese academics appears to be relatively modest, resulting in low research productivity across the VHE system (Harman et al. 2010; Nguyen 2014, 2015a, b; Pham 2010). Hayden and Thiep (2010) indicated that a small number of academics have research interests while the majority of academics focus on teaching only. So, the research productivity of academics across the VHE system, including that of academics at the two national and three regional universities, is considerably low. According to the Ministry of Education and Training, Vietnam currently has 24,000 people with a doctoral degree (Hoang 2016). Half of them are currently working at universities and research institutes and publish in the region with a total of nearly 2000 journal articles per year. This equates to one international journal paper published per five doctorates per year (Le 2016). This ratio counts for all international journal publications, irrespective of ranking and reputation of journals. If only high-ranking journals indexed by ISI or Scopus were considered, the result would be extremely low.

This low level of research productivity is largely due to academics in Vietnam being teaching-intensive. In Vietnam, prior to the 2000s, there was no expectation for academics at universities to research or disseminate findings. This is a consequence of the adoption of the educational model applied in the National Academy of the Soviet-Union. For many years, research has been exclusively implemented by research institutes which are members of either of two national research academies: the Vietnam Academy of Social Sciences or the Vietnam Academy of Science and Technology. Furthermore, research institutes serve specific purposes of different ministries (Nguyen 2014).

Table 10.2 compares the number of international refereed journal articles published by the Vietnamese researchers and those in other Asian countries in the period 2000–2016. It is noteworthy that the following information reflects the number of articles published in academic journals by all academics, researchers, and scientists from each country and have been indexed in the databases of Thomson Reuter. It is unable to extract the number of articles published by academics of HEIs only. Although the information does not reflect the actual number of articles published by researchers in each country because a majority of documents have not been indexed by Thomson Reuter, these Web of Science's documents are the most prestigious and valuable publications which reflect the highest quality and knowledge contribution of the work, so it is used here as an illustration for the research productivity of researchers in each country.

Within the ASEAN region, Table 10.2 shows that the number of refereed journal articles indexed in databases of Thomson's Web of Science from Singapore, Malaysia, and Thailand is much higher than that from Vietnam (192,857; 138,090; and 102,658 respectively compared to 26,025). The data confirms a comment made by a senior official at the Minister of Science and Technology in 2012 that Vietnam

Table 10.2 International refereed journal articles of researchers in East and Southeast Asia countries, 2000–2016

Country	Web of science Documents[a]	Times cited	Citation impact
China	2,931,257	21,593,261	14.20
Japan	1,770,279	22,272,763	13.98
Australia	916,289	12,806,056	13.90
South Korea	765,519	7,307,271	13.58
Singapore	192,857	2,680,476	12.58
Malaysia	132,090	679,793	11.13
Thailand	102,658	950,293	10.60
Indonesia	31,796	212,968	9.55
Vietnam	26,025	209,313	9.26
Philippines	18,814	199,501	8.31
Cambodia	2458	33,383	8.04
Brunei	1608	10,686	6.70
Laos	1591	17,707	6.65
Myanmar	1265	10,516	5.15

[a]The data were extracted from the Incites database of Thomson Reuter as of 21 November 2016

has the largest number of doctorate and masters' among ASEAN countries, but that the research capacity of Vietnamese academics with regard to their publications (research productivity) has been considered to be at the bottom of the list in the region (Giáo dục Việt Nam 2012).

When Vietnam is compared to China, Japan, Australia, and South Korea, the indexed refereed journal articles from such countries are extremely higher than those of Vietnam. This comparison is somewhat unfair as all of the countries in the comparison are developed countries that have a high GDP while Vietnam is still a developing country with a small GDP. Of course, the GDP of a country is not the only causal factor on research productivity of academics of a country, many other factors such as research environment of a university, research motivation, and research behaviours of academics highly impacting to academics' research productivity exist (Nguyen 2015a, b). But it is understandable that a correlation between the GDP and the public funding for research and development of a country in general and for HEIs in particular exists which in turn impacts the research productivity of researchers and academics. Currently, the annual expenditure for research and development in Vietnam accounts for only 2% of the total state budget. Moreover, according to Nguyen (2014), 'of the 2% budget allocation for research and development, only three-fifths were actually spent on research. The majority of the research funding was spent on paying salaries for more than 60,000 employees of all state-owned research institutes throughout the country. Nearly 10% of the total research and development funding was spent on research through various research projects carried out at both local and national levels' (p. 197). Interestingly, Lee et al. (2011) confirmed that the GDP is an important factor which is highly correlated with research productivity. Their empirical study even found 'a mutual causality between research and economic growth in Asia' (Lee et al. 2011, p. 465).

Regarding the citation impact of each country presented in Table 10.2, it can be seen that Vietnam ranks 11th out of 15 countries. From the presentation of the total number of Web of Science's documents and the citation impact of each country in Table 10.2, the data shows both quantity and quality of publications from Vietnam are still low compared with those of other countries in the same region. The research capacity of Vietnamese researchers and academics could be absolutely considered behind those of their counterparts in other countries.

Apart from tallying the total number of publications and citations of each publication produced by each academic, utilising the h-index is another well-known indicator to measure research productivity. It is mostly used to evaluate research performance of individual researchers and as such in the scope of this chapter, the h-index indicator is not taken into account to reflect the research capacity of academics.

In a comparative study undertaken in 11 countries in East Asia (Pham 2010), Vietnam's research productivity was found to be significantly lower than that of other countries in the region. Surprisingly, the study reported that the total number of international refereed articles from Vietnam is even fewer than the number of a single university in Thailand (such as Chulalongkorn University or Mahidol University).

The number of publications from Vietnam accounted for the research productivity of all researchers at the two national academies of Vietnam (Vietnam Academy of Social Sciences – Viện Hàn lâm Khoa học Xã hội Việt Nam, VASS) and Vietnam Academy of Science and Technology – Viện Hàn lâm Khoa học và Công nghệ Việt Nam, VAST) and hundreds research institutes which belong to ministries, provinces, and central organisations. In contrast, the role of academics at universities has been mainly teaching. This distinction is a barrier that restrains the research productivity of academics. Research has indicated that a large number of the government's research funding has been allocated to research institutes of two national research academies, while a very small amount has been allocated to hundreds of HEIs (Nguyen 2014). Information in Table 10.3 reflects the fact that two national academies receive large budget contributions from the government to undertake research and produce publications.

Table 10.3 The national budget for research and technology each year (VND Million)

Organisation	2011	2012	2013	2014	2015	2016
Ministry of Education and Training.	272,749	326,940	239,050	238,790	206,370	217,480
Vietnam National Academy of Sciences and Technology.	391,120	485,330	555,110	607,010	820,240	633,070
Vietnam National Academy of Social Sciences.	224,280	233,460	282,490	279,170	366,980	352,700
Vietnam National University Hanoi.	66,406	68,250	68,640	50,600	129,090	194,280
Vietnam National University Hochiminh city.	65,630	137,980	73,090	61,390	56,510	62,110

Source: Data has been collected from the website of the Government of Vietnam (Chính phủ 2016)

Table 10.4 The number of universities of each country ranked in the World's Top 400 in 2015–2016 and 2016–2017

Country	World's top 400 in 2015–2016	World's top 400 in 2016–2017
Australia	22	23
Japan	6	8
China	8	7
South Korea	8	9
Singapore	2	2
Malaysia	0	0
Thailand	0	0
Indonesia	0	0
Vietnam	0	0

Source: The Times Higher Education (2015b, 2016b)

Table 10.5 The number of universities of each country ranked in the Asia's top 200 in 2015 and 2016

Country	Asia's top 100 in 2015	Asia's top 200 in 2016
Japan	19	39
China	21	39
South Korea	13	24
Singapore	2	2
Malaysia	0	4
Thailand	2	7
Indonesia	0	1
Vietnam	0	0

Source: The Times Higher Education (2015a, 2016a)

In a recent review of science, technology and innovation in Vietnam, World Bank indicated that Vietnam has a low level of research productivity and income, weak performance of public-sector research, weak in the science and technology infrastructure as regards laboratories and research equipment (The World Bank 2016). Vietnam has, however, been endeavouring to build research universities in recent years and aims to have at least one research university to be ranked in the top World's 200 universities by 2020. However, until 2016 which is only four years off the point of 2020, Vietnam is yet to be listed in the world's top 400 universities (Table 10.4) or even in the Asian University Rankings Top 200 (Table 10.5).

However, there is good news for the VHE that the research productivity of academics at some young universities such as Ton Duc Thang University (TDTU) has significantly increased in recent years. TDTU is the first and only public university that is fully independent in finance from the Vietnamese Government. In recent years, this university has focused on academic research and invested vast amounts of money in research activities of its academics. It is also the first public university of Vietnam that is seeking and recruiting foreign academics, researchers, and

Table 10.6 International refereed journal articles of Ton Duc Thang University and regional universities

	2000–2005	2006–2010	2011–2016
Ton Duc Thang University	0	20	468
Hue University	85	135	272
University of Danang	10	24	140
Thai Nguyen University	No information found		

Source: IncitesTM Thomson Reuters (2016)

renowned scientists. Consequently, its number of international publications, particularly high-quality journal articles indexed by Thomson Reuter is significantly high and even higher than that of the other so-called leading universities of Vietnam (the case of three regional universities of Hue, Danang, and Thai Nguyen are used for an illustration).

Table 10.6 illustrates that TDTU had no indexed publication in Thomson Reuters's database in the period of 2000–2005, and only 20 publications in the period of 2006–2010. But, its research output from 2011 to 2016 is 22 times higher than that of the previous period with 468 publications. It is remarkable that TDTU's output is nearly doubled that of the number of Hue University and 3 times higher than that of the University of Danang. For unknown reasons, the research output of Thai Nguyen University has not been found in the Web of Science at the time of access but there is a belief that this university has some international publications.

Research Policies in Vietnam

Vietnam has recently launched a wide range of policies that emphasise the role of academic research for national advancement. As most Vietnamese people imbue a fondness for learning, Vietnam expects its academics to connect to the global academic system to conduct research in fields relevant to national development. The following main policies serve as a legislative framework to enhance academics' research capacity and productivity.

Higher Education Reform Agenda in Vietnam

Officially launched in 200, the Higher Education Reform Agenda (HERA) was to implement substantial and comprehensive renewal of the VHE during the period 2006–2020. It aimed to establish a robust higher education system that is forward-thinking by international standards, competitive, and appropriate to the socialist-oriented market system by 2020 (Chính Phủ 2005). It focuses on all aspects of the VHE including teaching and learning programmes, curriculum, academic qualifications, university governance, and academic research. Academic research has been emphasised in order to increase the research productivity of Vietnamese academics, in both quantity and quality, as well as both nationally and internationally. The HERA focuses on 'the development of an advanced research and development culture, with research and development activities to account for 25% of the higher education system's revenue by 2020 (currently it accounts for less than 2%)' (Harman et al. 2010, p. 3). In order to achieve that objective, the HERA suggests that Vietnamese Government spends at least 1% of the national budget to support research at HEIs. However, it is unable to realise this budget in the current financial constraints experienced by Vietnam at present. Furthermore, Nguyen (2014) indicated that if that 1% became available, it would still be very small because it would have to be divided across many colleges, universities, and research institutes.

The HERA also emphasises the need to link universities to enterprises in industry. The enterprises on the one hand play an important role as research product users for academics; on the other hand, they support academics in doing research by providing research funds and shared facilities. Although the HERA has some good points, it is considered an ambitious plan with many challenges. It has not been able to improve the research capacity of Vietnamese academics to a comparable international standard to date. This lack of attainment was, perhaps, largely due to the limited resources and finance allocated to support research and development in HEIs.

Strategy for Science and Technology Development Until 2020

On 11 April 2012, the Prime Minister of Vietnam approved the Strategy for Science and Technology Development for the period 2011–2020 (Thủ tướng Chính phủ 2012b). As Science and Technology play a crucial role in the development of a country, this Science and Technology Strategy serves as a means to increase the research capacity of the Vietnamese researchers in order to speed up the country's industrialisation and modernisation. It is expected that the government will spend more of the national budget on Science and Technology and increase the level of investment in research activities. Currently, Vietnam is striving to increase the total financial investment in Science and Technology from 1.52% of its GDP in 2015 to at least 2% of the GDP by 2020 (Hoang 2015).

Law of Higher Education

This inaugural Higher Education Law approved by the National Assembly of Vietnam on 18 June 2012 became effective on 1 January 2013. The Higher Education Law provides more autonomy to university governance such as strategic plan of development, international collaboration, training, and research. Particularly, the Law values the importance of the HE system in the development of Vietnam under the globalised forces. Particularly, it identified the importance of academic research and indicated that the development of research universities to meet the demands of globalisation, industrialisation, and modernisation is imperative (Quốc Hội 2013). Accordingly, the Higher Education Law requested that all universities in Vietnam be accredited by an independent organisation using a unique assessment provided by the Ministry of Education and Training. One of the most important assessment criteria is the academics' research productivity at an institution and the number of highly qualified academics who hold a doctoral degree.

Although the Higher Education Law emphasises the institutional autonomy of universities, the reality is not the same. In order to attract distinguished and highly qualified academics, universities should have autonomy to recruit academics and offer attractive salary packages to them. It is difficult to expect academics to perform well in both teaching and research and not offer an attractive and commensurate remuneration. Hence, the tight top-down control of the government and relevant ministries (education and training, finance, domestic affair) should be further reduced in order to provide more autonomous governance to universities.

Science and Technology Law 2013

In order to support the national socio-economic development and international integration, the Law of Science and Technology 2013 was approved by the National Assembly of Vietnam as the foremost policy in Science and Technology in Vietnam. It provides clearer information and latest regulations to meet the actual situations of the country. The Science and Technology Law 2013 emphasises the attraction, appropriate use, and value of researchers. It guides that research funding allocated to organisations and individuals becomes more flexible and that it is critical to build national research organisations which have international capacity, sufficient research infrastructures and mechanisms so that these research organisations can attract research collaboration with other foreign research organisations.

Research Programmes in Vietnam

To enhance the research capacity and productivity of the Vietnamese academics/researchers, the Government of Vietnam has built a number of research programmes as below.

Building Research Universities in Vietnam

Brew and Lucas (2009) and Faust (2013) mentioned that the research university is the place that generates and disseminates knowledge through research publications. The research university not only provides a qualified labour force for a society to meet the demands of industrialisation and modernisation of the country, but also conducts research to serve society (Altbach 2007). The research university connects closely with its communities, local and international, and plays an important role in dealing with imperatives of a country and of the world, for example diseases, financial crises, or natural disasters. As such, research universities have rapidly emerged 'making it possible for [their] countries to join the global knowledge society and to compete effectively in the sophisticated knowledge economies of the twenty-first century' (Altbach 2013, p. 316).

In order to promote research activities and research capacity of the Vietnamese academics, the Government of Vietnam has been building four strategic research universities with an international standard by 2020. They include Vietnam-Germany University (Đại học Việt-Đức), University of Science and Technology of Hanoi (Đại học Việt-Pháp), a university belongs to the University of Danang (potentially called Vietnam-United Kingdom University-Đại học Việt-Anh), and another university in Can Tho province. While the first two universities have been in the operation for a few years, the later ones are still being established. The funding announced for these universities mainly comes from an international loan provided by World Bank and Asian Development Bank. With the capital investment of USD100 million for each university, the Government of Vietnam expects them to become world-class universities and to improve not only the global rankings but also the ranking of the whole VHE in the future.

Project 322 and Project 911

The Project 322 began in 2000 for the period 2000–2010 and the Project 911 started in 2011 for the period concluding in 2020. These projects provide scholarships for academics at colleges, universities, research institutes, and some public organisations to study overseas at a postgraduate level. They aim to train 20,000 doctorates for Vietnam by 2020. The Vietnamese Government believes that academic graduates from overseas will have a significant and effective contribution to research and development of universities which are key to the knowledge economy. It is anticipated that knowledge and research experiences that abroad graduates gain will be transferred to their colleagues who have been inaccessible to overseas study. There is also an expectation of a linkage between domestic academics and academics at their overseas universities be maintained to foster future research collaborations. The academics graduating from overseas are expected to play key roles in undertaking research and producing publications. These projects help the HERA achieve its objective that at least 60% of academics at HEIs have a master's degree and at least 35% of them obtain a doctoral degree, as well as implement the aspiration of building research universities in Vietnam indicated in the Higher Education Law 2013.

The National Foundation for Science and Technology Development

The National Foundation for Science and Technology Development (NAFOSTED) was established in 2003 by the Vietnamese Government but it was not officially operated until 2008. This organisation is a member of the Ministry of Science and Technology. It serves as a non-profit office which facilitates research projects proposed by organisations and individuals from all universities and research institutes across the country. NAFOSTED provides research funds for researchers to conduct research projects. In particular, it aims to fund researchers to publish their research results internationally in high-quality journals. The following five statements indicate the missions of this newly established foundation:

- Build a durable, innovative, and conducive environment to research activities at universities and institutes;
- Improve the research capacity of young scientists and establish research centres that meet international standards;
- Enhance the quality of scientific research and increase the number of Vietnamese research published in ISI-covered journals;
- Encourage international cooperation for Vietnamese scientists to approach international research knowledge and to attract external funding to Vietnam's scientific projects; and
- Promote research efforts in enterprises, with a focus on core technologies development contributing to national economic growth and competitiveness. (NAFOSTED 2016b)

In order to achieve the goals, NAFOSTED, with a flexible funding mechanism (Nguyen 2015b), provides more opportunities for researchers to receive research funds. The funding is based on following criteria: (a) potential impact of the research, (b) originality and innovation of the work, (c) feasibility of the proposed research, (d) scientific capacity and expertise of the applicant, (e) expected results and scientific significance, and (f) research plan (NAFOSTED 2016a). Such criteria indicate that the funding mechanism of NAFOSTED apparently bases on the research capacity and productivity of applicants. In the context of declining public funding for research, this mechanism is considered to be more effective than the traditional model of fund allocations through administrative bodies such as ministries and provinces, which is ineffective and time-consuming. It is likely that the fund will not be equally distributed to organisations or researchers, but it will be based on the performance measure of academics and researchers. As long as the applicants are active and productive in research, their submission for a research grant is likely to be successful. Each research project's recipient is required to publish one or two articles listed in the index of ISI or Scopus depending on disciplines (Nguyen 2016).

Precisely, the successful implementation of these national initiatives is expected to improve the research capacity of the Vietnamese academics. However, in the current context of the VHE, the enhancement of research capacity of academics has encountered a plethora of challenges – the ones that require more effort and commitment of academics in addition to the strong support/investment from the government of Vietnam in general, and from MOET in particular.

Research Capacity, Policies, and Programmes in Australia

The following section will look at the research capacity of academics in Australia, and see how research policies and programmes currently existing in this country support Australian academics.

Research Capacity of Australian Academics

Unlike Vietnam, Australia is considered to have a strong research capacity internationally. The reform in HE of Australia started in the 1980s and had a strong focus on academic research (Li et al. 2008). The Government of Australia pays much attention and support to its HE system and attempts to build some best world-class universities in both teaching and research. The Australian universities have achieved international standards; they constantly seek to enhance their research capacity so that they are able to maintain and/or increase their world rankings.

On the one hand, the Australian universities must comply with national regulations, for example, undertaking research, in order to be labelled as 'university'. This is because the teaching-only institutions are not allowed to use the 'university' label (Bentley et al. 2014). On the other hand, Australian academics must do research in order to be identified as 'university academics' and confirm and maintain their academic identities. How much these academics engage in research depends on the missions assigned to academics by each university. For example, eight universities of Australia including University of Sydney, University of Melbourne, University of Adelaide, University of Western Australia, Monash University, Australian National University, University of Queensland, and New South Wales University formed an elite group called Group of Eight (Go8) to intensively collaborate in research. These universities are the sandstone universities of Australia and their research contributes significantly to Australia's social and economic development (Group of Eight Australia 2016). Another group of universities has formed a collaborative network called Innovative Research Universities (Sombatsompop et al. 2010). They aim to collaborate and support one another in undertaking national and international research (Innovative Research Universities 2016). Six universities have participated in the IRU including Griffith University, La Trobe University, Flinders University, James Cook University, Murdoch University, and Charles Darwin University.

Table 10.2 displays how the Australian academics have had 916,289 high-quality journal articles indexed by Thomson Reuter's database (ranked #3rd). However, it is ranked the second in terms of citation impact because articles by researchers in Australia have received the second largest number of the average number of citations a document has received. Apparently, the Australian academics are more productive than their counterparts in Vietnam because they spend more time engaged in research activities. In an international comparative study entitled *Changing Academic Profession* (CAP), Bentley et al. (2014) found that Australian academics spend on average 36% of their working time on teaching and 37% for research. As universities in the Go8 are research intensive and have long histories of training postgraduate students (doctoral level) and traditional research pathways, their academics were found to spend less time on teaching (31%) and more time on research (44%) compared with their colleagues at other universities. The following table illustrates the research productivity of academics at those universities. The number of international refereed journal articles indexed in the databases of Thomson Reuter for the period 2000–2016 is compared with the number of publications of two national universities and three regional universities of Vietnam to see the difference between the research productivity of academics in Vietnam and Australia.

The information contained in Table 10.7 reflects the academics of the Go8 universities being more productive than their colleagues at the IRU's universities.

Table 10.7 International refereed journal articles of academics in key Australia's and Vietnam's universities, 2000–2016

University	Web of science Documents	Times cited	Citation impact
University of Sydney	112,087	1,735,018	15.48
University of Melbourne	94,047	1,626,850	17.30
University of Queensland	83,443	1,424,806	17.08
Monash University	76,349	1,096,936	14.37
University of New South Wales	72,978	1,078,733	14.78
Australian National University	53,714	916,597	17.06
University of Western Australia	55,911	877,183	15.69
University of Adelaide	40,356	599,583	14.86
James Cook University	14,822	250,333	16.89
Griffith University	22,441	244,473	10.89
Flinders University South Australia	16,552	201,849	12.19
La Trobe University	17,636	194,485	11.03
Murdoch University	9146	119,399	13.05
Charles Darwin University	4229	64,127	15.16
Vietnam National University Hanoi	2114	18,358	8.68
Vietnam National University Hochiminh City	1217	5694	4.68
Hue University	492	2771	5.63
The University of Danang	174	653	3.75
Thai Nguyen University	No record found		

Although VNU-HN and VNU-HCMC of Vietnam have been considered as the two leading universities of Vietnam in terms of teaching and research, the number of international publications of academics from these Vietnamese universities is extremely low compared with the Australian counterparts. It is noteworthy that comparing the Vietnamese and the Australian academic research capacity and outputs appears to be rather superficial due to the stark differences, the local specificities and the unique dynamics existing in academic research field in these two countries, especially with regard to their research culture, research environment, and investments for research in each country. However, a contrastive analysis is necessary because it insinuates useful insights into the existing research and academic research capacity in Vietnam and Australia so as to identify the possible gap existing amongst universities labelled as 'research universities'. This information obtained from this contrastive analysis helps inform the educational leaders that changing a model of university from teaching-intensive to research-intensive appears to be challenging and that there is a long transition from a teaching university to a research university. This is because this transition requires not only the intention and determination of the key educational leaders, but also commands much joint-effort and commitment of both academics and educational leaders to bring about positive changes. Indeed, there is a whole spectrum between a teaching and a research university, and it takes universities years to shift from the first model to the second one. Clearly, transitioning from teaching-intensive to research-intensive university is unlikely to be achieved overnight, especially when the VHE is lagging behind regionally and internationally. Consequently, the goal set for HEIs in Vietnam to have at least a research university ranked in the world top 200 universities by 2020 definitely seems to be without reach in the short run.

Research Policies in Australia

Australia subscribes to a performance-based funding scheme which places accountability on academics and universities to produce research publications (Geuna and Martin 2003). This scheme emerged as a response to the knowledge economy, and it is effectively used to distribute research funding to universities based on their research performance. Li et al. (2008) emphasise that this funding scheme places enormous pressure on HEIs which necessitates the enhancement of their research capacity.

In 2015 the Government of Australia spent $9717 million in support of science, research and innovation of the country in which the research funding for higher education sector was $2828 million (Australian Department of Industry Innovation and Science 2015). The information reveals that within the amount of research funding for this sector, the government reserved AUD1,995.8 million for performance-based block funding. The more academics perform in research, the greater the amount of research funding is granted.

The research fund provided by the Australian Federal Government through the Australian Research Council (ARC) is complemented by each state to support academics and researchers. For example, Queensland State has a research fund called 'the Advance Queensland initiative' which supports researchers undertaking original work that will have a positive impact on Queensland. Academics at Queensland's universities can apply for a grant from this initiative, and their projects will help drive innovation and collaboration in new and existing industries and solidify the state's capacity and reputation as a global science and research leader.

The above-mentioned policies indicate that the Government of Australia emphasises the role of academic research to its national development through stimulating innovation and delivering solutions to the economic and social challenges facing the nation. As such, all Australian universities maintain a rigorous recruitment policy or framework to ensure their academics engage actively in research and contribute to research productivity.

Research Programmes in Australia

The following research programmes have been well established across the higher education of Australia and universities to ensure that academics are actively engaged in research activities which improve their research capacity and productivity.

Annual Review of Teaching and Research Performance

Academics in Australian universities are annually appraised for their research performance against what they have planned at the beginning of the academic year. The annual appraisal is an opportunity for the university to identify the strengths and weaknesses of its staff in order to provide appropriate support to maintain academic standards while advancing the university's strategic objectives in teaching and research. Through performance review, the university has an opportunity to have discussions about individual achievements, performance trajectories, development plans, and work profiles as well as leave plans or research plan.

Linkage Between Universities and Industry

Australian universities emphasise the importance of collaborations between the university and industry in undertaking research. Research universities make significant contributions to the development of the country because they not only generate knowledge, but also collaborate with business firms in industry to conduct joint research and development projects. The collaboration between universities and the

Australian industry is considered a necessary pathway to the development and prosperity of Australia. Cummings (2014) acknowledged that the linkage between Australian universities and industry is a good contribution to the knowledge-based economy.

Networking Among Universities

In 2009, the establishment of Collaborative Research Networks (CRN) heralded a significant policy initiative of the Australian Government's Department of Education and Training in improving the research capacity of academics. The CRN aimed to connect academics at less research-intensive universities with colleagues at research-intensive universities in order to develop their research capacity. This is an effective network in research collaboration through which less-experienced and junior academics/researchers have opportunities to learn from experienced academics/researchers (Australian Department of Industry Innovation and Science 2009). It is a channel to connect universities and research organisations with industry. One of the most important missions of the CRN is that 'researchers, businesses and governments work collaboratively to secure value from commercial innovation and to address national and global challenges' (Australian Department of Industry Innovation and Science 2009, p. 1). Further to this point, the establishment of CRN helps less research-intensive universities to develop their research capacity by collaborating with colleagues at more research-intensive universities. This network creates a linkage among universities in order to enhance the research capacity of academics in all linked universities (Bentley et al. 2014).

Other universities in the same broad field, such as technology form a group named Australian Technology Network to support one another in teaching and research. These universities also have a good relationship with industry so that their academics have more opportunities to receive research funding from industry. Intensive collaboration amongst members is essential for the ATN. Applying an end-user approach, these members particularly collaborate in research projects that address challenges of business, government, and industry so that the connection between them is very tight and effective.

Conclusion

Undertaking research and disseminating research findings tend to be amongst the most central functions of an academic at a university. As such, enhancing research capacity is considered to be important to benefit universities and communities worldwide. As highlighted in this chapter, the Vietnamese universities have to respond swiftly to the mounting pressure of transitioning from teaching-intensive to research-active universities. This is not an easy task when long-standing practices of the Vietnamese academics have been engrained in the strong tradition of teaching only.

The chapter has examined the research publications of the Vietnamese academics in a comparison with those of other countries. In particular, contrasting them with Australian counterparts help provide readers with a useful picture of the existing practices and contextualisation of where research productivity and publication is positioned globally. Drawing on the success of the Australian case, it appears that it remains a challenge for the Vietnamese academics to develop their research capacity and produce research publications that meet the international standard of publication as that of their counterparts in the region and the world.

To warrant enhanced research capacity for the Vietnamese academics and contribute to the country's social and economic development, the Government of Vietnam requires extra effort and attempt in formulating and implementing research policies to support the Vietnamese HEIs. Limited research capacity of the Vietnamese academics are resulted from the lack of highly qualified academics with a doctoral degree (particularly those trained overseas in a western and/or developed country), the constraint of low remuneration, a high teaching load, poor research resources, insufficient research infrastructure, and incentive policies for allocating time, financially and research support, as well as academics' perception of and comment for research instead of being burdened with the heavy teaching load (Harman and Ngoc 2010; Nguyen 2015a, b; Nguyen et al. 2016).

Australian practices of building research programmes showcase a good example and provide useful implications for Vietnam. Conditioned by financial constraints, the Government of Vietnam should call for the wider contribution of the society, including private and public organisations to promote research and development of Vietnam. Despite having been raised in the Science and Technology Law 2013, attracting immense industry research collaboration and support is a viable option. The Vietnamese universities must be more proactive in establishing and fostering research partnerships with research end-users in and outside of the organisations/ industry in a way that it garners mutual benefits. This partnership unfortunately remains pretty weak due to the ineffective tradition and culture of collaboration. If such a collaboration is enhanced, it enables employment opportunities (research jobs) and working places (to do experiments at industrial labs) for university academics.

Enhancing academics' research capacity requires a commitment from the academics and from the government and universities to keep academics' motivated, research productive, and committed to expanding the knowledge economy. Essentially, academics working at the Vietnamese universities should be autonomous and take lead in strengthening their research capacity and increasing their research productivity. This can be done by engaging in research activities that promote both the quantity and the quality of research publications.

Last but not least, the Vietnamese universities are required to continue providing a collegial environment that values high-quality teaching and research. The traditional practices of separating teaching from research and preferring one over the other need changing. Since teaching and learning are inextricably linked, as such each requires equal support, recognition, and opportunity to flourish. This means there must be a paradigm shift in reorienting the Vietnamese universities towards research-intensive ones; this is accorded with introducing a more comprehensive strategic research policy system, applying a more robust and transparent support system, offering additional incentive schemes for research staff, alongside with professional development strategies to uplift the research capacities for the Vietnamese academic staff.

References

Altbach, P. G. (2007). Empires of knowledge and development. In P. G. Altbach & J. Balan (Eds.), *World class worldwide: Transforming research universities in Asia and Latin America* (pp. 31–53). Maryland: Johns Hopkins University Press.

Altbach, P. G. (2011). The past, present, and future of the research university. In P. G. Altbach & J. Salmi (Eds.), *The road to academic excellence: The making of world-class research universities* (pp. 11–32). Washington, DC: World Bank.

Altbach, P. G. (2013). Advancing the national and global knowledge economy: The role of research universities in developing countries. *Studies in Higher Education, 38*(3), 316–330. https://doi.org/10.1080/03075079.2013.773222.

Australian Department of Industry Innovation and Science. (2009). *Powering ideas: An innovation Agenda for the 21st century*. Canberra: Autralian Department of Industry, Innovation, and Science Retrieved from http://www.industry.gov.au/innovation/InnovationPolicy/Pages/PoweringIdeas.aspx

Australian Department of Industry Innovation and Science. (2015). *Science, research and innovation budget tables for 2015–2016*. Canberra: Australian Department of Industry, Innovation and Science Retrieved from http://www.industry.gov.au/innovation/reportsandstudies/Pages/SRIBudget.aspx

Bentley, P. J., Goedegebuure, L., & Meek, V. L. (2014). Australian academics, teaching and research: History, vexed issues and potential changes. In J. C. Shin, A. Arimoto, W. K. Cummings, & U. Teichler (Eds.), *Teaching and research in contemporary higher education: Systems, activities and rewards* (pp. 357–377). London: Springer.

Brew, A. (2003). Teaching and research: New relationships and their implications for inquiry-based teaching and learning in higher education. *Higher Education Research & Development, 22*, 3–18. https://doi.org/10.1080/0729436032000056571.

Brew, A. (2006). *Research and teaching: Beyond the divide*. New York: Palgrave Macmillan.

Brew, A., & Boud, D. (1995). *Teaching and research: Establishing the vital link with learning*. Retrieved from: http://www.jstor.org.libraryproxy.griffith.edu.au/

Brew, A., & Lucas, L. (2009). Introduction: Academic research and researchers. In A. Brew & L. Lucas (Eds.), *Academic research and researchers* (pp. 1–12). New York: Open University Press.

Chính Phủ. (2005). *Nghị quyết số 14/2005/NQ-CP về đổi mới cơ bản và toàn diện giáo dục đại học Việt Nam giai đoạn 2006–2020* [Resolution no. 14/2005/NQ-CP on the fundamental and comprehensive reform of Vietnam higher education from 2006 to 2020]. Hanoi: Government of Vietnam.

Chính phủ. (2016). *Số liệu chi ngân sách nhà nước* [The allocation of state budget for ministries and public organisations of Vietnam]. Hanoi: Bộ Tài chính Retrieved from http://www.chinhphu.vn/portal/page/portal/chinhphu/solieungansachnhanuoc.

Cummings, W. K. (2014). The research role in comparative perspective. In J. C. Shin, A. Arimoto, W. K. Cummings, & U. Teichler (Eds.), *Teaching and research in contemporary higher education: Systems, activities, and rewards* (pp. 35–44). London: Springer.

Faust, D. G. (2013). *Drew Gilpin Faust address at commmencement 2013 of Harvard University.*

Geuna, A., & Martin, B. R. (2003). University research evaluation and funding: An international comparison. *Minerva, 41*(4), 277–304.

Giáo dục Việt Nam. (2012, December 5). *Việt Nam có quá nhiều tiến sĩ, nhưng ít phát minh* [Vietnam has too many doctors but few scientific publications]. *Giáo dục Việt Nam.* Retrieved from http://giaoduc.net.vn/Giao-duc-24h/Viet-Nam-co-qua-nhieu-tien-si-nhung-it-phat-minh-post101311.gd

Group of Eight Australia. (2016). *The Group of Eight: Australia's Leading Universities, leading excellence, leading debate.* Retrieved from https://go8.edu.au/

Harman, G., & Ngoc, L. T. B. (2010). The research role of Vietnam's Universities. In G. Harman, M. Hayden, & P. T. Nghi (Eds.), *Reforming higher education in Vietnam: Challenges and priorities* (Vol. 29, pp. 87–102). New York: Springer.

Harman, K., & Nguyen, T. N. B. (2010). Reforming teaching and learning in Vietnam's higher education system. In G. Harman, M. Hayde, & P. T. Nghi (Eds.), *Reforming higher education in Vietnam: Challenges and priorities* (pp. 65–86). Dordrecht: Springer.

Harman, G., Hayden, M., & Pham, T. N. (Eds.). (2010). *Higher education in Vietnam: Reform, challenges and priorities.* New York: Springer.

Hattie, J., & Marsh, H. W. (1996). The relationship between research and teaching: A meta-analysis. *Review of Educational Research, 66,* 507–542. Retrieved from http://www.jstor.org.libraryproxy.griffith.edu.au/

Hayden, M., & Thiep, L. Q. (2010). Vietnam's higher education system. In G. Harman, M. Hayden, & P. T. Nghi (Eds.), *Reforming higher education in Vietnam* (pp. 15–30). New York: Springer.

Hoang, T. (2015). *Bộ trưởng Nguyễn Quân "Có ba dạng đề tài xếp ngăn kéo"* [The Minister Nguyen Quan "There are three types of research projects which have not got practical implications"]. Retrieved from http://vnexpress.net/tin-tuc/khoa-hoc/bo-truong-nguyen-quan-co-3-dang-de-tai-xep-ngan-keo-3232704.html

Hoang, T. (2016). *Việt Nam có hơn 24000 tiến sĩ* [Vietnam has more than 24000 doctorates]. Retrieved from http://vnexpress.net/tin-tuc/giao-duc/viet-nam-co-hon-24-000-tien-si-3393238.html

Incites TM Thomson Reuters. (2016, 12/11/2016). *Incites organisations.* Retrieved from https://incites.thomsonreuters.com/#/explore/0/organization/*

Innovative Research Universities. (2016). *Collective research strengths.* Retrieved from http://www.iru.edu.au/research-strengths/collective-research-strengths.aspx

Jenkins, A., Blackman, T., Lindsay, R., & Paton-Saltzberg, R. (1998). Teaching and research: Student perspectives and policy implications. *Studies in Higher Education, 23,* 127–141. https://doi.org/10.1080/03075079812331380344.

Jensen, J. J. (1988). Research and Teaching in the universities of Denmark: Does such an interplay really exist? *Higher Education, 17,* 17–26.

Le, V. (2016, 16/06). *Một năm, 5 tiến sĩ mới có một bài báo quốc tế* [Five doctorates publish one international journal article per year]. *Quốc tế hóa giáo sư "nội": Chuyện dễ nói khó làm* [Internationalising the quality of 'domestic' professors: Easy saying but not doing]. Retrieved from http://vietnamnet.vn/vn/giao-duc/khoa-hoc/mot-nam-5-tien-si-moi-co-mot-bai-bao-quoc-te-309948.html

Lee, L.-C., Lin, P.-H., Chuang, Y.-W., & Lee, Y.-Y. (2011). Research output and economic productivity: A Granger causality test. *Scientometrics, 89*(2), 465. https://doi.org/10.1007/s11192-011-0476-9.

Li, B., Millwater, J., & Hudson, P. (2008). *Building research capacity: Changing roles of universities and academics.* Paper presented at the Australian Association of Research in Education (AARE) Conference, Brisbane.

Lindsay, R., Breen, R., & Jenkins, A. (2002). Academic research and teaching quality: The views of undergraduate and postgraduate students. *Studies in Higher Education, 27*, 309–327. https://doi.org/10.1080/03075070220000699.

NAFOSTED. (2016a). *Funding program in basic research.* Retrieved from http://www.nafosted.gov.vn/en/grant-program/Basic-Research/BS-sum-8/

NAFOSTED. (2016b). *Mission statement.* Retrieved from http://www.nafosted.gov.vn/en/about-us/Mission-Statement/Mission-1/

Nguyen, H. T. L. (2014). Research in Universities. In L. Tran, S. Marginson, H. Do, Q. Do, T. Le, N. Nguyen, T. Vu, T. Pham, & H. Nguyen (Eds.), *Higher education in Vietnam: Flexibility, mobility and practicality in the global knowledge economy* (pp. 187–207). New York: Palgrave Macmillan.

Nguyen, Q. H. (2015a). *Factors Influencing the research productivity of academics at the research-oriented university in Vietnam.* (Doctoral thesis), Griffith University, Australia.

Nguyen, T. L. H. (2015b). Building human resources management capacity for university research: The case at four leading Vietnamese universities. *Higher Education.* https://doi.org/10.1007/s10734-015-9898-2.

Nguyen, H. (2016). *800 triệu đồng cho một đề tài nghiên cứu vẫn còn rất khiêm tốn* [VND800 million for one research project is still fairly small]. Retrieved from http://dantri.com.vn/khoa-hoc-cong-nghe/800-trieu-dong-cho-mot-de-tai-nghien-cuu-van-con-rat-khiem-ton-20160527104413871.htm

Nguyen, H. T. N., Phan, L. N. H., Nguyen, T. T. S., Tran, N. A. L., & Nguyen, T. N. (2016). Vietnamese students' perception of employability: An empirical study. Paper presented at the Global Education Dialogue: Innnovation for employability.

Pham, H. D. (2010). A comparative study of research capabilities of East Asian countries and implications for Vietnam. *Higher Education, 60*(6), 615–625. https://doi.org/10.2307/40930314.

Quốc Hội. (2013). *Luật Giáo dục Đại học* [The law on higher education]. (08/2012/QH13). Hà Nội: Quốc hội.

Rice, R. E. (2006). Enhancing the quality of teaching and learning: the US experience. *New Directions for Higher Education, 133*, 13–22.

Sombatsompop, N., Markpin, T., Ratchatahirun, P., Yochai, W., Wongkaew, C., & Premkamolnetr, N. (2010). Research performance evaluations of Thailand national research universities during 2007–2009. *Information Development, 26*(4), 303–313.

The Times Higher Education. (2015a). *Asia University Rankings 2015.* Retrieved from https://www.timeshighereducation.com/world-university-rankings/2015/regional-ranking#!/page/0/length/-1/sort_by/scores_overall/sort_order/asc/cols/scores

The Times Higher Education. (2015b). *World University Rankings 2015–2016.* Retrieved from https://www.timeshighereducation.com/world-university-rankings/2016/world-ranking#!/page/0/length/25/locations/JP/sort_by/rank/sort_order/asc/cols/stats

The Times Higher Education. (2016a). *Asia University Rankings 2016.* Retrieved from https://www.timeshighereducation.com/world-university-rankings/2016/regional-ranking#!/page/0/length/25/locations/MY/sort_by/rank/sort_order/asc/cols/stats

The Times Higher Education. (2016b). *World University Rankings 2016–2017.* Retrieved from https://www.timeshighereducation.com/world-university-rankings/2017/world-ranking#!/page/0/length/25/locations/MY/sort_by/rank/sort_order/asc/cols/stats

The World Bank. (2016). *A review of science, technology and innovation in Vietnam.* Retrieved from http://www.worldbank.org/en/country/vietnam/publication/a-review-of-science-technology-and-innovation-in-vietnam

Thủ tướng Chính phủ. (2012a). *Quyết định của Thủ tướng Chính phủ về việc phê duyệt Chiến lược phát triển giáo dục 2011–2020* [The decision of the Prime Minister on the education strategic development plan 2011–2020]. (711/2012/QĐ-TTg). Hà Nội: Chính phủ.

Thủ tướng Chính phủ. (2012b). *Quyết định phê duyệt chiến lược phát triển khoa học và công nghệ giai đoạn 2011–2020 của Thủ tướng Chính phủ* [The decision of the Prime Minister on the approvement of the strategy for science and technology development for the period of 2011–2020]. (418/QĐ-TTg). Hà Nội: Chính phủ.

VNU-HCMC. (2016). *An overview of Vietnam National University – Ho Chi Minh city*. Retrieved from http://www.vnuhcm.edu.vn/Default.aspx?PageId=c486f71d-a0ad-4389-b6f2-6362a49b7d0a

VNU-HN. (2016). *An introduction about personnel organisation of Vietnam National University-Ha Noi*. Retrieved from https://www.vnu.edu.vn/home/?C2207

Westerheijden, D. F., Cremonini, L., & Empel, R. V. (2010). Accreditation in Vietnam's higher education system. In G. Harman, M. Hayden, & P. T. Nghi (Eds.), *Reforming higher education in Vietnam: Challenges and priorities* (pp. 183–195). New York: Springer.

Part V
HE Professional Development

Chapter 11
Teacher Competence Standardisation Under the Influence of Globalisation: A Study of the National Project 2020 and Its Implications for English Language Teacher Education in Vietnamese Colleges and Universities

Mai Tuyet Ngo

Abstract Being guided by the operational framework of the three key concepts of teacher competences, teacher standards and teacher competence standardisation, this chapter critically reviews, analyses and evaluates the national Project 2020s process of developing the English Teachers Competency Framework (ETCF) in Vietnam, its outcome and its fitness for purposes, based on which implications are proposed for Vietnamese colleges' and universities' ELT education.

Introduction

Under the influence of globalisation, changing demographics and technological advancements, the capacity of countries to compete in the global knowledge economy increasingly depends on whether they can meet a fast-growing demand for high-level skills. This has significant implications for education systems worldwide to make enormous efforts to improve their schooling quality and for higher education systems to improve their teacher education quality. No nation develops beyond the quality of its education system (Kumar and Parveen 2013) while the quality of any education system, as McKinsey and Company (2007) emphasised, "can not exceed the quality of its teachers" (p. 7); and the quality of its teachers cannot exceed the quality of its teacher education programs offered by colleges and universities. Teacher quality or teacher competence, as international research has revealed,

M. T. Ngo (✉)
College of Humanities, Arts and Social Sciences, Flinders University,
Adelaide, South Australia, Australia
e-mail: mai.ngo@flinders.edu.au

© Springer Nature Singapore Pte Ltd. 2019   199
N. T. Nguyen, L. T. Tran (eds.), *Reforming Vietnamese Higher Education*,
Education in the Asia-Pacific Region: Issues, Concerns and Prospects 50,
https://doi.org/10.1007/978-981-13-8918-4_11

is the single most important school-based factor that determines students' learning outcomes and schooling quality (e.g., Australian Professional Standards for Teachers 2016; Caena 2014; Goodwyn 2012; McKinsey&Company 2007). Any education system's aspiration is to have not one but many quality teachers or competent teachers in classrooms (e.g., Vesamavibool et al. 2015) and thus to have quality teacher education programs (Chari 2016) which is an essential contributing factor to quality teachers.

In the global context of rising international education standards (e.g., OECD 2011; Prime Minister 2012), having competent teachers becomes imperative and teacher competence standardisation should be at the centre of any nation's education reforms. The Vietnamese education reform is no exception. To implement its fundamental and comprehensive national education reforms, over the past decade, the Vietnamese Ministry of Education and Training (MOET) has taken various steps, one of which is to implement subject-specific teacher competence standardisation. The National Foreign Language Project 2020 (NFLP 2020) launched in 2008 by Vietnam's MOET specifically showcases the English language teacher competence standardisation. Moving towards achieving its ultimate aim of increasing foreign language proficiency which is currently low among ordinary people, the NFLP 2020 has given its top priority to developing foreign language teacher competence with its strong emphasis placed on English language and standardisation of English language subject teacher competence.

Within its limited scope and space, this chapter focuses on the NFLP 2020's English language teacher competence standardisation to investigate in what way it meets the needs of teacher education students in Vietnam who will become English language teachers. It also proposes implications for English language teacher education in Vietnamese colleges and universities. Being guided by the operational framework developed on the literature reviewed, this chapter critically reviews, analyses and evaluates the NFLP 2020's process of developing the English Teachers Competency Framework (ETCF) in Vietnam (i.e., the How), its outcome (i.e., the What) and its fitness for purposes (i.e., the Why), based on which implications will be proposed for English language teacher education in the Vietnamese colleges and universities.

This chapter is structured into three main parts. The first part presents some theoretical background on the three key relevant concepts of teacher competence, teacher standards and teacher competence standardisation; and the global influences on these theoretical concepts are also highlighted in this part. The second part focuses on the study of the NFLP 2020 and discusses the current practices of Vietnam's English teacher competence standardisation and English language teacher education in its own local context under the influence of globalisation; including critical analyses of the NFLP 2020's process of developing Vietnam's English Teacher Competency Framework (Vietnam's ETCF), its outcome (the ETCF's contents) and its fitness for the ETCF's intended purposes in the light of theoretical background. The third part concludes with some practical recommendations to improve the NFLP 2020's English teacher competence standardisation and implications for Vietnamese colleges' and universities' English language teacher education.

Theoretical Background

For a better understanding of the practices of teacher competence standardisation in any context, it is important to stocktake the relevant theoretical concepts. Drawing from recent literature, this chapter focuses on three relevant theoretical concepts including (1) teacher competences; (2) teacher standards; and (3) teacher competence standardisation. Definitions, purposes and advantages of those three key concepts as well as global influences on them are presented hereinafter, laying the strong foundation for developing the operational framework that guides the conduct of the study.

The Concept of Teacher Competencies

Competence or competency should be viewed as a holistic concept (Caena 2011) and can be generally defined as the dynamic combination of personal characteristics, knowledge, understanding, skills, behaviours and attitudes required for effective and efficient performance of a real-world task (e.g., Mrowicki 1986; Stoof et al. 2002). In the field of education, competences of teachers or teacher competences can generally be defined as descriptors of knowledge, skills and attitudes that teachers should have in order to perform their teaching professions in an effective and efficient way (Caena 2011; Karababa and Caliskan 2013). More specifically, teacher competences, as the European Commission (2014) further elaborated, are not only the subject knowledge but also a wide range of skills and attitudes – communication and collaboration skills, problem-solving skills, decision-making skills, creativity, critical thinking and positive attitudes towards learning that teacher and teacher educators need to master, as models for their students.

Being subjected to global influences, the definitions of teacher competences have now been widened to competences for teachers who also "need to be able to manage and generate changes" (Caena 2011, p. 9). The global expansion of teacher competences, as Caena (2014) added, has recently paid more attention to social responsibilities of teachers, roles of teachers as a social actor, the act of teachers' teaching construed as a result of negotiations between teachers and other educational actors and contexts, and more importantly, teachers' mental habits for reflecting, innovating and adapting to different students and contexts. Such aspects as teachers' awareness of relevant issues of the features and historical development of the subject area that they teach, disposition to change and commitment to promoting the learning of all students should thus all be taken into account when developing a model of teacher competences in the context of global change (Caena 2011).

The advantages of having teachers with high teacher competences are undeniable. International research consistently suggests that within education institutions, teachers with high competences play a central role in helping advance students' academic achievements and success (e.g., European Commission 2010, 2014; Jones

2014; McKinsey&Company 2007; Stoof et al. 2002). It follows that if an education system or a school aims to help their students achieve academic success, developing competences for their teachers and competence-based approach to teacher education are keys to success. Therefore, for teacher competence development, a list of teacher competences should describe, elaborate and explain what subject-specific teachers need to *know* and be able to *do* to help their students learn and achieve academic success (e.g., Bransford et al. 2005; Dudzik 2008; European Commission 2014). Such a list of teacher competences should be well embedded in any teacher education programs.

Notably, teacher competences should be viewed from "an incremental perspective" (Caena 2014, p. 2). The whole set of teacher competences, as European Commission (2014) highlighted, "cannot be fully mastered by any individual, let alone at the very beginning of the career." Indeed, teacher competences are not developed overnight, they are rather developed gradually over the teaching career of a teacher and also not every member of a teaching team will need all competences to the same degree in practice (Caena 2014). A continuum approach to teacher education that highlights teachers' professional continuum, linking entry/exit stages of initial pre-service teacher education, induction and in-service continuing teacher professional development) is therefore appropriate (European Commission 2014). It has been observed that across different cultures, school systems and universities' teacher education programs, there seems to be some consensus on *core* competence requirements or minimum competence requirements that all teachers and student teachers upon graduation must meet. The need for developing core (or minimum) teacher competences at an early career stage (for novice teachers) and developing additional competences at the later or more professional teaching stages (for more experienced teachers) are highlighted across the globe, especially among the EU (European Union) countries (Caena 2011; European Commission 2014), the ASEAN countries (SIREP 2010) and North American countries (OECD 2011).

The Concept of Teacher Standards

The current interest in standards can be traced to the early 1970s (Sykes and Plastrik 1993). A standard is often defined as a generally accepted principle (Australian Professional Standards for Teachers 2016; Goodwyn 2012). Standards, according to Sykes and Plastrik (1993) are tools often used to accomplish multiple goals, namely, as uniform measures to organise transactions, as rules monitored for compliance, as signals that convey information, as exemplars that represent ideals and as principles that direct action. When developing any standards, it is therefore important to determine the purpose(s) that it aims to accomplish. Its fitness for purpose(s), among others, is an important criterion to assess the effectiveness of any standards.

Teacher standards, according to the Australian Professional Standards for Teachers, are generally defined as "a public statement of what constitutes teacher quality" (Aitsl 2016). They articulate what an effective teacher looks like and what effective teaching and learning look like. Any initial teacher education (ITE) program, according to Aitsl (2018), "is accredited by demonstrating evidence against the nationally agreed Accreditation Standards and Procedures" that attach high importance to the Australian Professional Standards for Teachers. It is well documented that teacher standards constitute a critical component of essential learning conditions for achieving the educational goals of the nation (Kumar and Parveen 2013). Ingvarson (1998) usefully classified teacher standards into two main types. The first type refers to the basic tasks or duties of a teacher. This type, as Ingvarson (1998) observed, is often used by school administrators to appraise whether the teacher is doing the basic job. However, this type has its limitations as it fails to guide teachers where to improve in their specific areas of teaching. The second type of standards, according to Ingvarson (1998), refers to professional standards which are based on professional values and images of high-quality learning specific to subject fields. The global trend suggests that the latter type is more commonly used across the globe as it is more attached to the notion of professionalism and can often be used as the basis for professional development reforms. On this ground, this chapter concentrates on the latter type and follows Ingvarson (1998) who defines teacher standards as descriptors of what teachers are expected to know and be able to do to ensure students reach their learning goals. In this regard, teacher competence/competency, teacher standards and teacher competence standards are sometimes used interchangeably in both the literature and this paper.

The purpose of teacher standards, as AITSL (2016, 2018) suggests, is generally to present a common understanding and language for professional discussions and reflections on teacher preparation, practice and improvement. More specifically, teacher standards serve the purpose of (1) forming the basis for national consistency in many respects, including teacher performance and development; and/or (2) supporting the performance, development and professional learning of all teachers, thus contributing to the professionalisation of teaching; and/or (3) raising the professional status of teachers nationally. To assess the effectiveness of teacher standards, it is therefore important to take into account their fitness for purpose that they wish to serve.

It is worth noting that like teacher competences, there is a progression of teacher standards, meaning that a standard can be raised from one career stage to another. The Australian Professional Standards for Teachers are good examples illustrating standard progressions as they describe what is expected of teachers across career stages from the lowest level of being "graduate" to being "proficient" through to being "highly accomplished" and to the highest level of being "lead" across three domains of professional knowledge, professional practice and professional engagement (AITSL 2016). Therefore, teacher standards or teacher competence standards can be used as points of reference for each teacher to know which career stage he or she is in and what needs to be done to raise his or her current standards to the upper levels in the sequential career stages. Likewise, descriptors of teacher standards at each stage can be used as points of reference for teacher educators to appropriately design their pre-service and in-service teacher education programs to ensure that their student teachers have completed a qualification that meets the standards. For example, graduate teachers are awarded the qualification that meets the Graduate Standards.

As far as the process for establishing teacher standards is concerned, teacher standards are established as outcomes of a process of extensive research, expert knowledge, an analysis and review of standards in use, significant stakeholder consultation, including consultation with teachers, employers, professional associations and the public (e.g., European Commission 2014; SIREP 2010). In addition, once the standards are established, before they are rolled out and fully implemented (pre-implementation), they are required to undergo the validation process in which the standards are tested across systems and sectors, school types and geographical locations (e.g., Australian Professional Standards for Teachers 2016; SIREP 2010). For the during and post-implementation of teacher standards, monitoring and assessment are also recommended as required steps (SIREP 2010).

This whole process for establishing teacher standards has been commonly practiced in many countries. For example, the process of developing the Australian Professional Standards for Teachers, according to Aitsl (2018), was built upon the work of previous national frameworks and agreements and was informed by extensive research, expert knowledge, an analysis and review of standards in use by teacher registration authorities, employers and professional associations across Australia and significant consultation. Studying practices of developing teacher competence standards of 11 member countries of the Southeast Asian Ministers of Education Organization – SEAMEO, SIREP (2010) revealed the five-phase process consisting of (1) benchmarking with developed economies, (2) creating a team/technical working group/pools of experts at the Ministry level, (3) pilot testing of the first draft, (4) rolling out and full implementation of National Teaching Competency Standards, and (5) monitoring and assessment. To evaluate the effectiveness of a set of teacher standards, it is important to take into account whether all these five steps in the whole process have been taken to ensure that established standards have been well-informed by research, thoroughly analysed, reviewed by experts, well-consulted by both public and professional experts, and most importantly, validated or tested before implementation on a large scale, and monitored and assessed during and post implementation. An absence of any important steps suggested in this five-phase process may have a negative impact on the effectiveness of teacher standard implementation.

The Concept of Teacher Competence Standardisation

By establishing and putting into practice standards for teacher competence, an education system engages in the practice of teacher competence standardisation which refers to the process of outlining specific statements for each competence standard indicator (Fong et al. 2013). Teacher competence standardisation is often driven by the imperative that every teacher can and must achieve high standards to ensure every student reach the set learning goals. It is worth noting that though teacher standards as standardising tools may seem straight forward, the process of establishing and implementing teacher standards is a challenging and complicated process. Standard developers should therefore be well informed of the common purpose, the nature, the value and practices of teacher competence standardisation.

The common purpose of teacher competence standardisation is to provide guidance for teachers' self-professional development, teacher appraisal and teacher education programs (Fong et al. 2013; Goodwyn 2012). More specifically, as there are progressions of teacher standards by nature, teacher competence standardisation should inform teachers of both core competence standards requirements at the early career stages and of higher standards requirements at sequential career stages. Through a set of teacher competence standards that represents a coherent progression of standards, teachers at different career stages can self-assess their own competences and visualise their coherent teaching career paths for both their immediate and their long-term continuing professional development.

Advocates of teacher competence standardisation highlight it as a good practice and the value of descriptors of teacher performance through teacher standards. It is widely recognised to be a "one-size-fit-all" instrument which makes a difference and is often used as a positive lever to improve education quality on a large scale (e.g., Goodwyn 2012; Ingvarson 2005; SIREP 2010). However, teachers and teacher educators see major difficulties in maintaining standards (Biggs 1999); critics of teacher competence standardisation often view it as an unfeasible practice or at least a restrictive instrument that is used to control teachers and has a negative impact on teachers, especially on their identity, their autonomy, freedom and flexibility which are needed to be adaptive to learners' needs and teaching contexts (Darling-Hammond and Wise 1985).

Despite mixed views on standardisation of teacher competence, we are undeniably living in the "era of standardisation", in which teacher competence standardisation has received increased attention as a strategy for educational reform (Ingvarson 1998). Under the pressures of globalisation, standardising tools and processes have indeed crossed national borders in their expansion to numerous educational systems. Teacher competence standardisation, as SIREP (2010, p. 1) observed, has been "a global feature of the global education agenda". Therefore, there have been increasing demands for schools and higher education institutions across OECD countries, EU countries, ASEAN countries and others to seek regional consensus to use teacher competence standardisation as a powerful tool to lift their education quality as well as their teacher education quality (e.g., Caena 2011; European Commission 2013; Kelly and Grenfell 2004; Sykes and Plastrik 1993). It is highly recommended that training teachers to reflect on and develop their competences covered in the standards should be an integral part of both pre-service and in-service teacher education programs offered by higher education institutions.

An Operational Framework of the Study

For the advancement of students' academic performance and success, teacher competences, teacher standards and teacher competence standardisation are essential. Under
the influence of globalisation, teacher competence standardisation as a strategy for
education reforms is now the global practice without national borders. For better standardisation of teacher competences, the research literature suggests that special attention should be paid to the theoretical conceptualisation, practices of teacher competence
standardisation, the specific purposes that it aims to serve, and the "incremental"
nature of standards highlighting standard progression. In this study, in the light of the
reviewed conceptualisation of teacher competences, teacher standards and teacher
competence standardisation, an operational framework was developed for the study.

For an operational framework of the study, this study asserted that the practice of
teacher competence standardisation needs to take into consideration the *What* (i.e.,
descriptors of what teacher competences are), the *How* (i.e., the process of developing the teacher competences) and the *Why* (i.e., the purposes that the competences
aim to accomplish). For the *What*, the study follows Bransford et al. (2005) and
Ingvarson (1998) who all emphasised the importance of descriptors of what teachers need to *know* and be able to *do* to help students learn when developing teacher
competences. For the *How*, the study follows the European Commission (2014)
who advocates for a continuum or progression approach to developing core or minimum teacher competences for novice teachers at an early career stage and developing additional competences at the later stage for more experienced teachers. The
five-phase process consisting of (1) benchmarking with developed economies, (2)
creating a team/technical working group/pools of experts at the Ministry level, (3)
pilot testing of the first draft, (4) rolling out and full implementation of the National
Teaching Competency Standards, and (5) monitoring and assessment (SIREP 2010)
is a good starting point of reference for reviewing, analysing and evaluating the
NFLP 2020s current process of developing the English language teacher competencies in Vietnam. For the *Why*, this study takes into account the fitness for intended
purposes that the NFLP 2020 wishes to serve. Being guided by the operational
framework, the study on NFLP 2020s current practices of English language teacher
competence standardisation in Vietnam is presented.

The Study of Vietnam: The NFLP 2020 and Its Current Practice of English Language Teacher Competence Standardisation and Teacher Education

The Local Vietnamese Context and the Establishment of the NFLP 2020

A nation-wide review of the status quo of English language teaching throughout
Vietnam indicates that a majority of Vietnam's English language teachers are
unqualified to teach English (Bui and Nguyen 2016; Dang 2012; Nguyen 2013;

Nguyen and Bui 2016). Statistically, 83% of primary school teachers, 87% of lower secondary school teachers, about 92% of upper secondary school teachers, and about 45% of university lecturers (of English language subject) are not competent enough to teach English because of their low English Proficiency as revealed from a recent nationwide screening of teachers' English Proficiency (Nguyen 2013). The shortage of qualified English language teachers in Vietnam and its teachers' low English proficiency have not yet been effectively addressed (Bui and Nguyen 2016). These shortfalls have posed a big challenge for Vietnam and it is hardly surprising that ordinary Vietnamese people's English language proficiency is also low. According to Education First – the World's largest ranking of countries by English skills, Vietnam's English Language Proficiency ranked 39th out of 44 countries, which was nearly at the bottom with a very low English Proficiency Index (EPI) score in 2011 (Education First 2015); more recently it ranked 41th out of 88 countries (Education First 2019). Despite some recent improvements, Vietnamese population's English proficiency still remains lower than many countries in the region (Education First 2015) and it current position in Asia is 7th out 21 countries in the region (Education First 2019).

In response to Vietnam's low English proficiency, the Vietnamese Prime Minister officially issued in 2008 the Decision 1400/QD-TTg dated 30 September 2008 titled *"Approving the Project of Foreign Language Teaching and Learning in National Education System Period 2008–2020"*. The vision of the Decision 1400/QD-TTg is to improve human resource development and professional skills which emphasises foreign language proficiency (National Foreign Language 2020 Project 2014). In implementing the Decision, the Vietnamese MOET launched the National Foreign Language Project 2020 (NFLP 2020) in 2008. The management board of the NFLP 2020 is from the central government with its directors being the Minister and Vice-Minister of Education and Training and the representatives from ministries offices and related agencies, reflecting the Vietnamese government's firm political commitment to reforming foreign language education in general and English language education in particular across the whole national system.

The NFLP 2020 envisaged that by the year 2020, most of the Vietnamese graduates from vocational schools, colleges and universities would have gained the capacity to use a foreign language independently and confidently to further their chance to study and work in a multicultural environment serving the cause of industrialisation and modernisation of the country. Working towards achieving this aim, the NFLP 2020 highlights an urgent need to "renovate the teaching and learning of foreign languages within the national education system" (Prime Minister 2008). The NFLP 2020 is considered to be "the most remarkable language reform of the nation" (Bui and Nguyen 2016) and is viewed by many as an "ambitious" project (Nguyen 2013). However, whether it is achievable or not requires not only firm political commitment from the government and cooperation from all key stakeholders but also the project's willingness to reflect on and learn from its own current practices and the best international practices. This chapter focuses on English language teacher competence standardisation and is limited to reviewing, analysing and evaluating the NFLP 2020s current practice of English language teacher competence standardisation and its English language teacher education.

Globalisation and Global Forces

It is well documented that globalisation has made a considerable impact on the multi-dimensional aspects of societies, including Vietnam's English language education and English language teacher education. For English language education, English has been globally recognised as an international language of communication and work that would allow greater access to global developments in science, technology and business (e.g., Cabau 2009; Hanewald 2016; OECD 2011). In Asia, English skills are an integral part of many Asian countries' efforts to integrate with the global market economy for technological advancement and nationalism (e.g., Hanewald 2016; Kaplan et al. 2011; Kirkpatrick and Bui 2016). These global and regional forces highlight an urgent need for any education system across the globe to develop its average population who are equipped to work in a globalised economy where the English language is the international language of communication.

In Vietnam, though English was once the language of the enemy, it is now the language widely regarded as the most useful language for the nation and its people to realise their dreams of material success and privilege (Do 2006). In light of this, the NFLP 2020 has placed a strong emphasis on English language and is committed to improving and developing the English language capacity of the Vietnamese workforce in order to meet the demands for English speaking workforces and at the same time to help Vietnam fully integrate into the world of globalisation.

The new status of English has its practical implications for English language teaching and learning in Vietnam. The common status of English as an International Language (EIL) or English as a lingua franca now provides a broader intercultural communication across global contexts, including the Vietnamese context. As the context of English language learning and use changes, so does the English language teaching. Vietnam's context for teaching English, like other contexts across the globe, tends to shift from the context where English was not predominant in the social environment – English as a Foreign Language (EFL) in the past to the current context where English is now predominant in the social environment – English as a Second Language (ESL) and the context where English is used for broad intercultural communication – English as an International Language (EIL) and English as an Additional Language (EAL). There is thus an increasing need for more qualified ESL/EIL/EAL English language subject teachers and ESL/EIL/EAL teacher educators in Vietnam. The NFLP 2020 has to be aware of this changing nature of Vietnam's context of English language learning and use when developing competences for Vietnam's English language teachers in such new ESL/EIL/EAL contexts.

In addition, a recent overview of trends and issues in English language education in South East Asia reveals six common trends and accompanied issues (or hidden risks) (Hu and McKay 2012). These six trends and their accompanied issues across countries in East Asia, according to Hu and McKay (2012), are (1) the constant lowering of the starting age for formal English language education despite the findings of the recent comprehensive reviews of empirical research, highlighting that younger learners of the English language do not have the global advantage over older ones; (2) the increased prominence of English as a curricular subject which may have the possible negative impact on literacy learning in mother tongue and non-language subject learning; (3) a new orientation towards developing students' practical competence in using English for communication by promoting teaching methodologies of Western origins (i.e., Communicative Language Teaching – CLT and Task-based Language Teaching – TBLT) without giving due attention to the local pedagogical ecology; (4) the common movements to provide learners with some forms of immersion in English or an opportunity to use English for communicative purposes that may give rise to a wide array of issues including pedagogical effectiveness and Western ideological influences; (5) the gate-keeping role of English Proficiency in which English is a core component of high stakes assessments such as high school and university entrance examinations that may contribute to the dominance of English language competence as cultural and symbolic capital and creation of English knowing elitism; and (6) possible loss of cultural identity and integrity due to promotion of teaching English and English-speaking cultures. For the NFLP 2020's teacher competence standardisation, it is necessary for all key stakeholders to be well informed of all those six global trends and their accompanied issues in English language education, comprehend them and be competent in managing changes or hidden risks brought about by those six trends for the benefits of Vietnamese learners and the society at large.

As far as English language teacher education is concerned, globalisation brings about a global scenario in which there is not only a free movement of English language curriculum, textbooks and English language tests but also a free mobility of English language teachers (both qualified and unqualified ones) from native English-speaking countries in the West to non-native English speaking ones. Teacher mobility is a global phenomenon that poses its own risks. Vietnam has seen the free flows of unqualified English native teachers, mostly from the West, who have come to Vietnam and taken over the teaching jobs of Vietnam's qualified non-native English teachers. To prevent and control such unwanted flows of unqualified teachers from the West, it is, therefore, urgent for the NFLP 2020 not only to set standards for English language teacher competences, but also to quickly and strictly put them into real practice, especially for pre-service and in-service English language teacher education, native and non-native English language teacher recruitment and teacher appraisal throughout the nation.

Local Responses: The NFLP 2020s English Language Teacher Competence Standardisation and Vietnamese Colleges and Universities' English Language Teacher Education

In response to the influences of globalisation and the local context in which English proficiency among Vietnamese average adults (including Vietnam's English language teachers) is low, Vietnam's NFLP 2020 has intensified efforts in renovating

English language teaching and learning since the project's establishment. Under this project, the nation has seen a number of unprecedented activities and a number of major changes in English language education in Vietnam (Nguyen and Bui 2016). The NFLP 2020 Project has made various concurrent attempts, including adopting the Common European Framework of Reference (CEFR), establishing an English Language Proficiency Framework for Vietnam, setting English proficiency benchmarks for both English language subject teachers and students, beginning English instruction in grade 3, setting up the English Language Testing Center, University Courses in English (using English as a Medium of Instruction – EMI) and assigning key universities in the north, centre and south of Vietnam to provide continuous teacher professional development for English language teachers at all levels nationwide (Dang 2012; National Foreign Language 2020 Project 2014; Nguyen 2013; Prime Minister 2008). The most notable and most recent attempt is the NFLP 2020's recent development of Vietnam's English Teacher Competence Framework or Vietnam's ETCF which aims at standardising Vietnam's English language teacher competences and its allocation of financial resources for key universities in the North, Center and South of Vietnam to provide competence-based English language teacher education.

As far as English language teacher education in Vietnam is concerned, Vietnam's teacher education colleges and universities affiliated to Ministry of Education and Training (MOET) are normally responsible for designing and implementing their teacher education programs throughout the country. University lecturers from those colleges and universities are directly involved in English language teacher training in both pre-service and in-service programs which are approved by the MOET. Any changes in the contents of the English language teacher education programs offered by those colleges and universities must get official approval from the MOET. For many decades, the English language teacher education programs have experienced limited changes. It is important to note that the NFLP 2020 has mobilised human resources (i.e., teacher trainers, English language lecturers) from key English language teacher education colleges and universities in the north, centre and south of Vietnam to organise and implement nationwide professional development workshops for English language teachers.

Though the author was not involved in developing the ETCF from the beginning, the author was invited by the NFLP 2020's management board to be an English language teacher trainer and a material developer for delivering lecturers/presentations and compiling training materials for many teacher training workshops designed and organised by assigned universities to put the ETCF into real use throughout the country for the past 2 years from early 2014 till late 2015. Over the past 2 years, together with a team of English language educators, the author has had opportunities to work closely with both local and foreign English language educators who have been participating actively in English language teacher education from many different school levels from pre-school levels to tertiary ones. Such working opportunities allowed the author to make direct on-site observations, get access to relevant documents (i.e., two parallel versions of the ETCF, the ETCF Users' Guide, and the NFLP 2020's project documents profiling the meeting minutes, the procedures of developing the ETCF and its outcomes) and maintain direct regular contacts with Vietnam's English language teacher trainees, teacher trainers and English language educators. The author has thus gained insights in relation to the NFLP 2020's process of developing the ETCF, the contents and intended purposes of the ETCF itself and its assigned universities' English language teacher education. Such on-site observations, direct regular contacts, documentary analyses together with the theoretical backgrounds reviewed earlier can empower the author's critical analyses of the process of developing the NFLP 2020's ETCF, its content and its fitness for intended purposes in light of the operational framework developed earlier for the study, based on which implications are proposed for Vietnamese colleges' and universities' English language teacher education.

Within its limited space and scope, the aim of this chapter is to focus on the NFLP 2020's *process* of developing the ETCF (the How), its *outcome* – the contents of Vietnam's ETCF itself, (the What) and the ETCF's fitness for its intended purposes (the Why) and its implications for English language teacher education in Vietnamese colleges and universities.

The NFLP 2020's Process of Developing the ETCF: The How

The ETCF Users' Guide describes the development of the ETCF as a process of collaborating, drafting, reviewing, revising and adopting with collective efforts (National Foreign Language 2020 Project 2014). The author's knowledge and experience gained from on-site observations when participating in the NFLP 2020's project activities in 2014 and 2015 confirmed this process. The ETCF was first commissioned by the NFLP 2020 in the early 2010 and was then drafted for 3 years (2010–2012) by Dr. Diana Dudzik who was an international English education consultant (from the US Department of State's English Language Fellow Program). The ETCF was developed under the sponsorship of Resource Exchange International and the US Department of State, in collaboration with the leading Vietnamese English language experts from regional and national universities (National Foreign Language 2020 Project 2014). For drafting the ETCF, in-service teacher performance indicators were developed by the British Council in collaboration with a team of English teacher educators who are mostly university lecturers in the field of Teaching English to Speakers of Other Languages (TESOL) throughout Vietnam. The ETCF was then reviewed by the Vietnam National Institute of Educational Sciences with participants from leading universities and international partners. The ETCF was finally approved by a panel of experts from MOET and key English language educators/university lecturers in December 2012. At the time of this chapter being written, the ETCF is in the process of being rolled out and implemented on a nation-wide scale as a tool for the successful implementation of the NFLP 2020's English language subject teacher competence standardisation and ETCF-based English language teacher education programs offered by NFLP 2020's assigned universities.

For nation-wide implementation of the ETCF, since the ETCF was established in 2012, it can be observed that the NFLP 2020 has made efforts to inform and guide Vietnam's English language teachers (across school levels) of the ETCF and its users by organising many professional development workshops and programs for English language teachers throughout the country. Under the central management of the NFLP 2020, teaching materials, PowerPoint presentations, support activities and a users' guide have been compiled and used in such workshops in order to facilitate the implementation of the ETCF (Le and Ngo 2015).

In this study, to assess the NFLP 2020's process of developing the ETCF, due attention should be first drawn to the theoretical background reviewed earlier, especially the operational framework developed earlier in relation to the common process of establishing teacher standards. It can be observed that Vietnam's ETCF has gone through most of the steps suggested in the literature. Specifically, as the ETCF Users' Guide indicated, the development of the ETCF was fundamentally based on extensive research, analysis and review of not only the general teacher education research but also several international standards documents for foreign language teachers, including the Common European Framework Reference (CEFR), the American Council on the Teaching of Foreign Language (ACTFL) Program Standards for the Preparation of Foreign Language Teachers (2002 version), the TESOL/NCATE (National Council for Accreditation of Teacher Education) Teacher Education Standards (2010 version), the European Portfolio of Student Teachers of Languages (2007 version), and a Vietnamese project, the Hue University EFL Teacher Education Standards (2010 version). However, the question as to which components of the ETCF were developed with reference to which international standards document is still open for investigation and interpretation.

For a closer investigation of the NFLP 2020's process of developing the ETCF, it is important to refer to the five-phase sequential process reviewed earlier of (1) benchmarking with developed economies, (2) creating a team/technical working group/pools of experts at the Ministry level, (3) pilot testing of the first draft, (4) rolling out and full implementation of National Teaching Competency Standards, and (5) monitoring and assessment (SIREP 2010). Using this five-phase process as a useful point of reference, some observations can be made in relation to the development process of the ETCF. First, from the author's on-site observations and the NFLP 2020's documented activities, there is no evidence of benchmarking with developed economies, except for the fact that Diana Dudzik, the leader of the ETCF development team is an American by nationality.

Second, there was a lack of consultation with core English language subject teachers and universities' English language teacher educators/university lecturers themselves when conducting the second step of creating a team/technical working group/pools of experts at the ministry level. This lack of consultation was confirmed when the researcher had chance to have direct contacts with hundreds of core English language teachers from primary school levels to tertiary ones and English language teacher educators/university lecturers in the nationwide core teacher training programs from June to December 2015. It was evidenced that core English language teachers and teacher educators/university lecturers nationwide were not invited to any meetings in preparation for the development of the ECTF and thus struggled very hard to make sense of the ETCF upon its development and implementation. The NFLP 2020s meeting minutes show that for the development of the ETCF, the NFLP 2020 had consultations with a dedicated team of English professionals who are presidents, vice-presidents and teacher educators/trainers/university lecturers from the major foreign language and teacher education universities throughout Vietnam. However, there was no evidence of consulting directly with English language teachers and teacher educators/trainers/university lecturers who are the main change agents and the key implementers to put the ETCF into real life classroom practices. It may be argued that presidents, vice-presidents, teacher trainers, and language educators may be language teachers themselves but not all of them have English language teaching backgrounds. Even if they do, their perspectives might be different from those of everyday classroom teachers of English language and English language teacher educators/trainers/university lecturers who are the intended users of the ETCF and should thus have been invited to participate in the development of the ETCF right from the beginning. It is also the case for material developers and teacher trainers who are the ETCF's real users invited to be trainers of the NFLP 2020s English language teacher training workshops. From the author's on-site observations and the NFLP 2020s documents, there was no evidence that material developers and teacher educators/trainers/university lecturers for the NFLP 2020s nationwide workshops were invited to participate in the development of the ETCF.

Third, there were total absences of the third step of validating or pilot testing the ETCF for pre-implementation and of the fifth step of monitoring and assessment for during and post-implementation. Right after the ETCF was established in December 2012, it was immediately put into official use in January 2013 without any officially documented validation or pilot-testing efforts nor observable/documented efforts to monitor and assess the implementation of the ETCF in practice. Also, it is still open for interpretation whether the NFLP 2020 will have any real intention to take the fifth step of monitoring and/or assessing the implementation of the ETCF in the immediate or long-term future though it is highly recommended by both the literature and the best practice.

Absences of such critical steps in developing the ETCF may cause difficulty in putting it into use and can partly explain the reasons why teacher trainees and participants in the teacher professional development programs (in which the author participated and could make on-site observations) did struggle to understand the content of the ETCF, namely, its descriptors of domains, competencies and performance indicators. In many cases, English language teachers' resistance to many of the NFLP 2020's teacher development programs and to the use of the ETCF itself was also well documented in a recent research assessing the impacts of the NFLP 2020's activities on English language education and English language teacher education (Ngo 2014). Skipping such important steps in the process of developing the ETCF may consequently impact its nation-wide roll-out or implementation, causing difficulty in implementing the ETCF itself and more seriously, slowing down the process of standardising Vietnam's English language teacher competences.

The NFLP 2020s Outcome: Vietnam's ETCF Contents: The What

Vietnam's ETCF is the very first set of subject-specific standards in Vietnam complementing the general teacher standards (for all subject teachers from all school levels throughout the country) which were established by MOET's Professional Teacher Association (Cục nhà giáo) in October 2009. The ETCF claims itself to be a blueprint of knowledge, skills, values and processes that make up English teaching in Vietnam in the twenty-first century (Nguyen 2013). The ETCF's vision, as stated in the NFLP 2020 (2014, p. 8), is "to build the profession of English teaching beyond the level of technicians or teaching machines (giáo viên là những cái máy dạy) to practicing teachers with 'adaptive expertise'". Absences of important steps (i.e., the third step of validating and the fifth step of monitoring and assessment) in developing the ETCF raises important questions as to whether its contents sufficiently cover adequate knowledge, skills, values and processes that make up English language teaching in Vietnam. In addition, the co-existence of Vietnam's ETCF and Vietnam's general teacher competence standards, however, raises a number of concerns over why there needs to be two different sets of standards for English language teachers in co-existence, whether there are any similarities and differences (or contradictions) between them, whether these two standards have any linkages, which standards should be the main requirements for English language teachers to meet, and why English language teachers have to comply with more standards than other subject teachers and other foreign language teachers.

It is also worth noting that within the ETCF itself, there are two parallel versions: the pre-service version of 16 pages long (used for pre-service English teacher education) and the in-service version of 20 pages long (used for in-service teacher development and practicing teachers' self-assessment). Both versions of the ETCF were officially approved on 21st December 2012 by the MOET. The contents of both versions of the ETCF have five main domains of (1) knowledge of language, language learning and curricula content, (2) knowledge of language teaching, (3) knowledge of language learners, (4) professional attitudes and values in language teaching, and (5) practice and context of language teaching. The basic differences between these two versions, according to its developers, are that "the pre-service ETCF includes more rigorous and theoretical knowledge, the addition of more competencies, more rigorous performance indicators and teacher educator competencies" (National Foreign Language Project 2020 2014, p. 84). Such additional competencies in pre-service ETCF (which are not found in the in-service ETCF) are competencies for ethical testing and teaching, regional uses of English and English around the world. It is worth noting that while the pre-service ETCF is intended to be used to guide college and university English teacher education programs, the in-service ETCF is intended to be used to inform trainers/lecturers as they plan courses for practicing (in-service) teachers' ongoing development. However, there is almost no evidence of the ETCF-based approach taken to both pre-service and in-service English language teacher education in Vietnam's teacher education colleges and universities. As both versions are mostly similar in terms of format, contents and structures, the two parallel versions of the ETCF may overwhelm and confuse its users, particularly, English language teachers and teacher trainers, most of whom are participants in both pre-service and in-service teacher education programs.

The four common purposes of the pre-service/in-service ETCF are (1) pre-service/in-service teacher needs assessment, (2) pre-service/in-service teacher training program and curriculum evaluation, (3) pre-service/in-service teacher training program and curriculum improvement and (4) pre-service/in-service teacher self-assessment. The pre-service and in-service ETCF versions have a lot of practical implications for universities' teacher development programs which need to provide teachers with the opportunities to experience the values, processes, activities, classroom behaviours and roles that they are expected to use as well as to model effectively and teach in their classrooms. However, if both versions of the ETCF serve the same purposes for the same users, though at different career stages (pre-service or in-service stages), the question arises as to why they were not merged into one unified version (with special notes for different users at different stages) for the sake of simplicity and feasibility.

The NFLP 2020s Fitness for Purposes: The Why

Assessing the effectiveness of teacher standards, as mentioned earlier, needs to take into account teacher standards' fitness for purpose that they wish to serve. In the case of Vietnam, the NFLP 2020's ETCF was originally created to address the question of what Vietnam's English language teachers need to know and be able to do in order to equip Vietnam's English language learners with the skills and competences needed for the twenty-first century. A closer examination of the contents of the ETCF versions suggests that both versions wish to serve multiple-purposes of specifically providing ongoing professional development for pre-service/in-service teachers, mapping curriculum to ETCF, embedding competencies into courses, linking outcomes and assessments to competencies and providing a new apprenticeship for teachers-learners (Dudzik 2008) (These intended purposes are legitimate ones as they can help to ensure national consistency in English language teacher preparation development, and appraisal that are currently offered by teacher education colleges and universities and to support the professional learning of all English language teachers at all levels, contributing to the professionalisation of English language teaching in Vietnam. However, to sustain the ETCF's fitness for those intended purposes, both the ETCF's potential and the real users have to be well informed of all of those purposes and voluntarily take specific precaution actions to actively put the ETCF (as a useful tool for English language teacher preparation, recruitment and appraisal) into real practice to maximise its values. Apart from the nation-wide teacher training workshops which have been organised for short durations of 1–3 months for a large number of teachers from primary education levels to tertiary ones to inform users of the existence of the ETCF, its values and its purposes, there is no evidence of the ETCF's potential and real users putting it into real practice in teacher education colleges and universities nationwide.

To sum up, despite some critical analyses of the process of developing the ETCF, its outcomes and its fitness for purposes, the NFLP 2020's effort to establish the ETCF is a worthwhile effort for reforming Vietnam's English language teaching and learning practices. With the current practices of developing and implementing the ETCF, the NFLP 2020's English language teacher standardisation is moving in the right direction. However, to ensure its fitness for purpose and to keep all key stakeholders more focused on developing competences for English language teachers, and more importantly, to make the ETCF the foundation of English language teaching reforms, some improvements should be made, particularly to the process of developing the ETCF, the contents of the ETCF itself and to the national policies for implementing it in pre-service/in-service English language teacher education programs as well as nation-wide colleges' and universities' English language teacher education.

Conclusion

Recommendations for the NFLP 2020

Although the ETCF claims itself to be "a standardized, customizable and flexible tool" (The National Foreign Language Project 2020 2014, p. 17), this chapter attempts to investigate whether the NFLP Project meets the needs of teacher education students in Vietnam who will become English language teachers, make practical recommendations to the NFLP 2020's management board for further improvement of the development process, the content of the ETCF itself, the ETCF's fitness for intended purposes and to bring focus and vision to English language teacher development in Vietnam through a standardised tool of the ETCF. It also proposes practical implications for more standardised English language teacher education in Vietnamese colleges and universities.

First, regarding the process of developing the ETCF, it is recommended that the NFLP 2020 should actively engage Vietnamese English language teachers across school levels, and colleges and universities' English language teacher educators, especially those who are now participating in the teacher professional development workshops organised by the NFLP 2020 to get their practical insights and prompt feedback in relation to the ETCF's contents. Engagement of teacher trainers/educators/lecturers from colleges and universities into the ETCF development process can ensure that they fully understand the content, the process, the advantages and the philosophy of developing the ETCF before helping others (i.e., both in-service teachers and/or student teachers) understand it. In addition, getting teachers involved in developing the ETCF may give them the chance to voice their concerns and more importantly, to facilitate their professional learning and their later implementation of ETCF in practice. It would have been best if the NFLP 2020 had engaged English language teachers and teacher educators/trainers in the process of developing the

ETCF; however, it is not too late now to do so, especially when English language teachers and teacher educators/trainers are participants in many training workshops where their voices can be heard and their perspectives can be acknowledged and documented. If the ETCF is to be considered a strategic tool or instrument for Vietnam's fundamental reform of English language teaching and learning and English language teachers' professional development, the NFLP 2020 should recognise the important role of English language teachers who are the key change agents for reform implementation. The role of teachers as change agents in education reform (including the reform of English language teaching and learning) has been repeatedly emphasised in the literature (Fullan 2011; Hall and Hord 2010; Nguyen and Bui 2016). However, if the ETCF is considered a tool for English language teacher professional learning, it is important to note what Nguyen and Thu (2018, p. 231) in Chap. 12 argued that teacher professional learning must be "a collective activity and involve a wider community, not something that can be done solely individually" by either English language teachers or English language teacher educators/trainers alone.

In addition, it is recommended that both versions of the ETCF should be pilot-tested among their potential users and real users, namely student teachers, the English language teachers, teacher trainers, material developers to make sure that they all share the common language of understanding the ETCF. Through pilot-testing, the contents of the ETCF will be validated and appropriately revised to ensure its fitness for purposes. Given that the ETCF is now being rolled out, it is important for teacher education colleges and universities to take the ETCF-based teacher education by implementing it in both the pre-service and in-service teacher training programs; monitoring and assessment of the ETCF during and after its implementation is highly recommended by the NFLP 2020's experts.

Second, as far as the contents of the ETCF are concerned, the NFLP 2020 should be open to the best international practices to learn from other countries, especially from those where English is not a native language; rather English is used and learnt as an Additional Language (EAL) and/or English as an International Language (EIL). In addition, as the contents of both versions of the ETCF do not reflect progressions of the English language teaching profession, the ETCF should be understood as core teacher competency and should thus be re-labelled as Core English Teacher Competency Framework (CETCF) rather than using its current label as ETCF – English Teacher Competency Framework that may cause misunderstanding and potential resistance from many teachers. An alternative option is to take an incremental approach as well recommended in the literature by adding the progressions of competences articulated in the ETCF so that teachers at different stages of their teaching profession are aware of which stage they are in now and which stage they want to be or should be in the sequential professional career stages.

In terms of the number of standards, the two parallel versions of ETCF (pre-service ETCF and in-service ETCF) together with the general teacher competency standard established by Vietnam's Teacher Professional Association ("Cục nhà giáo") may raise a concern over the overwhelming "too many standards" phenomenon. In this regard, Sykes and Plastriks (1993, p. 7) asserted, "the proliferation of [too many] standards may lead not to stronger education for all children [in this case, all teachers or all student teachers], but to continuing discord and fragmentation… As policy makers create all these new standards, there is worry that the whole will not hang together." To develop a more coherent set of standards, it is recommended that both versions of the ETCF should be merged into one single set with particular reference to Vietnam's general teacher competency standards to avoid misunderstanding or confusion and to encourage English language teachers to change. In doing so, the ETCF can achieve what it promised to achieve which is to "help to bring consistency to the content and processes of teacher development among local, regional and international teacher training providers" (National Foreign Language Project 2020 2014, p. 35).

Last but not least, the pressures of globalisation and global forces reviewed earlier make it a matter of urgency for Vietnam to quickly revise and implement the final version(s) of the ETCF into Vietnam's English language teacher recruitment, training and teacher appraisal practices. The reform of Vietnam's English language teaching and learning practices can only achieve its goal if its teacher competence standardisation takes into account the cultural aspects of its local and national contexts and is implemented effectively and comprehensively on a large scale in Vietnam's English language education system, English language teacher education, and teacher recruitment practices.

Implications for More Standardised English Language Teacher Education in Vietnamese Colleges and Universities

The study of the NFLP 2020s English language teacher competence standardisation highlights both the global context and the local Vietnamese context in which the ETCF was developed as a standardising tool for teacher competence standardisation towards achieving the aim of renovating Vietnam's English language teachers which in turn can help renovate Vietnam's English language teaching and learning. Given its local demand and the global forces, the NFLP 2020s efforts to develop the ETCF are worthwhile efforts and the usefulness of its contents is well recognised. However, whether it can really help achieve its intended purposes of improving and developing Vietnam's English language teachers' competences depends very much on the improved process of developing the ETCF, the improved contents of the ETCF itself and its fitness for purposes as recommended above.

The findings of this study suggest that better standardisation of Vietnam's English language teacher competence requires the active participation of the English language teachers, the validation or pilot-testing of the ETCF (which was actually skipped in actual practice) before its nation-wide roll-out and very importantly, using, monitoring and assessing the ETCF in the immediate and long-term future. Unless English language teachers and teacher educators are well-informed of those competences articulated in the ETCF in the pre-service and in-service English language teacher education courses, and unless the ETCF is validated, used, monitored and assessed promptly, the NFLP 2020s task of standardising teacher competences might be a never-ending one. In other words, without a standard process (of developing the ETCF), a standard product (the contents of the ETCF), it would be hard for the NFLP 2020 to implement standardisation of English language teacher competence.

The findings of the study propose three main implications for the Vietnamese colleges and universities. First, it highlights the urgent need for Vietnamese colleges and universities to renovate and standardise their English language teacher education programs in which the ETCF should be well embedded. Without standard English language teacher education programs offered by Vietnamese colleges and universities, it would be difficult for Vietnam to implement English language teacher competence.

The second implication of the study proposes that English language teacher education colleges and universities in Vietnam should timely consider a shift from their current content-based approach to the new competence-based approach to English language teacher education. In such a new approach, the ETCF and all its five components of (i) knowledge of the subject; (ii) knowledge of teaching; (iii) knowledge of learners; (iv) attitudes and values; and (v) learning in and from practice (Dudzik 2008) should all be incorporated. To facilitate such incorporation, the existing model of English language teacher education models should be adapted and new models be developed to improve the college/university programs of English language teacher education at both undergraduate and postgraduate levels and to enhance the competences of teacher trainers/educators themselves.

The third implication of the study is that English language teacher education universities in Vietnam who are responsible for both pre-service and in-service teacher education should establish strong school-university partnership to keep colleges/universities well informed of school contexts, school teachers' current competences, the gap between their current competences and expected competences and professional development practices for English language teachers in the context of the English language teaching and learning reform in Vietnam. Such strong school–university partnership can help schools and universities that are keen on collaborating with each other with timely diagnosis, adequate treatment and assessment of school teachers' competences.

Concluding Remarks

This book chapter has attempted to put under spotlight a study on the NFLP 2020s English language subject teacher competence standardisation in Vietnam under the influence of globalisation, with particular reference to its process of developing the ETCF, its outcome – the ETCF itself, its fitness for purposes and its implications for universities' English language teacher education. However, there are obvious limitations to the chapter. The chapter took an inward approach to investigate in what ways the NFLP 2020 Project meets the needs of teacher education students in

Vietnam who will become English language teachers and focusing on the NFLP 2020s internal process and outcomes of the ETCF. In addition, critical analyses of the process, the outcome of the ETCF and its fitness for purposes in this book chapter seemed to be limited to the theoretical backgrounds reviewed, the operational framework developed by the author, the author's subjective observations and limited insights of English language teachers, (though in large numbers), with whom the author closely worked with and had direct frequent contacts with. The implications proposed in this study were based on the findings of the study focusing on the ETCF and competence-based approach to English language teacher education.

Further research is thus needed to take into account the perceptions of both the ETCF developers and users on a large scale and to take an outward approach to be more open to international practices, especially to other English non-native countries outside Vietnam that are more successful or at least ahead of Vietnam in achieving the similar goal of achieving higher English proficiency nationwide to see whether they have developed a similar ETCF and used it as a crucial driver for successful transformation of English language teaching and learning; and in case they do, how they have established and implemented it in practice to advance their English language education in Vietnamese colleges and universities. Countries such as Sweden, Denmark, The Netherlands, Norway and Finland in Europe, and Singapore, Malaysia, India and South Korea in Asia can offer invaluable lessons for Vietnam as these non-native English-speaking countries, especially those in Asia sharing many contextual and cultural similarities with Vietnam, have successfully achieved high English Proficiency Index Scores (Education First 2015). It is worth noting that the teacher competence standardisation is a global instrument for education reforms. It is important to consider localisation which emphasises not only theoretical backgrounds and local sensitivity to its own local Vietnamese cultural context but also its global awareness of international successes.

References

Aitsl. (2016). *What are the Australian professional standards for teachers?*
Aitsl. (2018). *Understand initial teacher education program accreditation.* https://www.aitsl.edu. au/deliver-ite-programs/understand-ite-program-accreditation
Australian Professional Standards for Teachers. (2016). *Standards.*
Biggs, J. (1999). *Teaching for quality learning at university.* New York: Society for Research in Higher Education & Open University Press.
Bransford, J., Deny, S., Berliner, D., Hammerness, K., & Beckett, K. L. (2005). Theories of learning and their roles in teaching. In J. Bransford & L. Darling-Hammond (Eds.), *Preparing teachers for a changing world: What teachers should learn and be able to do.* San Francisco: Jossey-Bass.
Bui, T. T. N., & Nguyen, H. T. M. (2016). Standardising English for educational and socio-economic betterment – A critical analysis of English language policy reforms in Vietnam. In W. W. Robert (Ed.), *English language education policy in Asia.* Cham: Springer.
Cabau, B. (2009). Language-in-education issues: Sweden as a study. *Educational Studies, 35*(4), 379–389.

Caena, F. (2011). *Literature review teachers' core competences: Requirements and development.*

Caena, F. (2014). *Initial teacher education in Europe: An overview of policy issues.* Brussels: European Commission.

Chari, C. (2016). *School-university partnerships in English language teacher education.* Cham: Springer.

Dang, T. C. (2012). *National foreign language project 2020 (E 2020 Project).* Paper presented at the teacher competency standardisation, Beijing.

Darling-Hammond, L., & Wise, A. E. (1985). Beyond standardisation: State standards and school improvement. *The Elementary School Journal, 85*(3), 315–336.

Do, T. H. (2006). *History of English language teaching in Vietnam.*

Dudzik, D. L. (2008). English policies, curricular reforms and teacher development in multilingual, postcolonial Djibouti. *Dissertation Abstracts International, 69*, 1652.

Education First. (2015). *EF English proficiency index 2015.*

Education First. (2019). *EF English Proficiency Index 2019.*

European Commission. (2010). *Common European principles for teachers' competences and qualifications.* Retrieved from Brussels.

European Commission. (2013). *Key data on teachers and school leaders in Europe.* Retrieved from Luxembourg.

European Commission. (2014). *Initial teacher education in Europe: An overview of policy issues.*

Fong, S. F., Ch'ng, P. E., & Por, F. P. (2013). Development of ICT competency standard using the Delphi technique. *Procedia – Social and Behavioral Sciences, 103*, 299–314.

Fullan, M. (2011). *The new meaning of educational change.* New York: Teachers College Press.

Goodwyn, A. (2012). One size fits all: The increasing standardisation of English teachers' work in England. *English Teacher, 11*(4), 36–53.

Hall, G. E., & Hord, S. M. (2010). *Implementing change: Patterns, principles and potholes.* Englewood: Prentice-Hall.

Hanewald, R. (2016). The impact of English on educational policies and practices in Malaysia. In R. Kirkpatrick (Ed.), *English language education policy in Asia.* Cham: Springer.

Hu, G., & McKay, S. L. (2012). English language education in East Asia: Some recent developments. *Journal of Multilingual and Multicultural Development, 33*(4), 345–362.

Ingvarson, L. (1998). Professional standards: A challenge for the AATE. *English in Australia, 122*, 31–44.

Ingvarson, L. (2005). Teaching standards: Foundations for professional development reforms. In M. Fullan (Ed.), *Fundamental change.* New York: Springer.

Jones, K. A. (2014). *Building competence: A case study in competency-based education.* Doctor of philosophy, University of Washington.

Kaplan, R. B., Richard, R. B., & Kamwangamalu, N. (2011). Why educational language plans sometimes fail. *Current Issues in Language Planning, 12*(2), 105–124.

Karababa, Z. C., & Caliskan, G. (2013). Teacher competencies in teaching Turkish as a foreign language. *Procedia – Social and Behavioral Sciences, 70*, 1545–1551.

Kelly, M., & Grenfell, M. (2004). *European profile for language teacher education: A frame of reference.*

Kirkpatrick, R., & Bui, T. T. N. (2016). Introduction: The challenges for English education policies in Asia. In R. Kirkpatrick (Ed.), *English language education policy in Asia.* Cham: Springer.

Kumar, I. A., & Parveen, S. (2013). Teacher education in the age of globalisation. *Research Journal of Educational Sciences, 1*(1), 8–12.

Le, V. C., & Ngo, T. M. (2015). *Putting the 'Competency framework for English language teachers' into practice: A guide for planning teacher personal professional development.* Hanoi.

McKinsey&Company. (2007). *How the world's best performing school system come out on top?*

Mrowicki, L. (1986). Project work English competency based curriculum. In J. Richards & T. Rodgers (Eds.), *Approaches and methods in language teaching.* New York: Cambridge University Press.

National Foreign Language 2020 Project. (2014). *Competency framework for English language teachers: User's guide.*

Ngo, T. M. (2014). *Assessment of impacts of the NFLP 2020 Project on Vietnam's English language teachers nationwide*. Hanoi.

Nguyen, H. T. M. (2013). *Vietnam's national foreign language 2020 project: Challenges, opportunities and solutions*. Forum 2013 Publication.

Nguyen, H. T. M., & Bui, T. T. N. (2016). Teachers' agency and the enactment of educational reform in Vietnam. *Current Issues in Language Planning, 17*(1), 88–105.

Nguyen, H. T. M., & Thu, N. D. (2018). Professional learning for higher education academics: Systematic tensions. In N. T. Nguyen & L. T. Tran (Eds.), *Reforming Vietnamese higher education: Global forces and local demands*. Dordrecht: Springer.

OECD. (2011). *OECD reviews of evaluation and assessment in education: Sweden*.

Prime Minister. (2008). *Decision 1400/QD-TTg approving the scheme "Foreign language teaching and learning in National Education system period 2008–2020"*. https://www.scribd.com/doc/237474972/National-Foreign-Language-2020-Project-English-Translations

Prime Minister. (2012). *Preliminary report: Malaysia education blueprint 2013–2025*.

SIREP. (2010). *Teaching competency standards in SouthEast Asian Countries: Eleven country audit*.

Stoof, A., Martens, R., van Merrienboer, J., & Bastiaens, T. (2002). The boundary approach of competence: A constructivist aid for understanding and using the concept of competence. *Human Resource Development Review, 1*, 345–365.

Sykes, G., & Plastrik, P. (1993). *Standard setting as educational reform* (Trends and Issues Paper No. 8). Retrieved from Washington, DC.

Vesamavibool, S., Urwongse, S., Hanpanich, B., Thongnoum, D., & Watcharin, K. (2015). The comparative study of professional standards for Thai teachers and for Asean teachers. *Procedia – Social and Behavioral Sciences, 191*, 2280–2284.

Chapter 12
Professional Learning for Higher Education Academics: Systematic Tensions

Hoa Thi Mai Nguyen and Thu Dinh Nguyen

Abstract Using activity theory as a theoretical framework, this case study identifies contradictions relating to the professional learning activities of academics in a higher education institute in Vietnam. Data were collected from in-depth interviews with a group of academics in order to gain in-depth understanding about their professional learning experience. The study puts forward implications for the design of a model for academics' professional development in the context of Vietnam.

Introduction

Reforms in higher education in Asian EFL (English as a Foreign Language) countries in general and in Vietnam in particular have brought about some remarkable changes under the pressure of regional and international integration (e.g. Harman and Nguyen 2010; Harman et al. 2010). In 2005, the Government of Vietnam approved Vietnam's Higher Education Reform Agenda (often referred to as HERA 2005), a plan for the comprehensive reform of the higher education system by 2020. By 2020, the higher education system should be "advanced by international standards, highly competitive, and appropriate to the socialist-oriented market mechanism" (Harman et al. 2010, p. 10). Such ambitious goals have presented the education sector with both opportunities and challenges (e.g. Le 2013; Pham 2010, 2012; Tran et al. 2014; Vallely and Wilkinson 2008) as higher education in Vietnam has been seen to lag behind regional and international standards (Pham 2013). The government made clear in HERA (2005) that one of its targets is to intensively develop academic staff and significantly increase the number of qualified staff in higher education. Thus, the issues of professional development of these staff are of great concern. There is apparent evidence that teacher

H. T. M. Nguyen (✉)
School of Education, University of New South Wales, Kensington, NSW, Australia
e-mail: hoa.nguyen@unsw.edu.au

T. D. Nguyen
University of Technology and Education, Ho Chi Minh City, Vietnam

© Springer Nature Singapore Pte Ltd. 2019   223
N. T. Nguyen, L. T. Tran (eds.), *Reforming Vietnamese Higher Education*,
Education in the Asia-Pacific Region: Issues, Concerns and Prospects 50,
https://doi.org/10.1007/978-981-13-8918-4_12

professional development and teacher lifelong learning can lead to teaching and learning improvements (e.g. Darling-Hammond 2006). In the context of reforming higher education in Vietnam, the support provided to academics is vital to enhance the quality of teaching and learning.

Despite multiple attempts to define characteristics of effective professional development (Guskey 2002, 2003), there is still disagreement about an effective model of professional learning (Cameron et al. 2013) and criteria for effectiveness in professional development among educational researchers and practitioners (Guskey 2002, 2003). While there exists consensus about the value and importance of teacher professional learning, the current literature fails to identify conditions that facilitate this learning (Clarke and Hollingworth 2002), and whether or not these conditions meet teachers' professional needs in assisting to advance their careers, especially in a specific context of change, such as in Vietnam. In a report on the academic profession in Vietnam, Pham (2013) noted urgently that a challenging task for the higher education system in Vietnam is to "create appropriate conditions for academics to undertake balanced activities and to develop their careers" (p. 188). A number of scholars (Harman and Nguyen 2010; Nguyen 2017; Pham 2001) stress the critical role of staff development training programs in enhancing the teaching and learning situation in higher education in Vietnam. Using activity theory as a conceptual and methodological framework, this study collected data from in-depth interviews with a group of academics in an institution in Vietnam to gain further understanding of their professional learning experiences.

Professional Learning

There has been a great deal of literature on professional development for teachers and their advancement (Richards and Farrell 2005; King 2004; Guskey 2003; Knapp 2003; Piggot-Irvine 2006). Generally, it encompasses both formal and informal opportunities for teachers to engage in certain activities whose aims are to enhance the effectiveness of their teaching, and student learning. Professional development can bring about excellence in teaching and doing research to tertiary institutions and, at the same time, ensure visible improvements in teaching and learning practices (Hattie 2003). In the context of globalisation, tertiary education plays an important role in providing a qualified workforce for highly competitive employment markets of the knowledge economy and the knowledge society (Day 2006). To meet such a goal, academics are expected to be change agents in this reform. This places more pressure for teachers/academics to be knowledgeable and able to deliver effectively the essential components of information contained in an updated curriculum and syllabi to their students in flexible ways (Nguyen and Tran 2018; Guskey 2002).

Unlike teachers in primary or secondary education who are often equipped with some form of pre-service education prior to their employment, teachers in higher education are recruited "on the basis of their knowledge, qualifications and experience in their subject areas, and lack pre-service teacher education" (Beaty 1998,

p. 8). This is even more complicated in the case of Vietnam, where, due to lack of teaching staff, many new graduates are appointed to work as academics without any proper and necessary preparation. Such academics have to bluff their way through the actual teaching even though they may have good knowledge about the discipline(s) or the subject(s) they are in charge of. In order to meet the quality requirement of teaching and learning, many tertiary institutions offer introductory courses about pedagogy together with a basic course about Internet and Communication Technology to provide new academics with tips and strategies to help them solve possible teaching problems (Newble and Cannon 2013). However, this alone is not sufficient for them to teach effectively in higher education as the lack of theoretical underpinnings of particular teaching skills means they can only apply tips and strategies mechanically (Hustler et al, 2003). This unique situation underlines the need for effective and relevant professional development.

There is evidence that professional opportunities for university academics in higher education in a number of places, including Vietnam, are often inadequately organised (Behari-Leak 2017; Collison et al. 2009; Chaudary and Imran 2012; Nguyen 2017; Phuong and McLean 2016). This is partly due to the fact that teachers are rarely taken into consideration in terms of needs, interest, impact or preference; teachers receive little support, mentally or financially, from their institution. Where some PL activities may appear supportive, in most cases they are top-down and transmissive (Zheng 2011; Chaudary and Imran 2012; Ulysal 2012), as policy makers and institution leaders are not aware of what teachers really wish to engage in and benefit from. These PD events therefore are one-off activities and have no bearing on teachers' later work (Behari-Leak 2017; Pham 2001; Diaz-Maggioli 2003; Harwell 2003). Therefore, there is a need for further studies which explore teacher professional learning experience.

Using Activity Theory to Conceptualise Teacher Professional Learning

In scholarship addressing the ways in which professional learning of teachers has been conceptualised, there are a variety of theories which view professional learning from different angles (Opfer and Pedder 2011; Philpott 2014). In this study, socio-cultural theory, more specifically activity theory (AT), is employed to shed light on concepts of teachers' professional learning. Socio-cultural activity theory is valuable because it allows the investigation of various socio-cultural-historical and interpersonal factors that shape teachers' learning. Socio-cultural theory purports that humans develop their activity, such as professional learning, through their participation with socially and culturally mediated artefacts (Vygotsky 1981). It allows researchers to investigate various socio-cultural-historical factors that shape teachers' learning. Few studies have applied socio-cultural theories to teacher professional learning, particularly in the context of Vietnam. Thus, this study adds to the

Fig. 12.1 The structure of
a human activity system.
(Engeström 1987, p. 78,
with permission from Yrjö
Engeström)

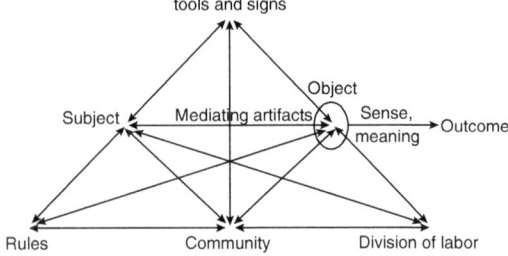

emerging body of ecological research on the higher education academics' learning
process as it seeks to understand the factors affecting their professional learning in
the context of Vietnam.

Central tenets of the theory used in the conceptualisation of this study are those
of activity theory. Activity theory posits individual thinking is shaped and reshaped
by participating in a specific environment which is influenced by present and historical contexts. Engeström, Miettinen and Punamaki (1999) advanced this notion to
include the activity system – an "object-oriented, collective, and culturally mediated
human activity" (p. 9). Professional learning is a "collective" activity because it
involves not just the teachers, but the school and the society in which the teachers'
professional learning occurs, and other members of systems with whom the teachers interact. It can be argued therefore that teacher learning is a complex process and
occurs in the context in which teachers live and work. Thus, any study of teacher
learning should be placed in its socio-cultural context.

Activity theory has been developed through three generations (Engeström 1987).
The first generation of CHAT (Cultural-historical activity theory) originated from
Vygotsky's claim that all human activities, including teacher professional learning,
are mediated by historical and cultural tools. This emphasises that learning is a social
process not an individual process. The second-generation CHAT was extended with
three elements: (1) rules; (2) community; and (3) division of labour (Engeström
1987) (Fig. 12.1). This generation of CHAT emphasises the role of community
within and for which the activity occurs, rules or norms (regulating the subject's
participation in an activity), and division of labour (the allocation of responsibility to
the community members in relation to the object) (Engeström et al. 1999). Roth and
Lee (2007) argue that what we are doing is part of what we normally do as a culture.
This generation of CHAT focuses on the role of the cultural and historical context of
the activity, and the interaction among these elements within a system. For teacher
professional learning to be an activity it must be a collective activity and involve a
wider community, not something that can be done solely individually. Thus the
nature of this activity can only be understood through locating it in a wider context
such as lecturing students, researching, working with others, and so on. In his proposal for a third generation of the theory, Engeström (2001) advocates a conceptual
tool "to understand dialogue, multiple perspectives, and networks of interacting
activity systems" (p. 135). The activity theory uses a joint activity system of at least
two interacting activity systems as the unit of analysis (Fig. 12.2).

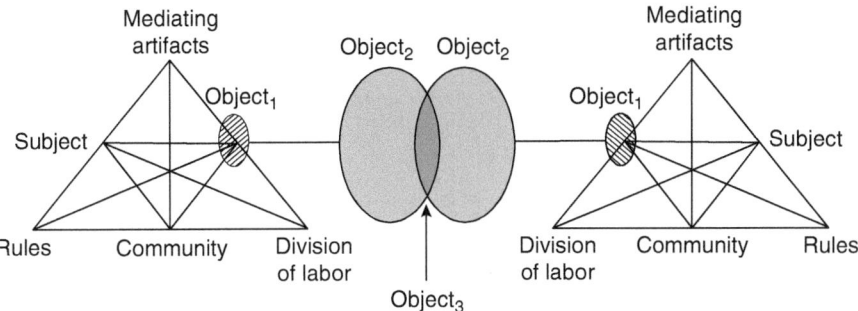

Fig. 12.2 Two interacting activity systems as the minimal model for the third generation of activity theory. (Engeström 2001, p. 136, with permission from Yrjö Engeström)

In this paper, focus is given to the second generation of CHAT, due to its concern with understanding human activity (teacher's professional learning in higher education) within a complex social context (higher education). It "allows for a focus at the level of individual teacher practices but also at the broader organisation level" (Murphy and Rodriguez-Manzanares 2008, p. 444). These tenets of the second generation of activity theory shape the conceptualisation, data collection and analysis in the present study. The use of activity and activity systems theory allows us to explore the complex settings in which teachers learn.

Research Design

This study used a case study research design to explore the professional learning experiences of a group of university academics to establish the conditions by which, and how, they were supported in developing their professional learning. Case study research design was employed to explore these issues in depth, as it complemented the aim of the study, which was to understand the tensions and contradictions facing university academics in the midst of changes in the education system in Vietnam. A group of academics constituted a case in this study. Although the findings are not generalisable, this collective case may contribute to "better understanding, perhaps better theorizing about a still larger collection of cases" (Stake 2005, p. 446).

An email was sent out to invite volunteer participants for the study. The participants are 10 volunteer university academics (6 male and 4 female) teaching different subjects (English, Automotive Engineering, Science, Electrical Engineering, Mechanical Engineering) at a university in the south of Vietnam. Two had PhD qualifications; the rest had Masters Degrees.

Data were collected from the in-depth semi-structured interviews. One-hour in-depth interviews were conducted by one of the researchers. Although a set of questions was prepared, the semi-structured approach allowed the researcher to be flexible and to follow the participants' leads (Merrian 1998). Utilising the semi-structured interview method was congruent with the nature of the research questions and research purposes. It helped to provide in-depth data for understanding the experience of participants.

Data Analysis

In order to further understand the tensions encountered and the factors affecting the academics' professional learning, the researchers began data analysis with the constant comparative method (Strauss and Corbin 2008). This analysis aims to report thematic findings represented in the participants' perceptions of the issues. The purpose of this study was to employ the elements of the activity system to identify barriers/enablers for professional learning activity that support/hinder the academics' professional learning in higher education in Vietnam. Therefore, in the next step of analysis, CHAT was used to explore the academics' professional learning experiences within higher education systems. A CHAT framework provided a useful structure in foregrounding and analysing practices and tensions. More specifically, in this study, Mwanza's (2002) model was used for the purpose of data analysis. Mwanza's (2002) model is practical in operationalising AT for data analysis as it maps out the descriptive tool for understanding what is happening in an activity system through AT-oriented questions. Following Mwanza's (2002) model for translating the activity systems, each question was adapted to match to an element in the activity system to help organise data from the activity framework.

This eight-step model (Mwanza 2002, p. 86) was used to guide the data analysis (Table 12.1).

These questions were used as pointers to interrogate the interview data.

Table 12.1 Eight-step model (Mwanza 2002, p. 86)

Identify the:	Questions to ask
Step 1 Activity	What sorts of professional learning activity are they interested in?
Step 2 Objective	Why is this professional learning activity taking place; what is it for?
Step 3 Subjects	Who is involved in carrying out this activity?
Step 4 Tools	By what means are the academics carrying out their professional learning activity?
Step 5 Rules and regulations	Are there any social/cultural/institutional norms, rules and regulations governing the performance of the activity?
Step 6 Division of labour	Who is responsible for what when carrying out this activity and how are the roles organised?
Step 7 Community	What is the environment in which the professional learning activity of the academics is carried out?
Step 8 Outcomes	What is the desired outcome from this activity

Following Mwanza (2002, p. 86)

Findings

In order to obtain basic understanding about the professional learning practice at a higher education institute in Vietnam, components of activity theory (second generation) were translated using the eight-step model. The information gathered is outlined as following.

The activity	For the purpose of the study, the activity of interest was professional learning
The object or objectives	To improve their teaching/research knowledge and skills
Subjects	The subjects involved in this professional learning activity were identified as single individual academics teaching at a higher education institute. They were passionate to seek ways to develop their professional learning
Tools	Funding, PL activities, English language proficiency, materials, technology
Rules	Workload, university requirements, family responsibility, time, daily teaching responsibility, working culture norms of the university
Divisions of labour	Individual lecturer's orientation University orientation
Community	Inside the university Outside the university
Outcomes	Dissatisfaction

The above information was used to produce the professional learning activity system of the academics as shown in Fig. 12.3.

Findings

The qualitative data from the interviews were analysed in accordance with the activity theory's concept of contradictions so as to explore the professional learning practice of the academics and the mediators which supports and/or hinders the professional learning activity. The information gathered about the professional learning activity of the academics was translated in terms of activity theory to produce the professional learning activity system as shown in Fig. 12.3. Using activity theory to frame the study and analyse the data, certain common themes that contradicted the objective of professional learning were identified and are discussed in the next section.

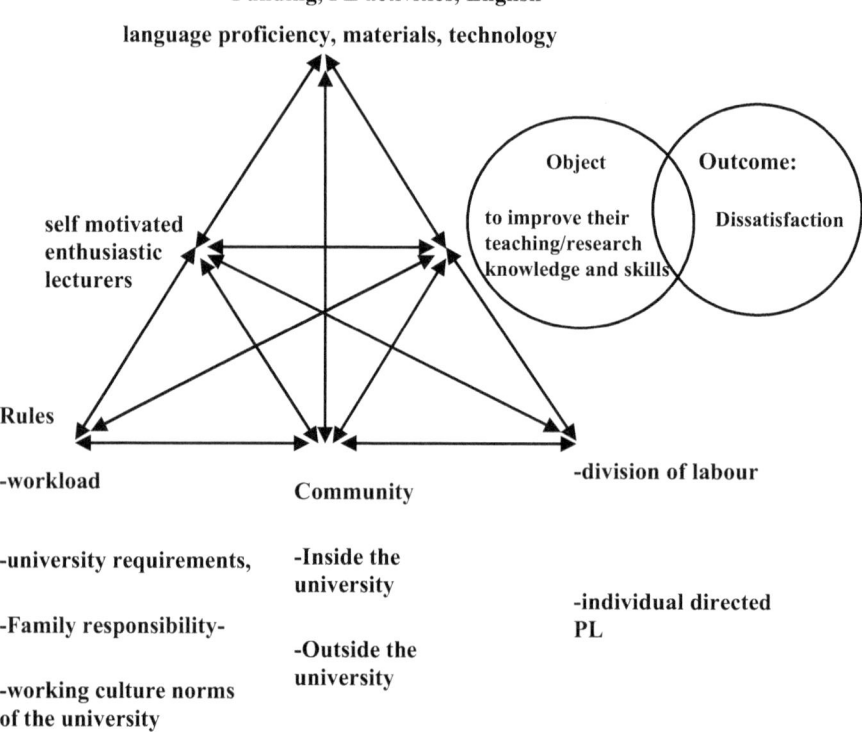

Mediating tools/artifacts

**Funding, PL activities, English
language proficiency, materials, technology**

**self motivated
enthusiastic
lecturers**

Object

**to improve their
teaching/research
knowledge and skills**

Outcome:

Dissatisfaction

Rules

-workload

Community

-university requirements,

-Family responsibility-

**-working culture norms
of the university**

**-Inside the
university**

**-Outside the
university**

-division of labour

**-individual directed
PL**

Fig. 12.3 Academics' professional learning activity system. (After Engeström 2001)

Lack of Resources

Within an activity system, the term, "tools", is referred to as the means which the subject employs to achieve the objective of the activity. Analysis with activity theory revealed that there was a tension between the academics' passion for learning and the limited resources (tools) at the university so as to render their professional learning less effective. A noticeable conflict between the subject and tools was identified in the professional learning activity system of the academics. All of the participants expressed great interest in developing their professional learning and regarded it as "a crucial part of their teaching career" (T4). Some of them elaborated as follows:

> To me, PD is a part of our professional life. We cannot miss it. We actually must do it, intrinsically or extrinsically, we must do it because we need to do better. If we want to do something better we need to learn from others or we need to reflect on what we've done. So professional development is a kind of daily activity, so we need to do it daily. (T1)

> PD, it's a must for everyone who pursues a career, for the sake of ourselves, our organisations, and those we aim to serve. It's also some source of motivation to nurture my love for my career and institutions. PD means better knowledge and teaching quality, more confidence and passion, more effective assessment, skillful research strategies, effective collaboration with colleagues and leaders within and outside the organisations, opportunities and experiences in working with diverse learners… (T6)

It can be seen that the subject was a group of self-motivated and enthusiastic academics. This interesting finding shows how motivated and passionate they were to pursue their goal to develop their professional learning. They were willing to further their study and were keen to participate in professional development opportunities such as workshops, short courses, mentoring, peer observation, etc (Joyce and Calhoun, 2013). Unfortunately, there were limited resources for the academics. These limitations, captured in the tool component of the activity system, included (a) limited funding; (b) limited PL activities; (c) limited language proficiency; (d) limited access to technology; and (e) limited learning materials, each of which is a hindrance to professional learning. One of the barriers frequently mentioned was the limited variety of PD activities. The academics reported that most of their university-initiated PL activities were decontextualised workshops and seminars. Therefore, they questioned the application of the knowledge from these workshops within their teaching practice. The participant academics expressed their need for more PL activities closely linked to their individual needs and contexts such as mentoring/coaching; action research, peer observation, and a community of practice model. Inevitably, they mentioned limited funding as a major barrier to accessing appropriate PL activity as they could not afford to attend conferences without financial support from their university. One lecturer expressed his concern, "cost-effectiveness is really a big problem for us. So just like we pay one hundred U.S. dollars for a conference and we're not sure whether we can learn something new or we can apply it or not so it's somehow a kind of very big prevention, I mean big constraint" (T1).

In addition to limited English proficiency, limited access to technology was another reported barrier to self-improvement. Lack of materials was also a major issue. Some academics complained that:

> Also difficult is access to literature in the field! Some materials we need are restricted by the copyright, or sometimes they cannot be found in Vietnam, so we need to order from other countries and maybe we are restricted by some kind of laws or something, it's hard to find the books. Sometimes the materials that we find are not very updated or something, we need to find something newer. (T3).
>
> This is a very big discussion point in my research because I cannot get access to sources of professional journals and literature. For every university they should have access to professional literature. Since being in this university, I have no access to professional articles. (T8)

In addition to the issue of funding, some of the academics identified the need for more ICT training opportunities, as increasingly the demands of their research and teaching have moved beyond face-to-face delivery modes. Lack of access to advanced technology supporting teaching and research was seen as a major hindrance to expanding their knowledge and improving their teaching.

ICT is very important to help bring the knowledge and also to help edit and compile the knowledge to make it easier for students to understand. And students can do that or study any time they like, and even they do not need to go to class, they still have everything and can pass the exams easily. With ICT we have to change the way we evaluate our students… because up to this time we don't evaluate just our students, we evaluate … their outcomes. (T8)

ICT is necessary in modern learning nowadays. I think it's a very good tool for teachers to enhance and improve their teaching methods, to use some new technology in teaching, for teaching and assessing student learning too. However, in UTE it is still limited because there is only one digital lab! (T9)

This is consistent with the observation made by Harman and Nguyen (2010) that academics in higher education in Vietnam "lack(s) skills and resources in order to take advantage of technological progress in teaching and learning modes" (p. 75). PL activities were also compounded by the academics' standard of English proficiency. Some of the academics believed that this prevented them from reading materials and establishing networks with other foreign colleagues in the region. Much more needs to be considered to improve English language proficiency of the academics as it is a valuable mediating tool for them to maximise their learning opportunities (Harman and Nguyen 2010; Songkaeo and Yeong 2016).

Organisation of Professional Learning Activities

Roles and responsibilities concerning PL was another issue which emerged from the data. There were two major types of PL activity identified by the academics, that is, self-generated PL activity such as furthering their degrees (Master and Doctor Degree) and reading related materials, and university organised PL activity such as workshops and seminars. These activities could take place either inside or outside the university and be run by other institutes and MOET (Ministry of Education and Training), and/or other foreign entities. While the academics had a high opinion of the PL activity they undertook independently, they expressed disappointment about the PL activities organised by their university as most of these were decontextualised and had little impact on their teaching. They agreed that a one-off workshop was not sufficient to improve their teaching practice. The following quotes support this argument.

Well, I must say PD activities are personal interests first because when I go there, I want to explore something new, and we want to explore the world of our field. The world is not about knowledge but the people inside that. So if I participate in the events which I don't really like it, actually I have no feelings in getting in contact with the others. So personal interests first. (T7)

Well, I sometimes took part in certain PD activities that I don't like, and I was forced to join by the university for sake of the university. But for those which I like, and I think they are useful, I attend because of my own knowledge, and for the future of my students. I am willing to attend. (T8)

All of the participants shared that they always had to seek information themselves to improve their teaching and research knowledge and skills by reading materials and searching information from the internet. They reported having to exercise their personal agency to source appropriate and relevant materials in order to develop their professional skills.

It can be seen that both the individual academics and their university were responsible for PL activities. However, it was reported that there was a divide between the individual academics' interest and the university's interest. From the individual academics' points of view, PL activities should be promoted and effectively supported by the University and the University did not pay much attention to scaffolding the PL activities to suit the individual academics' needs. Furthermore, insufficient support from the University for outside PL activities was possibly the biggest hurdle. One of the lectures was disappointed to say:

> So when I attended the conferences, I recognised one thing, that's how disadvantaged I was. I mean that I went along without much support from the leader from the authority. The other colleagues from international countries, I mean from other countries, they're all…given opportunities. Actually, they're given a lot of opportunities to go abroad, to learn from international colleagues, and even they're encouraged and they're given very favourable conditions to do so. (T1)
>
> Yes, lack of self-motivation, it does occur. However, when we participate in a kind of professional development events because the kind of professional development so if we like, we come to participate and it's not just about these events only… professional development is daily. So it doesn't mean that we will not go there, we will not develop ourselves. We can stay at home and learn the things we like. So the problem here is whether these kinds of professional development activities are closely related to our interest or not. (T3)

This interrogation into the division of labour (who is responsible for what roles) reveals the systematic tensions between the objectives and the division of labour. Given that the goal of PL is to improve the teaching/research practice, these divides in terms of roles were seen as a hindrance to the PL activity. The investigation showed that the academics and the university had different views on how to organise effective PL activity, highlighting the need for negotiation between the individual academics and the university.

Cumbersome Responsibility and Commitment

When analysing the PL practice of the academics it was necessary to consider how it was mediated by certain rules within the higher education context. The academics were less motivated to participate in PL activity, some because of workload and family responsibility (Bozzon et al. 2017) and others because of university requirements, time commitment, daily teaching responsibility, and working culture norms.

Lack of time was one of the most prominent factors reported to have a tremendous impact on the PD activities of the academics. They reported that the university did not provide them with release time to attend PL activities and that there were a lot of requirements from the university such as teaching and research output. This is one of the typical comments made by the participant academics

> Barriers? Yes, the first problem is time. I think, sometimes I want to attend a certain event but I cannot manage the time to do because of my workload. Actually for example, some courses are not affordable! And also lack of institutional support, I mean here, when I take part in some courses they don't offer many day off so it's very difficult. One more thing is family responsibility.
>
> I'll have to say that quite many academics are asking for support if they want to join in national or international conferences, mainly for the traveling fees, for their accommodation or other expenses. The problem is our university cannot support all. Besides, heavy workload is a real challenge. Like other colleagues, make-up lessons are terrible. (T10)
>
> Make-up classes. It's a burden for us after we come back from the conferences. We have to teach double or even more. (T1)

In addition, whilst being a dominant component of the teaching staff in the faculty, apart from teaching, the female academics have to do mundane work at home to take care of their families. Therefore, despite their willingness to actively participate in certain PD activities and events, they have to forsake some training courses and opportunities for career advancement, as one of them stated

> Yes, there are a lot of barriers. …family is also a big concern. It is really a conflict between family's need and career need. (T8)

Compounding the family and work responsibilities and commitments was the prevailing work culture at the university – reported to be less than collaborative. Some of the academics admitted that individual PL activities took place in isolation, as they did not normally share findings with other colleagues. On the one hand, they believed that an individual activity was very helpful for their own professional development. On the other hand, they perceived that the work culture at their university did not encourage collaboration in PL activities. Mentoring, peer observation, team/co-teaching were missing from the PL activities at the university. Most academics observed that they did not often work together to improve their professional learning. They tended to choose their own ways to enhance their professional learning, which limited opportunities for informal PL activities such as information sharing and co-learning. This partly can be explained by the lack of in-house professional learning activities which centre on the idea of community of practice.

In conclusion, the conditions of this activity brought about three tensions: (a) sustaining the academics' enthusiasm to develop their professional learning with a lack of resources; (b) attaining professional goals while experiencing less effective and limited PL activities; and (c) attaining professional goals while dealing with work-life balance and work culture. These tensions created a challenge to academics' undertaking PL activity (Lester 2015). The outcome of this was a feeling of dissatisfaction from the lack of effective PL activities to assist in advancing their careers.

Discussion and Suggestions

The aim of this chapter is to identify the tensions and contradictions in the professional learning activities of the participant academics in a higher education institute in Vietnam. The questions generated from activity theory were employed to identify major areas of contradictions within the PL activity system, that is, lack of resources, organisation of professional learning activities, and cumbersome responsibility and commitment. These three areas of contradiction show how the PL activities of the participant academics were hindered. These areas of contradiction raise critically important issues to be considered when designing PL activity to support academics' professional learning.

Limited resources are a great challenge for academic staff in developing their careers. That the academics lacked sufficient resources such as research funding, PL activities, English language proficiency, materials, and technology, raises the issue of how to assist them to overcome these hurdles for better engagement in PD programs which, in order to be effective, need to be "long-termed, comprehensive, goal-oriented, collaborative with adequate administrative support, and operational budget" (Richardson 2003, cited in Choi and Morrison 2014, p. 421). It is concerning that given that HERA 2005 has invested in the higher education system for the past years, the issue of resources has not been resolved (Hayden and Lam 2010; Pham 2010, 2015; Tran 2014). Pham's (2015) study also states that income and resources for research is a major reason academics want to leave the profession. This reinforces the need to increase financial, human, and technical resources for academics' PL in universities, such as providing financial support, enhancing ICT capacity and infrastructure, developing the academics' English proficiency and access to materials (ADB 2011; Songkaeo and Yeong 2016). The researchers agree with Pham (2010) who argues that "this can be done with investment from the government's budget, assistance by international loan projects or through cooperation with other partners on the market basis for shared utilisation" (Pham 2010, p. 63).

In addition to the perceived lack of resources, another finding was the academics' difficulty in pursuing PL activities due to the cumbersome responsibilities and commitments they experienced from different areas of their lives, and especially, the heavy teaching workload at the university. This resulted in little time for their professional development. This finding is highly relevant to the present context as a number of studies (Harman and Nguyen 2010; Pham 2012; Hayden and Lam 2010) found that the work/life burden is one of the most serious challenges for teachers in Vietnam. This is also seen as one of the critical factors in diminishing the academics' passion and enthusiasm for professional development. This finding not only demonstrates the tensions between the individual's desire for PL and the situational rules of the system, but also adds another indication of the academics' dissatisfaction with the higher education system. De-motivation to pursue PL activities may lead to the deterioration of the professional development pathway. Since a great majority of the academics in this university are young, they need more time for their teaching and learning, doing research, and community activity, which in turn will contribute to the development of both the university and them. This issue can only be solved by the individual endeavour of the academics who can see the value of their time investment into their career, along with systematic support from both the university and government in terms of release time for PL activities, and an appropriate compensation mechanism.

Regarding this objective, the data show that most PL activities are largely individually based and most PL activities which were conducted by the University and MOET were decontextualised and had very little value in developing professional learning. Individual PL activities such as reading and/or attending advanced degree programs to keep up with new information were considered as major PL activities which took place at the university. This finding is consistent with those in Vietnam and other countries in Asia (Phuong et al. 2015; Phuong and McLean 2016), which highlight the fact that higher education PL activity is mainly self-directed and lacks organisational support. This finding echoes the need for more support in order to achieve one of the objectives of HERA 2005, which is to create opportunities for professional development for higher education academics (Tran et al. 2014; Welch 2010). While academic staff members are strongly encouraged to further education for PhD degree to advance their teaching and research (Project 322, 2000; Project 911, 2010), professional learning seems to be ignored and receives little attention by MOET, the institutions, and even the academics themselves due to a variety of reasons. Sabbatical leave in foreign universities, a method to revitalize thinking (Pietsch 2011), enhances knowledge, updating teaching and research capacity (Iravania 2011), and establishing scholarly networks among universities in the world (Else 2015). Nevertheless, it is 'not available for academic staff members in Vietnam' (Le 2016, p. 31).

In addition, individual learning is critically important as it is linked to the individual need of each academic. However, in this study, this type of learning was reported to occur in isolation because the academics do not habitually work together and no collaborative culture can be created which results in them wanting to work by themselves. Such a work culture seems to discourage academics from supporting each other. Thus, they concentrated on improving their own learning through their self-generated PL activities such as self-study. One of the possible explanations can be the influence of traditional Confucian Heritage Culture (CHC) in education which places the teachers as the respectful authority of the knowledge with highly ranked social status. In a recent study which explores Vietnamese college lecturers' perceptions of face, Nguyen (2015) confirms that face-saving was firmly established in the participant Vietnamese lecturers' minds. They believed that "their profession holds an honorable and very important role and position in society" (Nguyen 2015, p. 211). Working in isolation is preferred as it may not expose them to the risk of losing face and public image. This contradicts the perceived core features of effective professional development, that is, collaboration and collegiality (Hipp et al. 2008; Servage 2008). Effective professional learning is nurtured in the collaborative working culture where the participants need to learn from and support each other. It is interesting to observe that in a number of our recent studies in Vietnam (Nguyen

2015), most of our research participants who participated in our collaborative mentoring projects seemed to be resistant to work with one another initially; however, later in the program, they became naturally committed to working with other teachers and valued peer collaboration and support (Vygotsky 1978). This supports the importance of the structured PL learning activities which are embedded in their workplace. It also echoes the need to move the PL activities beyond the individual level by implementing more activities which are embedded in a collaborative level of learning. The researchers challenge findings from Meng & Tajaroensuk's research (2013) that PD is just an individual lecturer's job and cannot expand to others through collaborative learning. If academics at tertiary institutions are provided with opportunities for professional development activities with collegiality and collaboration, they are more likely to feel ownership of the learning process (Diaz-Maggioli 2003). As such, their learning will certainly help develop their professionalism. Experience gained from participating in collaborative professional development activities will help create a bond and mutual learning among academics, which in turn facilitates their exchanging and sharing of knowledge, understanding to support each other in work, and research for professional advancement (Timperley 2008). Also, through collaborative learning, teachers at tertiary institutions are able to "interpret certain education issues of interest and concern upon their actual understanding and lenses" (Viskovic 2006, p. 336). Besides, academics should be made aware of the importance and benefit in exchanging and sharing knowledge and understanding as well as collaboration in the workplace in order to achieve better results in teaching (Kelly 2006). DuFour (2004) opined that teachers' knowledge and understanding may not be sufficient for them to deliver a good lesson to enhance students' understanding, and it is important that they need to learn from each other. This is a daunting task for leaders in the higher education system, to create this kind of learning culture in the workplace. Therefore, effective professional development demands sufficient institutional support and external support alike (Cole 2012) alongside the provision of varied and effective professional development model(s) and opportunities for teachers to select, design, implement, and evaluate the activities they participate in (Pleschova et al. 2012). Kennedy (2014) suggests a number of different PD models in practice. Such models may manifest themselves in a flexible combination of top-down strategies like training courses, and workshops (transmission) to coaching and mentoring (transitional) and CoP and action research (transformation) (Kennedy 2014) as teachers need time to adapt themselves to self-initiated and self-supported professional development.

Another hurdle the academics experienced was attending PL activities which were decontextualised and did not fit their needs. This study aligns with other studies (Villegas-Reimers 2003; Schwille et al. 2007) by providing evidence that PD events targeting teachers in higher education are still delivered in the form of face-to-face seminars, conferences, or short training courses. These types of PL activities are exposed to criticism because of their inherently brief, fragmented and decontextualised nature (Diaz-Maggioli 2003), and failure to assist teachers in transforming theory into classroom practice (Cole 2012). Vietnam has adopted a top-down approach in which professional development has always been designed and implemented with little consideration of teachers' needs, interests, and contextual factors. This approach with activities such as conferences, seminars, and system-based courses has proved to be of little effect (Ling and Mackenzie 2001; Diaz-Maggioli 2003), and therefore, should be replaced with more interactive and collaborative models, such as team teaching, mentoring, community of practice, and collaborative action research (Burbank and Kauchak 2003; Chaudary and Imran 2012; Cirocki et al. 2014; Nguyen 2017; Nguyen and Baldauf 2015; Vo and Nguyen 2010). Evidence from a number of studies (Vo and Nguyen 2010; Nguyen and Baldauf 2015; Nguyen 2017) in Vietnam shows that the PL activities of the academics in higher education in Vietnam could go beyond the one-off PL activity to a more collaborative and transformative PL activity such as mentoring (Nguyen and Baldauf 2015; Nguyen 2017), and critical friends' groups (Vo and Nguyen 2010). Vo and Nguyen (2010) via their study, conclude that a Critical Friends Group (CFG) seems useful for academics of English in Vietnam to share and exchange ideas about their profession, mutual learning and assisting each other in professional development in a comfortable manner. In addition to face-to-face collaborative professional learning activities, online PL activities can be implemented to support and sustain interaction and ongoing contact among the participant academics. These types of PL activities can be more accessible and flexible (Sorensen and Takle 2004). Employing a blended learning approach to develop professional learning activities for academics can maximise their opportunities to develop their professionalism effectively and efficiently.

Being active in a variety of PL activities which sustain collaboration and learning could help them to find the effective strategies for their own academic development (Austin and Sorcinelli 2013). The study raises the issue of academics' voices and agency in developing their own PL activity. It is very difficult for them to be committed to PL activity if they are not heard and their roles are passive in this process. As Kennedy (2016) advocates the shift in professional development on more "nuanced understanding of what teachers do, what motivate them, and how they learn and grow" (p. 974). As discussed in the findings, some of the academics even said that it was a waste of time to participate in activities which did not assist in developing their professionalism. This stresses the need for a shared vision and plan in developing higher education academics' professionalism in order to maximise the individual's agency in initiating their own PL activity (Lester 2015) while utilising support from the university and/or higher levels such as MOET. The university is urged to empower academics to become change agents in their own professional learning by negotiating a PL plan which will accommodate their needs and by choosing an appropriate PL process which will fit the context in which they are working.

This study suggests an urgent need to negotiate the shared responsibility between the university and individual academics in order to accommodate both the needs of individual academics and the requirements of the university. Thus, support from the university is extremely necessary. In other words, this study supports the claims by Kennedy (2005) that a PL model should maximise both "an individual endeavour related to accountability" and "a collaborative endeavour that supports transformative practice" (p. 235). A point of interest is that the interviewees had indicated certain models of professional development suitable to specific stages of their career. Such a preference for varied professional development models, to a certain extent, emphasises the need to increase the capacity for professional autonomy. Wells (2014) argues that one of the key elements in effective PL for teachers is that they are empowered to take an active role in the change process.

Conclusion

This study highlights the need to be sensitive to the issue of context and academics' professional agency and needs when designing appropriate PL programs for academics. The participants in this research expressed diverse views on professional development and no one model fits all. Therefore, any proposed model of PD should take into account individual academics' needs, current teaching and learning workload, research, and, of course, internal and external support. Additionally, although not mentioned by the research informants in this study, it appears that the low staff-high student ratios have burdened individual Vietnamese academics. This issue has posed similar problems to academics as mentioned in the vast majority of the PL research literature.

More specifically, when analysing the academics' PL activity in terms of activity theory, certain common themes emerge that highlight the tensions and contradictions in the academics' professional learning system. These themes raise critical issues to consider when designing and implementing PL activity for HE academics in the context of Vietnam amid educational reform. The key issue in this chapter is that HE academics' PL activity requires tremendous efforts from both individual academics and the university to solve these systematic tensions. From AT analysis, the PL activity needs to address:

- The need to have sufficient resources
- The need to be sensitive to the issue of context which is compounded by certain rules in the system, negatively affecting PL activity
- The need to empower the academics by providing more opportunity to negotiate and have shared visions and a plan for their own PL

To comply with the standardisation of teaching and learning at higher institutions in Vietnam currently and also with the pressure of regional and international integration (Harman and Nguyen 2010), academics at universities should be made aware of professional learning as a response to professionalism (Evans 2002; Hargreaves and Fullan 2000), and as a demand of individual career advancement. Professional development also plays a central role in enhancing quality teaching and learning (Hargreaves and Fullan 2000). In order for academics to achieve expected outcomes in professional development according to their agenda, it is imperative that tertiary institutions provide them with necessary supporting conditions to actively engage in varied PD activities in order to acquire and develop professional competencies throughout their careers. A flexible combination of top-down and bottom-up PD is imperative to establish a sustainable environment for PD (Hayes 2014), and to remove potential barriers to teachers' engagement in PD activities. The effective professional learning of academics requires support at national, university-based and individual levels of provision, places on the learning of teachers in their context, and meets their evolving needs.

As mentioned above, this chapter describes a small-scale research study which focuses on the tensions and contradictions of the academics in the Vietnamese higher education. Due to its small-scale research, the results cannot be applied to other tertiary institutions and therefore it cannot be generalised in other situations. It would better to conduct a larger scale investigation with a larger number of participants from different universities, only then will the results provide the readers a more comprehensive view on the beliefs and attitudes towards professional development, teachers' professional needs, their preferences, and potential barriers, upon which suggestions of a feasible model of professional development can be made with a view to enhancing teachers' quality teaching and professional skills. Therefore, the results may possess certain limitations regarding generalization of results as potentially in qualitative research (Tsang 2014; Yin 2014).

Acknowledgements This research was supported under Australian Government's Endeavour Executive Fellowship Awards. We would like to express our appreciation to Associate Professor Susan Goodwin (The University of Sydney) and Dr. Tony Loughland (The University of New South Wales) for their excellent support.

References

Asian Development Bank (ADB). (2011). *Higher education across Asia: An overview of issues and strategies*. Mandaluyong City: Asian Development Bank.

Austin, A. E., & Sorcinelli, M. D. (2013). The future of faculty development: Where are we going? *New Directions for Teaching and Learning, 2013*(133), 85–97. https://doi.org/10.1002/tl.20048.

Beaty, L. (1998). The professional development of teachers in higher education: Structures, methods and responsibilities. *Innovations in Education and Training International, 35*(2), 99–107.

Behari-Leak, K. (2017). New academics, new higher education contexts: A critical perspective on professional development. *Teaching in Higher Education, 22*(5), 485–500. https://doi.org/10.1080/13562517.2016.1273215.

Bozzon, R., Murgia, A., Poggio, B., & Rapetti, E. (2017). Work–life interferences in the early stages of academic careers: The case of precarious researchers in Italy. *European Educational Research Journal, 16*(2–3), 332–351.

Burbank, M. D., & Kauchak, D. (2003). An alternative model for professional development: Investigations into effective collaboration. *Teaching and Teacher Education, 19*(5), 499–514.

Cameron, S., Mulholland, J., & Branson, C. (2013). Professional learning in the lives of teachers: Towards a new framework for conceptualising teacher learning. *Asia-Pacific Journal of Teacher Education, 41*(4), 377–397. https://doi.org/10.1080/1359866X.2013.838620.

Chaudary, I. A., & Imran, S. (2012). Listening to unheard voices: Professional development reforms for Pakistani tertiary teachers. *Australian Journal of Teacher Education, 37*(2), 88–98.

Choi, D. S.-Y., & Morrison, P. (2014). Learning to get it right: Understanding change processes in professional development for teachers of English learners. *Professional Development in Education, 40*(3), 416–435. https://doi.org/10.1080/19415257.2013.806948.

Cirocki, A., Tennekoon, S., & Calvo, A. (2014). Research and reflective practice in the ESL classroom: Voices from Sri Lanka. *Australian Journal of Teacher Education, 39*(4), 24–39.

Clarke, D., & Hollingsworth, H. (2002). Elaborating a model of teacher professional growth. *Teaching and Teacher Education, 18*(8), 947–967.

Cole, P. (2012). Linking effective professional learning with effective teaching practice. *Australian Institute for Teaching and School Leadership*, 1–26. Retrieved May 4, 2015. http://www.aitsl.edu.au/docs/default-source/default-document-library/linking_effective_professional_learning_with_effective_teaching_practice_-_cole

Collinson, V., Kozina, E., Kate Lin, Y. H., Ling, L., Matheson, I., Newcombe, L., & Zogla, I. (2009). Professional development for teachers: A world of change. *European Journal of Teacher Education, 32*(1), 3–19. https://doi.org/10.1080/02619760802553022.

Darling-Hammond, L. (2006). Constructing 21st-century teacher education. *Journal of Teacher Education, 57*(3), 300–314. https://doi.org/10.1177/0022487105285962.

Day, C. (2006). Change agendas: The role of teacher educators. *Teaching Education, 15*(2), 145–158.

Diaz-Maggioli, G. (2003). *Professional development for language teachers*. EDO-FL-03-03. ERIC Digest. Retrieved on April 7, 2015, from http://unitas.org/FULL/0303diaz.pdf

DuFour, R. (2004). What is a 'professional learning community'? *Schools as Learning Communities, 61*(8), 6–11.

Else, H. (2015). *Sabbaticals: No longer so open-ended or available?* Retrieved on March 25, 2018, from https://www.timeshighereducation.com/features/sabbaticals-no-longer-so-open-ended-or-available/2019616.article

Engeström, Y. (1987). *Learning by expanding: An activity-theoretical approach to developmental research*. Helsinki: Orienta-Konsultit.

Engeström, Y. (2001). Expansive learning at work: Toward an activity theoretical reconceptualisation. *Journal of Education and Work, 14*(1), 133–156. https://doi.org/10.1080/13639080020028747.

Engeström, Y., Miettinen, R., & Punamaki, R. L. (1999). *Perspectives on activity theory*. New York: Cambridge University Press.

Evans, L. (2002). What is Teacher development? *Oxford Review of Education, 28*(1), 123–137.

Guskey, T. R. (2002). Does it make a difference. *Educational Leadership, 59*(6), 45–51.

Guskey, T. R. (2003). Analyzing lists of the characteristics of effective professional development to promote visionary leadership. *NASSP Bulletin, 87*(637), 4–20. https://doi.org/10.1177/019263650308763702.

Hargreaves, A., & Fullan, M. (2000). Mentoring in the new millennium. *Theory Into Practice, 39*(1), 50–56.

Harman, K., & Nguyen, T. N. B. (2010). Reforming teaching and learning in Vietnam's higher education system. In G. Harman, M. Hayde, & P. T. Nghi (Eds.), *Reforming higher education in Vietnam: Challenges and priorities* (pp. 65–86). Dordrecht: Springer.

Harman, G., Hayden, M., & Nghi, P. T. (2010). Higher education in Vietnam: Reform, challenges and priorities. In G. Harman, M. Hayden, & P. T. Nghi (Eds.), *Higher education in Vietnam: Reform, challenges and priorities*. Dordrecht: Springer.

Harwell, S. (2003). *Teacher professional development: It's not an event, It's a process*. Florida: CORD.

Hattie, J. (2003). Teachers make a difference what is the research evidence? In *Professional learning and leadership development*. New Sydney: NSW DET.

Hayden & Lam (2010). Vietnam's higher education system. In G. Harman, M. Hayden, & P. T. Nghi (Eds.), *Reforming higher education in Vietnam: Challenges and priorities* (pp. 15–30). Dordrecht: Springer.

Hayes, J. (2014). *The theory and practice of change management*. London: Palgrave Macmillan.

HERA. (2005). *Vietnamese Government Resolution on substantial and comprehensive renewal of Vietnam's Tertiary Education in the 2006-2020 period. No 14/2005/NQ-CP.*

Hipp, K. K., Huffman, J. B., Pankake, A. M., & Olivier, D. F. (2008). Sustaining professional learning communities: Case studies. *Journal of Educational Change, 9*(2), 173–195. https://doi.org/10.1007/s10833-007-9060-8.

Hustler, D., McNamara, O., Jarvis, J., Londra., & Campbell, A. (2003). *Teachers' Perceptions of Continuing Professional Development: Research Report RR429.* Institute of Education. Manchester Metropolitan University, UK.

Iravania, H. (2011). Analyzing impacts of sabbatical leaves of absence regarding faculty members, University of Tehran. *Procedia – Social and Behavioral Sciences, 15*, 3608–3615. https://doi.org/10.1016/j.sbspro.2011.04.343.

Joyce, B., & Calhoun, E. (2013). *Models of professional development: A celebration of educators.* Thousand Oaks: Corwin.

Kelly, P. (2006). What is teacher learning? A socio-cultural perspective. *Oxford Review of Education, 32*(4), 505–519.

Kennedy, A. (2005). Models of continuing professional development: A framework for analysis. *Journal of In-Service Education, 31*(2), 235–250.

Kennedy, A. (2014). Models of continuing professional development: A framework for analysis. *Professional Development in Education, 40*(3), 336–351. https://doi.org/10.1080/19415257.2014.929293.

Kennedy, M. M. (2016). How does professional development improve teaching? *Review of Educational Research, 86*(4), 945–980. https://doi.org/10.3102/0034654315626800.

King, H. (2004). Continuing professional development in higher education: What do academics do? *Planet, 13*(1), 26–29. https://doi.org/10.11120/plan.2004.00130026.

Knapp, M. S. (2003). Chapter 4: Professional development as a policy pathway. *Review of Research in Education, 27*(1), 109–157. https://doi.org/10.3102/0091732X027001109.

Le, H. (2013). Vietnamese higher education in the globalisation context: A question of qualitative or quantitative targets. *The International Education Journal, 13*(1), 17–29.

Le T. K. A. (2016). *Developing the Academy in Vietnam: An investgation of the formation of academic identity by university lecturers in Vietnam* (PhD thesis). Southern Cross University, Lismore, Australia

Lester, J. (2015). Cultures of work–life balance in higher education: A case of fragmentation. *Journal of Diversity in Higher Education, 8*(3), 139–156.

Ling, L. M., & MacKenzie, N. (2001). The professional development of teachers in Australia. *European Journal of Teacher Education, 24*(2), 87–98.

Meng, J., & Tajaroensuk, S. (2013). An investigation of tertiary EFL teachers' problems in their in-service professional development. *Journal of Language Teaching and Research, 4*(6), 1356–1364.

Merrian, S. B. (1998). *Qualitative research and case study application in education.* San Francisco: Jossey-Bass Publishers.

Murphy, E., & Rodriguez-Manzanares, M. A. (2008). Using activity theory and its principle of contradictions to guide research in educational technology. *Australasian Journal of Educational Technology, 24*, 442–447.

Mwanza, D. (2002). Conceptualising work activity for CAL systems design. *Journal of Computer Assisted Learning, 18*(1), 84–92.

Newble, D., & Cannon, R. (2013). *Handbook for teachers in universities and colleges.* London: Routledge.

Nguyen, T. Q. T. (2015). The influence of traditional beliefs on Vietnamese college lecturers' perceptions of face. *Journal of Education for Teaching, 41*(2), 203–214. https://doi.org/10.1080/02607476.2015.1031542.

Nguyen, H. T. M., & Baldauf, R. B., Jr. (2015). Beginning teachers: Supporting each other and learning together. *Teacher Education and Practice, 28*(1), 75–89.

Nguyen, H. T. M. (2017). *Model of mentoring in language teacher education*. Switzerland: Springer.

Nguyen, N.T & Tran, L.T (2018). Global forces and local demands in the Vietnamese higher education In N. T. Nguyen & L. T. Tran (Eds.), *Reforming Vietnamese Higher Education: Global Forces and Local Demands*. Dordrecht: Springer.

Opfer, V. D., & Pedder, D. (2011). Conceptualising teacher professional learning. *Review of Educational Research, 81*(3), 376–407.

Pham, H. H. (2001). Teacher development: A real need for English departments in Vietnam. *English Teaching Forum*, *39*(4). Retrieved from http://exchanges.state.gov/englishteaching/forum/archives/2001/01-39-4.html

Pham, T. N. (2010). The higher education reform agenda: A vision for 2020. In G. Harman, M. Hayden, & P. T. Nghi (Eds.), *Reforming higher education in Vietnam: Challenges and priorities* (pp. 51–86). Dordrecht: Springer.

Pham, T. L. P. (2012). The renovation of higher education governance in Vietnam and its impact on the teaching quality at universities. *Tertiary Education and Management, 18*(4), 289–308. https://doi.org/10.1080/13583883.2012.675350.

Pham, T. N. (2013). *The academic profession in Vietnam*. Paper presented at the RIHE International semina report.

Pham, T. N. (2015). Academic career development in Vietnam. In *Paper presented at the international conference on the changing academic profession project 2013*. Hiroshima: University.

Philpott, C. (2014). *Theories of professional learning: A critical guide for teacher educators*. Northwich: Critical Publishing.

Phuong, T. T., & McLean, G. N. (2016). The experiences of Vietnamese university faculty in relation to their faculty development. *Asia Pacific Education Review, 2016*(17), 599–608. https://doi.org/10.1007/s12564-016-9454-5.

Phuong, T. T., Duong, H. B., & McLean, G. N. (2015). Faculty development in southeast Asian higher education: A review of literature. *Asia Pacific Education Review, 16*(1), 107–117. https://doi.org/10.1007/s12564-015-9353-1.

Pietsch, T. (2011). What's happened to sabbatical leave for academics? *The Guardian*. Retrieved March 31, 2018, from http://www.theguardian.com/higher-education-network/blog/2011/oct/05/sabbatical-leave-for-academics

Piggot-Irvine, E. (2006). Establishing criteria for effective professional development and use in evaluating an action research based programme. *Journal of In-service Education, 32*(4), 477–496.

Pleschova, G., Simon, E., Quinlan, K. M., Murphy, J., Roxa, T., & Szabó, M. (2012). *The Professionalisation of Academics as Teachers in Higher Education*. European Science Foundation,1-32, retrieved from http://www.esf.org/fileadmin/Public_documents/Publications/professionalisation_academics.pdf.

Prime Minister of Socialist Republic of Vietnam. (2000) Project 322/2000 / QD-TTG dated April 19, 2000. Approval of the Scheme on "Training of cadres and scientists at foreign establishments by state budget".

Prime Minister of Socialist Republic of Vietnam. (2010). Project 911 / QĐ-TTg dated June 17, 2010. Approval of the scheme on "Training for Lecturers with Doctoral degree for for Universities and Colleges in the Period 2010–2020".

Resolution No 14/2005/NQ-CP, 2 November 2005, on "the Substantial and Comprehensive Renewal of Vietnam's Tertiary Education in the 2006-2010 Period" (usually referred to as the Higher Education Reform Agenda, (HERA)).

Richards, J., & Farrell, T. (2005). *Professional development for language teachers: Strategies for teacher learning*. Cambridge: Cambridge University Press.

Roth, W.-M., & Lee, Y.-J. (2007). "Vygotsky's neglected legacy": Cultural-historical activity theory. *Review of Educational Research, 77*(2), 186–232.

Schwille, J., Dembélé, M., & Schubert, J. (2007). *Global perspectives on teacher learning: Improving policy and practice*. Paris: International Institute for Educational Planning (IIEP) UNESCO.

Servage, L. (2008). Critical and transformative practices in professional learning communities. *Teacher Education Quarterly, 35*(1), 63–77.

Songkaeo, T. Y., & Yeong L. H. (2016). *Defining higher education issues and challenges in Southeast Asia/ASEAN within the international context- THP literature review*. Retrieved from http://www.headfoundation.org/papers/2016_-_2)_Defining_Higher_Education_Issues_and_Challenges_in_Southeast_AsiaASEAN_within_the_International_Context.pdf

Sorensen, E. K., & Takle, E. S. (2004). A cross-cultural cadence: Knowledge building with networked communities across disciplines and cultures. In A. Brown & N. Davis (Eds.), *Digital technology: Communities and education* (pp. 251–263). London: Routledge Falmer.

Stake, R. E. (2005). Qualitative case study. In N. K. Denzin & Y. S. Lincoln (Eds.), *The Sage handbook of qualitative research* (3rd ed., pp. 433–466). Thousand Oaks: Sage Publications.

Strauss, A., & Corbin, J. (2008). *Basics of qualitative research: Techniques and procedures for developing grounded theory* (2nd ed.). Thousand Oaks: SAGE.

Timperly, H. (2008). *Teacher professional learning and development* (Educational practices series – 18). Belley: Imprimerie Nouvelle Gonnet.

Tran, T. T. (2014). Governance in higher education in Vietnam – a move towards decentralization and its practical problems. *Journal of Asian Public Policy, 7*(1), 71–82. https://doi.org/10.108 0/17516234.2013.873341.

Tran, L., Marginson, S., Do, H., Do, Q., Le, T., Nguyen, N., et al. (2014). *Higher education in Vietnam: Flexibility, mobility and practicality in the global knowledge economy*. New York: Palgrave Macmillan.

Tsang, E. W. K. (2014). Generalizing from research findings: The merits of case studies. *International Journal of Management Reviews, 16*(4), 369–383.

Uysal, H. H. (2012). Evaluation of an in-service training program for primary-school language teachers in Turkey. *Australian Journal of Teacher Education, 37*(7), 14–28.

Vallely, T. J., & Wilkinson, B. . (2008). *Vietnam higher education: Crisis and response*. ASH institute for democratic governance and innovation, Harvard Kenedy School. Retrieved from http://www.hks.harvard.edu/innovations/asia/Documents/Higher Education Overview112008.pdf

Villegas-Reimers, E. (2003). *Teacher professional development: An international review of the literature*. Paris: International Institute for Educational Planning.

Viskovic, A. (2006). Becoming a tertiary teacher: Learning incommunities of practice. *Higher Education Research & Development, 25*(4), 323–339.

Vo, L. T., & Nguyen, H. T. M. (2010). Critical friends group for EFL teacher professional development. *ELT Journal, 64*(2), 205–213. https://doi.org/10.1093/elt/ccp025.

Vygotsky, L. S. (1978). *Mind in society: The development of higher psychological processes*. Cambridge, MA: Harvard University Press.

Vygotsky, L. S. (1981). The genesis of higher mental functions. In J. V. Wertsch (Ed.), *The concept of activity in soviet psychology* (pp. 144–188). Armonk: Sharpe.

Welch, A. R. (2010). Internatonalisaton of Vietnamese higher education: Retrospect and prospect. In G. Harman, M. Hayden, & P. T. Nghi (Eds.), *Reforming higher education in Vietnam: Challenges and Priorities* (pp. 197–213). Dordrecht: Springer.

Wells, M. (2014). Elements of effective and sustainable professional learning. *Professional Development in Education, 40*(3), 488–504. https://doi.org/10.1080/19415257.2013.838691.

Yin. (2014). *Case study research: Design and methods*. Thousand Oaks: Sage.

Zheng, H. (2011). Dilemmas in teacher development in the Chinese EFL context. *Journal of Cambridge Studies, 7*(2), 2–15.

Chapter 13
Revisiting "Teacher as Moral Guide" in English Language Teacher Education in Contemporary Vietnam

Linh Thuy Le and Leigh Gerrard Dwyer

Abstract Based on larger scale qualitative research on the role of Vietnamese Teachers as Moral Guides (TMG), this chapter pinpoints the conflicts and negotiations surrounding moral perceptions and professional identity of English language pre-service teachers (ST) and teacher educators (TE). It also highlights issues for teacher education, urging explicit encouragement of TEs to enact their TMG roles through caring relationships while enhancing STs' understanding of morality and development of teacher identity.

Introduction

The idea of 'teacher as moral guide' (TMG), the traditional identity of Vietnamese teachers, remains a core value in Vietnam today. However, as an English language teacher and teacher educator, the primary author of this chapter has observed the problematic effects of the decline in teacher morality, the changing nature of teachers' moral roles, and the moral tensions in contemporary society, associated with ELLT (English Language Learning and Teaching), globalisation and the tensions of the teaching profession in Vietnam. This has triggered her research interest in the social dimension of English language teacher education among higher education institutions and the formation of teacher identity. A particular concern of this study is Vietnamese pre-service teachers' (ST) perceptions of their moral guiding role, how they position themselves and how they are positioned as teachers of English after graduating, in conjunction with values emanating from the English-speaking world, the practice of ELLT and the moral duties of a Vietnamese teacher. More specifically, attention is paid to how meanings of TMG are identified and

L. T. Le (✉)
Federation Technology Institute, Melbourne, VIC, Australia

L. G. Dwyer
Melbourne Polytechnic, Melbourne, VIC, Australia

© Springer Nature Singapore Pte Ltd. 2019
N. T. Nguyen, L. T. Tran (eds.), *Reforming Vietnamese Higher Education*,
Education in the Asia-Pacific Region: Issues, Concerns and Prospects 50,
https://doi.org/10.1007/978-981-13-8918-4_13

refined during the processes of these student teachers' linguistic and pedagogical development, an issue currently underplayed in teacher-education forums.

Context of Research

Teacher Morality in the Teaching Profession in Vietnam

Recent literature and empirical studies have highlighted the vital role of morality (also see: Chaps. 1, 2 and 9) in Vietnamese education (Doan 2005; Phan 2008; Phan and Le 2013; Phan and Phan 2006; Phan et al. 2011; Rydstrom 2001, 2003). Phan (2008) provided a thorough review of the concept of morality and teachers' roles in Vietnamese ideology, culture and history from the perspectives of Taoism, Buddhism, Cao Dai and Confucianism (see also: Chaps. 2, 4, 7 and 12) to modern times with a wide range of concrete examples in Vietnamese poetry, folklore and culture. These empirical studies have proved that in Vietnamese society, teachers are respected for their role in teaching students how to be morally good, and they experience high social status as well as high expectations from society to be role models. Morality is regarded as the foundation for all teaching and resonates deeply with the Confucian doctrine "first morality, second knowledge", which is a guiding principle of Vietnamese education.

In modern Vietnam, Ho Chi Minh's (1959) ideology (also see: Chap. 2, pp. 34–35) is interwoven into the education system, emphasizing the enormous role of education in improving and developing the young. For Ho Chi Minh, teachers must be morally and intellectually good people to produce moral students: "good and evil are not inherent, but mostly due to education" (also see: Chaps. 1 and 9).

Vietnam's *Education Law* (also see: Chaps. 1, 3, 8 and 10) states that the aim of education is to produce people of "good morality" and "intellect" (Socialist Republic of Vietnam, Article 27). Implicit in the Law, teachers themselves are required to teach morality, as well as knowledge. Article 35 of the *Constitution of Vietnam* states that "education's objective is to foster and nurture the personality, human qualities [and] imbue with …. good virtues…" (p. 7)

The *Education Law* (The Socialist Republic of Vietnam, 2005) clearly identifies the role, tasks and rights of the teacher in Articles 15, 70 and 72, in which the teacher must have:

(a) good moral, mental and ideological qualifications
(b) the standardised level in the profession
(c) good health as required by the profession
(d) a clear curriculum vitae (pp. 30–31)

This Law clearly stipulates the education of moral values as the primary mission of Vietnamese education.

In other contexts, Campbell (1997) states that societal concerns about morality in contemporary life connect with renewed interest in moral education and character education (p. 255) (also see: Chap. 2, p. 35); while Narvaez and Lapsley (2008) assert the implicit moral influence of teachers in classrooms "when they select and exclude topics, when they insist on correct answers, when they encourage students to seek the truth of the matter, and when they establish classroom routines, form groups, enforce discipline, and encourage excellence" (p. 2). The implicit moral influence identified by Narvaez and Lapsley was also identified in this chapter (see discussion of teachers as role models). Increasing demands have been made of teachers to have moral influence on young people (Sylwester 1997; Lickona 1998; Dweck 1999 cited in Cummings et al. 2007); however, for decades, the moral aspect of teaching has received less attention in comparison to the technical aspect (Bárcena et al. 1993; Blase 1983). In their research report, Lovat and Toomey (2007) found that students and teachers of teacher education programs are not provided with courses explicitly designed for moral development. A report by the Character Education Partnership (2000, cited in Benninga 2003, p. 6) identified only three university teacher education programs in the USA that offered their student teachers (STs) the knowledge and professional skills to integrate character education into classroom practices. Character formation is intrinsic to classrooms and schools and an inescapable part of the teacher's craft (Hansen 1993; Jackson et al. 1993; Lapsley and Narvaez 2006). A quarter of states in the USA have mandated character education for students and hundreds of schools have incorporated it into their curriculum. In this context, practising moral education is not only a concern for Vietnam but also for teachers worldwide.

Moral Roles of Vietnamese Teachers and TMG

In Vietnam, teachers have two dominant roles: teacher of knowledge and of moral values. The word "teacher" or "*Thay/Co giao*" in the Vietnamese language literally means the person who teaches, and culturally means the one who is a moral educator. The teacher is second in the top three people in society "King-Master-Father"; even more respected and important than one's father. Vietnamese teachers have also been identified in Phan (2008) as:

- moral guides
- sources of productive activity
- providers of knowledge
- role models
- spiritual guides
- moral educators
- moral agents

Phan emphasises the moral guide role as dominant, and as a traditional attribute of Vietnamese teachers. As moral guides, teachers must be mindful of their character, behaviour and manner, and develop themselves to be more moral. Being a

Vietnamese teacher means not only being a moral guide but also being someone who tries to become a better person.

In a case study with five Vietnamese-American pre-service teachers of English in Canada by Nguyen (2008), the Vietnamese identity of teacher as moral guide was found to be dominant despite being away from Vietnam for a long time. Nguyen (2008) concluded that there are three factors contributing to the professional image of these overseas Vietnamese teachers. These were their personal histories, their belief systems and their schooling experience.

In another study with 150 university students in Vietnam and 60 university students of English in China, Phan et al. (2011) explored students' perceptions of English language teachers as moral guides in these two nations, with special focus on the issue of maintaining and reviving morality through ELT classes. The findings showed the students' continuing expectations about their English language teachers as moral guides despite rapid social changes. The process of teachers identifying their role amid the tensions of global and local cultures deserves more study in actual teaching and learning contexts with an emphasis on local and global appropriation.

Phan and Le (2013) provided a critical analysis of the moral dilemmas in ELT that the teachers were experiencing and the conflict between performing their professional ELT role as a facilitator, and upholding the TMG expectation.

TMG has been examined with different groups of Vietnamese ELT teachers, whether they are pre-service or in-service teachers, locally or overseas trained and working in or outside of Vietnam (Nguyen 2008; Phan 2008; Phan et al. 2011). The findings confirm that Vietnamese teachers of English, wherever they are, see themselves as moral guides, and expect to play that role. How they interpret such a role and enact it in their work practices is at times a painful but important process to understand.

Moral Issues in Vietnam's Social and Educational Context

Since Vietnam's Open Door policy started in 1986, dramatic socio-cultural changes have taken place, including increased social tensions and the unsettling of shared moral values in society, especially among young people (Doan 2005; Le 2009a, b). The movement away from traditional social values among the younger generation has been partly a result of the current status of moral education in the Vietnamese education system (Doan 2005) and concomitant issues of quality teacher education (Le 2009a, b; Pham 2001).

The current culture of teacher education institutions is thought by some to be morally problematic and to have a negative impact on pre-service teachers' perceptions of teacher morality (Le 2009a, b; Pham 2001). For example, during and after the practicum, pre-service teachers showed disappointment in their supervising teachers and mentor teachers, whom they expected to be role models (Le 2009b). A survey on "welfare systems in Vietnam with the goal of progress and social justice" (as cited in Le 2009b) showed quantitatively that society and students do not respect teachers as much as before.

The Ministry of Education and Training (MOET) has taken action by implementing the "Codes of Ethics" (MOET 2009). It is ironic that teachers whose mission it is to educate students about being morally good citizens now need to be re-educated in morality themselves. However, teacher morality cannot be addressed simply by issuing official regulations. The matter calls for in-depth exploration, especially within the field of teacher education in Vietnam.

Methodology

This study adopted a qualitative case study methodology, with a full acknowledgment of the limitations such as the small number of participants, the inability to measure the scale of a problem, as well as the different attributes that account for the structural differences between different groups of participants. In addition, results from a single case investigation cannot provide scientific generalization, and there were constraints on the length of time for conducting the study. However, the choice of this methodology is in accordance with Stake (cited in Denzin and Lincoln 2005), who claims that designing a case study is "to optimize understanding of the case rather than to generalise beyond it" (p. 443). This research does not attempt to deal with the causal relationship of a phenomenon but to "sophisticate the beholding" (Stake 1995, p. 45) of the phenomenon through the participants' perspectives. This study also aims to depict an in-depth picture of how the teachers as moral guides are identified during the English language teaching and learning process, so a qualitative case study best suits this purpose.

Given that case studies are holistic in their approach, the case study reports firstly need to be open to alternative interpretations from the readers and represent alternative views within the research data. Conflicting views or alternative perspectives or truths are part of the real life of social interactions; the case study reports should reflect these differences. It is therefore necessary that the researcher accesses more than one form of data so that he or she is able to present the complexities of the case studied and the varying interpretations.

Furthermore, case study is complex in that it attempts to represent the many/multiple truths outlined in the field of social research where the aim is to broaden understandings of the world as the participants and researchers see it. Therefore, many aspects and layers of the case should be considered in the interpretation of data (Kemmis 1980). Researchers undertake the research with the aims of increasing their understanding of the phenomenon and adding to the breadth of knowledge of the case, so the report must be written in ways that enable the readers to engage with the material and its context.

In these respects, the study has employed a variety of data collection instruments and a multiplicity of analytical tools to understand the participants' perspectives of the phenomenon studied. In the next section, we will elaborate on (1) how data were collected, analysed and (2) how positioning theory, discourse theory and discourse analysis were workable tools of inquiry.

Research Participants and Data Collection

Qualitative research requires a careful and purposive collection of participants. "Maximum variation sampling" which provides good qualitative data (Creswell and Clark 2007, p. 112) has been used in an effort to include males and females in this study. The sample consists of STs of English who were in their third and fourth year of the English language teacher education program, and English language TEs. Participants were purposively chosen from three of the most prestigious and well accredited teacher education universities in Vietnam. The number of participants who voluntarily and actively followed the research process by the end of the data collection period included 10 teacher educators and 19 student teachers. These participants varied in age, social, personal and geographical background, as well as teaching and learning experiences.

Multiple data sources were used not only for the triangulation of data to ensure the construct validity of the research (Merriam 1998; Mertens 2005; Patton 2002; Yin 2009) but also for the richness and depth of data interpretation. According to Yin (2009) and McMillan (2008), multiple forms of data collection are a major strength of case study data collection. In addition, Flick (2002) affirms that the combination of multiple methodological practices in a single study is best understood as a strategy that adds rigour, breadth, complexity, richness and depth to any inquiry. In light of these features, the data for this study were collected from semi-structured interviews provided before participants' teaching practicum, journal writing and diary-keeping during the teaching practicum with an aim to "reflect an attempt to secure in-depth understanding of the phenomenon in question" (Denzin and Lincoln 2005, p. 5). Participants were enthusiastically responsive to questions, providing real examples and speaking frankly about their experiences.

Data Analysis and Interpretation

Data analysis included interview transcripts, journal entries, diaries and field notes. Data collected were first coded following thematic analysis (Boyatzis 1998) and case study analysis (Merriam 1998, 2009; Yin 2009). Thematic analysis involves two levels of interpretation: the semantic and the latent and or interpretive levels. In order to obtain both a description of what the participants have said or written and the interpretation of their perceptions and identification of TMG, the study employs the combination of semantic and latent thematic analysis procedures (Braun and Clarke 2006). The analysis tries to make sense of meaning from the surface to the underlying layer, which fits well with the constructionist paradigm where broader assumptions and theories can be made from the data. This method at the level of thematic analysis is indeed close to discourse analysis, which was used and addressed later. In order to obtain a thick description of each case and a bigger picture of my data, "Pattern matching and explanation-building" (Yin 2009, pp. 136 & 141) was used as the data analysis method.

Deep sense of the coded data then was made and analysed with the deployment of self and other positioning theory (Harré and Langenhove 1999), d/Discourse analysis (Gee 2004, 2005), and the central concept of "morality" and "morality as an identity filter" (Phan 2008).

Positioning Theory as a Tool of Inquiry

Positioning theory is the idea of discursive practice and its supposition that individuals (also see 'individualism': Chaps. 1 and 2) are active developers of their identities, thus identity is discursively produced (Harré and Van Lagenhove 1999). One positions oneself or is positioned by others in verbal and non-verbal discourses at the local, institutional and societal levels (Glazier 2009). All institutions, according to Holstein and Gubrium (2000), can offer their members access to different kinds of narrative resources for identity construction.

Harré and van Langenhøve (1999) also claim that positioning theory applies to "the study of local moral orders as ever-shifting patterns of mutual and contestable rights and obligations of speaking and acting" (p. 1). In other words, positioning theory is the study of the way rights and duties are ascribed, attributed and justified to and by individuals in local social groups, which is very relevant in the current context of teacher identity.

Positioning theory was particularly useful for this study since the analysis focused on the participants' positioning of selves and others around the responsibilities and the moral issues of teachers in the contemporary social and the EIL (also see: Chap. 11) context, from which the collective professional identity for the Vietnamese teachers of English was constructed and aligned with the global and local norms. It was a lens through which English language learning and teaching (ELLT) was positioned and negotiated in the STs' identity development as reported in their narratives.

Subject Positions

Subject positions are considered to be central in the construction of understanding of one's world and one's place in it, and therefore would be useful in understanding the creation of professional teacher identity (Søreide 2006). Søreide reminds us that when participants describe and make reference to these accessible subject positions they also place themselves in certain positions which is visible in their narratives and through the way the participants evaluate and talk about the relevance of the subject positions in question, and in turn helps one to understand teacher identity formation as a process of narrative positioning.

Self and Other Positioning

Davies and Harré's (1990) ever-negotiable definition of self implies that an individual's role is reconstructed when one is positioned in conversation, and this position is a representative of self. Reeves (2009) adds that people negotiate identities continually when they "take up, assert, and resist identity positions that define them" (p. 35). As a result, in a discursively constructed identity, the positions people give themselves are intertwined with the positions they ascribe to others (Reeves 2009); consequently, positioning forms the heart of identity work.

The employment of positioning to analyse the data in this chapter include: (i) Reflexive positioning (self-positioning) referring to a person's assertion of an identity position for the self (Davies and Harré 1990); (ii) Interactive positioning (other-positioning) ascribing an identity position to another; (iii) Deliberate/ intentional positioning assigning identities to others that are complementary to the self (Harré and van Langenhove 1999).

Through these positionings, an understanding of how the STs position themselves and position others as teachers, and how they are positioned by other people in the role of teachers can be obtained. The STs' conceptualisation of TMG and professional identity was explored through several narratives in which they expressed their ideas and points of views from different positions.

Discourse/Discourse Analysis

Discourse was found to be relevant to the interpretation of data due to its close relationship with identity. Discourse analysis helps "comprehend exactly what people are doing with, and through language as they speak" (Bartlett 2008, p. 169). Language is not the only tool we use to both reveal and understand ourselves; our emotional reactions, attitudes and behaviours also contribute to this sense of self and how we present ourselves to others. These tools together with words can be a form of discourse that needs to be accounted for as the spoken words does not exist on its own. Seen in this way, Gee's (1996) definition of big D (Discourse) has informed the interpretation of data as well. According to Gee (ibid), "D"iscourse incorporates many activities and actions, both internal and external, along the mind-body-spirit continuum and an individual brings certain subjectivities to a discursive act while at the same time the discourse affects the individual engaging in it.

In Gee's (2004) opinion, the basic premise of the discourse analysis is: *How* people say or write things (form) helps constitute what they are doing (function). In turn, what they are saying (or writing) helps constitute *who* they are being at a given time and place within a given set of social practices (their socially situated identities). Finally, *who* they are being at a given time and place within a given set of social practices, produces and reproduces, moment by moment, our social, political, cultural and institutional worlds (p. 48). Social practices are practically routine activities through which people carry out (partially) shared goals based on (partially) shared (conscious or unconscious) values. This connection between identity and discourse provides a tool of inquiry for this study of TMG.

Findings and Discussion

Søreide's (2006) framework of subject positions as narrative resources and identity construction enabled the narrative of professional identity of Vietnamese STs in this study to be explored through two mechanisms:

- identification with and recognition of the available subject positions (positive positioning);
- distancing, opposition and/or rejection of the available subject positions (negative positioning).

The positions that STs are placed in relative to the position of TMG may lead to defining and characterising STs in ways that explain their differential treatment and views on the image of teachers. When asked to discuss TMG, they positioned themselves through what they revealed in the interviews and narratives. As positioning oneself always implies a positioning of the other (Harré and van Langenhove 1999), once participants' membership was established and accepted, how their stories positioned others became the focus.

Identification/Recognition of TMG and Teacher Morality

This section presents data collected from the first interview and journal entries of STs, showing their perceptions of teaching and teachers' roles. Firstly though, it is necessary to understand what the informants meant "morality" to be. Their understanding was compatible with Rich's (1992) and Phan's (2008) definitions of morality in an educational context.

> That which is moral therefore relates to the principles of right conduct in behaviour. To say that a certain act is immoral means that it is unvirtuous or contrary to morality because it does not conform to principles of right conduct. (Rich 1992, p. 97)

Rich's view of morality, which has been applied to the United States Education context, is similar to Phan's definition in her study of Vietnamese teachers' identities. According to Phan, morality refers to "socially acceptable and proper behaviour and manners" (p. 5). The synthesis of these views was a common ground from which the research findings could be analysed.

Dual Roles

Through positioning themselves and others as teachers, participants identified the dual role of teachers as being moral guides as well as subject qualified. All participants described having a dual responsibility with one aspect of the dual role being to teach the curriculum and academic skills, and the other being to teach the whole person and to be an integral part of their students' moral and character development. This is evidenced in the following excerpts of both ST and TE interviews.

> I think, the aim of teaching is not just teaching academic information, but …more than that, it is also educating a morally good person (Thuy, ST, 1st interview)

> Teachers everywhere have the responsibility of developing students' morality (Khanh, TE)

Aside from imparting knowledge, in most responses concerning teachers' responsibilities, the interviewees had a clear recognition of teachers being a moral guide. Some participants even positioned teachers as parents.

> As a moral guide, teachers are like parents who teach you to be man…. They not only teach knowledge but also educate a child to become a good person. (Ngoc, ST, 1st interview)

> The role of the teacher is very similar to that of a mother who always nurtures and educates her children. (Do, ST, 1st interview)

One of the factors affecting participants' portrayal of TMG is their belief in teachers' capacity to affect students' moral growth. The participants' positioning is similar to Bergem's (1990) findings about the teacher as an educator, whose way of living, behaving and acting could have great impact on growing individuals. Another ST remarked that:

> Teachers are essentially required to be moral guides. (Dang, ST, 1st interview)

Similarly, when positioning themselves as a teacher, Thu and others saw their dual roles as the model of teaching and the model of living.

> Besides teaching well, what is more important is to build up good characters for my students, educate them to be a good person. (Thuy, ST, 1st interview)

STs constructed several subject positions in which TMG and teachers as role models became the most prominent. TEs' interviews supported the literature about the dual roles of teachers (see: Carr 2000; Lumpkin 2008; Rich 1992; Socket 1993).

Teachers as a Standard of Excellence: Both Professional and Personal

Participants understood that a good teacher must be a person of good morality. The sort of teacher described by participants is similar to the term "teacher with character" as described by Lumpkin (2008) whose study suggested that the teacher with character is a role model for students. According to Rich (1992, p. 96), teachers must be worthy role models for the purpose both of guidance and imitation, which was an opinion widely echoed by participants through the term "moral model" (to refer to their expectations of a teacher).

> Teachers must be perfect as a *moral model*, for example not violating social standards. (Thu, ST, 1st interview)

> Teachers should be kindhearted, friendly, fair, sympathetic and empathetic ... Teachers should be a *moral model* for students to look at and follow. (Thuy, ST, 1st interview)

> You must be a person of good morality. You must be perfect in every field. (Dang, ST, 1st interview)

> You must be morally perfect in every way so that you are free from being criticized. (Thuy, ST, 1st interview)

Phrases like "must be perfect", "in every way" and "in every field" occur repeatedly in the informants' discourse on teacher morality, which is a sign of the absolute expectation of teachers to be TMG.

These views are also consistent with those found in the literature such as Campbell's (2008b) "renewed professionalism in teaching" (p. 601). In addition to subject knowledge, teachers must demonstrate their "ethical knowledge" in practice through their actions (p. 603).

The informants identified deviations from norms that should be avoided with regard to professional appearance, speech and conduct. Dang and Trieu showed their consciousness of teacher language by using "must not" to indicate the strong prohibition for teachers to avoid such taboos:

> Teachers mustn't use bad language in front of students. (Trieu, ST, 1st interview)

The data replicate the way Carr (2000) and Goodwyn (2005) see teachers as moral agents who represent their own models through their dress, speech and work ethics. According to Hoa, vulgar language and violence are also unacceptable.

> A teacher as moral guide must be the one who has a proper manner in classroom, who never shouts, offends or insults, or uses violence. The teacher must be fair and respectful. (Hoa, ST, 1st interview)

Consistent with Goodwyn (2005, p. 168), participants of different generations shared the view that appearance is an important factor for teachers. Both STs and TEs recognised non-conformity with professionally recognised dress codes as unacceptable among Vietnamese teachers.

> Teachers are not allowed to wear casual clothes in the classroom. (Truong, TE)

It would not be easy to accept teachers wearing scanty outfits. (Dang, ST, journal)

Teachers' professional identity is not only self-perceived, it is also externally imposed, and personal domains including behaviour, family life, social connections and even dress codes are subject to scrutiny.

The participants believed that the teacher's family is more conventionally judged than that of other professionals with regard to the growth and success of their children, and their daily practices (Do and Thuy, ST), such that teachers' family lives are a significant matter of concern for their students.

Teachers should lead a model life with a good family. If he is a good model in class but not a good husband, this will influence his image. (Thuy, ST, journal)

In their journals, Dang and Do (STs) shared the view that it was not easy for Vietnamese teachers to lead normal social lives. For example, Dang felt that:

Teachers shouldn't go to places such as bars or nightclubs because these places are unsuitable. (Trieu, Thuy and Dang, ST)

Participants recognised that the strictness of social expectations on the teaching profession has been reduced, but teachers were still required to follow socially approved professional standards.

Reported instances of deviation from these standards ranged from alcohol abuse or sexual misconduct to inappropriate clothing. Many of these offences would today, in Carr's (2000) contention, be regarded as private or personal concerns, but in the informants' perceptions, they are destructive to the professional image of the teacher. By building up a collective identity of idealised Vietnamese teachers, the participants include and construct their own individual identities (Jenkins 2008).

In Chap. 12, Ngo offers a critical lens into the introduction of the new Vietnam English Teacher competency standardisation as is commissioned by the NFLP 2020. She generally refers to a raising of professional standards among trainee teachers, including professional attitudes and values in language teaching.

Teacher Morality as Vocational Calling

The data showed TMG as being interpreted in different ways. For instance, Hoa, Chi, Ngoc and Thuy agreed that TMG relates to when the teacher imparts knowledge and monitors students' progress while Quyen and Thu associated TMG more with the teacher being an example for the students in their behaviour.

The teacher must set a good example in behavior. (Thu, ST, 1st interview)

According to STs, teachers have a dual role, but despite this, the teacher has but one identity, which is 'moral guide'.

Through their positioning of self and others, participants in this study recognized 'teacher morality' as the shaper and filter of their personal and moral identities. Data revealed that what makes Vietnamese teachers' roles distinctive from other professions is the emphasis on the role of morality in defining the whole teacher.

> The STs clearly perceived their moral model role as essential and distinctive. (Quyen, TE)

> Teachers teach the way they are. Their every move causes publicity so they must be very good to be a role model. (Tran, ST, 1st interview)

The STs identified morality as the fundamental ingredient in constructing teacher identity.

The TEs highlight that the Vietnamese teachers today can adopt modern teaching and living styles but they must uphold the traditional moral standards/TMG for Vietnamese teachers (Truong and Bach, TEs). In this sense, professional identity is not only self-constructed but also socially regulated. The finding resembles and extends the previously cited scholarly conversation of teacher identity in Rich (1992), Phan and Phan (2006) and Phan (2008), where meanings associated with TMG and/or the moral role of today's ELT teachers are socially and linguistically reconstructed by all parties involved with the teachers themselves playing a major role in this process.

The teacher, who is not modelling behaviour for students, whether intentionally or not, will be deemed immoral. Immorality is evinced through the inadequate discharge of responsibilities and negligent attitudes to work.

> For me, being a teacher, you should be caring and responsible to your students by carefully planning your lesson, making it interesting to help the students learn. Some teachers just use the same outdated lesson plan and repeat the same routine every day … that is not a moral teacher. (Quyen, TE)

While many participants found it hard to respond to questions about morality requirements for teachers, Do, together with some other STs (Thuy and Minh), as well as TEs (My and Bach), believed that teacher morality had a connection to the strength of character. In this way, their identity as an individual overlapped with their identity as teachers regarding morality. In choosing the teaching profession, they believed that their personality features were suited to the requirements of the job.

> I am quite confident, humorous, and patient. (Ngoc, 1st interview)

> Teaching is suitable for my personality. (Minh, journal)

With regard to the TEs' views, My and Bach, who have been teaching for more than 20 years, asserted that they had those special qualities of teachers by nature. My found herself suited to the job and had almost no difficulties in responding to its duties and requirements, while Bach admitted his personal features made him easily accepted as a teacher. In this case, the personal and the professional pervaded each other, and personal morality seemed to be additive and supportive to that of the professional morality.

> I am a dignified person who has rather a serious way of living, so I don't feel it difficult to play the role of moral guide for students. I hate lies and dishonesty. … I do not have to follow any models of good or bad … I think, I myself know what is right and what is wrong. I was born to be a teacher. (My, TE)

> I am easily recognized as a teacher from my appearance and manner. I think that I am most suitable for teaching, not any other job. (Bach, TE)

Analysis showed the participants' perceptions of teacher morality as being an essential factor in the composition of a Vietnamese teacher, which mirrors Phan's (2008) conception of 'morality as an identity filter.' She argues that the personal and professional identities of Vietnamese teachers are negotiated and constructed through the lens of teacher morality.

Teaching is a vocation for these participants; and consistent with the social conception of TMG, individuals with characters consistent with TMG are drawn to the profession. They cultivate themselves whilst in the role so that they develop the whole self which has both private and professional aspects. Morality is significant in STs' identity construction, as their choice of teaching as their preferred profession is firmly linked to the motivation to better themselves both personally and professionally (as whole people).

> I got the motivation to perfect myself, to learn more, achieve more knowledge, to be better at teaching. Becoming a teacher is a motivation for me to perfect myself in terms of personality and knowledge. (Thu, 1st interview)

It is evident that the STs equate becoming a teacher with becoming a better person. Developing oneself to be a model for others is the way the student teachers understand that their professional lives will shape their personal lives. Teachers who are drawn to teaching want to develop themselves and do not feel forced to conform to TMG.

However, not all teachers are drawn to teaching as a vocation; for those who are, it fits with TMG, but data indicated that it is not the case for all teachers. This idea is demonstrated in the case of another TE, Mai, who confessed that she felt uncomfortable because her parents, who were teachers, pressured her to become one. Mai said:

> I was born in a teaching family and my parents influenced me a lot because they were teachers too. They taught me that … I should become a role model. They wanted me to become a teacher. They think teachers must conform to very strict rules, have good knowledge of subject matter and their personal lives should be a model for students to follow. The way they wear clothes, speak, and behave in front of people should adhere to a strict standard. (Mai, TE)

The account of Mai (TE) exemplified the perceived hardship of a teaching career and the high expected moral standards. According to Mai, upon joining the profession, one has to change features of one's overall identity and adapt to the new culture and new practices. With regard to the teaching profession, morality implicitly governs, directs and shapes both the personal and professional identity as reported in Phan (2008). Mai was an example for those people who entered the profession without vocational calling but were forced to identify with TMG in tandem with high society's expectations.

Resistance/Opposition to TMG

Teaching Profession as a "Sacred World"

There was evidence of resistance to the TMG role identity throughout the data. For the informants, teaching is identified as different from other professions due to the complexity and nature of the demands entailed in the role of teachers. This view is supported by Goodwyn (2005) and Sockett (1996) who argue that the teachers see themselves as unique among other groups. Dang, a senior ST in his fourth year, emphasised the moral role of teachers as the most prominent difference:

> Teachers must be different from other professions from their appearance, to attitudes and behaviours, in both academic and social life, in and out of the school context, in all settings they must be *models*. (Dang, ST, 1st interview)

Talking from experience, Bach (TE) disclosed some of the uneasiness that he felt for Vietnamese teachers, placed in prominent positions and charged with what he called the role of 'saint':

> There are many requirements that make me feel uneasy. Being a teacher, you must be decent and conform to standards in every way…you must be a model in your social and personal life … Thus, the teacher is placed in a very high position, like a saint… so teachers can't be corrupt or dishonest. (Bach, TE)

Another teacher educator advised her students to not follow the job if they were not very good at subject knowledge and morality. For her, those who do not have an interest in or commitment to TMG, should work in a different profession. She explained:

> As a teacher, when you make a moral mistake, it could entail serious consequences and have an impact on many people. You must be perfect to be respected. (My, TE)

The teaching profession was described as a 'sacred world', with the requirements for entry being unattainable for many STs (Phan and Le 2013), and the most significant factor to affect this view being the requirement to be a moral model. 'Saintly' expectations regarding teachers' morality, coupled with multiple pressures and tensions of social change as well as the 'sacred' status of the profession made the participants feel a lack of confidence enacting and responding to this role.

The Lack of Self Confidence

Positioning themselves as a teacher, the ST participants found themselves unable to respond to the responsibilities and moral requirements for teachers, some decided not to pursue the teaching profession:

> I am afraid that I cannot respond to the required moral responsibilities and requirements to be a teacher …. I admire the teaching profession, but I think I am not good enough to be a teacher. (Chi, ST, 1st interview)

The STs kept personal distance sufficient to make the moral role less threatening because they judged themselves as not morally good enough. They kept distance from being a moral guide in every context by limiting the role to just within the school environment.

> The teacher needs to act as a moral guide when they are in class and in front of students; outside class, they can do whatever they want. (Chi, ST, 1st interview)

STs were mindful of the responsibilities of the job, but as far as their personalities were concerned, they were apprehensive of not being able to meet such exacting and onerous obligations. There is internal resistance from STs towards the moral role, which has a link to a deficit in the respondents' self-confidence.

Among TEs, the opposition to TMG was evident from the way they demonstrated their understanding of the job requirements as well as the way they understood themselves, expressing their consciousness of TMG but showing opposition towards this role. For instance, Khanh (TE) although an experienced educator with 25 years' experience, still lacked the confidence to be a model.

> I am conscious of my role as a model, a moral model … but I am not brave enough to consider myself as a model for others to follow. (Khanh, TE)

In his refusal to identity as moral model for students, Khanh emphasised the students' autonomy with regard to following their teachers' model or not.

> I cannot force my students to follow me, to follow the way I behave. It is up to the students' choice who or what they follow. (Khanh, TE)

Thanh and Mai with less than 10 years of teaching experience were also not confident and opposed to the traditional model.

> I never think of myself as a model of morality. I never expect others including my students to follow the way I behave. (Thanh, TE)

> It is not my duty to care about students' morality because they are grown up enough to know what is right and what is wrong. (Mai, TE)

This positioning showed an opposition to the conventional understanding of teachers' roles. TEs want their students to be selective in learning and copying their examples. From the inner voices of TEs, it can be seen that modern teachers leave autonomy to their students and raise the questions of whether the current teacher education program provides sufficient input to empower the education students' agency in moral reasoning and judgment while empowering TEs to confidently enact this moral education role.

Personal Voice

The constraints of teacher morality are loosened when it comes to a personal voice. Positioning themselves as teachers, the STs were opposed to social norms regarding teachers' morality and made the point that people look too highly upon teachers.

Thuy asserted that she did not care about teachers' personal lives while Dang said that it was unfair to expect highly of teachers and see them as some kind of superhero or saint. The relativity of morality is seen here with the proposition that humans are imperfect, and as teachers are human, they live their own lives and have their own freedom.

> Teachers are also normal people; they have the rights to do whatever they want. (Trieu, ST, 1st interview)

The participants valued freedom for the teacher as an individual and agreed that the TMG model is too strict. The process of self-positioning can itself be the catalyst for teachers to revise their stance. Initially, Hoa and Thuy positioned teachers as perfect models but then, they revised their stance as follow:

> I don't want teachers to be like a robot who must be perfect in every way … if so, nobody wants the job. (Thuy, ST, journal)

> Teachers have their own life…they do not have to take responsibility for students' lives. (Hoa, ST, journal)

The STs felt sorry for teachers who are forced to live up to TMG standards. In distancing and creating more space, they are seeking to limit the meaning of teacher to the giver of subject knowledge more so than moral knowledge.

As an experienced TE, Kim had to struggle to build a teacher image in her own way, rather than be shaped by others or by collective norms:

> Recently coming back from the UK, I found myself destabilised as a teacher so I looked at myself again and lots of ideas were still inside my mind. I gave up all teaching jobs and looked at myself again to work out whether other teachers see me better as myself or as a teacher, but it seems that they still want me to be a teacher. (Kim, TE)

There is a strong personal voice here where the collective identity imposes on the individual. It made Kim felt uncomfortable and reluctant:

> As a teacher you have to think of yourself as role model to be a good teacher and a good citizen. Actually, I am not a role model for my students to follow, but if I can, I try to the best of my ability to be a person that my students can think of as a good one. I am just a normal person. (Kim, TE)

Positioning herself as a normal person, Kim resisted playing the moral model role although she was aware of keeping and maintaining a professional image. Interestingly, she knows the expectations but she thinks she is not good enough despite trying to be good. Ironically, her words are what a humble and moral person might say.

Resistance to TMG was also reflected in the way the participants described their expectations and redefinition of teachers' TMG roles. Although teacher morality is still valued, the moral guide role meaning has shifted. For example, by positioning the teacher as just a regular person who teaches, and thus positioning himself as "an individual rather than a teacher", Khanh viewed the moral guide as follows:

> You can help even the weakest student to learn, to achieve their goal, then you are a moral guide. (Khanh, TE)

In this sense, the moral role becomes limited to teachers' responsibility for students' learning and knowledge development with little or no concern about developing students' morality. Mai implicitly highlighted the teachers' role of being models and inspirers of knowledge and inquiry.

> I think teachers should be role models. To be a role model, they should be very good at English and have very good teaching skills first. (Mai, TE)

The informants accepted the teacher's responsibility to master knowledge of subject matter, but they were concerned about morality being expected. In his rejection of himself being a moral model, Bach (TE) insisted on the core values and dignities that the teacher should maintain. He said:

> I think that teachers must be a model in their behaviour and their conduct. They can have modern style but must behave in the way teachers are supposed to. Although they can be dynamic, mobile and modern … they must uphold the standards for Vietnamese teachers. (Bach, TE)

This point of view reflects what Nguyen (2018) highlights in Chap. 2 (p. 19) about the essentialist perspective of identity that treats Vietnamese identities as being coherent and the oneness that remains fairly stable and unchanged throughout a person's life.

Morality is the marker of Vietnamese teacher identity, but the meaning was modified and redefined by the respondents. It is still the element that brings them a sense of belonging to the Vietnamese teacher community. Moreover, the data show that Vietnamese teachers are expected to uphold the national standards that represent Vietnamese people and are set by law. Vietnamese teachers' national identity has been reinforced in the views of the participants:

> Traditional teachers in Vietnam were expected to be model of morality for students, and the value still exists, however it has changed. Now I cannot tell the students you should behave this way or that way. (Khanh, TE)

Many participants hoped that they could be a model for the students to imitate and to learn from in certain ways, but they were uncertain of being able to be the perfect models.

There is a shift in the meaning of TMG that was evident through the participants' hesitation to fully adopt the TMG model. The conventional and traditional meaning of TMG, therefore, can now be understood as facing opposition and unwelcoming attitudes on the one hand and as developing and changing on the other (partly as a result of those attitudes).

Teachers as moral agents are a universal notion with shared meanings, which influences teachers everywhere in their conception of their missions and roles. Fenstermatcher (1990) when elaborating on teachers as moral agents argues that teachers are specifically responsible for the proper and appropriate moral development of their students (p. 133). There are moral qualities to a teacher's action, and morality might have a considerable impact on the morality of the students. Teachers' conduct in the classroom is a moral matter, so their behaviours and characters are the models for their students to see, to understand and to follow

(p. 135). Therefore, in his views, teachers must pay attention to these and unceasingly develop their moral characters.

Beyer (1997) defines teaching as a field of "reflective moral action" and teachers as "moral agents" where teachers engage in practices contributing to the creation of a better educational and social world. For her, such teachers are, indeed, genuine professionals (p. 253). This proposition echoes with Sockett's (1993) views of professional teachers as moral agents. In addition, the teacher should possess such moral qualities as "humility, courage, impartiality, empathy, open mindedness, enthusiasm, judgment and imagination", accompanied with other related virtues like "honesty, sense of justice and care" (Campbell 1997, p. 256). Teachers transmit moral messages through professional ethical practice in classrooms and schools. The teachers' moral agency is not just reflected through their self-conscious decision making in formal instruction but is also implicit in their act of teaching. It is demonstrated and practised both consciously and unconsciously.

Sockett (1993) contends that "professional teachers are expert because of their professional virtue" (p. 90). The professional teacher as described by Sockett is a moral individual working as a teacher. Campbell (2008a) also agrees with Sockett (1993) that teachers play a dual and inseparable role as a moral individual and as a moral educator. Increasingly, the literature has addressed the necessity for educators to regard their professional responsibilities as basic moral imperatives (see Campbell 2008a).

Hansen (1998) brings a more comprehensive description of this role, arguing that a teacher as moral agent must be one who is "caring, compassionate, thoughtful; consequentialist, or has outcome-based views" and must be responsible "to produce students with moral qualities like civic mindedness or cultural sensitivity, and so forth" (p. 644). However, Hansen (1998) also indicates that not all teachers can identify with this role. Many teachers see themselves as moral guides and play out the role without expressing it in those words or not, whereas others, especially pre-service and novice teachers do not identify with that role. They identify themselves rather as teachers of a specific subject or as developing children's cognitive capacities.

The data showed that a traditional TMG involves not only responding to universal norms and moral requirements but also facing more specific social restrictions and demands.

Conclusion

This chapter has shown how TMG has been perceived by Vietnamese pre-service teachers and teacher educators of English at several universities of teacher education. The meanings of TMG and of the moral role of EIL professionals – who tend to have more chances of being exposed to global values and ideologies – are known to be socially and linguistically reconstructed. This case study has explored whether EIL practices and the global integration process have impacted on the formation of professional identity of Vietnamese ELT teachers in the current milieu of Vietnam. The study reports that ELLT seems not to have exerted a negative impact on the culture and values of its learners. Rather, it empowers their economic, intellectual and cultural capital, and contributes to the development of their identities.

Although modern teachers have multiple roles, the historical and conventional role of Vietnamese TMG is the most prominent in the participants' positioning of this own identity. TMG has been reinforced as the identity marker of Vietnamese teachers, even if they do not like it or are not confident about it. The findings have also validated the significance of ELT teachers' roles in educating and nurturing the young generation to become global citizens who have the skills of thinking, higher orders of thinking, innovativeness and creativity, but who are also critically aligning with the target of citizenship education in the twenty-first century as suggested by W. O. Lee (2012).

Moreover, there is a conflict in becoming a teacher and functioning in the paradigm of TMG as well as the shifting image of Vietnamese teachers that focuses on teachers being moral in a less explicit way. Morality has not only proven to be a filter in the identity formation process (Phan 2008) but has been identified as an aspect of the vocational calling to the teaching profession. How this identity is constructed has been revealed both through the respondents' identity positioning and by their resistance to the imposed identity of the role. The TMG identity remains socially perpetuated and regulated to this day.

In this chapter, how TMG is perceived has been examined in relation to the issues it raises for teacher education universities in Vietnam. The research results show, there is a group of participants who saw TMG as a way to improve teaching quality, and there is another group of STs drawn to a moral life who enter the profession, so they have no quarrel with meeting society's high expectations. There is yet another group who are pressured to join the teaching profession or who join it without vocational calling. For them, TMG is an issue that may subside if the standard TMG moral definitions are softened but left unattended. This issue may affect the TMG identity from within. Society's expectation is a problem for this group because they may be ambivalent about morals but interested in academia. Another group of experienced teacher educators reflects that they do not accept or meet the requirements of TMG after being in the profession for some time. For them, TMG is seen as a powerful tool for change that can affect the profession from within. These different perspectives about TMG can have an impact on teacher identity formation and will shape the future of teacher education in Vietnam.

Findings from this study have also contributed a new way of understanding TMG with tensions and expectations from the STs' and TEs' positionings with a shifting image of ELT teachers in terms of their moral guidance roles. It has pinpointed a number of conflicts and negotiations around moral perceptions and professional identity work through the dialectic positioning of self and others. The research puts forward issues for teacher education, urging the explicit encouragement of TEs to enact their TMG roles through a caring relationship while enhancing STs' understanding of morality and development of moral identity.

References

Bárcena, F., Gil, F., & Jover, G. (1993). The ethical dimension of teaching: A review and a proposal. *Journal of Moral Education, 22*(3), 241–252. https://doi.org/10.1080/0305724930220305.

Bartlett, T. (2008). Wheels within wheels, or triangles within triangles: Time and context in positioning theory. In F. M. Moghaddam, R. Harré, & N. Lee (Eds.), *Global conflict resolution through positioning analysis* (pp. 169–187). New York: Springer.

Benninga, J. S. (2003). *Moral and ethical issues in teacher education* (Eric digest). Washington, DC: ERIC.

Bergem, T. (1990). The teacher as moral agent. *Journal of Moral Education, 19*(2), 88–100.

Beyer, L. E. (1997). The moral contours of teacher education. *Journal of Teacher Education, 48*(4), 245–254.

Blase, J. J. (1983). Teachers' perceptions of moral guidance. *The Clearing House, 56*(9), 389–393.

Boyatzis, R. E. (1998). *Transforming qualitative information: Thematic analysis and code development*. Thousand Oaks/London/New Delhi: SAGE Publications.

Braun, V., & Clarke, V. (2006). Using thematic analysis in psychology. *Qualitative Research in Psychology, 3*(2), 77–101. https://doi.org/10.1191/1478088706qp063oa.

Campbell, E. (1997). Connecting the ethics of teaching and moral education. *Journal of Teacher Education, 48*(4), 255–263.

Campbell, E. (2008a). Teaching ethically as a moral condition of professionalism. In D. Narváez & L. Nucci (Eds.), *The international handbook of moral and character education* (pp. 601–617). New York: Routledge.

Campbell, E. (2008b). The ethics of teaching as a moral profession. *Curriculum Inquiry, 38*(4), 357–385.

Carr, D. (2000). *Professionalism and ethics in teaching*. London: Routledge.

Constitution of Vietnam. On www at http://www.vietnamlaws.com/freelaws/Constitution92(aa01).pdf. Accessed 11 May 2015.

Creswell, J. W., & Clark, V. L. P. (2007). *Designing and conducting mixed methods research*. Thousand Oaks/London/New Delhi: SAGE Publications.

Cummings, R., Harlow, S., & Maddux, C. D. (2007). Moral reasoning of in-service and pre-service teachers: A review of the research. *Journal of Moral Education, 36*(1), 67–78.

Davies, B., & Harré, R. (1990). Positioning: The discursive production of selves. *Journal for the Theory of Social Behaviour, 20*(1), 43–63.

Denzin, N. K., & Lincoln, Y. S. (2005). *The SAGE handbook of qualitative research* (3rd ed.). Thousand Oaks: Sage Publications.

Doan, D. H. (2005). Moral education or political education in the Vietnamese educational system. *Journal of Moral Education, 34*(4), 451–463.

Fenstermatcher, G. D. (1990). Some moral consideration on teaching as a profession. In J. I. Goodlad, R. Soder, & K. A. Sirotnik (Eds.), *The moral dimension of teaching* (pp. 130–151). San Francisco: Jossey-Bass Publishers.

Flick, U. (2002). *An introduction to qualitative research* (2nd ed.). London: SAGE.

Gee, J. P. (1996). *Social linguistics and literacies: Ideology in discourses* (2nd ed.). London: Taylor& Francis.

Gee, J. P. (2004). Discourse analysis: What makes it critical? In R. Rogers (Ed.), *An introduction of critical discourse analysis in education*. Mahwah/London: Lawrence Erlbaum Associates.

Gee, J. P. (2005). *An introduction to discourse analysis: Theory and method* (2nd ed.). London/New York: Routledge.

Glazier, J. A. (2009). The challenge of repositioning: Teacher learning in the company of others. *Teaching and Teacher Education, 25*(6), 826–834. https://doi.org/10.1016/j.tate.2008.11.014.

Goodwyn, A. (2005). Professionalism and accountability. In A. Goodwyn & J. Branson (Eds.), *Teaching English: A handbook for primary and secondary school teachers*. Abingdon/Oxon/New York: Routledge Falmer.

Hansen, D. T. (1993). From role to person: The moral layeredness of classroom teaching. *American Educational Research Journal, 30*, 651–674.

Hansen, D. T. (1998). The moral is in the practice. *Teaching and Teacher Education, 14*(6), 643–655.

Harré, R., & van Langenhove, L. (Eds.). (1999). *Positioning theory: Moral contexts of intentional action*. Malden: Blackwell.

Ho, Chi Minh. (1959). Bài nói tại lớp học chính trị của giáo viên [A lecture at a politics class for teachers]. In The Institue of Marxism-Leninism and Ho Chi Minh ideology studies Hồ Chí Minh – full version, 2000 (Vol. 9, pp. 497–502). Hanoi: National political publishing house.

Hoang, H. (2010). *Giá trị sống đang bị chao đảo* [The value of life is being shaken]. Retrieved April 1, 2010, from http://tuoitre.vn/Ban-doc-viet/371214/Gia-tri-song-dang-bi-chao-dao.html

Holstein, J. A., & Gubrium, J. F. (2000). *Constructing the life course*. New York: General Hall, Inc.

Jackson, P., Boostrom, R. E., & Hansen, D. T. (1993). *The moral life of schools*. San Francisco: Jossey-Bass.

Jenkins, R. (2008). *Social identity* (3rd ed.). London: Routledge.

Kemmis, S. (1980). The imagination of the case and the invention of study. In H. Simons (Ed.), *Towards a science of the singular*. Norwich: University of East Anglia/Care Occasional Publications.

Khanh, A. (2009). *Dao duc nha giao* [Teacher morality]. Retrieved January 15, 2010, from http://www.rfa.org/vietnamese/in_depth/Teachers-ethics-issue-kan-10112009104855.html

Khue, T. (2009). Học lễ từ trong gia đình [Learning morals from family education]. *Tuoi Tre online* [The youth online]. Retrieved January 13, 2010, from http://www.tuoitre.com.vn/Tianyon/Index.aspx?ArticleID=353435&ChannelID=118

Lapsley, D. K., & Narvaez, D. (2006). Character education. In A. Renninger, I. Siegel, W. Damon, & R. Lerner (Eds.), *In handbook of child psychology* (Vol. 4, pp. 248–296). New York: Wiley.

Le, M. T. (2009a). *Năm 2010, giáo viên sống được bằng lương?* [by 2010, can teaches live on their salaries?]. Retrieved January 13, 2010, from http://www.tuoitre.com.vn/Tianyon/Index.aspx?ArticleID=353434&ChannelID=118

Le, M. T. (2009b). *Nghề giáo hiện nay: nghề "oan trái"* [Teaching professions in the modern time: a "dilemma" career]. *Tuoi tre online*. Retrieved January 13, 2010, from http://tuoitre.vn/Tuoi-tre-cuoi-tuan/355261/Nghe-giao-hien-nay-nghe-%E2%80%9Coan-trai%E2%80%9D.html

Lee, W. O. (2012). Education for future-oriented citizenship: Implications for the education of twenty-first century competencies. *Asia Pacific Journal of Education, 32*(4), 498–517. https://doi.org/10.1080/02188791.2012.741057.

Lovat, T., & Toomey, R. (2007). *The 'double helix' relationship between quality teaching and values education: Emerging issues for teacher educators*. Paper presented at the 2007 Australian Teacher Education Association National Conference.

Lumpkin, A. (2008). Teachers as role models teaching character and moral virtues. *Journal of Physical Education Recreation and Dance, 79*(2), 45–49.

McMillan, J. H. (2008). *Educational research: Fundamentals for the consumer* (5th ed.). Boston: Allyn and Bacon.

Merriam, S. B. (1998). *Qualitative research and case study applications in education* (Rev. and expanded. ed.). San Francisco: Jossey-Bass.

Merriam, S. B. (2009). *Qualitative research: A guide to design and implementation*. San Francisco: Jossey-Bass.

Mertens, D. M. (2005). *Research and evaluation in education and psychology: Integrating diversity with quantitative, qualitative, and mixed methods* (2nd ed.). Thousand Oaks: Sage Publications.

Ministry of Education and Training (MOET). (2009). *Quy dinh ve dao duc nha giao* [Codes of ethics].

Narvaez, D., & Lapsley, D. K. (2008). Teaching moral character: Two alternatives for teacher education. *The Teacher Educator, 43*(2), 156.

Ngo, M. (2018). Teacher competence standardization under the influence of globalisation: A case study of the National Project 2020. In N. T. Nguyen & L. T. Tran (Eds.), *Reforming Vietnamese higher education: Global forces and local demands*. Dordrecht: Springer.

Nguyen, H. T. (2008). Conceptions of teaching by five Vietnamese American preservice teachers. *Journal of Language, Identity & Education, 7*(2), 113–136.

Nguyen, N. T. (2018). Cultural modalities of Vietnamese higher education. In N. T. Nguyen & L. T. Tran (Eds.), *Reforming Vietnamese higher education: Global forces and local demands*. Dordrecht: Springer.

Patton, M. Q. (2002). Qualitative interviewing. In M. Patton (Ed.), *Qualitative research and evaluation methods* (pp. 339–427). Thousands Oaks: SAGE Publications.

Pham, H. H. (2001). Teacher development: A real need for English departments in Vietnam. *English Teaching Forum Online, 39*(4), 4.

Phan, L. H. (2008). *Teaching English as an international language: Identity, resistance and negotiation*. Clevedon/Buffalo: Multilingual Matters.

Phan, L. H., & Le, T. L. (2013). Living the tensions: Moral dilemma in English language teaching. In T. Seddon & J. Levin (Eds.), *Routledge world year book of education 2013* (pp. 220–235). London: Routledge.

Phan, L. H., & Phan, V. Q. (2006). Vietnamese educational morality and the discursive construction of English language teacher identity. *Journal of Multicultural Discourses, 1*(2), 136–150.

Phan, L. H., Phan, V. Q., & McPherron, P. (2011). English language teachers as moral guides in Vietnam and China: Maintaining and traditionalizing morality. In J. Ryan (Ed.), *Education reform in China: Changing concepts, contexts, and practices* (pp. 132–157). London: Routledge.

Reeves, J. (2009). Teacher investment in learner identity. *Teaching and Teacher Education, 25*(1), 34–41.

Rich, J. M. (1992). The teacher as an exemplar. *The High School Journal, 75*(2), 94–98. https://doi.org/10.2307/40364545.

Rydstrøm, H. (2001). 'Like a white piece of paper'. Embodiment and the moral upbringing of Vietnamese children. *Ethnos, 66*(3), 394–413.

Rydstrøm, H. (2003). *Embodying morality: Growing up in rural northern Vietnam*. Honolulu: University of Hawai'i Press.

Sockett, H. (1993). *The moral base for teacher professionalism*. New York: Teachers College Press.

Sockett, H. (1996). Can virtue be taught? *The Educational Forum, 60*(Winter), 124–129.

Søreide, G. E. (2006). Narrative construction of teacher identity: Positioning and negotiation. *Teachers and Teaching: Theory and Practice, 12*(5), 527–547.

Stake, R. (1995). *The art of case study research*. Thousand Oaks: Sage Publications.

Yin, R. K. (2009). *Case study research: Design and methods* (4th ed.). Thousand Oaks: Sage Publication.